Endorsements

I can only imagine the depth of impact that many will experience through this pathway to freedom outlined so profoundly by Craig. This is an instruction manual for any intentional caregiver who is interested in seeing individuals find complete healing of their whole being physically, emotionally and spiritually. This is a helpful manual illustrated with true stories to provide life changing experience for the personal reader who deeply desires freedom in their inner being. The truth of God's Word comes alive with potential as God truly desires to see every man woman and child experience the fullness of peace and become all they were ever created to be. Faith to Freedom is an amazing gift to the body of Christ.

Bishop Lloyd Hoover, Fellowship of Anabaptists Churches,
Executive Director of The Potter's House

Craig Snow has given us a well-written and easy-to-read book on a much needed topic. We all need restoration and rebuilding. We must move beyond conversion into full freedom in Christ. God's salvation is multifaceted and He wants to apply the work of Christ deep inside each of us. This book will help you find your way into greater freedom and health.

Dr. Barry Wissler, President, HarvestNet International

We would be very hard-pressed to find a more comprehensive manual on the biblical truth of salvation and the freedom that God has provided for each of us to enjoy in this life. This book is packed with biblical insight, great stories that testify to truth, and practical steps toward embracing all God has for us through Jesus Christ. Enjoy the book and watch God work!

Kevin Eshleman, Lead Pastor, Ephrata Community Church

In Faith to Freedom, Craig Snow addresses the subject of working out our soul's salvation. Jesus not only forgives us, He also frees us from the power of sin by His shed blood. This book advances the Kingdom of God by helping us live out our freedom through the power of the Holy Spirit. It provides a step by step study guide to help us walk out our newfound life in Christ and equips us to help others live free as well. I recommend it as a resource for small groups seeking to grow spiritually mature.

Eugene Weaver, President, Global Christian Ministry Forum

So many believers have no idea why certain areas of their lives always seem to trip them up. Sadder yet, many others do not even realize they are in bondage because they have never truly walked in freedom. Faith to Freedom is a must read for anyone who desires freedom, a healthier walk with God, and healthier human relationships. Pastor Craig draws on decades of study and practical experience to write a masterpiece of education and inspiration.

Deryl Hurst, Senior Pastor, Dove Westgate Church

Testimonies

Claustrophobia was keeping me from doing many things and it kept getting worse. I was excited to hear about Faith to Freedom. This healing ministry helped me learn to see myself through the eyes of God. It broke chains of deception that kept me in bondage to fear. I have been craving Him more than ever.

Darlene Eager, Owner of DC Eager Emergency Services, LLC

I was initially skeptical about Faith to Freedom. I was never one to go into the past to fix the present. Two things changed my mind. One is the gentle way the ministry was handled. Secondly was the coupling of prayer and a prophetic voice. This was an effective way to dig up old bitter roots, help repair flaws in my thinking, and plant fresh seeds of life into my soul. Freedom is not an event but a journey. FTF was very helpful in directing me toward greater freedom in my journey with the Lord.

Dennis Scalese, Pastoral Care, Ephrata Community Church, Lancaster, PA

In all my life I never had an encounter with the Holy Spirit that directly healed and set me free from areas I had not realized the enemy was still operating. This ministry brings freedom in all the areas of a person's life that are bound. Breaking past bondages, this ministry releases people into the freedom to become a child of the Living God.

Robert M. Weatherholtz, Associate Director of the Potters House Ministry

FAITH TO FREEDOM

A pathway to wholeness manual

CRAIG SNOW

Faith to Freedom

By Craig Snow
© 2020 Craig Snwo

Published by
Partnership Publications
A Division of House To House Publications
Lititz, Pennsylvania 17543

ISBN-13: 978-1-7330137-1-0
ISBN-10: 1-7330137-1-7

Unless otherwise noted, all scripture quotations in this publication are taken from the Holy Bible, New International Version (NIV).
© 1973, 1978, 1984 by International Bible Society. Used by permission of Zondervan Publishing House. All rights reserved.

Printed in the United States of America

Dedication

I dedicate this book to my big brother, my Lord and Savior, Jesus Christ, who prompted me and guided me in the writing of this book.

I dedicate this book to my family: To my wife Yvonne who has patiently, unselfishly, and generously supported me in ministry over many years, allowing me to invest in others; to my son, Adam who has taught me more about freedom than he will ever realize; to my daughter, Rachel who shares my heart for doing ministry in the name of Jesus Christ; and to my sister, Brenda, my late mom, Ida, and Dad, Meredith, and my extended family for their love and support over many decades of shared life.

Acknowledgements

I want to thank my wife, Yvonne and my children, Adam and Rachel for their ongoing love, keeping me grounded in practicing what I preach. I extend my heart-felt gratitude to my daughter-in-law, Carrie, for her painting depicting Faith to Freedom. I am indebted to the people of St. Andrews U.C.C. and Swamp Christian Fellowship for giving me the privilege to serve as their pastor and for the life lessons they have taught me. I am grateful to DOVE Westgate Church for modeling many of the concepts presented in this book. I am thankful to HarvestNet International for the many ways they have imparted grace to me. I am grateful to pastors and lay people I pray with on Tuesday mornings and my Amish friends I pray with on Friday mornings for their friendship and shared vision for revival. I want to express my appreciation to my small group that has heard much of what is in this book and has been a constant encouragement. I want to express my gratitude to the many colleagues and friends who have interacted with me around the development of this book and for those who have written an endorsement. I am especially thankful for my cousin, Kim Powell, for her encouragement and input. Also, I am grateful to Beth Sahd whose technical support has been immeasurably helpful. Finally, I am most appreciative for Sue Shank who has been my partner in ministry for over twenty-five years. Together the Lord has blessed us with revelation upon revelation and grace upon grace.

FOREWORD

Some years ago, I had the privilege of speaking at a leadership conference sponsored by my pastor friend Craig Snow. I was impressed with Craig's shepherd's heart and love for the body of Christ. I learned that he carries a mandate from the Lord to help believers walk in true freedom through Christ, and then be trained and equipped to help others find the same freedom. He has received a clear revelation that our God does not want us to live under the fear of oppression, but in complete freedom.

Faith to Freedom is a culmination of what Craig has learned over many years as he has watched the Lord bring freedom, healing, and deliverance to many. He has learned key biblical insights into healing and deliverance and puts these truths within our reach.

This book is practical and Bible-based. As a manual, it provides steps toward the attainment of emotional, spiritual, and mental freedom. Craig includes many testimonies from his own life and ministry. He explains how freedom is primarily a spiritual matter conceived in the mind of God and realized in the human heart. A person can be confined to a prison cell, yet be free in spirit.

Craig explains that we are a slave to what we fear. But the good news is, Jesus sets us free from oppression with His truth and love. In Christ, we are no longer slaves to fear or shame. We are adopted sons and daughters of God (Romans 8:15). God calls us to live out the gospel of freedom. Unfortunately, there is often a massive gap between what Christians have learned to expect from the gospel and what they actually experience.

Faith to Freedom presents both the "why" and the "what" for biblical freedom. Ministry apart from sound doctrine invites disaster. I love the way Craig delves into the nuts and bolts of ministry, all the while helping us understand the need for a culture of freedom. He teaches us that in the absence of the healing and deliverance ministries, the church does not look much different from the world.

This means we must grow in our experience of health, security, contentment, and sense of well-being. In this regard, salvation is continual and progressive. Many Christians believe and yet they don't believe. They vacillate between faith and unbelief. They believe with their head, but not with their heart. Craig teaches us that true faith and action are inseparable. If we do not do what the Lord says, we don't really believe in Him.

Craig helps us understand that anxiety is fear without a known cause. It is the accumulation of pain and unease that stems from concerns that remain uncertain or unfounded. Anxiety dominates modern life. It is produced by rapid change, information overload, mistrust for authority and government institutions, breakdown of the family, and instant media exposure to world crises that include terror, natural disaster, crime, and conflict.

- Fear says: "I am afraid I will always be alone and unloved." Faith says: "God loves me and draws me to Himself" (Jeremiah 31:3).

- Fear says: "I can't help being overwhelmed." Faith says: "These feelings are not valid. They are a bluff to my mind and body, not grounded in truth" (Psalms 27:3).

- Fear says: "I am afraid of failure." Faith says: "I can do all things through Christ who strengthens me" (Philippians 4:13).

The list goes on.

Jesus did not come to make us religious. He came to set us free from all spirits that keep us captive to sin. *"If the Son sets you free, you are free indeed."* (John 8:36). Jesus came to restore us to a right relationship of freedom with the Living God.

We learn in *Faith to Freedom* that knowing our true identity in Christ is crucial to breaking any false identity Satan and the world want to place on us. Instead of letting the opinions of others define us, we must believe the truth of what God says about us. Believing the truth found in God's Word is what sets us free from lies and false identities. Craig's book helps us to do this.

Many in the coming years will praise God for the wealth of spiritual and practical wisdom found in the pages of this book. Thank you, Craig, for sharing your life with us and for sharing key biblical insights about healing and deliverance. It is made practical so that all of us can follow in your steps of finding freedom and helping others find it as well. Thank you for your obedience to the Lord in writing this helpful and crucial book.

Larry Kreider

International Director

DOVE International

CONTENTS

Section 4: Constructing A Culture of Freedom

Appendices

Introduction

"You, my brothers and sisters, were called to be free.
But do not use your freedom to indulge the flesh;
rather, serve one another in love."
Galatians 5:13 NIV

"Live as people who are free, not using your freedom as a
cover-up for evil, but living as servants."
1 Peter 2:16 ESV

The Bible champions God as a Liberator—One who brings freedom to His people. At the very core of God's character is a heart for freedom. In 2 Corinthians 3:17, Paul makes it understandable, *"Now the Lord is the Spirit, and where the Spirit of the Lord is, there is freedom"* (NIV). God wants His people to live with the same freedom He enjoys. He does not want them to live under fear of oppression, and demonstrates this again and again. He raised up Moses to free slaves from Egypt (Exodus 9:1). He proclaimed liberty to debtors in the year of Jubilee (Leviticus 25:10). He delivered Israel from their enemies as recorded in the book of Judges. He miraculously delivered King Hezekiah from Assyria (2 Kings 20:6; 2 Chronicles 32:20-22). He released Israel from captivity in Babylon (Ezra 1:1-11). The priest Zechariah prophesied the birth of John the Baptist with the words, *"God has come to help his people and set them free"* (Luke 1:68, 74 GNT). Most importantly, God sent a Messiah who would, in the words of Isaiah, set all people free from spiritual bondage (Isaiah 61:1). This promise was fulfilled in the birth of Jesus Christ.

Cultural norms, laws, and governing systems have much to with expanding or limiting individual freedoms. However, the configuration of social and political entities devised by man do not represent freedom. Freedom is primarily a spiritual matter conceived in the mind of God and realized in the human heart. A person can be confined to a prison cell, yet be free in spirit. People may riot or revolt in an attempt to overthrow an oppressive government, but like moving pieces on a chess board, this only achieves the repositioning of power brokers. Unless there is change in the human spirit, oppression remains. Government systems intended to treat people with equity and fairness are only as just and free as the people who are in power.

There are spiritual forces behind every human act of oppression. These evil forces incite the fear of man. They pervert and corrupt justice. They need to be confronted and overcome. You are a slave to what you fear. The good news is that Jesus sets us free from oppression with His truth and love. In Him, we are no longer slaves to fear or shame. We are adopted sons and daughters of God (Romans 8:15). God calls us to live a gospel of freedom. Unfortunately, there is a massive gap between what Christians have learned to expect from the gospel and what they actually experience.

In the scriptures above, both Paul and Peter remind Christians that their faith in Christ is a call to freedom. This freedom does not license one to indulge in the sinful nature; instead, it is a mandate to serve others in love. Serving others in love requires freedom from sin. James 1:27 puts it this way, *"Religion that God our Father accepts as pure and faultless is this: to look after orphans and widows in their distress and to keep oneself from being polluted by the world."* Today, many Christians are eager to show God's love through charitable acts of service but have lost sight of the urgency to free themselves of spiritual pollution. They have faith but need to discover freedom. They are saved but are not free.

For the average Christian, salvation is a reward for having made a personal decision. They have decided to make Christ their Savior and are assured of going to heaven. Out of gratitude and obedience to God, they show kindness to others, and consequently feel confident in their spiritual condition and destiny. This is all well and good, but it also begs the question: How likely is it for a believer to become spiritually: complacent when he already knows he is going to heaven?

Think of it this way: what would motivate a believer to change his thinking, to sacrifice his comfort, to alter his habits, and to abandon his fleshly desires, when he is already convinced that—without any additional effort—he is good enough to inherit a mansion in the sky? Why would he put himself through all the pain and stress of personal transformation? Why would he want to rid himself of worldly pollution when heaven is already in sight? Why would he want to die to himself when he already has eternal life? Could it be that an earthly life lived in freedom is better than one lived in bondage? Could it be that the freedom found in Christ is better than being held captive to the destructive forces of darkness? Could it be that a life dedicated to freedom is living on a higher plain, one in which the love, joy, peace and blessing of heaven is experienced in the here and now?

Without teachings in freedom one can easily become complacent, self-satisfied, and apathetic. Faith can lose its urgency. Spiritual matters become optional and the call to usher in the kingdom fades away in a fog of mundane business. Neglect of the inner life results in the person being more defined by the world than by the Word. He may get into heaven, but heaven has not yet gotten into him. For this reason, it becomes necessary to remind people that salvation is not merely mental assent to believe in a Savior, it is a lifestyle made possible by a gospel of freedom.

At the beginning of His public ministry, Jesus announces the kingdom of God is near (Matthew 3:2). He declares that living in this kingdom is good news. He promises a life of freedom. He makes it clear that the Holy Spirit is upon Him and that He has come to set captives free from the oppression of sin, death, and evil (Luke 4:18-19).

Later in His ministry, Jesus gives grace and power to His disciples to live as free men and set others free. He gives them the gift of the Holy Spirit, thus providing both the motivation and the means to change people from the inside out. In this way, they are made heirs to everything that belongs to Him. Sin, failures, or inadequacies no longer define them. Shame and fear do not shackle them. The chains are broken. There is no need to excuse or hide from sin. In Christ they are free from condemnation (Romans 8:1). Reconciled to God, they can be honest with themselves and with others.

Through the presence and power of the Holy Spirit, life takes on an expectant hope and positive change. Pride, jealousy, and selfishness lose their appeal as believers grow in grace and truth. The living Word of God renews hearts and minds. A culture of honor emerges that looks a lot like heaven. Believers do not seek to compete, dominate, or incriminate, but to serve and love each other. Relationships take on a quality of harmony and unity envied by the world. This is the kingdom Jesus proclaimed and the one He died for.

All of this sounds wonderful and tranquil, except for one daunting fact. Within any body of believers, there still exists sinful behavior and evil practices. There is still an ongoing war between spirit and flesh. Individuals suffer from despair, anxiety, rejection, loneliness, torment, woundedness, addictions, and inner turmoil. The church still struggles with conflict and disunity. Pride supplants humility. Blame, bitterness, and belligerence reside in the heart. Gossip and venom fly from the tongue. Sexual perversion is tolerated. Consequently, outsiders charge Christians with hypocrisy and a lack of authenticity. The church becomes a place to avoid rather than embrace.

One of the most significant barriers to unity, healthy relationships, and life-giving community is pretense. We pretend we don't struggle with sin. On the outside we put on a good-looking face of righteousness. On the inside, self-righteousness, judgment, jealousy, resentment, lust, fear, depression, a critical spirit, selfish ambition, and unbelief fill our souls. The harsh reality is that where defilement of spirit goes unrecognized and demons are ignored, oppression abounds.

In such an atmosphere, honor, trust, and respect slowly erode. Vision and energy fade as people lose hope for the abundant life. Such pretense leads to the practice of religion and an emphasis on 'doing' over 'being.' The focus of the church becomes protocol, politics, problems, and programs rather than righteousness, relationship, reconciliation, and restoration. Institutional success is elevated above spiritual growth. Tasks and events take precedent over prayer and presence. Corporate goals take priority over soul development. The Board Room takes preference over the Throne Room. Information overshadows transformation. Revelation succumbs to reason. Compassion is reduced to joyless duty.

But we are not without hope! God is all about revival. Despite all the flaws found in the church, God is continuously at work, transforming her to reflect the character of His Son. In 2 Corinthians 3:18 Paul states: *"But we all are being transformed into the same image from glory to glory, just as from the Lord, the Spirit."* Jesus is still working to present Himself with a pure bride without stain or wrinkle (Ephesians 5:27).

The good news is that Jesus is incrementally setting us free from pretense, deception, and rationalization. He is setting us free from the corruption of the world and lies of demons. He is still depositing truth and grace into our lives. John 8:36 declares: *"So if the Son sets you free, you will be free indeed."*

The purpose of this book is to apply the power of the gospel to our frail and corrupted lives. As we revisit biblical truths and implement practical strategies, both as individuals and the local church, we are empowered to carry out the Apostle Paul's admonition, *"Therefore, beloved, since we have these promises, let us cleanse ourselves from everything that defiles body and spirit, perfecting holiness in the fear of the Lord"* (2 Corinthians 7:1).

Most people wait until they experience a crisis, like a broken marriage, financial ruin, or drug addiction before they seek help with getting their life in order. Instead, it is my hope that believers will see healing and deliverance as an ongoing way of life. My hope is that readers will experience the fulfillment of Jabez's Prayer. *"And Jabez called out to the God of Israel, 'If only You would bless me and enlarge my territory! May Your hand be with me and keep me from harm, so that I will be free from pain.' And God granted the request of Jabez"* (1 Chronicles 4:10, BSB). May the contents of this book bless you to keep the faith and live free.

At the beginning of this writing project I thought I could simply outline practical ways people can be set free from bondage. However, the further I went into the project, it became evident that I needed to provide some theological underpinnings as well. The first part of the book deals with the "Why and the What." It provides a theology for freedom and lays a foundation for achieving it. Ministry in the absence of sound doctrines invites disaster. Therefore, it is appropriate to engage in some fundamental theology first.

The second half of the book focuses on the "How-To" and delves into ministry nuts and bolts, plus the need for a culture of freedom.

My sincere desire is to help local churches restore souls and set them free to do ministry in the power of the Holy Spirit. I pray the truth in these pages will help people move from a faith in Jesus that merely gets them into heaven to a freedom in Jesus that brings heaven to earth. My hope is that readers will gain a new vision and a dynamic faith, setting them free for positive life change. In turn, the church will also be more fruitful, producing mature disciples.

Scripture tells us to forget the past because God is doing a new thing (Isaiah 43:19). God's ways and thoughts are higher than our ways and thoughts (Isaiah 55:9). God does not always work the way we expect. Moses had never seen a burning bush or witnessed the opening of the sea before God gave him these experiences. Peter was not familiar with walking on water or collecting money from a fish. My hope is that by reading this book, you will be open to encounter God in new ways. I pray this book will strengthen your faith, moving you past your current personal experience and logic, into a realm of revelation and power that results in freedom.

A list of questions suitable for a small group discussion is provided at the end of each chapter. The facilitator can address them in numerical order or pick and choose according to time constraints. Resources in the Appendix can help expand understanding and make application to the biblical practices.

"Freedom is the oxygen of the soul."

– Moshe Dayan

1

Why This Book?

Personal Background

As long as I can remember, I have been a Christian. I was baptised as an infant and later at the age of twelve, I was baptized by immersion. My family on both sides were church attenders. I grew up believing that Jesus died for my sins, and by faith in Him, I was saved. My family's example most impacted my life. They were the ones who shaped my beliefs and values. From age twelve on, I believed I would be going to heaven when I died. However, I was constantly plagued by guilt for sinning over and over again. I would sin and ask for forgiveness, only to do it over again. I felt trapped. I knew there had to be something more, and I developed an insatiable desire to search for that something more. I did not realize it at the time, but I was following Jeremiah's admonition, *"You will seek me and find me when you seek me with all your heart"* (Jeremiah 29:13).

During those early teen years, I thought of God as transcendent. He was some supernatural being in outer space, all-knowing and all-powerful, who was watching me and keeping score when I did something wrong. That understanding kept me morally constrained, but it did not bring much peace. To make sense of my world, I went to college seeking insight into myself. Trying to find my purpose and place in this life, I enrolled in classes like philosophy, sociology, and psychology. I graduated from Towson State University in 1974 with a Bachelor of Science degree in Psychology.

In March of 1975, I took a group of youth on a weekend retreat. On that retreat, my life took a surprising turn. During a time of collective prayer, each student gave thanks for something positive they experienced over the weekend. As the prayers began to my left, everyone closed their eyes and bowed their heads, except for me. I looked across the room, and a white cloud appeared over the head of one of the young people. It was brighter than the sun. Within the cloud were shiny sparkles of silver and gold, glistening in the light. The cloud was the shape of an upside-down triangle. I heard a voice coming out the cloud. The voice said, "My name is Jesus, and this is where I live." I immediately began to cry as I remembered a phrase from a hymn we would often sing in church, "You ask me how I know He lives? He lives within my heart." At that moment, the presence of Jesus became real, convincing me that everything I had learned from the Bible was true. God was no longer an intellectual concept, a force that governed the universe; rather he was a Spirit that lived in me. I could hear His voice. The whole experience put me on a spiritual high that lasted for three weeks. I was so filled with hope and love my family thought I had fallen into some kind of a cult.

This encounter created in me a hunger and a thirst to understand the Word of God better. I spent the next year fervently reading the Bible, going to conferences, attending prayer meetings, and getting involved in outreach. I witnessed to people and saw miracles happen. One day when I was reading my Bible, I turned to Ephesians chapter four. Something peculiar happened. I came upon verses 11 and 12 which state: "*And he gave some, apostles; and some, prophets; and some, evangelists; and some, pastors and teachers; For the perfecting of the saints, for the work of the ministry, for the edifying of the body of Christ*" (KJV). Those words seem to leap off the page and into my heart. They became deeply embedded in my soul. I had no idea what was going on, but soon I would get some hints.

Through some carefully orchestrated God appointments, I met some remarkable people and attended certain events that propelled me to explore the possibility of becoming a pastor. Within a year, I was a seminary student. I fully expected to learn how to make disciples who would know Jesus as Savior and Lord. I was not prepared for the challenges ahead of me.

Throughout my seminary education, I continued to have many encounters with the Holy Spirit. These spiritual encounters sustained me. The rigors of intellectual argument continually challenged my simple faith. My experience of the supernatural was constantly bumping up against the rational explanations of biblical accounts. However, throughout my seminary years I never lost my intrigue with the passage in Ephesians chapter four. In fact, that intrigue only intensified as I began to look at the passage in the original Greek language.

One word mystified me. I could not make sense of it. In the King James Version, it says "perfecting of the saints for the work of ministry". The Greek word for "perfecting" is the word, *katartismos*. It is translated in English to mean "complete furnishing, equipping." At that time when I thought of equipping someone for the work of ministry, I thought about acquiring biblical knowledge, learning sound doctrine, and developing skills that would enable me to be a pastor. After all, isn't that what seminary is all about? However, I discovered that the word *katartismos* was also found in other passages. In Matthew 4:21 and Mark 1:19, James and John are in a boat mending their fishing nets. In both references the Greek word for "mending" is *katartizo*, the verb form of *katartismos*. These multiple meanings were very puzzling.

I could not make sense of how mending or repairing broken fishing nets had anything to do with equipping people for pastoral ministry. Going further, I discovered a passage in Galatians 6:1 that uses the same word. It says, "*Brothers and sisters, if someone is caught in a sin, you who live by the Spirit should **restore** that person gently. But watch yourselves, or you also may be tempted*" (emphasis mine). The Greek word for "restore" is also *katartizo*. Again, I was mystified. What does "restoring" people from sinful behavior have to do with equipping people for ministry? Sinful people are doing ministry all the time. And what connection did that have with mending broken nets?

For twenty-six years serving as a local church pastor, I remained perplexed. I could not understand how repairing broken nets and restoring sinful people had anything to do with equipping people for the work of ministry.

In 2005, I went through a spiritual cleansing process and was delivered from demonic spirits. At that point I received revelation. The word *katartismos* finally made sense. Equipping the saints for ministry is not merely the acquisition of Bible knowledge and developing pastoral skills such as preaching, counseling and administration. More fundamentally, it is the restoration of broken souls. It is healing inner hurts. It is deliverance from demonic lies hidden in the unconscious mind. It is dismantling false identities and reconstructing true identities. It is equipping broken souls to live by the Spirit rather than the sinful nature. A properly restored, repaired, and mended soul functions as God intended. The soul set free from bondage is empowered to live out God's purposes and destiny. A restored soul equips a person to do ministry in the Spirit rather than the flesh.

Since 2005, I have come to see that equipping the saints involves more than educating people in the scriptures, giving money, programing fellowship events, planning potluck meals and doing humanitarian deeds. Equipping sets souls free from suffering, corruption, deception, and distortions. It has a supernatural, restorative, healing, and transformational quality.

After retiring from the pastorate in 2016, I earnestly gave myself to this ministry. Over the past few years, I have seen the life-giving power of the Holy Spirit set people free at deeper and deeper levels. This has given me pause to think how I could have implemented this ministry when I was a pastor.

During the 1980s and 1990s, numerous people would say to me, "You need to write a book." My response was always the same. "I have nothing to say that has not already been said." Then in 2017, I was leading a training event to activate students for ministry. During one of the sessions, I took the role of the person receiving ministry. The Holy Spirit revealed I had received a word curse that prevented me from stepping out to write a book.

The Spirit stimulated a memory of something that happened during my college days. As a student, my English Professor had given me a writing assignment. When the paper came back, there was more red ink on it than white space. I went to the professor to talk about the paper. She said to me in matter-of-fact terms, "You will never be a writer." Her words stung. They were like a knife piercing my heart. Believing her words were true, I never thought I had the ability to write a book. However, after breaking off that word curse, I was set free to begin to write. With fear and trembling and with a great deal of dependence on the Holy Spirit, I have undertaken this writing project.

Admittedly, I considered giving up many times. However, the gift of prophecy inspired me to persevere. Three different prophets whom I did not know, on three different occasions, said they saw me writing books and manuals that would advance the kingdom of God. Those prophetic words served as encouragement and confirmation that I was doing what the Lord put in my heart forty years earlier.

Woven throughout these pages are lessons learned, not only from my personal experience but from others who have found freedom. I am most grateful to them, for they have taught me much about freedom found in Jesus Christ.

Christians Need Freedom Too – A Pastor's Story

Kyle is the Senior pastor of a congregation in Reading, Pennsylvania. He grew up in a Christian home. His father was a pastor. Kyle went to seminary and became a pastor as well. At age thirty-eight he came to see me and my associate, Sue Shank, in search of deliverance from anger and rage.

Just prior to his coming, a fellow pastor and his wife were involved in a motorcycle accident. Sadly, the pastor's wife died, and his friend lost a leg. This incident triggered deep-seated anger within Kyle, causing him much misery and frustration. He realized that his temper was out of control. Kyle is a man of faith who has dedicated his life to developing the faith of others. Yet he was in bondage to the sin of anger. He had faith, but he was not free. This is what he had to say about his deliverance experience.

Last year, during the summer of 2016, I found myself to be an angry person. I was short-fused with those I wished to have the most patience. I was easily frustrated and overwhelmed, and I lived without proper emotional margin.

I wasn't violent, but I was a jerk, reacting to situations in ways that did not reflect the man I want to be and to become.

All of this led me to Restoring the Foundations, and to Pastor Craig Snow and Sue Shank. What transpired over the course of the next several hours was nothing short of extraordinary. It is hard to put that time into a sequence of events as if it is simply a program with a series of steps, but I will try to describe what took place.

After brief greetings and prayer, we talked for an hour or so in a way that was similar to a counseling session. At the great risk of sounding like a Christian cliché, all I can say is that Jesus showed up. I became aware, not through therapy, but by the conviction of the Holy Spirit, that the murder in the summer of 2001 of my mentor, Dr. Janet Rahamut, was the root of my pain and the cause of my anger. To understand my encounter with Jesus, I need to provide context for the event that He sought to heal.

As a young, single student beginning seminary, that murder made me question whether or not I could trust God with my future. The pain reopened the year before when a pastor friend lost his wife and his leg when a drunk driver struck their motorcycle. Now, however, I was not a young student with my life in front of me. I was a husband, a father of two wonderful boys, a pastor, a homeowner, etc. Now I questioned whether I could trust God with my present.

All too often, I trick myself into thinking that it takes heaven and earth to move mountains in order for a young, fit, reasonably-minded person to die. This was one of the occasions that stripped away my illusions. I was reminded of how fleeting life can be, how the best and most fervently prayed over of plans can end in a moment, often with little to no warning.

There are any number of ways I could have interpreted this realization, but I allowed a lie of Satan to take root near the core of my being—that God was not a good father; He was instead bad and negligent.

As the Holy Spirit made me aware of this during our counseling, I had the closest thing to a vision that I have ever experienced. I saw myself and Jesus sitting across the table from each other in the dining room of Dr J (what we affectionately called Dr. Rahamut). As I felt His love and peace, I handed Him all the bitterness, anger, resentment, and unbelief that had built up in my spirit, and I received His forgiveness and healing.

As I was struggling to trust Him, the most difficult area related to my two sons. What if something happened to them? Yet in that moment I felt the security of the Holy Spirit and I saw myself lean across the table and hand a picture of my sons to Jesus. He embraced me, poured His love over me, and tucked the picture of my sons into the folds of his robe, right next to His chest, near His heart.

If all of this sounds sensationalized or unbelievable, I can simply say that I was bound but now I am free. While I still struggle with sin and even anger at times, I am a changed man. Those close to me agree that I am more Christ-like. I am sold on the power and anointing that God pours out through the process of Restoring the Foundations."

What is Restoring the Foundations?

This is Kyle's testimony. However, there are hundreds, even thousands, of others like it. Restoring the Foundations (RTF), is a healing and deliverance ministry established by Chester and Betsy Kylstra. Betsy was a social worker and Chester was an engineer. Together, under the leading of the Holy Spirit, they were directed to develop a systematic and integrated approach to inner healing and deliverance. Based on biblical principles, they identified four areas that contribute to emotional, physical, psychological and spiritual dysfunction. These include: Sins of the Fathers and Consequential Curses (generational curses), Ungodly Beliefs (lies), Soul Spirit Hurts (trauma) and Demonic Oppression (defiling or unclean spirits). Through the application of forgiveness, confession, repentance, renunciation, receiving grace, pouring out your complaint and other biblical teachings, all offered in the spirit of prayer, the person experiences freedom at the core of their being. It was through this process that Kyle had an incredible encounter with Jesus, setting him free from deep seated anger.

I am incredibly grateful to the Kylstra's for the groundbreaking work they did in establishing a systematic approach to healing and deliverance. Back in 2005, their close friends, John and Leslie Kindler, introduced me to this life-giving ministry. Being set free from generational curses myself, I went on to receive training in this ministry of healing and deliverance. Today, even though I am retired from the pastoral ministry, I continue to minister to people like Kyle who are searching for freedom in their life. I refer to my ministry as Faith to Freedom. I believe God not only wants His people to have faith in Him, but also to enjoy the freedom He provides.

Do you have an anger problem? Do you struggle with lust? Do you battle depression? Do you wrestle with shame and guilt? Do fear and anxiety paralyze you? Do you feel defeated by a string of broken relationships? Are you feeling insignificant and jealous of others? Do you have to be right about everything? Do you feel insecure or driven to prove your worth? Do you desire peace but continually feel stressed out? Do you comfort yourself with food, alcohol, drugs, sex or entertainment? Do you feel compelled to work all the time? Are you competing and in conflict with those close to you? Are you easily offended? Do you feel rejected? Does your life lack purpose? Do you have goals but feel something is hindering them? Do you pray but feel that your prayers are not making much difference? Are you attending worship, yet your soul remains dull and lethargic? If you can identify with any of these, maybe you are a person of faith who needs to be truly set free. Salvation fully lived bears the fruit of freedom. John 8:36 declares, "*So if the Son sets you free, you will be free indeed.*"

A Need to Recover Restoring Ministries

In my view, there is a great need to restore the healing and deliverance ministry back to the church. These are the ministries that set people free through applying the truth of the Word and the power of the Spirit. This ministry cannot be relegated to the periphery of congregational life and treated as optional. It is central to the mission of the church and essential to the health of believers. Apart from the ministry of healing and deliverance, the Kingdom of Heaven cannot manifest fully here on earth. This is why Jesus devoted so much of His time to training His disciples to heal and cast out demons. Ancient documents, both secular and religious, reveal it was common for every Christian to be able to cast out demons.

Many Christians are living defeated lives and are desperate for cleansing, healing, and deliverance. They want to know their faith can make a difference in the quality of life. Learning theology, Bible study, spiritual disciplines and fellowship are all needed, but people are hungering for something more. They want to experience the goodness of God for themselves. They want to experience the abundant life Jesus promised.

In the absence of the healing and deliverance ministries, the church does not look much different than the world. In fact, many view the church negatively, labeling it as irrelevant, judgmental, intolerable, and archaic. Perhaps the severest criticism levied against Christians is they are hypocritical. Believers pretend to follow Jesus, but their lifestyle and behaviors are in stark contrast to the teachings of Jesus. Sermons expound, "All have sinned and fallen short of the glory of God" and "Grace is sufficient for all things." Yet the prevailing culture in many churches is one of accommodation, neglecting hidden sin, ignoring the reality of evil and giving a superficial nod to repentance. All of this points to a lack of accountability. The emphasis is on changing behavior rather than spiritual realities rooted in the heart. Consequently, little change is occurring in the character of the believer, reducing Christian morality to the same behavioral modification practiced by the world.

What Current Studies Reveal

Over the last twenty years, studies conducted by evangelical sociologist George Barna have shown that attitudes and behaviors between Christians and non-believers are virtually the same. Surveys show no difference in such things as handling debt, divorce, viewing sexually explicit materials, giving money to the poor, drugs prescribed for depression, use of profanity in public and much more. When it comes to living self-indulgent lifestyles, there is little to no difference between Christians and the world.

These characteristics are the antithesis of the early church. New Testament writers clearly advocated a separation from the world based on a life of holiness. Hebrews 12:14 states, *"Make every effort to live in peace with everyone and to be holy; without holiness no one will see the Lord."* Even more importantly, Jesus himself prayed that His disciples would not to be identified with the standards of the world. *"I'm not asking you to take them out of the world, but to keep them safe from the evil one. They do not belong to this world any more than I do. Make them holy by your truth; teach them your word, which is truth"* (John 17:15-17 NLT).

In an interview conducted by Homiletics Online, George Barna made the following observations when asked, "Do we really want to know what it means to act like a Christian?"

There are a couple of things that go into that. One of them is that we're happy to take the label of Christian and not have to deal with the responsibility. Part of that is because of an absence of leadership in churches. You see, most of the churches in America have no God-given vision that they're centered on. And so, what do we wind up doing? We revert to playing the religious game. Let's have **more programs**, let's get **more people in the seats**, let's build a **bunch of buildings**—all the things about which the world would say, 'Ah, that's success.' This has nothing to do with God's equation of 'Are you holy? Are you obedient? Are you serving? Do you want to be like Christ?' So, we've missed the boat there. We've got to have the leadership component.[1]

Barna went on to say that educational research shows that 60 to 70 percent of behavior change comes from modeling. As the person finds someone they can trust, they watch them and starts to imitate them. He asserted this is a missing component in the Church today.

We know that less than 10 percent of all Christian families ever spend time studying the Bible and praying together. Less than 10 percent. So, what does that mean? It means that most Christian families are saying to the local church, 'Here are my kids. You deal with them and I'll do my best to get them there next week. That's my contribution.' So that's not enough.[2]

Finally, Barna made the observation that the things that have the most influence over people's thinking and behavior are movies, television, the internet, publishing, public policy officials and parents—not the church!

Missing the Mark

Recently, Lindsay Putney, a beautiful twenty-eight-year-old woman from my small group, gave a testimony to her church. She had just completed a study in the Gospels and had come to a new realization. On the brink of tears, she confessed, "My life looks nothing like Jesus' life." She further explained that all her life she believed that Jesus was God who came to earth to show man how to live. And as his followers, we are to imitate Him. But she discovered a greater truth. Jesus was a man living on the earth, showing us how to live like God. The Holy Spirit that made the man Jesus to be God was the same Holy Spirit that dwelt in her. Previously, she had mistakenly thought she could not live like Christ because He was divine and she was human. The reason her life didn't look anything like Jesus' life was because she was trying to follow Jesus on her own strength rather than in the power of the Spirit. She had missed the mark and asked the question: "How did this happen?"

Based on Barna's research and the above comments, it is evident that the church in America has missed the mark when it comes to implementing Jesus' teaching on salvation and equipping people to live a life like Jesus. Instead of proclaiming a gospel that demonstrates the Spirit's power, the church has opted for social programs designed to address human appetites. Although most churches are preaching orthodox Christian doctrine, personal belief systems are not being integrated into these teachings. I think it is fair to say that the numerical and spiritual decline in today's church reflects the Apostle Paul's warning to Timothy regarding the state of the church in the last days. Paul wrote:

> But mark this: There will be terrible times in the last days. People will be lovers of themselves, lovers of money, boastful, proud, abusive, disobedient to their parents, ungrateful, unholy, without love, unforgiving, slanderous, without self-control, brutal, not lovers of the good, treacherous, rash, conceited, lovers of pleasure rather than lovers of God – having the form of godliness but denying its power. Have nothing to do with such people (2 Timothy 3:1-5).

I have observed that while salvation is preached in most churches, there is a lack of power to set captives free from sin and evil. There is a form of religion but little to no spiritual power to overcome the sinful nature. Christians, in general, have biblical knowledge but do not grasp how to make salvation fully operative in their lives. Consequently, they live well below their potential spiritual inheritance in Christ Jesus. Settling for contentment in what Christ has already done at conversion, they lose out on further blessings that come from walking in the Spirit. As apathy sets in, hunger and passion for God begins to wane. Good works and orthodox teachings remain, but as Revelation 2:4 warns, they have forsaken their first love.

For evidence of this, one needs to look no further than the emphasis on church programs over the pursuit of God's presence, or the emphasis on performance over prayer. Prayer meetings are the least attended meetings in the church. Doing good things is important, but it must be governed by our being one with Christ. Otherwise salvation becomes a matter of works rather than grace.

Salvation, properly understood, includes power to set people free from worldly bondages. Believers have power to overcome evil with good. Teaching the gospel apart from power does not stand up against the temptations and schemes of the evil one. It leaves the church weak and undistinguishable from those in the world. On the other hand, where the Spirit of the Lord is there is liberty (2 Corinthians 3:17).

Before going further, it is important that I clarify my intentions. Although my words may seem critical and my attitude a bit cynical, I can assure you that is not what is in my heart. I do not want to bash, put down, or dwell on the deficiencies of the modern church. Sometimes we can exaggerate the negatives and magnify the shortcomings to the point of inflicting discouragement. I love the church. She is the body of Christ. The last thing I want is to offend the bride of Christ. However, if the bride is to be ready for the coming of the bridegroom, she must be brutally honest and willing to apply the healing salve of Truth to for removal of her blemishes. I sincerely hope that in the pages that follow, you will find reason to rejoice. I hope you will become as giddy as a radiant bride, getting ready for the bridegroom's arrival.

First and foremost, discipleship is about a growing love relationship with God. Jesus taught that the greatest commandment is to love God. From that relationship, we are equipped to love our neighbors. Unfortunately, our capacity to love our neighbors dwindles when our relationship with God is weakened. A. W. Tozer wrote, "Orthodox Christianity has fallen to its present low estate from the lack of spiritual desire. Among many who profess the Christian faith. scarcely one in a thousand reveals any passionate thirst for God."[3] "But it is wholly impossible to love the unknown. There must be some degree of experience before there can be any degree of love. Perhaps this accounts for the coldness toward God and Christ evidenced by the average Christian. How can we love a Being whom we have not heard nor felt nor experienced?"[4]

For more information regarding Restoring the Foundations and other freedom and deliverance ministries that are impacting the church, consider the following.

Restoring the Foundations: 1-828-696-9075 www.RestoringTheFoundations.org. Additional ministries include: Cleansing Streams, Freedom in Christ, Truly Free, House of Healing Ministries, Be in Health.

Discussion Questions

1.   Before reading this chapter, how did you think about freedom? What pops into your head when you hear the word freedom? How has this chapter provoked or expanded your thinking? In what ways has it stretched your understanding of what freedom means for your faith?

2.   Have you ever stopped to consider what salvation means for you while you live on earth or have you mainly had a heavenly perspective of salvation? What has the church taught you about salvation?

3.   The author shared some ways God has spoken to him. How has God spoken to you? What impact have God's messages to you had on the trajectory of your life? Have these words created any ongoing questions in your heart?

4.   What stood out to you about Pastor Kyle's testimony? If Pastor Kyle needed freedom from his past, do think other Christians could benefit from a healing and deliverance ministry as well? How do you see your family and friends benefiting from this kind of ministry? Do you need more freedom? What keeps you from it?

5.   The author believes churches need to re-instate the healing and deliverance ministry. Do you agree or disagree? Why? What hurdles need to be overcome in order to this to happen?

6.   George Barna's study revealed there is little to no difference between the morals of believers and non-believers. What do you think your church should do about that? What could you do to help turn things around?

7.   The author asserts that one reason the church has missed the mark in equipping believers to live like Jesus is the failure to teach the full meaning of salvation. Do you agree or disagree with this view? Why or why not?

8.   The author asserts that salvation fully embraced bears the fruit of freedom. What does salvation have to do with freedom? How does a person leverage faith in order to realize freedom? What does the presence of the Spirit have to do with freedom?

Endnotes

1. http://www.homileticsonline.com/subscriber. Interviews/barna.asp
2. Ibid.

2

Salvation Results in Freedom or Freedom Results in Salvation Which Is It?

Salvation Is More Than A Ticket to Heaven

Christianity teaches that Jesus is the Savior of the world (John 3:16). He acquired salvation for those who believe in His life, His death on the cross and His resurrection from the dead (Romans 10:9). By His grace He has saved our souls (1 Peter 1:9). Okay—but what does a saved soul look like?

For many Christians, salvation means having faith in Christ to forgive sin and having hope of going to heaven when you die. This belief brings much consolation. It helps people endure many trials and troubles in this life, knowing they will eventually leave this world for a better one. While this is true, salvation involves much more than having your ticket punched for heaven.

Biblical salvation entails a sense of health, wholeness, safety, prosperity, peace and well-being in the present. It means freedom from the power of sin, freedom from the lies of the world, freedom from the oppression of evil, and freedom from the fear of death. God's Truth sets us free (John 8:31-32). This freedom produces an unshakeable hope, an unexplainable peace, and an unspeakable joy (1 Peter 1:8).

This freedom enables Christians to live as conquerors instead of victims (Romans 8:37). No longer are they slaves to fear (Romans 8:15). They are free to be the children of God (Galatians 4:7). Their identity is based on the fear of the Lord rather than the fear of man. Jesus lived his life based on the fear of the Lord. The Prophet Isaiah declared the Messiah would fear the Lord and even take delight in the fear of the Lord (Isaiah 11:2-3). Just as Jesus feared the Lord, believers must do the same to enjoy the blessings of salvation.

Paradoxically, fearing the Lord is what sets captives free from the fear of humiliation, rejection and threats that comes from man. John Newton eloquently wrote of this truth in his beloved hymn, *Amazing Grace.* The second stanza says:

> *'Twas grace that taught my heart to fear (the fear of the Lord)*
> *And grace, my fears relieved (fears of the world)*
> *How precious did that grace appear*
> *The hour I first believed.*

The fear of the Lord is integral to salvation. Oddly enough, it is the fear of the Lord that results in a long and good life (Psalm 34:11-22). This is the blessing God wants his children to have. In John 10:10 Jesus said, *"My purpose is to give them a rich and satisfying life"* (NLT). Salvation then, is not only about a future life in heaven, it is about abundant life in the present made possible through faith and the freedom found in Christ.

In this chapter we will explore more fully what it means to be saved. Without a complete understanding of salvation, Christians lose out on what God intends for their lives. A brief word study will help us grasp the concept of salvation as expressed in both the Hebrew and Greek languages.

How the Bible Defines Salvation

The Hebrew word for "save" in the Old Testament is *yasha.* It is a verb meaning "to defend, deliver, help, preserve from destruction, rescue, be safe, bring salvation, save and get victory." These words depict life here on earth as well as life in heaven.

Yasha is a root word for the noun *Yeshuwah* which means "something saved, deliverance, aid, victory, prosperity, health, salvation, welfare." The word *Yehowshuwa* is a noun for the name Joshua meaning "God saves."

Yeshua is the Hebrew word derived from *Yehowshuwa.* It is the Hebrew name for Jesus which means "to rescue or deliver." Jesus is the one who brings salvation to humanity. He is the Savior who frees us from sin, death and evil. Life lived in Him brings a sense of victory, prosperity, security, health, and well-being to a person's life.

There are two Greek words in the New Testament for "save." They both are equivalent to *yasha* in the Old Testament.

The first word is *sozo.* It is a verb meaning "to heal, deliver, protect, save, preserve, do well or prosper, and be made whole." It not only communicates the idea of victory over death via eternal life for the soul, but also victory in every area of our earthy life. *Sozo* is found fifty-four times in the gospels. It is used in three different ways:

1. Fourteen times as deliverance from disease or demon possession.
2. Twenty times as rescue of physical life or some impending peril or death.
3. Twenty times as spiritual salvation of the soul.

The second word is *soteria*. It is the noun form of *sozo*. It also refers to salvation including such concepts as deliverance, preservation, restoration, safety, security against danger, bodily health, and a sense of well-being. *Soteria* is found forty-six times in the New Testament.[1]

Based on this word study, it is evident that salvation entails a sense of health, wholeness, safety, prosperity, peace, well-being, and restoration to be experienced by believers in the here and now.

The Goal of Salvation is Christ

The premise of this book is that we who are saved experience a growing sense of well-being as we commune with Christ and submit to His authority. As we surrender our will to His and open our hearts to receive His grace, He sets us free from the power of sin, the lies of the world, and the oppression of evil. Salvation is about becoming like Christ. In John 13:15, as Jesus washed the disciples' feet, He said, *"For I have given you an example, that you also should do just as I have done to you."* Jesus later explained, *"A new commandment I give you, that you love one another: just as I have loved you, you also are to love one another"* (John 13:34). Essentially, as we put into practice the faith Jesus practiced, we are free to enjoy the salvation He came to give us.

Paul understood the goal of salvation was to live free in Christ (Galatians 5:13). He made living like Christ his utmost prize. He wrote: *"I don't mean to say that I have already achieved these things or that I have already reached perfection. But I press on to possess that perfection for which Christ Jesus first possessed me.... I press on to reach the end of the race and receive the heavenly prize for which God, through Christ Jesus, is calling us"* (Philippians 3:12-14 NLT).

A Revealing Question: Why Did Jesus Come to Earth?

For many years now, I have attended a Friday morning prayer meeting with a group of Amish and Mennonite leaders. We pray for revival and the health of the church. One morning the question arose: "Why is there is so much division in the body of Christ when we all share in salvation?" A discussion about denominational differences ensued. A second question followed: "How is it that we all believe in Christ, but never reach unity?" One pastor spoke up saying, "Whenever you have people who have part of the truth and treat it as though it were the whole truth, there will always be division." William Wood puts it this way, "Heresy begins when you embrace one truth at the exclusion of another."

Unity will not be reached until people stop heralding their truth as superior to truths held by other believers. At the heart of this kind of thinking is spiritual pride. Believing we know it all causes one group to judge another group, leaving the Body of Christ fractured. Declaring certain beliefs as absolute, while minimizing or negating other truths, separates and divides the Body of Christ.

The same is true for individuals. If we have personally experienced a portion of the gospel, it does not mean we have experienced all God has for us. God is constantly revealing more and more of His truth and grace. Every Christian faces the challenge of how to keep his limited knowledge from becoming the absolute standard by which to judge others and at the same time hold fast to his knowledge so as not to compromise his faith. To reach such a balance requires both openness and discernment. The question arises: how can believers discern good from evil without becoming judgmental, self-righteous, or self-condemning? The answer is not found in dogma but in a humble relationship with Christ. As Christ sets believers free from self-centeredness, sin, and evil, we are less driven by pride and more controlled by the Spirit. When we surrender to the Spirit, we are guided by love and truth.

Could it be that unity and personal wholeness stem more from truth and love, born out of freedom from sin, than conformity to a particular doctrine, theology, or practice? Could submission to the Spirit be the means through which we can reconcile differences of opinion with others and conflicts from within? After all, God's Word does say, *"If we walk in the light, as he is in the light, we have fellowship one with another, and the blood of Jesus Christ his Son purifies us from all sin"* (1 John 1:7 ESV).

Doesn't this suggest that when we are not in unity with each other, someone is out of alignment with the Spirit? Consequently, we are not free. The scripture declares, *"Now the Lord is the Spirit, and where the Spirit of the Lord is, there is freedom"* (2 Corinthians 3:17). The good news is that where the Spirit reigns we are free from self-deception, selfish ambition, and toxic relationships.

Could it be that divisions arise more from quenching and grieving the Spirit than from disagreements themselves? Could it be that we resist the Spirit more than we recognize? Could it be that by purifying our hearts of sinful attitudes we would be free to love one another more perfectly? 1 Peter 1:22-25 says, *"Now that you have purified yourselves by obeying the truth so that you have sincere love for each other, love one another deeply, from the heart."*

While discussing this dilemma of disunity in the church in our Friday fellowship, we asked ourselves: "How should we pray for freedom from sinful attitudes in the body of Christ?" We discussed the need for humility and repentance from pride. However, another question then surfaced. "What *are* the reasons Jesus came to earth?"

Like most Christians, my friends stated several reasons. They said such things as Jesus came to seek and save the lost. He came to forgive us of our sins. He came to give us eternal life. These responses point to the central concept of Christianity: salvation. However, salvation is so multi-faceted that these answers barely scratch the surface of the significance of this divine gift. Let's go deeper.

What the Scriptures Reveal About Salvation

Knowing it is Jesus who provides us with salvation, I thought it helpful to research the reasons why Jesus came to earth. I found at least fifty-four. Various authors have compiled different lists, some shorter and some longer, identifying why Jesus came to earth. John Piper has written an excellent book explaining many reasons why Jesus came to die.[2] Here below is a simplified list of why Jesus came to earth with supporting verses.

- **Jesus Christ came into the world to save sinners.**
  1 Timothy. 1:15; Hebrews 9:26

- **Jesus Christ came into the world to call sinners to repentance.** Mark 2:17

- **Jesus Christ came to proclaim the good news of the Kingdom.**
  Luke 4:18, 43; Mark 1:38.

- **Jesus Christ came into the world that men might have abundant life.**
  John 10:10

- **Jesus Christ came into the world to fulfill the law and prophets.**
  Matthew 5:17

- **The Father sent Jesus to bless us by turning us from our iniquities.**
  Acts 3:26

- **Jesus came to disarm and destroy the devil and his works.**
  Colossians 2:15; Hebrews 2:14; 1 John 3:8

- **Jesus came to display God's wisdom to rulers and authorities in heavenly places through the church.** Ephesians 3:10

- **Jesus came to give eternal life.** John 6:51

- **Jesus came to give us the Holy Spirit for our freedom.**
  John 14:16-17, Matthew 3:11; John 8:32; 2 Corinthians 3:17

- **Jesus came to free us from false identities, making us sons and daughters by the Spirit of adoption.** Galatians 4:6; Romans 8:15; Hebrews 2:10

- **Jesus came to give spiritual gifts to believers through the Holy Spirit.**
  1 Corinthians 12:11; Ephesians 4:11

- **Jesus came to heal our sickness and comfort the broken hearted.**
  Isaiah 61:1-3; Isaiah 53:5

- **Jesus came to free us from every kind of sin and make us clean.**
  Titus 2:14; 1 John 1:9, Ephesians 5:25-26

- **Jesus came to set captives and the oppressed free.** Luke 4:18

- **Jesus came to reconcile man back to God and give him a ministry of reconciliation.** 2 Corinthians 5:18

- **Jesus came that we might die to sin and live to righteousness.**
  1 Peter 2:14

- **Jesus came to free us from the futility of our ancestry.** 1 Peter 1:18-19

- **Jesus came to free us from guilt, purifying our conscience with his blood.**
  Hebrews 9:14

- **Jesus came to unleash the power of God in the gospel.**
  1 Corinthians 1:18; Romans 1:16

- **Jesus came to rescue us from the final judgment.**
  Hebrews 9:28; 1 Thessalonians 1:10

- **Jesus Christ came into the world to Judge the world.**
  John 9:39; John 5:22-23

- **Jesus came to provide for our justification** (made righteous in the sight of God). Romans 5:9; Romans 3:24; Romans 3:28

- **Jesus came to fulfill the prophecy from Ezekiel to give us a new heart and new spirit.** Ezekiel 36:24

- **Jesus came to deliver us from our enemies and those who hate us.**
  Luke 1:71-75

For a complete list see John Piper's book *Fifty Reasons Why Jesus Came to Die.*

Salvation is Multi-faceted

As you can see, Jesus came into the world to fulfill many purposes. This makes it evident that salvation is multi-faceted. It includes themes of redemption, forgiveness, faith, truth, reconciliation, restoration, justification, sanctification, new identity, holiness, gifts, power and authority, kingdom, ministry, eternal life, judgment, defeat of Satan, cleansing, healing, deliverance, and a new heart—all of which contribute to freedom. Faith in the gospel of Christ is not limited to the forgiveness of sins and the hope of eternal life. It is much more encompassing. It impacts both heaven and earth. It has both spiritual and physical ramifications. It provides freedom for daily living.

Salvation Comes by Word and Spirit

The gospel of Jesus Christ is not just a collection of good moral teachings. The gospel is more than a cognitive narrative. The gospel is the Word of God; it is both alive and powerful (Hebrews 4:12). It has the power to set people free from sin and the consequences of sin here and now. It has the power to deliver people from evil. It has power to release captives, to open the eyes of the blind, and to bring relief to the oppressed. It removes guilt and restores innocence. It has power to cleanse and heal. It impacts the spirit, soul, and body. The gospel reveals what life is like in the kingdom when it is proclaimed and demonstrated under the unction of the Spirit (1 John 2:20).

What makes the Word alive and powerful? It is the Holy Spirit. 1 Thessalonians 1:5 declares: *"For our gospel did not come to you in word only, but also in power, and in the Holy Spirit."* When the Word is taught apart from the power of the Spirit the impact of the gospel is minimal. When the Spirit is present there is power to free people from the constraints of corruption, giving them new life—a life filled with faith, hope and love.

Any time we limit the gospel to forgiveness of sins and the promise of heaven, we greatly reduce its power to set people free. This lack of understanding is a major reason why so many Christians live a lifestyle like that of the world. They readily believe that Jesus died for their sins but the idea that they can live free from sin does not occur to them. They know God desires to give them new life, but they are unaware of what freedom looks like or how to get there. Because of this ignorance, many Christians resign themselves to live in bondage to fear, anger, jealousy, rejection, discouragement, discord, or self-deception. Other Christians strive for comfort, indulgence, and self-gratification. Still others are held captive to self-righteousness, pride, competition, and control.

These believers are stuck in what the Apostle Paul calls a carnal life. They know Jesus as Savior, but not as Lord. They have received the Holy Spirit, but their attitudes and behaviors still resemble that of the world. Their Christian walk is far below what God intends for it to be. They have not yet learned to be the "overcomer" Jesus calls them to be (1 John 5:4; Revelation 2-3). They live more in the flesh and less in the power of the Holy Spirit. Their faith promises them hope of heaven, but they live defeated lives on earth. Their lives are more characterized by hang-ups, habits, and hindrances than by freedom. They suffer from broken relationships and lack purpose, peace, direction, confidence, hope, joy, love, zeal, and motivation to witness. However, when believers gain a more complete understanding as to why Jesus came to earth, their picture of the Christian life becomes clearer and their expectations radically change. They realize they can live as overcomers. They desire more of God and willingly surrender to the leadership of the Holy Spirit.

When Christians experience the power of the Spirit to overcome sin and evil, the desire for freedom explodes. Indifference gives way to excitement. No longer do they resist the Spirit. Suddenly they become open to revelation that heals and delivers. Intimacy with God in prayer becomes a priority. Conversations with the Lord become as precious as the air they breathe. That portion of the Lord's Prayer that was once repeated from rote memory during worship, *"Thy kingdom come; Thy will be done on earth as it is in heaven"* is no longer a mechanical recitation. It now comes to life. It becomes an urgent petition for God to break through and make the kingdom of God real in their lives. Out of the fertile soil of prayer spring divine encounters. These encounters translate into fresh testimonies bearing witness to the glory of the Lord.

A Vison for the Kingdom

I said earlier that Jesus came to earth to do at least fifty-four things. A friend once asked me, "Of the fifty-four reasons Jesus came to earth, which one is primary?" Without hesitation I said, "Jesus came preaching the good news that the kingdom of God was near" (Mark 1:14-15; Luke 8:1; Matthew 4:23).

He asked, "Why this reason over all the others?" To answer, another question needed to be asked: "What is the good news of the kingdom?" In a word, the answer is freedom: freedom from sin and evil, freedom for love, joy, peace, and much more. All the other reasons support this primary purpose. Some may say Jesus came to show us God's love. That is true, but without freedom, God's love can never be realized. Sin and evil dominating our lives nullifies love. Freedom must come first. Freedom in Christ results in salvation.

Jesus came to give humanity a vision for freedom. He spoke of it in terms of the kingdom of God. He revealed what it takes to see it, and how to enter it (John 3:3). He taught about and modeled the kingdom, and He made it accessible. He taught about it in the Sermon on the Mount and in His telling of parables. He modeled it in His many acts of deliverance and healing. He made the kingdom accessible by His death on the cross and resurrection from the dead. He made living in the kingdom palpable through the gift of the Holy Spirit.

Having been anointed with the Spirit, Jesus set out to model kingdom living. Matthew 4:23 says, *"Jesus traveled throughout the region of Galilee, teaching in the synagogues and announcing the Good News about the Kingdom. And he healed every kind of disease and illness"* (NLT). Acts 10:38 makes a similar claim, *"And you know that God anointed Jesus of Nazareth with the Holy Spirit and with power. Then Jesus went around doing good and healing all who were oppressed by the devil, for God was with him"* (NLT).

To experience life in the kingdom one must not only have faith in Jesus, but also have a faith like Jesus and do the things Jesus did. This requires an intimate friendship with Him. This means living in the presence of God, like Jesus lived in the presence of the Father. At a minimum, this requires holding fast to the conviction that we are God's offspring. *"For in Him we live and move and have our being"* (Acts 17:28). We are children of the King. He has put His spiritual DNA into every one of His sons and daughters. They are recipients of His royal character. This is what Jesus meant when he said, *"The Kingdom of God can't be detected by physical signs. You won't be able to say, 'Here it is!' or 'It's over there!' For the Kingdom of God is already among you"* (Luke 17:20-21).

Paul further clarified the nature of God's kingdom when he wrote, *"For the kingdom of God is not a matter of eating and drinking, but of righteousness, peace and joy in the Holy Spirit"* (Romans 14:17). Dear friend, the kingdom of God cannot exist only in your head. It must also be in your heart and demonstrated in your lifestyle. The character of God is made evident in two ways: putting into action a supernatural love for people and having a pure heart marked by righteousness.

Our righteousness comes not by good works but through faith in Christ who makes us righteous (Romans 3:22). Through Christ's atoning work on the cross, we are made right with God. We are justified. We are saved. Jesus becomes our Savior. However, our soul still needs to be cleansed from the corruption of the world. Having faith like Christ makes us victorious over the world (1 John 5:4). We become like Him through the sanctifying work of the Holy Spirit. Our life begins to take on the righteousness of Christ. (For an explanation of the difference between faith in Christ and faith of Christ see the work of R. T. Kendall[3], David Reagan,[4] and Collin Hansen[5]).

Jesus promised that those who hunger and thirst for His righteousness shall be filled (Matthew 5:6). When believers come to see themselves as having been made righteous and have a desire for more of Christ's righteousness, they take on a new identity. They understand themselves to be a kingly priest who rules on earth (Revelation 5:10). They begin to exercise the authority given to them by Christ. After owning this identity, they no longer settle for anything less than the pursuit of complete holiness.

Having once been reluctant to admit their sin, they are now zealous to have it exposed and die to it. The scriptural command to *"Be holy, because I am holy"* (1 Peter 1:16) is not an impossibility; it is an exciting daily pursuit. When a congregation takes on this mindset, revival breaks out under the anointing of the Holy Spirit. In such an atmosphere the presence, power, and love of God manifest, advancing the kingdom of God. This is the vision Jesus has for His people. He promises, *"Seek the Kingdom of God above all else, and live righteously and he will give you all you need"* (Matthew 6:33 NLT).

Obedience Fosters Freedom

It is essential to have an in-depth understanding of what Jesus envisioned for us. But that alone is not sufficient to experience freedom from worry and anxiety. Jesus makes this clear in a parable at the end of His Sermon on the Mount. The parable describes a man who built his house on a rock. The rock represents foundational truths Jesus just taught. These teachings keep a person safe, free of fear when the storms of life hit. He said in Matthew 7:24, *"Everyone who hears these words of mine and puts them into practice is like a wise man who built his house on the rock."*

Experiencing the freedom that salvation offers necessitates more than being familiar with Jesus' teachings; we must put them into practice. James 1:22 says, *"Do not merely listen to the word, and so deceive yourselves. Do what it says."* In salvation we accept Jesus as both Savior and Lord. He not only rescues us from sin and death, He also becomes our Master. Submitting to Jesus' authority the way Jesus submitted to the Father's authority is paramount to realizing freedom.

A Call to Restore

As you can see, the idea of being free from disease, demons, fear, and death is not only included in biblical salvation, it is at the very core of its meaning. Jesus, the author of salvation, came not only to forgive sinners but to release captives and to set the oppressed free (Luke 4:18-19). His ministry of cleansing, healing, and deliverance needs to be restored to the church. It is not enough for it to operate on the perimeter as a counseling service. It needs to become central to the life of the church. It needs to be incorporated into the church's DNA. It is a ministry that begins with conversion and extends throughout the disciple-making process. The next chapter discusses freedom received from conversion.

Discussion Questions

1. What assumptions have you had regarding why Jesus came to earth? Among the reasons listed, which ones caught your attention?

2. What does salvation mean to you personally? What does a saved soul look like? What connection does the fear of the Lord have with salvation?

3. How does the Bible define salvation? Do you believe that freedom results in salvation or does salvation result in freedom? Explain the difference.

4. Of the reasons Jesus came to earth, which one do you think is primary? What role does the written Word have in salvation? What role does the Spirit have in salvation?

5. What do you think happens to a person when they experience the Holy Spirit's power to set them free from sin and evil? What causes one's desire for freedom to grow or wane? What can a church do to help keep the desire for freedom active and growing? What role does healing and deliverance play in revival?

6. What is the connection between freedom, salvation, and the kingdom of God? Do you see any danger in preaching one to the exclusion of the others? What place does obedience to God have in salvation?

Endnotes

1. Part 1 of Sozo Series ... https://www.pinterest.com/pin/396457573441214732/
2. John Piper, *Fifty Reasons Why Jesus Came to Die* (Crossway Books, Minneapolis, MN, 2006).
3. https://rtkendallministries.com/the-faith-of-christ
4. http://www.learnthebible.org/the-faith-of-jesus-christ.html
5. https://www.thegospelcoalition.org/article/faith-in-christ-or-faithfulness-of-christ-whats-the-difference/

3

Freedom Begins with Conversion

Conversion: A Divine Transaction

Throughout my years as a pastor, I would meet Christians who were looking to become a member of a church. In my New Members' Class, I would ask them to share their conversion testimony. The details of their stories would vary, but a few things remained consistent. They would explain how they had a sense of peace, joy, cleansing, hope, and belonging. They often mentioned release from heaviness and a new beginning. They frequently reported having positive emotional reactions and warm feelings. Whereas all of these are common and valid experiences, something more significant happens at conversion. Several spiritual transactions occur that have eternal consequences. The following paragraphs offers some insight into the freedom these transactions afford.

The word *convert* means "to change from one state of being to another." Water is converted to steam. Inches can be converted to centimeters. U.S. dollars can be converted to British pounds. Spiritually speaking, conversion happens when we trade our old sinful nature for the new nature Christ provides. God's Holy Spirit enters our spirit and we become new creations. Our spirit is regenerated. Our lives take on new meaning, new perspective, new direction, new purpose, and new identity. Our natural tendency is to live life to please ourselves. That changes upon conversion. Our souls are restored to a right relationship with God, and we desire to please Him by exercising faith in Christ. Surrendering our life to Christ's Lordship, we no longer live for ourselves; we live to glorify God.

In the Old Testament, the Hebrew word for *converted* means "to turn back or to return." It also translated as "restore," as in Psalm 23:2, *"He restores my soul."* The idea is that at conversion, we return to the original state in which God created us. Although once separated from Him because of sin, our relationship with Him is restored. Our fellowship with God returns to what it was like in the Garden of Eden before Adam sinned. So, the first significant thing that changes at conversion is our residence. Our area code is transferred back to God's Kingdom. This transfer occurs through several spiritual transactions, outlined below.

Conversion frees us to transfer our citizenship back to the kingdom of God.

The Apostle Paul describes this transference in his letter to the Colossians. *"He delivered us from the domain of darkness and transferred us to the kingdom of His beloved Son"* (Colossians 1:3 ESV).

In other words, we are no longer under the authority of the devil, who is the "prince of this world." We are under the authority of Jesus Christ, the King of kings. We no longer belong to Satan. Instead, we become the possession of God, paid for by the blood of Jesus Christ. No longer are we captive to sin and the devil. Conversion allows us to enjoy God's intimate presence, setting us free to live the abundant life characterized by *sozo*—salvation. We are free to enjoy His blessings, receive His love and live with confidence in His goodness and mercy. Through the indwelling of the Holy Spirit, our desire for righteousness supplants our desire for self-centered living. Even though we continue to struggle with sin in this world, we are free from being defined by it. Even though we live in this world, we are not of this world. Our citizenship is in God's kingdom. No longer are we sinners going to hell; rather we are saints who sometimes sin on our way to heaven. How does this happen?

At conversion we are forgiven of our sin. One of the reasons Jesus came to earth was to save God's people from their sins.

Matthew 1:21 declares, *"And she will bring forth a Son, and you shall call His name JESUS, for He will save His people from their sins"* (NKJV).

Before Christ's death on the cross, a person's sins were covered by the shed blood of animals offered as a sacrifice. This was done in accordance with the Law of Moses. However, God established a New Covenant through Christ's death on the cross. Jesus became the perfect sacrifice, taking the place of animal sacrifices. His shed blood became the once and for all offering that paid the price for the forgiveness of sin.

Hebrews 9:26 says, *"But he has appeared once for all at the culmination of the ages to do away with sin by the sacrifice of himself."*

Jesus modeled forgiveness throughout His ministry. He extended forgiveness to those who exhibited faith and to those who did not. Luke 5:20 records, *"When Jesus saw their faith, he said, 'Friend, your sins are forgiven.'"*

Luke 23:24 declares, *"Jesus said, 'Father, forgive them, for they do not know what they are doing.'"*

Interpersonal forgiveness was not emphasized in the Old Testament. It was believed only God could forgive sins (Luke 5:17-21). But Jesus was very concerned that people learn to forgive each other. He taught His disciples the importance of interpersonal forgiveness and gave them authority to forgive.

Matthew 6:14-15 says, *"For if you forgive other people when they sin against you, your heavenly Father will forgive you. But if you do not forgive others their sins, your Father will not forgive your sins."*

Matthew 18:21-11 says, *"Then Peter came and said to Jesus and asked, 'Lord, how many times shall I forgive my brother or sister who sins against me? Up to seven times?' Jesus answered, 'I tell you, not seven times, but seventy-seven times.'"*

John 20:23 says, *"If you forgive anyone's sins, their sins are forgiven; if you do not forgive them, they are not forgiven."*

The consequences for refusing to forgive is to be put in a prison to suffer torment. Jesus made this clear in the parable of the unforgiving debtor in Matthew 18:34-35. *"In anger his master turned him over to the jailers to be tortured until he should pay back all he owed. This is how my heavenly Father will treat each of you unless you forgive your brother from your heart."*

At conversion we are set free from the wrath of God.

"For the wrath of God is revealed from heaven against all ungodliness and unrighteous of men, who by their unrighteousness suppress the truth" (Romans 1:18 ESV).

"Because of your stubbornness and unrepentant heart, you are storing up wrath for yourself in the day of wrath and revelation of the righteous judgment of God" (Romans 2:5).

"Therefore no one will be declared righteous in God's sight by the works of the law... for all have sinned and fall short of the glory of God, and all are justified freely by his grace through the redemption that came by Christ Jesus" (Romans 3:20-24).

"And He Himself is the propitiation [atoning sacrifice] for our sins and not for ours only but also for the whole world" (1 John 2:2 ESV; 1 John 4: 10 ESV; Hebrews 2:17 ESV). Note: New International Version uses "atoning sacrifice."

From birth, we have lived in a sinful world. Our natural bent is to reject the holy God and to live life to please ourselves. Our sinful nature is the opposite of God's character. We have treated God as our enemy. Like rebellious children, we have refused to honor God as our heavenly Parent. We deserve His wrath, punishment, and condemnation. There is no gift, sacrifice, or service that will appease God's anger. Yet, because of Christ and His redeeming work on the cross, we are liberated from God's wrath.

Because Christ took our punishment, we are no longer condemned. He paid the price for our sin debt. Christ fulfilled God's requirement for justice so we no longer need to fear the wrath of God. God's wrath is satisfied, appeased, and atoned for by God Himself through Christ's sacrifice on the cross. No matter how bad you may feel, it is liberating to know God is no longer angry with you!

At conversion we are set free from blame, guilt, and shame. All legal guilt is removed. Because of Christ, we have peace with God. God no longer remembers our sins, and we can boldly enter His throne room without fear.

"Therefore, since we have been justified through faith, we have peace with God through our Lord Jesus Christ, through whom we have gained access by faith into this grace in which we now stand" (Romans 5:1-2).

"Surely, he took up our pain and bore our suffering, yet we considered him punished by God, stricken by him and afflicted. But he was pierced for transgressions, he was crushed for our iniquities; the punishment that brought us peace was on him, and by his wounds we are healed" (Isaiah 53:4-5).

"Their sins and lawless acts I will remember no more. And where these have been forgiven, sacrifice for sin is no longer necessary. Therefore, brothers and sisters, since we have confidence to enter the Most Holy Place by the blood of Jesus" (Hebrews 10:17-19).

"Let us then approach God's throne of grace with confidence, so that we may receive mercy and find grace to help us in our time of need" (Hebrews 4:16).

Because of Christ's atoning death on the cross, we have peace with God. We need not worry about being good enough or worthy enough. From God's standpoint, all guilt and shame are washed away, restoring the relationship that was once lost due to Adam and Eve's sin. Having accepted Christ as our Savior and Lord by faith, our spirits are regenerated, making communion with God possible. Because Christ's Spirit is now within us, we have direct access to the most holy place, the presence of God. Christ's redeeming work on the cross relieves His followers from carrying any burden of guilt or shame. We can boldly enter God's throne room through prayer, expecting to receive God's mercy and grace. We are able to hear God speaking to us.

At conversion, we are free from all accusations of moral wrong and offense.

Because Christ justifies us, we are no longer considered guilty nor are we condemned. We are declared righteous, even though we are not innocent.

"There is no judgment against anyone who believes in him. But anyone who does not believe in him has already been judged for not believing in God's one and only Son" (John 3:18 NLT).

"For our sake he made him to be sin who knew no sin, so that in him we might become the righteousness of God" (2 Corinthians 5:21 ESV).

"Therefore, there is now no condemnation for those who are in Christ Jesus" (Romans 8:1).

"Who will bring charge against those whom God has chosen? It is God who justifies. Who is he that condemns? Christ Jesus, who died – more than that, who was raised to life – is at the right hand of God and is also interceding for us" (Romans 8:33).

"For all have sinned and fall short of the glory of God, and are justified by his grace as a gift, through the redemption that is Christ Jesus, whom God put forward as propitiation by his blood, to be received by faith" (Romans 3:23-25 ESV).

"If we claim we have no sin, we deceive ourselves and are not living in the truth. If we confess our sins, he is faithful and just and will forgive us our sins and purify us from all unrighteousness. If we claim we have not sinned, we make him out to be a liar and his word is not in us" (1 John 1:8-10).

"If our hearts condemn us, we know that God is greater than our hearts, and he knows everything" (1 John 2:20).

To be justified is to be acquitted of sin and declared righteous. We are declared blameless before God. It is as though we never committed any sin at all. We are considered completely innocent, even though we continue to sin. We are absolved of all guilt and are no longer condemned. Having Christ's righteousness imputed to us, striving for God's approval is laid to rest. Being justified, we no longer need to resist the truth pridefully. Instead, we are free to face our sinful nature, humbly confess our sin, receive mercy, and be cleansed from unrighteousness. We can then confidently repent and change our way of thinking to conform to the mind of Christ. In this way, we can expect to receive imparted righteousness through the transforming work of the Holy Spirit.

As we yield to the sanctifying work of the Holy Spirit, our lives begin to reflect the righteousness of Christ. Our lives advance from glory to glory, from grace to grace. Though accusations of condemnation will continue to harass us—from Satan, our peers, the church, society in general, and from our own conscience—still the truth remains. Only God's opinion ultimately matters. We should not allow any opinion to define us except His. In this way, we can live free of condemnation with a hunger and thirst for righteousness.

At conversion we are set free from the anguish of separation and alienation. We are reconciled to God.

"For Christ also suffered once for sins, the righteous for the unrighteous, to bring you to God. He was put to death in the body but made alive in the Spirit" (I Peter 3:18).

"All this is from God, who through Christ reconciled us to himself and gave us the ministry of reconciliation" (2 Corinthians 5:18 ESV).

Ever since Adam committed the original sin, humanity has been estranged from God. The entire purpose of the gospel is to bring us back to a right relationship with God. Through Christ, we are reunited with God so that we can enjoy His presence forever. We no longer are His enemies; instead, we live to glorify Him. At conversion, we regain a friendship with God and recover a sense of belonging, security, and intimacy. Romans 5:11 declares, *"We also rejoice in God through our Lord Jesus Christ, through whom we have receive reconciliation."* Psalm 16:11 says, *"In God's presence we are filled with joy and with eternal pleasures."* In God's presence there is no sorrow. There is joy, peace, and harmony.

If the gospel only offered forgiveness of sin, afforded justification, brought us atonement, saved us from the flames of hell, provided eternal life, and produced health and prosperity without the enjoyment of God's presence, it would fail to be good news. We are created to be in a love relationship with God. Reconciliation makes that possible.

At conversion we are set free from fatherlessness.

"The Spirit you received does not make you slaves, so that you live in fear again; rather, the Spirit you received brought about your adoption, to sonship. And by him we cry 'Abba, Father'" (Romans 8:15).

"Because you are his sons, God has sent the Spirit of his Son into our hearts, the Spirit who calls out, 'Abba, Father'" (Galatians 4:6).

Through adoption, we are no longer slaves to fear. We are sons and daughters of God, adopted into the family of God. The Spirit of His Son enters our hearts. We take on a new identity and name, the same name as God's only begotten Son. His name is Christ. Our name is *Christian* which means "followers who belong to Christ." Through adoption, we come to know who we are. We are His sons and daughters. No longer are we defined by abandonment, loneliness, isolation, or an orphan spirit. We are not only in God's family; the Father loves us with an everlasting love. He promises that He will never leave nor forsake us. He takes pleasure in us and grants us full legal rights to everything that belongs to Him. We are co-heirs with Christ. Through Christ we have access to every spiritual blessing in heavenly places (Ephesians 1:3 ESV).

Conversion sets us free from the legalism of the Old Covenant.

"God made us adequate as servants of a new covenant, not of the letter, but of the Spirit; for the letter kills, but the Spirit gives life" (2 Corinthians 3:5-6).

The Old Covenant required strict adherence to Jewish traditions and religious rules and practices. These practices included dietary laws, festival observance, animal sacrifices, and religious codes of behavior. At conversion, a New Covenant, based on the Spirit, replaces these religious traditions.

The New Covenant brings new life. It prescribes walking in the Spirit, as opposed to striving, to keep a behavioral code. Keeping man-made regulations and laws is powerless to give life. Legalism cannot curtail immorality. It only serves to heighten temptation. Even spiritual disciplines like Bible study, giving, and church attendance can be reduced to a legalistic endeavor. Although these disciplines can help foster spiritual growth, they do not guarantee a Spirit-filled walk. The law of God is necessary to provide moral standards and guidelines, but to live in freedom requires grace found in the New Covenant.

At conversion, we are set free from the past.
We are at a place of new beginning. We are born again.

"Therefore, if any man be in Christ, he is a new creature: old things are passed away; behold, all things are become new" (2 Corinthians 5:17 KJV).

"Don't you know that all of us who were baptized into Christ Jesus were baptized into his death? We were therefore buried with him through baptism into death in order that, just as Christ was raised from the dead, through the glory of the Father, we too may live a new life.… For we know that our old self was crucified with Him so that the body of sin might be done away with, that we should

no longer be slaves to sin, because anyone who has died has been freed from sin" (Romans 6:3-6).

"Jesus replied, 'Very truly I tell you, no one can see the kingdom of God unless they are born again'" (John 3:3).

Once Jesus is the leader of our life, things of the past no longer define who we are. The old self is put to death, and a new life begins. Past failures, regrets, losses, sins, and disappointments no longer define us. No matter how terrible we think we are, we are not beyond His redeeming. No matter how bad we have messed up, Jesus gives us a uniquely different kind of life. It is like a caterpillar that is transformed into a butterfly. We go from a slow crawling earthly specimen to a glorious creature set free to float on air. Life is lived in a whole different way. A fresh perspective shapes our purpose, feelings, desires, and understanding. Life takes on new direction and significance. Our worth is not determined by performing to meet the expectations of men. Rather, we live by a higher standard. Psalm 40:8 declares: *"I delight to do your will, O my God, and Your law is within my heart."*

While we may occasionally sin, we are no longer enslaved to sin. No one lives a sinless, perfect life, but the redeemed Christian sins less and less while hating sin more and more. Sin surrenders its power to God's love. The flavor of sin becomes less appetizing as we taste the goodness of God. His blessings become far more satisfying than the desires of the flesh. The attractions of the world grow strangely dim in the light of His righteousness. In Christ, we live with hope that something beautiful is being made of our life.

At conversion we are baptized and set free from corruption of the world.

"And now why are you waiting? Arise, and be baptized and wash away your sins, calling on the name of the Lord" (Acts 22:16).

"And this water symbolizes baptism that now saves you also—not the removal of dirt from the body but the pledge of a good conscience toward God" (1 Peter 3:21).

"Christ loved the church and gave himself up for her to make her holy, cleansing her by the washing with water through the word; and to present her to himself as a radiant church, without stain or wrinkle or any other blemish, but holy and blameless" (Ephesians 5:25b-27).

According Romans 3:23, each one of us is born into this corrupt world as a sinner. When we are converted, we are born again by the Spirit (John 3:21).

Our dead spirit is made alive with Christ by the grace of God. In baptism, our sins are washed away through faith in Christ. Our old nature is buried, and we rise to new life in Christ. We become new creatures; our spiritual DNA changes. The Holy Spirit regenerates our spirits. Positionally and legally, we have been declared innocent by the Judge. Our debt has been paid, and we are set free by God's proclamation. Christ sets us frees from the penalty of sin and gives us the promise of heaven when we die.

However, as long as we live in this corrupt world, we are subject to temptations and remain at war with sin and evil. We must learn to overcome the power of sin through obedience to the Word and cooperation with the Spirit. In this way, we experience the benefits of salvation. This is what Paul meant when he said, *"...work out your salvation with fear and trembling"* (Philippians 2:12).

Through water baptism, we are received into Christ's church. Baptism testifies to the truth that we are beneficiaries of Christ's work. Through baptism, we declare we have received forgiveness of sin, citizenship in the kingdom and a new birth through the indwelling Spirit. We affirm a peaceful relationship with God the Father through reconciliation, a new identity by adoption and a new covenant based on grace through faith. Additionally, we avow a good conscience towards God through the washing away of sin and a restored innocence through justification. However, conversion is just the beginning of a transformation process by which we move from faith to freedom.

At conversion we are redeemed.

The word for "redeem" in the Bible is *agorazo*. It is a marketplace term that means "to buy back." In ancient times it referred to buying back a slave. Through Christ's sacrificial death on the cross, we are bought back from being slaves to sin and death. We are set free from bondage. God's very nature is one of redemption evidenced by sending His Son to redeem the church. The scriptures indicate:

- **The LORD is a God full of redemption** – Psalm 130:7-8
- **Jesus is prophesied as the Redeemer** – Luke 2:38
- **The church has been purchased by the blood of Jesus** – Acts 20:28

Benefits of redemption include:

- **Peace with God** – Romans 5:1; Colossians 2:20
- **Freedom from the curse of the law** – Galatians 3:13
- **Deliverance from the bondage of sin** – 1 Peter 1:14-19; Titus 2:14-15
- **Eternal life** – Revelation 5:6-9

- **Adoption into the Family of God** – Galatians 4:5
- **Forgiveness of sins** – Ephesians 1:7
- **Declared righteous** – Romans 5:17
- **Indwelt by the Holy Spirit** – 1 Corinthians 6:19-20

Understanding these spiritual transactions occur at conversion strengthens faith, so that when feelings of doubt come creeping in, you can remain strong in the assurance of your salvation.

In the next chapter we will look at freedom that goes beyond conversion. This freedom empowers us to mature, moving toward Spirit-filled living.

Discussion Questions

1. Conversion means a change in substance. What changes in a person when he or she is converted to the Christian faith?

2. When a person is converted, he or she may or may not have an emotional experience. What was your experience? How has your life changed?

3. Can you name the spiritual conversions that occur at the time of conversion? Why is it important for every Christian to know about them?

4. Which one of the transactions identified above is the most significant for you? Which one do you question the most? What questions do you have about these spiritual transactions?

5. All these transactions carry with them the promise of being set free. What difference do these invisible transactions make in the way you, as a Christian, should live your life?

6. With these transactions taking place at conversion, why does Paul say we need to work out our salvation with fear and trembling (Philippians 2:12)?

7. Knowing that Jesus has already forgiven you, do ever struggle to forgive yourself? Is it harder to forgive yourself or others? Why? How has forgiveness enabled you to gain freedom from past mistakes and sin?

8. Do you agree that unforgiveness runs in opposition to God? Have you ever considered unforgiveness as a refusal to use the authority Jesus gave you? What happens when you fail to forgive?

9. How does it make you feel knowing you have been bought with a price? How do you feel knowing you are redeemed by Christ's shed blood?

4

Freedom:
A Step Beyond Conversion

How Can It Be?

When I was pastor of Swamp United Church of Christ, one of our elderly members became severely ill and was admitted to Lancaster General Hospital. I went to visit and pray with him. We talked about things that mattered to him, namely his wife and his faith. We talked about life and death. At a very sober moment in the conversation, he posed a serious question: "Reverend Snow, how can it be? You live your entire life by what you believe to be right, only to find out near the end, you have been doing it wrong all along?" The question caught me a bit off guard. However, I assured him that as Christians, we are always learning. There is always more truth to be revealed and incorporated into our lives. Meanwhile, God's grace is sufficient.

At the time, this seemed like a satisfactory answer. However, several years later I realized how inadequate my explanation was. It is human to miss the mark. It is quite another to realize why. My answer failed to factor in Satan's power to deceive. A personal encounter with evil opened my eyes to this greater truth. It is not only our insufficiency that keeps us doing things wrong. It is also the devil's interference.

Up until that time, I had not considered the importance of being personally set free from Satan's lies. Of course, I recognized the need to be doctrinally correct and to live my life based on the truth of Scripture, but I did not consider the significance of Satan's influence on my daily thinking patterns. It was disturbing to me to think that Christians can live their entire lives believing orthodox doctrine and still be deceived without knowing it.

Then in 2005, by the grace of God, light was shed on my conundrum. I received ministry from John and Leslie Kindler, cleansing my soul from defiling spirits that had kept me in bondage to religious attitudes and perceptions. I began to understand the significance of what the Apostle Paul called strongholds (2

Corinthians 10:4) and the need to renew my mind (Romans 12:2). Even though I had publicly confessed Christ at age twelve and had been baptized in the Spirit for decades, I began to notice demonic influences in my life. From that point on, my thinking changed. I began to interpret Scripture from a different world-view. Until we are set free from Satan's influence in the way we think, biblical knowledge, although having some benefit, will not be sufficient to allow us to experience the full measure of salvation God intends.

In the previous chapter, I explained the doctrine of salvation, focusing on what happens at conversion. We receive forgiveness sins, the washing away of guilt and shame, and Christ's Spirit. The righteousness of Christ is accredited to us and we are given a new identity. At conversion, we receive all of this plus the promise of heaven—but that is just the first step.

To personally realize salvation, there is more. We must learn to apply these truths to our lives (James 1:22). It is through the appropriation of these truths that we are set free from the power of sin and evil and empowered to enjoy the benefits of salvation.

When Christ's righteousness is imputed to us, we no longer need to strive for God's approval. Because we are justified, pride will no longer drive us to re-sist the truth. Instead, we are free to face our sinful nature, humbly confess our sin, and confidently repent. At that point, we receive an installment of imparted righteousness through the transforming work of the Holy Spirit. As we yield to the sanctifying work of the Holy Spirit, our lives advance from grace to grace, reflecting God's glory.

This chapter will focus on freedom that goes beyond conversion and extends into practical living. Even though we believe in Christ and are saved, we must demonstrate our faith daily. This faith is what Paul means when he says in Romans 1:16, *"the gospel of Christ is the power of God to bring salvation to everyone who believes."* The message of the gospel is not only to convert un-believers but also to enable believers to realize salvation's benefits, resulting in ever-increasing security, contentment, and a sense of well-being. In this regard salvation is continual and progressive.

At conversion, we decide to believe in Christ. We know him as Savior. But that is not the end of the story. Faith in Christ takes us a step further, requir-ing us to have an awareness of the Holy Spirit's presence and learn to submit to Him. At this point, we come to know Christ as Lord. Through obedience to the Spirit, we move from believing *in* Christ to believing *like* Christ. We move from imputed righteousness to imparted righteousness. The more we listen to the Spirit's voice and obey God's Word, the more holy we become. This involves crucifying the flesh and cleansing ourselves from impurities. The more we die to self and purify ourselves from defilements, the more of God's glory rests upon us. This process is what Paul referred to as *"being saved through the sanctifying work of the Spirit"* (2 Thessalonians 2:13).

This process defines discipleship, transforming us from a carnal Christian to a spiritual Christian. Gradually, our lives begin to reflect the truth, grace, power, and love of Christ. In this way we work out our salvation with ongoing reverence for God (Philippians 2:12).

Scriptures describe this progression in a variety of ways.

We move from grace to grace.

"For of His fullness we have all received, and grace upon grace" (John 1:16 NASB).

We move from glory into the same glory.

"But we all, with unveiled face, beholding as in a mirror the glory of the Lord, are being transformed into the same image from glory to glory, just as from the Lord, the Spirit" (2 Corinthians 3:18 NASB).

We move from faith into more of the same faith.

"For in it {the gospel of Christ} the righteousness of God is revealed from faith to faith; as it is written, 'But the righteous man shall live by faith'" (Romans 1:17 NASB).

The Scriptures teach we are to become progressively more and more like Christ. The Apostle Paul wrote more than one-third of the New testament. He said of himself: *"Not that I have already obtained all this, or have already arrived at my goal, but I press on to take hold of that for which Christ Jesus took hold of me"* (Philippians 3:12). Paul did not allow himself to become complacent. He realized there was always more of Christ to be assimilated into his life. In another instance Paul wrote, *"As you therefore have received Christ Jesus the Lord, so walk in Him, having been firmly rooted and now being built up in Him and established in your faith"* (Colossians 2:6-7).

We are instructed in the Word to become mature saints. No longer can we remain spiritual babies drinking milk. We must become mature adults eating spiritual meat. No longer do we rely on our own moral reasoning based on what we can understand and see. Instead, we look to what is unseen. Paul writes in 2 Corinthians 4:18, *"So we fix our eyes not on what is seen, but on what is unseen, since what is seen is temporary, but what is unseen is eternal."* According to Ephesians 1:17-21, this means we look to the unseen Holy Spirit for wisdom and revelation. As the eyes of our heart are opened, we come to know the power of Christ to overcome sin and evil. Through empowerment of the Spirit, we are strengthened to live righteously with the same kind of rule, authority, power, and dominion as the resurrected Christ. The goal is to leave behind the carnal life in order to live a victorious Spirit-filled life. When we submit to Christ, there is always more peace, more joy, more love, more grace, and more fruit.

Hudson Taylor's Belief

Hudson Taylor was twenty-one years old when he went to China in 1853 as a missionary. He had no formal theological education, but had a complete commitment to obey the Scriptures and a reliance on revelation by the Holy Spirit. He lived his life abiding in Christ, desiring the fullness of God. He is most remembered for saying: "Depend upon it, God's work done in God's way will never lack God's supplies." He came to realize that living in union with Christ always results in more. Scriptures make this point in the following ways (emphasis mine):

- 1 Thessalonians 4:1, *"As you received from us how you ought to walk and to please God, just as you are doing, do so **more and more**."*

- 1 Thessalonians 4:10, *"Concerning brotherly love...we urge you, brothers, to do **more and more**."*

- 2 Peter 1:2-3, *"May God give you **more and more** grace and peace as you grow in your knowledge of God and Jesus our Lord"* (NLT).

- Philippians 1:9, *"It is my prayer that your love may abound **more and more**."*

- Ephesians 5:18-19, *"Be filled [**continually filled**] with the Spirit, addressing one another in psalms and hymns and spiritual songs, singing and making melody to the Lord with your heart."*

- Ephesians 3:16-19, *"May the Father grant you, according to the riches of his glory, to be strengthened with power through his Spirit in your inner being, so that Christ may dwell in your hearts through faith – that you, being rooted and grounded in love, may have strength to comprehend with all the saints what is the breadth and length and height and depth, and know the love of Christ that surpasses knowledge, that you may **be filled with all the fullness of God**."*

Any view of the Christian life that does not promote the "more and more" teachings of Scripture is defective and lacking power. To remain content with a little is not in keeping with God's desire to give you "more and more."

This is where the idea of freedom comes into full view. The *more* we assimilate Christ into our life, the *more* we are free from the powers of sin and evil. The *more* freedom we assimilate into our lives, the *more* we are free to enjoy spiritual blessings of heaven on earth.

In Galatians 5:1 Paul wrote, *"It is for freedom that Christ has set us free."* And in Romans 6:18 he declared, *"You have been set free from sin and have become slaves to righteousness."* In other words, at conversion, we are set free from the eternal consequences of sin. But, more than that, because Christ's Spirit is alive within us, we can live free from the power of sin. We can live free of negative effects of sin and evil right now.

This is good news, but it is not without its challenges. The forces of sin and the temptations of Satan are still actively trying to draw us back into our old sinful ways. We are in a continual state of conflict. The world incessantly seeks to have us conform to its pattern. The devil never stops tempting. Even more daunting is the realization that our old sinful nature has not completely died. We continue to battle with all of these. As Paul put it in Romans 7:15, 21 *"For what I want to do I do not do, but what I hate I do…. When I want to do good, evil is right there with me."*

Paul tells us we are at war with the law of sin within us, including public sins, private sins, and sins of which we are not aware. Psalm 19:12 states, *"But who can discern their own errors? Forgive my hidden sins."* It is shocking to know we are not even aware of our sins. These hidden sins are covered over by deceitful desires, denial, avoidance, rationalization, blame-shifting, and ignorance. In recognition of this fact, Paul says we are to be free of these things. In 2 Corinthians 4:2, he writes: *"We have renounced secret and shameful ways; we do not use deception, nor do we distort the word of God. On the contrary, by setting forth the truth plainly we commend ourselves to everyone's conscience in the sight of God."*

Sprinkles on the Face

One Sunday morning, in the middle of worship, Wes Dudley, stood up to give a prophetic word to our congregation. He read from 1 John 1:5-8.

"This is the message we have heard from him and declare to you; God is light; in him there is no darkness at all. If we claim to have fellowship with him and yet walk in the darkness, we lie and do not live

out the truth. But if we walk in the light, as he is in the light, we have fellowship with one another, and the blood of Jesus, his Son, purifies us from all sin. If we claim to be without sin, we deceive ourselves and the truth is not in us."

Wes then recounted what occurred a few days earlier. He was out on his porch when his four-year-old son came out with a yellow sprinkle on his face. It was a deposit leftover from eating a donut found in the kitchen. Wes asked his son, "What have you been doing?" The boy innocently answered, "Nothing." Wes queried again, "Have you been eating?" The boy sheepishly replied, "No." With that denial, Wes took the conversation to another level. "You have a yellow sprinkle on your cheek." Wes then gently removed the sprinkle and showed it to his son. In a loving fatherly way, he confronted his son with the evidence of his crime. He gently instructed the little boy to always be truthful. It was a teachable moment not only for his son, but now also for the congregation. Numbers 32:23 declares, *"and be sure your sin will find you out"* (KJV).

Anyone with small children can identify with this scenario. It is a striking example of human nature. Even at a young age our sinful nature seeks to do what the Apostle Paul calls *"suppress the truth"* (Romans 1:18). We try to pretend that we are innocent. But the truth is, we all have sprinkles on our faces. All of us have sin in our lives, both the saved and unsaved.

We all have sin we want to keep private, so we pretend it doesn't exist. We all have sin buried deep within that we have forgotten. However, if we fail to acknowledge hidden sin, we become subject to its power. Over time, unconfessed sin forms what the Bible calls strongholds (2 Corinthians 10:4). Strongholds are patterns of thought, attitudes, feelings, and beliefs that are based on lies and that prevent us from walking out our faith in Christ (see chapters 16 and 17 for more exposition). Whenever we live under this deception, we miss out on God's greater good. Proverbs 28:13 states, *"He who conceals his transgressions will not prosper."*

Spin Doctoring Prevails

Apart from hard-hearted people who don't care, I think most people like to be seen in a positive light. We all have a need to be accepted and are therefore reluctant to confess our sins to others. We fear rejection and do not want others to know about our private life. We feel embarrassed and vulnerable. We assume that if people knew who we really were, they would not like us or might even take advantage of us. Instinctively, we seek to protect ourselves. However, when fear becomes bigger than our faith we drift into dishonesty or even idolatry. So, out of self-protection, we become spin doctors, bending facts in our own favor, while pointing out the faults of others. When the truth finally hunts us down, we feel cornered. We will dodge, distort, deflect, deny, equivocate, excuse, and even lie. When that does not work, we will accuse, blame, and slander others.

Today's Cultural Climate

Sadly, this reality is defining our culture today. Harsh political discourse and crude commentary fill the airways, marring the social climate. Bullying, belittling, and mocking are rampant in our schools. Poisonous posts on social media pollute the atmosphere with cursing and accusation. TV pundits levy exaggerated criticisms and caricature defaming those with whom they disagree. Comedians lace their jokes with vile sarcasm and slander. Clever putdowns and satire are weapons of choice to ridicule people who are disliked. Political candidates are demonized for their policies, and their character is maligned. Demeaning and disparaging comments are made about their families; vicious insults and repugnant language are common fare. A spirit of anarchy hovers over the nation as folks have lost trust and respect for authority. People have become numb to these verbal assaults and no longer trust the media as a source of non-biased reporting.

In many quarters of our society, this meanness has not been limited to verbal abuse but has risen to levels of physical violence and sexual abuse as well. Recently, a PG movie made for children, *Show Dogs,* featured canines suffering sexual indignities in order to fight crime. Linda Crockett wrote an article in the Lancaster Newspaper characterizing the movie as normalizing sexual abuse.[1] I was appalled when I read that the movie taught children it was okay to have their private parts touched.

There seems to be no end to the physical and emotional pain being inflicted on people of all ages. We live in a hurting society. Tragically, the more people get hurt, the more they hurt others. As people feel increasingly threatened, degraded, neglected, and hopeless, the result is a downward spiral of depression, anxiety, drug addiction, violence, and suicide.

Consequently, the average life span of Americans has decreased in recent years. The Bible warns that the wages of sin is death (Romans 8:23). All of this can portend a gloomy future for our country, but it doesn't have to. If the church would preach and practice a gospel of freedom, things could change. It needs to be said, however, that preaching such a gospel comes with a cost.

I grew up in the 1960s, an era of organized crime, political assassinations, civil rights, happy hippies, riots, and Vietnam protests. But even in such a contentious atmosphere, there were standards of restraint and decorum. Dr. Martin Luther King epitomized this as he successfully married civil unrest with nonviolent protest. His message was one of freedom, justice, equality, and love. As with all prophets, he called for radical change. It is unfortunate that his vision for a more harmonious society was met with violence. He was murdered while standing on a hotel balcony in Memphis, Tennessee. His life and death have had great impact on me. I now realize that his call for justice will not be met until spiritual freedom is achieved. The church needs wake up to this truth.

Looking back on those days of social upheaval and conflict, I recall that manners and honor were the norm. I remember an occasion when, as a young boy, my mother instructed me to wash my mouth with soap for lying about a fight I had with a playmate. Today, that kind of discipline would not be acceptable. It would be considered abusive. However, in the absence of such discipline, preserving the dignity of others has become a relic of the past. Jettisoned is the importance of honor and respect, replaced with political correctness, militant self-promotion, slander, slurs, and organized aggression. People no longer feel free to disagree for fear of being personally attacked. The "cancel culture" has become normative. No matter how spurious the methods used against an opponent, they can be justified if they produce the desired results.

A sense of repulsiveness and hopelessness has gripped the American psyche. Suicide is the leading cause of death among our youth, largely due to bullying on social media and lack of hope for the future. Life is one big put down, reducing advocacy to smear tactics even among the sophisticated elite. Some radicals have taken to the streets, pretending to care about the plight of their neighbors. They raise their voices and fists in angry protest. But in reality, the cry for social justice is a ruse, disguising their own hostility. Railing against injustice with malicious rhetoric only serves to reveal the darkened condition of one's own heart. Burning down buildings belonging to innocent people indicates more interest in destruction than justice. Criticizing someone else's wickedness without first removing the log in one's own eye may temporarily win an argument, but ultimately it is a malignant cancer on society. Proverbs 18:21, states, *"Death and life are in the power of the tongue, and those who love it will eat its fruits"* (ESV).

When we come under verbal attack, our natural response is to defend ourselves. In retaliation, we will unscrupulously gossip and hurl insults back. This is true of believers as much as it is of unbelievers. It is easy to magnify the sins of others yet remain blind to our own. Softening our own sins with mild verbiage while excoriating others with scathing sarcasm not only creates a relational divide, we grow dangerously close to losing our souls. Such hypocrisy is deadly. Jesus taught us that using words filled with contempt and enmity puts us in danger of hell fire (Matthew 5:22). Sadly, this is the human condition and part of the carnal nature.

The Carnal Nature Exposed

The carnal nature takes many forms and sin is manifested in a variety of ways. Many overt sins including murder, rape, theft, sexual abuse, beatings, kidnapping, torture, and the like are destructive and ruinous to society. Both believers and pagans recognize these sins as terrible.

Another tier of sins includes drunkenness, addiction, prostitution, adultery, divorce, cheating, and gambling. These are injurious but not as egregious, a nuisance but tolerable.

Other sins are more private and personal in nature. They tend to be more subtle and insidious. These include jealousy, envy, resentment, lust, anger, gossip, greed, lies, slander, and manipulation. These are offensive and personally upsetting.

Some sins affect our character, deeply embedded in the soul. They are neither criminal nor illegal, but they are spiritually lethal. The Bible identifies these sins as self-centeredness, self-righteousness, self-protection, self-reliance, self-promotion, self-justification, self-importance, and self-ambition. In a single word, these sins are all rooted in pride. Pride is one of the most deadly but well-hidden sins. There are other covert sins like self-pity, judgmentalism, worry, anxiety, and grudges, but pride is the most duplicitous. It is something readily seen in others, but not recognized in ourselves. Like a stealth bomber flying under radar, it unleashes its payload of destruction without detection. The Bible warns how disastrous it is. *"Pride goes before destruction, a haughty spirit before a fall"* (Proverbs 16:18).

Pride along with envy, anger, lust, greed, gluttony, and sloth have traditionally been considered deadly sins. Pride is the chief of these sins through which all others enter the mortal soul. Pride is an excessive belief in your own abilities, attributes, and appearance that interferes with your relationship with God and people. Pride is one of seven sins that God hates (Proverbs 6:16-19).

John Amodeo Ph. D., MFT wrote an article entitled, "Why Pride Is Nothing to Be Proud Of" in *Psychology Today* (June 2015). He says, "We've all been repelled by people who have an inflated view of themselves. They may talk about themselves excessively and rarely show interest in others…. Pride is often driven by poor self-worth and shame. We feel so badly about ourselves that we compensate by feeling superior. We look to others' flaws as a way to conceal our own. We relish criticizing others as a defense against recognizing our own shortcomings."

St. Augustine said, "It was pride that changed angels into devils; it is humility that makes men as angels."

Thomas Aquinas said this of pride "inordinate self-love is the cause of every sin…. the root of pride is found to consist in man not being, in some way, subject to God and his rule."

Overcoming the Carnal Nature

When you remove issues of competition, achievement, and status, people work better together. That is, when pride and selfish ambition are eliminated, people work better together to achieve much. As someone pointed out, "there is no letter 'I' in the word team." As long as no one cares who gets the credit, there is no end to what we can achieve.

Jesus desires that we be set free from our carnal nature. He wants to liberate us from all sins, known and unknown, secret and public. He desires that believers honor, serve, and love one another by hearing the truth. Jesus said, *"You shall know the truth and the truth will set you free"* (John 8:32). This truth comes through reading the scriptures and using human reasoning apply them. This is good, but using logic alone is not sufficient to grasp the truth. Relying on human reasoning, we are apt to rationalize our sins away. We can reason away portions of the Bible all together. We can dismiss those verses that make no sense and ignore those with which we disagree. Evil can appear as good through the distorted interpretation of the Scriptures. Jeremiah 17:9 identifies this limitation as part of the human condition. He says: *"The heart is deceitful above all things and beyond cure. Who can understand it?"*

However, when truth is appropriated through revelation, darkness is dispelled. The Indwelling Holy Spirit shines His light on our hidden sins, revealing them to be what they are, truly evil. The Spirit confronts both our self-conceit and self-deceit with truth. But there is more. His piercing Word is joined with mercy and love. Together they form a powerful one-two punch of amazing grace. Delivered under conviction, we confess our sins and receive forgiveness. Jesus then cleanses us from all unrighteousness (1 John 1:9). He purifies our hearts and renews our minds so that we can overcome sin's self-defeating way of life. This enables us to live in this world but not be of the world (1 John 2:15-17).

When we cooperate with the Holy Spirit, Jesus accomplishes His mission to set us free so that we can fulfill our God-given purpose and destiny which are already written in the books of Heaven. Jesus not only gives us faith to believe in Him, He goes one step further. He sets us free to be like Him. He calls us not only to have faith in His grace to save us from hell, but to be holy as He is holy (1 Peter 1:15). Through this transforming process, we become citizens in His heavenly kingdom.

Christ not only delivers us from evil, He empowers us to live righteously in the service of others. James 1:27 declares, *"Religion that God our Father accepts as pure and faultless is this: to look after orphans and widows in their distress and to keep oneself from being polluted by the world."* To love the poor, care for those in distress, and keep ourselves from being polluted by the world, we must learn to overcome sin, first within ourselves, and secondly, within others.

Overcoming the pollution in the world requires more than good intentions; it requires supernatural power. We have access to this power through the indwelling Holy Spirit. But that is not all. To overcome the world, we must also overcome the destructive forces of Satan, requiring an additional outpouring of divine power. The Bible calls this outpouring the baptism of the Holy Spirit.

In the next chapter we will take a closer look at the role the Holy Spirit has in setting us free.

Discussion Questions

1. What would it be like to live your entire life a certain way as a Christian, only to find out in old age you missed the mark? How could this happen? What role do evil spirits and strongholds play in missing the mark?

2. What is the difference between believing *in* Christ and believing *like* Christ? What must happen for that shift to take place?

3. Hudson Taylor believed that there was always something more to the Christian life for him to discover. What Scriptures validate this belief? What has been your experience of going from faith to faith, grace to grace, glory to glory?

4.   The author asserts everyone has sprinkles on their face. Everyone has sin and it will eventually find you out. Yet, we consistently suppress the truth. Why is that? What needs to happen for a person to stop spin-doctoring the truth?

5.   At the heart of our carnal nature is pride. What makes it so hard to see pride in ourselves but so easy to detect in others? In what ways do you engage in "status management?" What are some of the ways a person can overcome the carnal nature?

6.   In following the example of Jesus Christ, Dr. Martin Luther King paid a heavy price for preaching freedom. What price do you think you will pay if you embrace a gospel of freedom? How would your life change? What would be the benefit? How could your commitment for freedom impact your family and your church?

Endnotes

1. Linda Crocket, Lancaster Newspaper (LNP), June 8, 2018.

5

The Role of the Holy Spirit in Freedom

How are We Set Free?

In the previous chapter, we saw that the salvation begins at conversion with forgiveness of sins. However, salvation is not a one-time event. It is a daily occurrence. *"Today is the day of salvation"* (2 Corinthians 6:2). Being forgiven of sin is not the same as being free from sin. Something more is required if we are to experience the abundant life Jesus gives. Paul wrote in Galatians 5:1, *"It is for freedom that Christ has set us free."* In other words, the reason Jesus forgives us and sets us free from the penalty of sin is so that we can live free from the powers of sin and evil. How is this accomplished? It is through the power of the Holy Spirit. The Apostle Paul makes this clear in writing to the Corinthian Church. He says, *"For the Lord is the Spirit, and wherever the Spirit of the Lord is, there is freedom"* (2 Corinthians 3:17).

At conversion, God's Spirit is deposited into the believer. Our spirit becomes regenerated. The promised presence of the Holy Spirit seals our salvation (Ephesians 1:13). Our bodies become a temple that houses the indwelling Holy Spirit (1 Corinthians 6:19). All these transactions are invisible. However, when Paul refers to the freedom brought by the Holy Spirit, he is referencing the manifest presence of God. Here the glory of God is revealed through the release of His power. A tangible, observable change occurs in the believer. Paul describes this change as a letter written on the human heart (2 Corinthians 3:3-9). The ministry of the Holy Spirt authors a new life story. The Spirit gives us assurance of our salvation and empowers us to live like Christ. In 2 Corinthians 3:18, Paul declares, *"And we all, with unveiled face, beholding the glory of the Lord, are being transformed into the same image from one degree of glory to another. For this comes from the Lord who is the Spirit"* (2 Corinthians 3:18).

This transformation does not occur by human effort, seeking to comply with the letter of the law. In 2 Corinthians 3:6, Paul states that letter of the law kills, but the Spirit gives life. Any attempt to live by a legal code, conform to moral principles or to eliminate the sinful nature apart from the ministry of the Spirit is futile. The gospel is not about behavior modification. Such efforts do not produce the righteousness of Christ. You can't make yourself righteous any more than you can save yourself. Only through the supernatural power of the Holy Spirit can the believer enter the glory of Christ. Here is a case that illustrates the point.

In the Spring of 2018, Katie, a forty-year-old woman and mother of two, came to see Sue and me. She was seeking emotional and spiritual help. Katie is a Licensed Psychologist and a Christian. She had been experiencing severe anxiety and debilitating fear. In the following testimony, Katie describes how the power of the Holy Spirit set her free. She writes:

> I now experience God in an exponentially more profound way. It has been life changing and brings me to my knees every time I think about the immense mercy our Savior can pour out on us. We just have to allow Him to dissolve the enemy's strongholds. In this way we allow more of His grace in our lives. I recall Pastor Snow saying that deliverance ministry reclaims and clears out space in our bodies and spirits so that there is more room for the Holy Spirit. The experience is amazing. I can *feel* His strength and presence in my body now. I am no longer pleading the scripture verses. I would often recite verses over my life, but now I can *feel* their truth. *"I can do all things through Christ who strengthens me"* (Philippians 4:13) is now a fact, no longer a wish. I can feel the draping of the robes of righteousness (Isaiah 61:10) on my body. I sit taller in my chair, understanding and sensing, deep in my spirit, that I *am* royal and I *am* chosen (Peter 2:9). His grace is unending. Now, when I struggle, I give it to the Lord and He never fails. He not only takes my burdens; He blesses me abundantly in response. I cannot believe I am worthy of the riches He has shown me. And of course, I am not. But Christ has shown me that if I trust Him with everything I have, He will do the same. What an awesome God! What are you waiting for? If God is for us, then who can be against us? (Romans 8:31).

Katie's testimony illustrates that knowing the Word of God is not the same as experiencing the power of God. There needs to be a balance between knowledge of the Scriptures and the ministry of the Spirit. It has been said, "If you have all Word and no Spirit, you dry up. If you are all Spirit and no Word, you blow up. But if you have Word and Spirit, you grow up." Intellectual knowledge of the

Bible alone is not enough to create the power of God's life-giving words. Jesus said, *"The words I have spoken to you are spirit and they are life"* (John 6:63b). To experience the life-giving power of the Word of God, we need to understand who the Holy Spirit is and how to cooperate with Him.

The Holy Spirit is the third person of the Trinity. He is holy and unseen. Like breath and wind, He is invisible, but real and powerful, nonetheless. He is the manifestation of divine power. He creates. He formed the world and recreates people in accordance with the Word of God (Genesis 1:2; 2 Corinthians 5:17). In the Old Testament, God promised to place His Holy Spirit upon and into believers (Ezekiel 11:19; 36:26, Joel 2:28). In fulfillment of that promise, Jesus told His disciples He would ask the Father to send the Holy Spirit to them. He promised that the Spirit who was among them would also be in them (John 14:16, 25). Just as the Holy Spirit played an essential role in Jesus' life, enabling Him to set captives free from sin and death, the same would be true of his followers.

The following identifies the various roles the Holy Spirit plays in the acquisition of freedom.

The Holy Spirit Is our Regenerator.

John 3:5; Ezekiel 37:1-14; Ephesians 2:1-5

Before Christ entered our life, we were spiritually dead. But through the Holy Spirit, we have been given new life. Our spirit has been regenerated. We are born again, as new creations, through the transference of divine energy. We receive Christ's spiritual DNA. The very Spirit that was in Christ is now in us. The Holy Spirit gives us confidence that we are the sons and daughters of God. We become heirs with Christ and have eternal life. The Spirit in us serves as a seal of our salvation.

The Holy Spirit is our Adopter. He transfers to us the divine nature.

Romans 5:5; Romans 8:15-16; 2 Timothy 1:7; 2 Peter 1:3-4

Christ's ministry on the cross accredits His righteousness to us. Through it, we gain favorable standing with God as God declares us righteous. This is called imputed righteousness. Because Christ imputes His righteousness to us, we are given access to God through the Holy Spirit. God the Father adopts us into His family. We no longer fear God's judgment but call Him our Daddy (Romans 8:15-16). The Spirit works within us, both to will and to do His good pleasure (Philippians 2:13). As we submit to the Spirit's control, He produces the attributes of Jesus Christ within us. The Bible identifies these attributes as the fruit of the

Spirit (Galatians 5:22-23). According to Romans 8:6, He gives us life and peace. This impartation is referred to as recreated or imparted righteousness. We take on His divine nature (2 Peter 1:3-4).

The Holy Spirit Is Our Purifier, Refiner and Sanctifier.

Luke 3:16; Matthew 3:13-17; 1 John 1:9; John 16:7-11; Galatians 5:16-26; 2 Corinthians 10:4

The Holy Spirit helps us live holy lives by separating wheat from the chaff, truth from lie, sin from righteousness (Matthew 3:13). He shines His light into our dark hearts and reveals hidden sin. Like fire burning up chaff, He purifies our souls. He cleans out wrong attitudes, negative habits, and impure thoughts. He brings conviction to unbelief. As we confess our sins, He washes us clean from all unrighteousness (1 John 1:9). He sets us free from the law of sin and death (Romans 6:2). Additionally, He demolishes strongholds as we take every thought captive to Christ (2 Corinthians 10:4-5). He reveals God's standard for righteousness and demonstrates God's judgment over Satan. Submitting control to the Holy Spirit and resisting the devil forces demons to flee (James 4:7). The presence and power of the Holy Spirit enables us to be set free from bondage. We experience life in the Kingdom, as righteousness, peace, and joy. Going through various trials and testing of faith, the Holy Spirit purifies our soul, leaving a rich deposit of godly character. With this life-giving hope, our one desire is to continually purify our self so that more of Christ's glory may rest on us (1 John 3:3). This is called sanctification (2 Thessalonians 2:13-14).

The Holy Spirit is our Revealer and Guide.

John 14: 26; 1 John 2:27; John 16:13-15; Romans 8:14

The Spirit has access to all the wisdom and knowledge of God. Being in a right relationship with him, He guides us into truth—enabling us to grow and mature spiritually (John 14:26). He mixes gentleness with correction, so that we learn discipline. He is our teacher (1 John 2:27) and provides us with revelation. Knowing the past, present and future, He guides us into the truth (John 16:13-15). As we listen, He shows us where to go and what to do. He functions like a built-in GPS, guiding us in the way and the will of God. He does not speak for Himself. His goal is to glorify Jesus Christ in us.

Romans 8:14 declares, *"For all who are being led by the Spirit of God, these are sons of God."* As a believer, you have access to the guidance of the Holy Spirit.

To follow the Holy Spirit's guidance, we must learn to hear His voice, discern His gentle promptings, respond to His subtle nudges, and be obedient to His leadings. All of this is subjective and can be misappropriated. For this reason, testing these impressions with Scripture is necessary. These promptings are never contrary to God's written Word and are always in accordance with God's character and nature. They are further tested by two or three witnesses.

We can have confidence in these inner promptings because Jesus promises us the Holy Spirit will lead us into all truth (John 16:13). Apart from the Holy Spirit, we are prone to be led by human nature and into the world's thinking. If we rely solely on our own understanding without revelation from God, we are likely to choose wrong paths. Proverbs 14:12 ESV warns, *"There is a way that seems right to a man, but its end is the way to death."* On the other hand, if we allow the Spirit to guide us, we will live. Paul writes, *"If you live according to the flesh, you will die; but if by the Spirit you put to death the misdeeds of the body, you will live"* (Romans 8:13).

The Holy Spirit is our Uniter.

Acts 2:1-47; 1 John 1:6-7

Acts 2:42 says that after the disciples were baptized by the Holy Spirit three thousand people were converted. They all *"continually devoted themselves to the apostles' teaching and to fellowship, to the breaking of bread and to prayer."*

The Greek word for fellowship is *koinonia,* which can be translated as "partnership." This partnership is a supernatural grace that enables Christians to love one another the way Jesus instructed them to love. He told His disciples, *"Love one another as I have loved you"* (John 15:12). Jesus' love is supernatural and pure.

This supernatural grace comes as a result of living the truth. In 1 John 1:6-7, we learn, *"If we claim to have fellowship with Him and yet walk in the darkness, we lie and do not live out the truth. But if we walk in the light, as He is in the light, we have fellowship with one another, and the blood of Jesus, His Son, purifies us from all sin."*

Acts 2 reports that after the pouring out of the Spirit, no one was in need. The people shared their possessions unselfishly and shared meals together. Many were converted when they witnessed this loving community. This kind of unity fostered a sense of belonging and family that brings God's blessing (Psalm 133).

Before Jesus died, He prayed for His disciples to know this kind of unity. *"I pray that they will all be one, just as you and I are one – as you are in me, Father, and I am in you. And may they be in us so that the world will believe you sent me"* (John 17:21).

Where people live out the truth in the power of the Holy Spirit, there is no divisiveness. Instead, unity becomes a powerful witness to the presence and love and of God. *Koinonia* is not the same as gathering for fun social events. Rather, it promotes an intimacy rooted in the presence of the Holy Spirit. This intimacy is what attracts unbelievers to Jesus. Fellowship is not intended to turn the church inward on herself. It is an outreach designed to share the gospel through loving relationships.

Just as Jesus proclaimed the gospel with *dunamis* power, healing the sick and working of miracles, he does the same with *koinonia* power. He binds hearts and minds together, knitting them in love. In such relationships, the fruit of the Spirit is evident and gives witness to Christ's presence.

The Holy Spirit is our Intercessor.

Psalm 30:2; Romans 8:22-27

While Jesus is praying for us in heaven, the Holy Spirit is praying for us on earth.

Paul writes that the Holy Spirit within us intercedes for us with groanings too deep for words (Romans 8:26). The Spirit does this because we are ignorant and weak. We don't know what to pray for or how to pray. We don't know what we need. Because the Spirit knows the mind of the Father, He prays on our behalf according to the Father's will. He can communicate with the Father in ways that we cannot.

Just as the entire creation groans waiting to be fully redeemed from the curse of sin, we groan for the full redemption of our bodies (Romans 8:22-23) through the Holy Spirit who prays for us.

Romans 8:26-27 states, *"Likewise the Spirit helps us in our weakness. For we do not know what to pray for as we ought, but the Spirit himself intercedes for us with groaning too deep for words"* (ESV).

Because of sin, we live in a broken world. We ourselves are broken vessels. Our fragile bodies, though weak, contain the Holy Spirit (2 Corinthians 4:7). Living in this defective world, we are subject to pain, suffering, evil and disaster. When these negative realities come upon us, we can become distressed, depressed, confused, fearful, irritable, restless, and anxious. We can feel overwhelmed, not knowing how we got in such a condition. Neither do we know what to do about it.

But the Holy Spirit knows all about our condition. He knows what our needs are and how they can be taken care of. He knows how to petition the Father to fulfill God's plans and purposes in our lives. This gives us hope and encouragement.

All this intercession by the Spirit gives us a measure of freedom from worry. It is encouraging that we can receive help without knowing every aspect of God's will. It is uplifting to know that someone understands when we don't understand ourselves. We can have confidence God will act on our behalf when we can't articulate our problem. It is heartening to know that when hardship befalls us, we have someone fighting for us. We can be patient with ourselves, knowing that the Holy Spirit knows our hearts and is working to free us from corruption. We can have hope in the future because the Holy Spirit is working things out for our good.

The Holy Spirit is our Comforter.

John 14:16-18; John 20:22

Before Jesus died on the cross, He had intimate conversations with His closest disciples. He sought to comfort them by telling them in advance what was going to happen. He told them He no longer considered them servants, but friends (John 15:15). Although He would no longer be with them, He would not leave them as orphans. He would ask the Father to send to them the Holy Spirit, who would be their Comforter. The Spirit would come alongside them to assure them they were not alone. He promised to leave His peace with them (John 14:27). After Jesus' resurrection, He appeared to them. Huddled together behind a locked door, He greeted them with peace. He breathed on them and said, *"Receive the Holy Spirit"* (John 20:22). Then, just before He ascended into heaven, He assured them again He would be with them to the end of the age (Matthew 28:20).

The Spirit comforts us with a peace that passes understanding. In response to prayers of thanksgiving and petition, His peace will guard our hearts and minds (Philippians 4:6-7).

In 2 Corinthians 1:4, Paul encouraged us to comfort others with the same comfort we have received from God. He says, *"For as we share abundantly in Christ's sufferings, so through Christ we share abundantly in comfort too"* (ESV).

The Spirit comforts us through collective prayer, giving us boldness to testify when threatened (Acts 4:29-31).

The Spirit comforts us as we live in the fear of the Lord (Acts 9:29-31).

The Spirit comforts us by stirring our hearts. In 2 Timothy 1:6, Paul writes to Timothy to comfort him, reminding him to stir up God's gift, also known as the gift of the Holy Spirit. Paul reminds Timothy that the Holy Spirit instills power, love, and self-control. In Romans 8:15, Paul puts it another way, saying that as children of God we are no longer slaves to fear. In Romans 5:3-5, he says we rejoice in our suffering, because God has poured out His love into our hearts by the Holy Spirit. In pouring out God's love, the Holy Spirit comforts us.

The Spirit comforts us by giving us the assurance of salvation. The very awareness of the Holy Spirit's presence gives us the comfort of knowing we have eternal life (1 John 5:12-13).

The Spirit comforts us by reminding us of the words of Jesus (John 14:26). Jesus said, *"In the world you will have trouble but be of good comfort, I have overcome the world"* (John 16:32). John reaffirms this truth when speaking of the antichrist spirit. He declared: *"Little children, you are from God and have overcome them, for he who is in you is greater than he who is in the world"* (1 John 4:4).

The Holy Spirit gives us spiritual gifts.

Exodus 31:2-5; 1 Corinthians 12:4-11; Ephesians 4:7-16; Romans 12:6-8; 1 Peter 4:10

In order to live the Christian life, to be Christ's witnesses and carry out Christ's mission and ministry, the Holy Spirit distributes a variety of spiritual gifts to us according to His grace (I Corinthians 12:4-11). These gifts are a manifestation of the Spirit. They are used to build up the church in love and to give evidence to unbelievers that Jesus Christ has power to save. The Holy Spirit gives us access to these gifts. We are instructed to desire and seek His gifts, especially the higher gift of prophecy (I Corinthians 12:31; 1 Corinthians 14:1). These gifts give us purpose and enable us to contribute to the Kingdom of God in loving cooperation with other members of the body. Each gift is uniquely important and plays a vital role in the church. We are to be good stewards of these gifts because they are an expression of God's grace (1 Peter 4:10).

In the Old Testament, the Holy Spirit anointed Bezalel and others with knowledge and skills of craftsmanship to build articles for the tent of meeting. The Spirit came upon others to prophesy and to exercise leadership.

The New Testament identifies three categories of spiritual gifts.

1. **Motivational gifts shape a person's perspective on life and how they view their role in the church.** They are the motivation behind one's words and actions. Examples of these gifts are found in Romans 12:3-8.

2. **Ministry gifts describe what a person does to serve and meet the needs of others.** Examples in Ephesians 4:11-13 and 1 Corinthians 12:27-31.

3. **Manifestation gifts go beyond natural endowments.** They demonstrate God's supernatural power. Examples found in 1 Corinthians 12:7-11.

The Holy Spirit is our Empowerer.

Luke 24:35-59; Acts 1:4-8

Jesus told His disciples that being baptized in the Holy Spirit involved being *"clothed with power from on high"* (Luke 24:49). He told them to wait in Jerusalem for the gift the Father had promised. He said, *"You will receive power when the Holy Spirit comes upon you; and you will be my witnesses"* (Acts 1:8). When the Spirit came on the day of Pentecost, they heard rushing wind, saw flames of fire, spoke in other languages, and were infused with divine energy. They were given supernatural abilities. They were fearless, filled with courage and boldness. They proclaimed the gospel in word and deed. Like Jesus, they healed sickness and cast out demons. They were able to see and hear from the invisible realm. They gave their lives to martyrdom in Christ's service and lived a radical lifestyle, different from the world. The disciples were empowered to live like Christ and commissioned to be His representatives. The Holy Spirit empowers us to do the same today. The Spirit is the same yesterday, today and forever (Hebrews 13:8). There is no variation or turning in God (James 1:17).

The Holy Spirit is our Deliverer, Healer and Restorer.

Luke 4:18-19; Acts 10:38

The Father poured out the Holy Spirit upon Jesus enabling Him to minister to the sick and oppressed. Upon Jesus' baptism in the Jordan River, the heavens opened and the Spirit came on Jesus in the form of a dove. Then the Father pronounced His favor upon Jesus (Matthew 3:17). The Spirit immediately drove Jesus into the wilderness to be tested by the devil (Matthew 4:1). After having passed the test, Jesus returned to Galilee with the Holy Spirit's power (Luke 4:14). He used that power to do good and to heal those who were oppressed (Acts 10:38). It was that same power of the Holy Spirit that enabled the disciples to heal and cast out evil spirits. Jesus told them, "As the Father has sent me, I am sending you" (John 20:21). He told them they would do the very things He had been doing (John 14:12-14). He said that those who believe shall be followed by signs, speak in tongues, heal the sick, and cast out devils (Mark 16-18). The Holy Spirit still does these things today.

The Holy Spirit Makes the Difference

The role the Holy Spirit plays in our lives is vital and amazing. He is a gift that keeps on giving. Living in a broken, pain-filled world, the Spirit works on our behalf to free us from all that negatively affects us. The Scriptures say that it is the anointing of the Holy Spirit that breaks the yoke of oppression (Isaiah 10:27). Just because a counselor is a Christian, that does guarantee that his or her counseling will be effective. Knowing the Word, having degrees, or being likeable do not make him or her effective. These things can never substitute for the ministry of the Holy Spirit.

Through the Holy Spirit, the kingdom of God is manifested in the life of the believer (Luke 17:21). It is the power of the Spirit that sets us free from sin and evil. This is good news, but there is a catch. Sadly, many Christians fail to benefit from this work of grace. Why? They fail to cooperate with the Spirit. Each time we selfishly refuse to listen, ignore His leading, and disobey His directives the greater we distance ourselves from Him. The Holy Spirit is a person who has feelings. He can be offended. Although He will never leave us completely, He will take a step back. He will not partner with sin. He is holy and will use the Word to reprove, correct, encourage, and forgive us. But He does not gloss over or tolerate sin. Our lack of cooperation with the Spirit keeps us in bondage. It takes away our strength, steals our joy, inhibits our growth, and weakens our witness. When we offend the Spirit, we distance ourselves from his presence, power, and love. There are at least six ways we offend and sin against the Holy Spirit.

Offending the Spirit

1. **The Holy Spirit is grieved.** The word *grieve* means "to make sorrowful or sad." When believers exhibit unforgiveness, bitterness, anger, slander, unwholesome talk, screaming, malicious behavior, or foul and abusive language, the Spirit is grieved (Ephesians 4:29-32).

2. **The Holy Spirit is lied to and tempted.** To *lie* is to "pretend or deceive" and to *tempt* is to "test." Ananias and Sapphira pretended to be devoted to God, but they were not. Their words did not reflect their true hearts.

Selfishness and the love for money consumed them. They tested the Holy Spirit's integrity by trying to impress others with their holiness. Whereas they wanted to make a good reputation for themselves, in truth they had wrong motives and faulty character (Acts 5:1-10).

3. **The Holy Spirit is blasphemed.** To *blaspheme* is to "speak of someone as evil." To speak of the Spirit as evil is to reject the gift of eternal life. When a person's heart is so hard that he or she rejects or turns away from this grace, he or she decides his own fate. Rejecting salvation makes this sin unforgiveable, not because of God's lack of grace, but because the person will not receive it (Matthew 12:31-32).

4. **The Holy Spirit is resisted.** People who resist the Spirit refuse to accept the message of the gospel. Their pride will not allow them to acknowledge their need to be saved (Acts 7:51).

5. **The Holy Spirit is insulted.** To insult the Spirit is to treat the blood of Jesus as unholy. The person who commits this sin dismisses the great price Jesus paid for salvation as irrelevant and inconsequential. This person fails to appropriate the gift of salvation (Hebrews 10:29).

6. **The Holy Spirit is quenched.** To *quench* means to "extinguish, stifle, or suppress." Generally, it refers to putting out fire. The Spirt is depicted as fire in the Bible. Failure to deal with sin snuffs out the Spirit. Failure to feed on the Word, pray, listen, obey, worship, and fellowship lead to apathy, indifference and self-will. These douse the flame of the Holy Spirit (1 Thessalonians 5:19).

Specific Ways We Quench the Spirit

- We teach people that God does not speak to human beings nowadays.

- We freely indulge our sinful desires, hardening our hearts until we can no longer hear God speaking to us. We neglect spiritual disciplines.

- We tell the Spirit we will do what He wants later—or when we get old.

- We intentionally disobey the commands of Scripture.

- We pretend to be better than we really are.

- We ignore the guidance of our conscience.

- We are more concerned what people think than what God thinks about us.

- We think because we have grace, it doesn't matter whether we obey God or not.

- We let pride keep us from doing anything that we consider humbling or embarrassing.

- We quench the Spirit by programming everything to the point that we do not allow the Spirit to speak.

- We engage in corrupt talk along with bitterness, anger, clamor, and slander.

- We neglect to ask the Holy Spirit to fill us and strengthen our inner being.

- We rely on rules, regulations, and policies rather than the Holy Spirit.

- We rely on human talent and knowledge and neglect the Holy Spirit's illumination and empowerment.

- We despise prophetic utterance and suppress spiritual gifts.

- We fear the Spirit's supernatural work, rather than discerning and testing it.

- We treat the Holy Spirit as an abstract power rather than a divine person.

- We fail to acknowledge that we are adopted sons of the Father.

- We shut down free expression in worship, preventing heartfelt passion for the Lord.

- We treat worship and prayer as an event rather than a lifestyle.

Powerless Christianity

Americans cherish freedom. Our nation was birthed out of a desire to be free from tyrannical oppression. We celebrate our independence on the 4th of July. We place great value on free speech, freedom of religion, and freedom to bear arms. At sporting events, we salute the flag while the national anthem is played in tribute to those who have died defending our civil freedoms. Yet American Christians remain in bondage. Why? The church has subscribed to a powerless Christianity. Many do not walk in the power of the Spirit.

Charles Kraft, in his book *Confronting Powerless Christianity,* makes a compelling case that the church in the developed world needs to undergo a paradigm shift. He persuasively argues for and demonstrates how the church can appropriate the power of Jesus to heal and free others from emotional and spiritual wounding. Kraft points to the fact that Jesus was a healer and that He promises His followers would also bring healing (John 14:12). Jesus commissioned His disciples to go into all the world to proclaim the gospel and assured them they would drive out demons and make people well through the laying on of hands (Mark 16:15-18). Jesus gave His disciples power and authority to do these things (Luke 9:1, John 20:21). Kraft argues that while the church today shows love, empathy and gives humanitarian aid to hurting people, it does not know the power of God to bring healing and deliverance to those in bondage.[1]

Similarly, John Bevere, in his book, *Killing Kryptonite*, asks "Am I settling for living below what I am created for? Are we, the collective church truly experiencing God's presence and power to change our communities?" To put it bluntly, why aren't we experiencing what we read about in the New Testament?

Wherever Jesus went, He changed communities. So did His disciples. The Scripture says that the early church turned the world upside-down (Acts 17:6 NKJV) and had no needy people in their midst (Acts 4:33-34). Bevere further states that Jesus instructed His disciples to seek first the kingdom of God and His righteousness, then everything else would be given to them (Matthew 6:33). The New Testament teaches that where the presence and power of God are manifested, there is no need.

The reason the modern church lacks power is because it fails to do the things the early church did. In other words, the church lacks power because it is full of sin and evil. The envy, jealousy, gossip, strife, competition, comparison, pride, control, and division that we find in the world are also in the church. Failing to cleanse itself of these defilements through repentance, the church quenches the Holy Spirit. People will presume they are walking in the light when they are actually like Ichabod (1 Samuel 4:21); the glory has departed.[2]

As the church relies on corporate planning and social programs instead of the Holy Spirit, she is rendered less powerful. Yes, the church believes in Jesus, but is not free to demonstrate the power of Jesus. This reduces religion to a form of godliness while denying its power (2 Timothy 3:5). Real freedom comes when we have power to live as we should, not as we please. This is a struggle all Christians go through. Like the Apostle Paul, we struggle doing the evil things we don't want to do, and not doing the good things we want to do (Romans 7:14-25). To overcome this struggle, we need to let go of self-sufficiency and rely on the power of the Holy Spirit.

Unlike the early church that allowed God to rule, many Christians today seek to tame the Holy Spirit. They want to muzzle Him and constrain Him by their own way of thinking. They want to remain in control. For the most part, the church has adopted a Greek model rather than a Hebrew model of living. The Greeks relied on reason and analysis for wisdom. The early Hebraic church relied on revelation and obedience for wisdom. For a comparison of Greek and Hebraic thought in matters of faith, see Appendix A.

Knowledge of God's Word without faith results in dead programmatic religion rather than life-giving freedom (Hebrews 4:2). To be honest, most churches in America have been compromised. They are weak and timid in their witness because they have intellectualized the Scriptures rather than surrendered to the Holy Spirit. Evangelism is reduced to a program or social event that targets consumers rather than being a way of life. We must admit the church today does not resemble the early church in which believers were ready and willing to die for their faith.

Yet the promise remains for those daring enough to be open to the manifestations of the Spirit's power. For more information on receiving the power of the Spirit see the article written by Michael Bradly.[3]

Next we will examine what it takes to cooperate with the Spirit.

Discussion Questions

1. What did you learn about the Holy Spirit that you did not know before? How does the Holy Spirit set people free from sin, the world and evil?

2. What connection do you see between the ministry of the Holy Spirit and the need for people to be set free? In what ways does the Holy Spirit help in the fight against sin, the world, and evil? How do spiritual gifts contribute to spiritual freedom?

3. How have you experienced God's presence and power? In what areas of your life do you sense a need for more of the Holy Spirit's ministry?

4. What are some of the most common ways people offend the Spirit?

5. Western culture has adopted more of a Greek rather than a Hebraic mindset. What impact does this have on a believer's ability to relate to the Holy Spirit?

Endnotes
1. Charles Kraft, *Confronting Powerless Christianity*, (Chosen Books, Bloomington, MN, 2002).
2. John Bevere, *Killing Kryptonite: Destroy what Steals your Strength*, (Messenger International Inc., Palmer Lake, CO, 2017).
3. Michael Bradly, How to Receive the Baptism of Holy Spirit, https://www.bible-knowledge.com/how-to-receive-the-baptism-of-the-holy-spirit/

6

The Role of Faith in Freedom

Jesus's Kind of Faith

In the previous chapter I spoke about the role of the Holy Spirit in freedom. Without the Spirit there is no freedom. But how do we receive the Holy Spirit? How do we cooperate with the Spirit? We do it the same way we received salvation. It is by faith. *"So then as you received Christ Jesus as Lord, continue to live in Him"* (Colossians 2:6).

Everything we receive from God, from the moment we are born again until the time we die, is by faith. Paul tells us that *"The just shall live by faith"* (Romans 1:7) and the writer of Hebrews reminds us that *"It is impossible to please God without faith"* (Hebrews 11:6). Jesus pleased God by exercising faith as He trusted the Father. Jesus' faith was not mere intellectual assent. Jesus' faith led to obedience. James 2:19 says, *"You believe that God is one. You are doing well! Even the demons believe that, and shudder"* (BLB). In other words, demons believe there is a God but are in terror because of their disobedience. In contrast, James describes Abraham as one who was obedient to God even to the point of being willing to sacrifice his son, Isaac. Jesus' faith was one of trusting the Father even to the point of sacrificing Himself on the cross to set others free. In this chapter, we look at the role faith in the acquisition of freedom.

Most Christians do not often think about Jesus as having faith. They assume that because He was divine, He automatically knew what was on the mind of God. Yet the writer of Hebrews tells us that we are to look to Jesus, the author and finisher of our faith (Hebrews 12:2). This means He is the originator of the faith. He gives saving faith to every believer (Ephesians 2:8-9). He sustains it, watches over it, and cares for it, so that faith accomplishes its purpose in our spiritual journey (Philippians 1:6). There is one true faith and that is the faith of Jesus (Ephesians 4:5). With this faith we are to pray (Mark 11:24). It is this faith for which we are to contend (Jude 3). We are to examine ourselves to make sure we are still practicing this faith (2 Corinthians 13:5).

Biblical faith involves complete trust, unquestioning confidence, and obedience to God. This is what Jesus embodied. It is more than intellectual assent, for even demons believe in God and tremble (James 2:19). Biblical faith demonstrates reliance on God's goodness and grace.

Jesus lived His life trusting in the goodness of the heavenly Father. He lived in complete obedience to the Father's will, even when it meant suffering on the cross. By example, He taught His disciples the necessity of faith in life and in death. He declared, *"With God all things are possible to those who believe"* (Mark 9:23). He affirmed the faith of those who demonstrated faith on behalf of another (Luke 5:20). He admonished those who had little faith (Matthew 6:30, 8:26, 16:8), yet assured His disciples that even a little faith could move mountains (Matthew 17:20). He marveled at the Canaanite woman and the Centurion soldier who had great faith (Matthew 15:21-28, 8:10). He asked those who sought His help if they had faith (Mark 9:22-23). He recognized the role of faith in healing (Mark 5:34, Luke 17:19). He did not perform many miracles where there was no faith (Mark 6:5). He questioned whether men would have faith when He returns (Luke 18:8).

Clearly Jesus was a man of faith. It was inherent in His character. We know this because Jesus was full of the Spirit and part of the fruit of the Spirit is faith (Galatians 5:22). Like every other godly character trait, Jesus modeled faith for His disciples.

Over the past several years, there has been a debate among scholars whether the phrase "faith in Jesus" or "faith of Jesus" is the better translation in various New Testament scriptures. (See Romans 3:22; Galatians 2:16; Galatians 3:22; Revelation 4:12; 2 Timothy 3:15; James 2:1). The problem stems from the same Greek word being used for both "in" and "of". According to Greek grammar, these prepositions can be interchangeable based on the context. The KJV and the NET renders these texts "faith of Jesus." The NIV and most other modern versions translate the texts "faith in Jesus." This small difference has significant implications. In the first instance, the emphasis is on having the faith of Jesus at work in the believer. In the second instance, the emphasis is on believing what Jesus has done for the believer. I am of the persuasion that the gospel incorporates both understandings. In other words, when a person has faith in Jesus, this also includes Jesus' faithfulness at work in them. If we emphasize one over the other, we suffer a fundamental loss.

The New Testament instructs us that faith in Christ Jesus is the means of salvation. John 3:16 teaches that whoever believes in Jesus as Savior shall be saved. By believing in Jesus' atoning work on the cross they would be made righteous and enjoy the benefits of salvation. Calling people to believe in Jesus as their Savior is the focus of most preachers, particularly those of an evangelical bent. Indeed, this is the good news of the gospel—but there is more to the gospel than simply trusting in Jesus' work for us.

Believing involves more than intellectual agreement. There is also the invitation to participate in the life of Jesus by way of a spiritual relationship. Because Jesus places his Spirit in every believer, we are expected to live out our faith as He did. In other words, we are to demonstrate the same absolute faith in God the Father that Jesus demonstrated. When practicing this kind of faith, we can expect to reflect not only Jesus' perfect love for others and His overcoming sin, but also His resurrection power.

By receiving the Holy Spirit at conversion every believer can demonstrate faith like Jesus did. As Christ overcame the world through the exercise of faith, we too can overcome the world. Revelation 3:21 states, *"To the one who is victorious, I will give the right to sit with me on my throne just as I was victorious and sat down with my Father on his throne."* Even though we are still in the flesh, with an inherited desire to sin, the Holy Spirit helps us to overcome this natural human propensity. By appropriating faith given to us by the Holy Spirit, we can be set free from the law of sin (Romans 7:22-23). Indeed, this is the victory that overcomes the world, even our faith (1 John 5:4).

Revelation 12:11 captures the need for both faith in Jesus and the faith of Jesus. In referring to Satan, it says, *"They triumphed over him by the blood of the Lamb and by the word of their testimony."* This means that by believing in Jesus' blood sacrifice on the cross we are saved. But we are also saved from Satan's power by the word of our testimony. Our testimony reflects Jesus' faith at work in us, which is obedience to God's Word as we use the spiritual authority given to us to rebuke Satan. James captures both of these principles when He says, *"Submit yourselves, then, to God. Resist the devil, and he will flee from you"* (James 4:7).

Jesus Models Freedom Through Faith

Jesus showed us how to live in freedom by faith. He did this by demonstrating how life is to be lived in the Holy Spirit, free of sin and evil. Jesus was the Messiah. He was anointed with the Holy Spirit (Luke 4:18). He was full of the Holy Spirit and was led by the Holy Spirit (Luke 4:1). Jesus put faith in the

Holy Spirit to lead Him and reveal to Him what the Father was saying and doing. Jesus said, *"Truly, truly, I say to you, the Son can do nothing of his own accord, but only what he sees the Father doing. For whatever the Father does, that the Son does likewise"* (John 5:19 ESV). Jesus taught His disciples to have faith in what He said, because it was a word coming from the Father (John 8:28 ESV). He told them that if they believed, they would do the very things He was doing (John 14:12). Holding fast to this promise is what made the early church function in supernatural power.

The way we cooperate with the Spirit is through faith in what He is saying. God speaks to us by way of revelation through reading Scripture, participating in conversations with fellow believers, hearing sermons, receiving mental impressions, hearing an inner voice, and experiencing dreams and visions. Additionally, God reveals Himself to us through books, testimonies of others, prophecies, sacraments, symbols, spiritual encounters, circumstances, answered prayer and in many other ways. The key to experiencing freedom is to trust in the leading of the Holy Spirit. The Spirit is Truth. It is the Spirit of Truth that sets us free from sin and death.

In John 8, Jesus explains that everything He says and does is based on revelation from God the Father. Verse 30 tells us that many Jews believed in Jesus as the One God sent. He then tells those who believed that if they would continue to have faith in His word, they would be set free from death due to sin of unbelief. As strange as it may seem, people who have faith in Jesus can also display unbelief. Perhaps the greatest struggle believers have in their quest for freedom is unbelief. They can believe with their heads but have unbelief in their hearts.

Freedom Comes When Faith is Anchored in Jesus Christ

Romans 8:2 states, *"For the law of the Spirit of life in Christ Jesus has set you free from the law of sin and death."* In other words, we are set free from the problem of sin, the power of sin, and the penalty of sin as long as Jesus remains the object of our faith.

Faith is only as good as the object in which we have faith. On April 30, 1976, Evelyn Mooer, an experienced climber, affixed a rappelling rope to a pipe grating on top the Mark Twain South County Bank. She thought this would be an easy rappel, but she plummeted to her death. The problem was that the pipe grating was not anchored.[1] She put faith in an unreliable object. Faith that is not properly anchored to what is true and reliable will fail no matter how sincere it is. Freedom comes when you put faith in Jesus Christ. He is the one true liberator.

Jesus has power to liberate.

There are powerful evil forces on earth and in the heavenlies. They seek to kill, rob, and destroy God's people (Ephesians 6:12; John 10:10). But Jesus has disarmed them and has made a spectacle of them on the cross (Colossians 2:15). In Jesus, God became human. Through His sacrificial death, Satan's power, the power of death, was broken (Hebrews 2:14). Jesus is the only one with power to save (Acts 4:12). He has the power to give us His divine nature, liberating us from the corruption of the world (2 Peter 1:3-4).

Jesus has the authority to liberate.

God has given Jesus all authority over heaven and earth (Matthew 28:18). He is the head of all rule and authority (Colossians 2:10). God has given Jesus the authority to grant eternal life (John 17:2). Satan has deceived some Christians. They believe his lies, convincing them they have no right to live and have no right to freedom. The truth is Jesus has all the credentials and authority needed to grant them life and freedom.

Jesus has the truth to liberate.

To be set free from sin's deceitful desires and Satan's lies we need to encounter the truth. To be set free from sin, we need to be told the truth about sin. We must know the truth about our captivity and about God's deliverance. Jesus said, *"I am the way, the truth and the life"* (John 14:6). He said, *"If you abide in my word, you are truly my disciples, and you will know the truth, and the truth will set you free"* (John 8:31).

Jesus has the perseverance to liberate.

Those who follow Jesus will endure many losses, setbacks, detours, defeats, and disappointments due to sin and evil in the world. However, Jesus gives us encouragement. He said, *"I have told you these things, so that in me you may have peace. In this world you will have trouble. But take heart! I have overcome the world"* (John 16:33). Paul further promises, *"Being confident of this, that he who began a good work in you will carry it on to completion until the day of Christ Jesus"* (Philippians 1:6).

In Jesus, all God's covenants and promises are fulfilled. He came that we may have life and have it abundantly (John 10:10). He endured great suffering but completed the work the Father gave Him to do (John 17:4; Hebrews 3:1-6). His faithfulness is constant. It never changes. He is the same yesterday, today and forever (Hebrews 13:8). He promises to be with His disciples to the end of the age (Matthew 28:20). His love never fails and never gives up.

Freedom Comes Through Faith in the Scriptures

Romans 10:17 declares, *"So then faith cometh by hearing, and hearing by the word of God."*

I grew up in the church but attended public schools. As a result, I had many doubts and questions as to the truthfulness and reliability of the Bible. Teachings of evolution conflicted with the Bible's account of creation. The idea of a woman having the right to abort her child conflicted with the Biblical teaching that God creates life and that my body is not my own.

This incongruity between my education and the Bible was not settled until I was twenty-five years old and attended a youth retreat. It was the first time I openly discussed my beliefs about God. Initially, I felt a bit awkward, but as the weekend progressed, I became more relaxed. I previously described this divine encounter in the introduction. I saw a brilliant white cloud, sparkling with silver and gold, out of which a voice said, "My name is Jesus, and this is where I live." Remembering the words of a common hymn, "You ask me how I know he lives, he lives within my heart," I knew for sure that the Bible was absolutely true and that his Spirit lived in me.

No longer did I have any doubts about the reliability of the Bible. I knew the unexplainable stories of creation, the fall of man, miracles, healings, angels, and supernatural beings were somehow real and true. I came to realize that what I did not understand about the Bible in my mind was not because the Bible was faulty, but my understanding was limited. I discovered I could trust the revelation contained in the Bible even when it was not compatible with the assumptions and philosophies of learned men. Because I had experienced the presence of Jesus in what the Bible identifies as *Shekhinah* glory (Exodus 25:8, 29:46), I became hungry to learn more about the mysteries, truths, and promises of God in His Word. No longer would I allow reason alone to define reality. Proverbs 3:5 says, *"Trust in the Lord with all your herat and lean not on your own understanding."*

Having faith in the Scriptures set me free from the confines of secular humanistic thinking and moral relativity. I developed an insatiable appetite for more and more Spirit-filled illumination from the Bible. That hunger still lingers today. Jesus said, *"Man does not live by bread alone but by every word that proceeds from the mouth of God"* (Luke 4:4). The Scriptures contain words that give life. They not only reveal who God is but also serve as a framework by which to understand reality. They are the source of a Christian worldview. They provide a standard for morality, a guide for relationships, and strategies to overcome temptations. They provide foundational truths on which to construct a positive self-identity and they tell us how to meet the human need for security, significance, and acceptance.

Once you have settled in your heart that God's Word is absolutely true and reliable, you will be free from doubt. You are free to pursue a life of obedience and submission without fear. Making the Scriptures your primary authority for life will set you free from false philosophies of men, desires of the sinful nature and the deceit of Satan.

Freedom Is Purchased with the Currency of Faith

What is faith? The Bible defines faith in Hebrews 11:1, *"Now faith is confidence in what we hope for and assurance about what we do not see."* The Contemporary English Version translates this verse as *"Faith makes us sure of the things we hope for, to be certain of the things we cannot see."* In other words, faith without doubt is the basis on which we can confidently expect God to act. Through faith, we can be certain something will happen without first having seen it accomplished. In contrast, where there is doubt or a lack of faith, nothing will happen. God will not respond. A man who doubts is double-minded. He is unstable and will not receive anything from the Lord (James 1:6-8).

Faith is the currency by which we obtain salvation. It is the means or basis by which we claim the benefits of being saved. The primary benefit of being saved is freedom from sin, evil, and death. Remember, where the Spirit of the Lord is, there is freedom.

Imagine you want to buy a certain item in a local store. You call ahead to make sure they have the item and you ask for the price. They confirm that the item is in stock and tell you what it costs. You check your wallet to make sure you have enough money. Having sufficient funds, you make your way to the store, fully believing the item is as good as yours. Arriving at the store, you give the clerk the means of exchange, the amount of money required. The clerk gives you the item and you possess it. You no longer need the money because the item is in your hands. Compare this with salvation by faith. Our faith is like the money. It is the basis of exchange by which you possess salvation. Although we have not yet fully received all the benefits of salvation, including our place in heaven, we have confidence and the assurance that we are saved because of our faith in Christ Jesus, who has already paid the price for our salvation (1 Peter 1:3-9).

Paul speaks of this transaction as the "law of faith" (Romans 3:27). In Romans 3 he explains salvation is obtained through the law of faith, not through compliance with Old Testament law. The law of faith supersedes the law of the Torah or moral law. In verse 27, he declares no one can boast of their works because all have sinned. Only by faith in the works of Jesus is there any reason to boast. Faith is a law by which we attain the promises of God. Promises include forgiveness, justification, salvation, healing, deliverance, freedom, and others.

As Christians, we receive everything by faith. Faith provides us with salvation, healing, the Spirit, and spiritual gifts. The writer of Hebrews tells us how the Israelites failed to receive the promise of God because they did not exercise faith in what God promised them. They did not mix faith with the Word. Hebrews 4:2 NKJV says, *"Indeed the gospel was preached to us as well as to them; but the word which they heard did not profit them, not being mixed with faith in those who heard it."* When you hear the Word of God, it must be received with faith if it is to be of any benefit.

Just as both the laws of gravity and motion govern the physical world, the law of faith governs the spiritual world. Through the application of the law of faith in accordance with God's Word, will, and nature, the Lord will always fulfill His promises. God keeps His covenants and His word. He is not a man that He should lie (Numbers 23:19). A mature Christian knows that God never changes. His love never fails. He is worthy of being the object of our faith.

Sometimes people mistakenly put their trust in faith itself rather than in God, which is nothing more than wishful thinking. Faith is not a means to get what you want done in heaven; it is a means by which God's will is done here on earth. This is what Jesus taught when He prayed, *"Your kingdom come. Your will be done, on earth as it is in heaven"* (Matthews 6:10).

Measures of Faith Keeps You Free from Pride and Torment

The Bible speaks of different measures of faith. God has given to every Christian a measure of faith for salvation, amounting to enough trust to be saved. However, He gives some people the gift of faith. This gift is an extraordinary confidence in the promises, power, and presence of God that enables them to take heroic stands in doing God's work. In addition, God bestows varying measures of faith upon ordinary Christians. This measure of faith enables them to live and minister in accordance with God's purposes. In Romans 12:3-8, Paul is concerned about Christians *"thinking of themselves more highly than they ought to think."* To keep believers free of pride, he says spiritual gifts are allocated to men by God.

In the same way, God gives to each person a measure of faith by which to use those gifts so that no one can claim credit or boast in the way they serve the Lord. Paul humbly said this about himself: *"I am what I am by the grace of God"* (1 Corinthians 15:10). Similarly, in Ephesians 2:8-9, Paul states we are saved by grace through faith, not by works. Just as God gives spiritual gifts, faith itself is a gift given by God to be used with humility.

When believers have this understanding of faith, they can remain humble. They can work alongside each other free of competition, jealousy, envy, or regret. In addition, they can be free of judging others who have weak faith. Paul instructs that we are not to judge those who have weak faith in disputable matters (Romans 14:1). The truth is no one can do anything of eternal consequence apart from the grace and the faith that God gives.

As John the Baptist said, *"a man can only receive that which is given to him from heaven"* (John 3:27). In other words, any success we have as Christians is due to the grace of God at work within us. Paul put it this way in writing to the Philippians, *"for it is God who works in you to will and to act in order to fulfill his good pleasure"* (Philippians 2:13). Succinctly stated, God gives us faith to use His gifts to accomplish His will. Believers who have stopped comparing their gifts and faith with others are free to be content. Appropriating God's gifts in proportion to faith, believers are free to do their part in the body of Christ without any sense of inferiority or superiority.

Choosing to Appropriate Faith Brings Freedom

God gives sufficient faith for complete freedom. John says, *"Every child of God defeats this evil world and we achieve this victory through faith"* (1 John 5:4 NLT). However, people do not always appropriate their faith, or they appropriate it for some things and not for others. For example, some folks have faith to believe they are saved, but do not have faith to leave family and home to become a missionary. Some have faith to go to worship every Sunday but lack faith to lead a ministry. Some have faith to give a small amount of money to God but not to tithe. Some have faith to believe there is a hell but lack faith to witness to others. Some have faith to pray privately but not publicly. Some have faith that God hears them when they pray but lack faith to believe they can hear God when He speaks. Some have faith to receive healing but not to cast out demons. Some have faith in the authority of the Word of God but no faith in spiritual gifts. They have faith to believe God can do anything but lack faith to believe they can speak in tongues or prophesy. The following incident makes the point.

Not long ago, I met a young, twenty-seven-year-old woman who spent much of her childhood in a secular foster program. She became a Christian in her mid-teens. She suffered from an eating disorder, had been addicted to alcohol and drugs, and often cut herself. She was separated from her husband and children and had suffered a failed pregnancy. With a diagnosis of a mental disorder, she was considering suicide. She could hear demons, but not the voice of God. Although she had accepted Jesus as her Savior, she was convinced she was condemned to hell due to her destructive actions. She did not believe she could be forgiven and thought committing suicide would rid her of the pain. Her plan was to sacrifice herself to make up for the terrible things she had done. Secretly, she had flashbacks of the face of her unborn child, whom she believed she had murdered through her drug use.

Strange as it may seem, she had faith in miracles of healing and deliverance because she had witnessed those things in her church, but she did not have faith to believe God had forgiven her for all her sin. It took quite some time, but through prayer ministry and deliverance, she eventually renounced this lie. She proclaimed the truth that Jesus is the only person God required to die for sin.

God has endless amounts of faith to give to people, but each person must choose to appropriate it. The exercise of faith occurs along a continuum. Scriptures reveal that people can exercise great faith, little faith, doubt, no faith, or unbelief. Even Christians can exhibit unbelief, as was the case with this young woman. She could not believe God could forgive her.

Doubt and Unbelief Nullifies Freedom

Ken Davis, a Christian comedian and author, tells a funny story in his book *Fully Alive*. When in college, he was to deliver a speech that would be graded on creativity, persuasiveness, and making his point in a memorable way.

Ken titled his talk "The Law of the Pendulum." For twenty minutes, he presented the principles of physics that govern a swinging pendulum. He stated that because of friction and gravity, the pendulum could never return to a point higher than the point of release.

He demonstrated this by attaching a child's toy to a three-foot string, then tying one end of the string to the top of the blackboard with a thumbtack. Pulling the string to one side, he marked on the blackboard the spot of release. When the toy swung back, he marked the height of the toy on the blackboard. He did this until the toy stopped.

Ken turned to the class and asked how many believed that the law of the pendulum was true. The entire class, including the professor, raised their hands. Thinking the presentation was over, the professor began to walk to the front of the room. But Ken had not finished. Hanging from a steel beam in the middle of the room was a 250-pound weight attached to a 500-pound test parachute cord. Ken asked the professor to sit with the back of his head against a concrete wall. He then lifted the 250-pound weight within an inch of the professor's face.

He once again explained the law of the pendulum, emphasizing that the 250-pound weight would fall short of the professor's face upon its return. He asked the professor if he still believed in the law of the pendulum. After a pause, the professor weakly nodded his head and whispered, "Yes."

Ken released the weight. It swung across the room and then returned, at which point Ken reported he had never seen anyone move as fast as the professor who dove out of the way. Ken turned to the class and asked, "Does he believe in the law of the pendulum?" The class unanimously answered, "No!" The professor put more faith into his feelings and his personal perceptions than in the law of the pendulum.

Like this professor, many Christians believe—and yet, they do not believe. They vacillate between faith and unbelief. They believe with their head but not with their heart. To believe with the head is to use reason, logic, intellectual understanding, and sensory perceptions. To believe with your heart is to have assurance in what God has said and to obey whether it makes sense to the mind or not. Isaiah 55:9 declares, *"As the heavens are higher than the earth, so are my ways higher than your ways and my thoughts than your thoughts."* Heart faith is choosing to believe God regardless of the circumstances, situation, or other limitations. Noah demonstrated heart faith when he built an ark without any empirical evidence that a massive flood was even possible. He simply obeyed God. Charles Spurgeon once said, "Unbelief will destroy the best of us, faith will save the worst of us." To overcome unbelief, we need to believe in our hearts.

Freedom Requires Believing with the Heart

Biblically speaking, the heart is the inner man, also known as the soul and spirit of a person. The word, "spirit" in Hebrew is *ruach.* In Greek, it is *pneuma.* Unlike the physical body, it is the unseen part of a person that never dies. When we are born again, the Holy Spirit is fused with the human spirit and is given eternal life with God. An unsaved person is eternally separated from God because they have not been reconciled to God and have not received His

Spirit. When a person is saved, the Holy Spirit takes up residence within. The Spirit interacts with a person and enables godly living to the degree in which the person submits to the Holy Spirit.

The Hebrew word for "soul" is *nephesh*. The Greek word is *psyche*. The mind, will, and emotions comprise the soul. It is the seat of personality and includes such things as attitudes, beliefs, and character traits. The soul's activity is concentrated in the brain, heart, and stomach. These organs have a high concentration of neurons that process everything we experience.

To believe with the heart not only includes the processing of objective data with the logical faculties of the brain but also the subjective components of our being, including feelings, attitudes, expectations, beliefs, values, and will. Before we accept something as true, it filters through all these areas. The end product determines how we organize and give life meaning. Romans 10:9 declares, *"If you declare with your mouth, 'Jesus is Lord,' and believe in your heart that God raised him from the dead, you will be saved."* If salvation is to have any personal meaning, it cannot simply be an intellectual concept; it must involve the heart where the emotions, will, values, and beliefs reside.

Initially, when we receive the gift of salvation, we do so by confessing Jesus as the Son of God, making Him Savior and Lord. We ask for and receive God's forgiveness. We receive the Holy Spirit and believe with our heart in Jesus' empowering grace, taking on a new life and a new identity. After conversion, we transform into this new identity by further confessing and receiving forgiveness for our transgressions. Through repentance, we grow in Christlikeness. Ephesians 4:22-24 refers to this process as taking off and putting on. It is taking off the old self with its deceitful desires and putting on the new self that reflects the righteousness and holiness of Christ.

Freedom Requires Faith in God's Forgiveness

If forgiveness is to accomplish its cleansing work in this process, it must occur not simply in the head but also in the heart. Otherwise, forgiveness is nothing more than a mental concept that has no real effect on the way a person organizes and gives meaning to life.

Just as we are instructed to forgive others who sin against us from our heart (Matthew 18:35), so, too, we must receive forgiveness in our hearts to realize freedom. We must also forgive ourselves at the heart level. If we do not let forgiveness impact our will, feelings, and attitudes, we will have no peace and faith will not have done its work. To be assured of God's forgiveness, it must take up residence in the heart where it has meaning and significance.

The Christian life cannot be lived apart from the reality that we are in a constant battle with sin and evil. Whereas Jesus has come to take away our sin and destroy evil, He calls us into His service to live out this victory. By exercising faith in His forgiveness, we overcome these destructive powers. If we do not, we fall prey to temptation and suffer defeat. Consequently, feelings of guilt, shame, and torment follow. God provides a way out of this bondage. He sets us free from these negative feelings through forgiveness. As promised in 1 John 1:9, *"If we confess our sins, He is faithful and just and will forgive us our sins and purify us from unrighteousness."* Forgiveness precedes purification.

The problem is that even after we have confessed our sins and asked for forgiveness, we don't always feel cleansed. We continue to berate ourselves. We beat ourselves up with guilt and conclude that God is still angry with us. Instinctively, we feel someone must pay for wrongs committed. We have an innate desire for justice. To satisfy that need, we might excuse and defend ourselves, might blame others, or decide we are indeed guilty and must pay the penalty. We condemn ourselves.

Of course, this is unnecessary because Jesus has already paid the debt for all our sin on the cross. The problem is that we can confess our sin and not apply faith to God's forgiveness. Faith involves activating our will to believe that God has indeed forgiven us, turning a deaf ear to doubt and unbelief. Faith involves believing that God is more merciful than we can imagine or deserve. Faith dares to believe that God has removed our transgressions as far as the east is from the west (Psalm 103:12). Believing that we are forgiven involves more than agreeing with an intellectual proposition. Applying faith to forgiveness takes place in the heart.

Freedom Requires a Test of Faith

James wrote, *"Consider it pure joy, my brothers and sisters, whenever you face trials of many kinds, because you know the testing of your faith produces perseverance. Let perseverance finish its work so that you may be mature and complete, not lacking anything"* (James 1:2-4).

One of the reasons God permits trials is that it tests the authenticity of our faith. Trials purify us and show what we really believe deep down in our hearts. People often think they have faith when in fact they do not. Jeremiah 7:9 says: *"The heart is deceitful above all things and beyond cure. Who can understand it?"*

True faith can only be substantiated by going through a trial. If faith remains intact after going through a season of adversity, we can be assured our faith is real. In fact, faith is like a muscle. It grows stronger with stretching and exercise. Putting faith through a strenuous workout can be exhausting and no fun. We can grow weak and discouraged when our strength fails. We feel like giving up. However, even if our faith proves inadequate and our hearts condemn us, we can still have hope because God is greater than our hearts. He knows everything (1 John 3:20).

In times of adversity, it is helpful to remember that faith occurs along a continuum: great faith, little faith, doubt, unbelief, or no faith at all. For example, the centurion soldier had great faith (Matthew 8:10). Crossing the sea in a storm, the disciples had little faith (Matthew 8:26). There were times the disciples demonstrated faith, at other times little faith and sometimes unbelief. A good example is Peter. When Jesus called him, he had faith to step out of the boat into the lake. Miraculously, he walked on water, but in a matter of seconds he looked at the wind-tossed waves, became afraid, and began to sink. Jesus reached out to him saying, *"O you of little faith, why did you doubt?"* (Matthew 14:31). When a man brought his son to Jesus for healing and Jesus asked if he believed, the man said, *"I believe. Help my unbelief."* After Jesus healed the boy, the disciples asked Jesus why they could not cast the demon out. He told them they had *"little faith"* (Matthew 17:16-20; Mark 9:28-29).

Jesus was constantly teaching His disciples to grow their faith. He was teaching them to have faith for the impossible. When He appeared after His resurrection, the disciples were frightened and thought He was a ghost. He said to them, *"Why are your hearts filled with doubt?"* (Luke 24:38 NLT). On another occasion He said, *"Truly I tell you, if anyone says to this mountain, 'Go, throw yourself into the sea' and does not doubt in their heart but believes that what they say will happen, it will be done for them. Therefore, I tell you, whatever you ask for in prayer, believe that you have received it, and it will be yours"* (Mark 11:23). Through these experiences, Jesus was teaching His disciples how to live in His kingdom by faith. Faith must be cultivated. It cannot be taken for granted.

Freedom Requires Perseverance in the Faith

The fight for freedom is a life-long battle. We can never let our guard down. Peter warns us to always be alert and sober-minded because our enemy, the devil, prowls around like a roaring lion looking for someone to devour (1 Peter 5:8). Similarly, Jesus instructs us to always be vigilant. He exhorts us to watch and pray so that we will not enter temptation (Matthew 26:41). The devil is relentless in his pursuit to take us captive.

Christians are always vulnerable to Satan's schemes and attacks. You can be a mature, life-long follower of Jesus and still fall into one of Satan's traps. Those who have been delivered from drug addiction can have a relapse many years after having been clean. Those who have been set free from pornography can have a setback with one little peek. Some believers can fall away from practicing the faith for a time, entering a "backslidden state," only to return later. Still others can reject the faith altogether, becoming apostate (Hebrews 6:4-6; Jude 1:6). These are people who once believed, but turn away, reject, and deny Christ. Essentially, they renounce their faith. Peter refers to such people as those who succumb to heresies that lead them to deny the Master who bought them (2 Peter 2:1).

Charles Templeton is a modern-day example of this. After being an acclaimed evangelist, the caliber of Billy Graham in the 1940s and 50s, he renounced his faith in 1956 and remained an atheist until his death in 2001. In 1996, he published *Farewell to God* in which he explains his reasons for leaving the Christian faith. His fall from faith began with embracing the theory of evolution.

The Christian life is not meant to be lived alone. We cannot win the battle for our soul by ourselves. We need others to support, correct, and encourage us. We need someone to fight for us when we are weak and worn. In Galatians 6:9, Paul writes, *"Let us not grow weary in doing good, for at the proper time we will reap a harvest if we do not give up."* To keep us from giving up, we need others to mentor and counsel us with words of love and truth. Adversity, hardships, suffering, sickness, loss, threats, false teachings, persecution, betrayal, rejection, tragedy, and unmet expectations can trigger fear, doubt, and unbelief, leading to setbacks and relapses.

Paul wrote to the Corinthians, *"Grace and peace to you from God our Father and the Lord Jesus Christ… the God of all comfort, who comforts us in all our troubles, so that we can comfort those in any trouble with the comfort we ourselves have receive from God"* (2 Corinthians 1:2-4). We need to develop an unshakeable resolve to extend comfort, never giving up on each other. Jesus never gave up on His disciples when they disappointed Him, denied Him, and deserted Him. Jesus never wrote them off. We must never overestimate the strength of our faith, thinking we have "arrived." Instead we must always persevere in pursuit of Christlikeness, both for ourselves and others.

Freedom Requires Faith To Be Taught

Even though the disciples failed many times to grasp the importance of faith, Jesus trained them time and time again. This required great patience and belief on Jesus' part. The truth is, His disciples continued to struggle with unbelief right up to Jesus' ascension into heaven. Matthews 28:16-17 records that after His resurrection, the eleven disciples went to the mountain in Galilee to meet Jesus. Even as they worshipped Him, some doubted. Amazingly, even though some still doubted, He commissioned them to go into the world to make disciples. To help them overcome any lingering unbelief, He further promised that He would be with them until the end of the age. Jesus had more faith in His disciples than they had in themselves!

Although it took a lot for the disciples to learn the importance of faith, it eventually stuck. Having learned their lesson, they taught others. For example, the writer of Hebrews instructed his readers to have faith by recounting how an entire generation of Israelites died in the wilderness because their hearts were hard with unbelief. They did not enter the land of milk and honey that God promised because they were afraid and disobedient. They missed God's blessing because they did not add faith to the Word of God (Hebrews 3-4:2).

Hebrews 11 underscores the kind of faith needed to please God. The author provides a long list of Old Testament heroes who accomplished great things through faith. Peter, in his epistles, encourages believers to stand firm in the faith (1 Peter 5:8) as they face persecution, trials, false teachers, and Satan's attacks.

The Apostle Paul also taught the importance of faith. He writes to the Romans underscoring the faith of Abraham: "*Without weakening in his faith, he faced the fact that his body was as good as dead – since he was about a hundred years old – and that Sarah's womb was also dead. Yet he did not waver through unbelief regarding the promise of God, but was strengthened in his faith and gave glory to God*" (Romans 4:19-21). He instructs the Ephesians to take up the shield of faith to counter the attacks of Satan (Ephesians 6:16).

James explained the consequences of a lack of faith. "*But when he asks, he must believe and not doubt, because he who doubts is like a wave of the sea, blown and tossed like the wind. That man should not think he will receive anything from the Lord; he is a double-minded man, unstable in all he does*" (James 1:6-8). Doubt or double-mindedness will get us nothing from God. God desires to bless us with freedom, but without faith, we cannot receive it. If we are afraid, anxious, rebellious, or unbelieving, we block our own blessings.

Everyone has faith in something. When we turn on a light switch, we have faith the lamp will go on. When we approach a busy intersection in our car, we have faith the traffic lights will keep us from getting hit by traffic. When we board an airplane, we have faith the pilot will fly us safely to our destination. Relying on our physical senses, reason, and knowledge, we put our faith in what we see and understand. But how do we put faith in that which we do not see? How can we have faith in an invisible God? The following illustration addresses the question.

Imagine a father lifting a trap door in the floor of his house that leads to his basement. He slowly lowers himself to the basement floor. There is no light in the basement except that which comes through the trap door from the room above. His curious daughter, looking for her father, shouts to him, "Daddy, are you down there?" He replies, "Yes I am." She asks, "Can I come down too?" He answers, "Sure, just sit on the edge of the trap door and jump. I will catch you!" She does as her father instructs but she is scared. She doesn't want to move. She hesitantly says, "Daddy, I can't see you." He responds, "I know dear, but I can see you. Jump and I will catch you." Believing the words of her father, whom she cannot see, she leaps into the darkness, lands safely into her father's arms. Her fear is overcome.

This little girl knew her father's love. Even though she could not see his face, she had faith in her father's words. This is how we need to be with God. We can be free of fear and unbelief when we know God loves us. We can do things we never thought possible. We can have a quality of life based on the promises of God that far exceeds the empty promises of this world. We are free to leap into another realm—the kingdom of God. The Father's love sets us free to look past the dangers of this world and into the unseen promises. The early disciples found that with each test of faith, they grew stronger until they met the final test in which they were set free from fear of persecution and death.

Freedom Depends More on Faith than Understanding

One of the difficulties in having faith in God, is learning to trust his Word rather than our own feelings and experiences. David trusted God and His Word. In 1 Samuel 17: 41-51, David was confronted by Goliath. All the soldiers in Israel's army were intimated by Goliath's taunts and paralyzed with fear by his threats. David saw the same giant, heard the same taunts, and felt the same indignation, but he responded differently. David had faith in what God said was true. The facts were that Goliath was bigger, stronger and a more experienced warrior, but David believed God's promises were stronger than Goliath's threats.

David was influenced more by God's Word than his own perceptions and fears. Consequently, his faith gave him victory.

We usually do not choose which Goliath's we will face, but we can choose whether we respond in faith or in fear. David learned to respond in faith to big problems because he had learned to apply faith in small problems. He exhibited boldness and courage when others were afraid because his earlier life experience built within him a strong belief that God was with him. He was convinced he would kill Goliath, because the God who gave him previous victories over the lion and the bear would also enable him to defeat this seemingly impossible foe. As God proves Himself faithful again and again, the more we will trust Him to bring us into freedom. And the more we experience freedom, the more we want.

Freedom Requires Hearing and Doing

The Bible says Jesus came proclaiming the kingdom of God (Matthew 3:2, 4:23; Luke 11:20). In the Sermon on Mount, He teaches what life in the kingdom is like and concludes by saying, *"Therefore everyone who hears these words of mine and puts them into practice is like a wise man who built his house on the rock"* (Matthew 7:24-27). When the winds and rain of adversity come, the house still stands on a firm foundation. Those who do not put Jesus' words into practice are like those who build on the sand. When the winds and rain of adversity come, the house crashes. Jesus sums up this teaching by encouraging listeners to hear His words and to do what He says.

The Christian life involves both hearing and doing. However, most of us want to add a third step. We want to hear, understand and then we decide what to do. We make our choice based on our own understanding, but this is not what the Bible instructs. Proverbs 3:5 says, *"Trust in the Lord with all your heart, and lean not on your own understanding; in all your ways acknowledge Him, and He will make your paths straight."* We must learn to trust God with things we don't understand, in other words, to live by faith.

Much of what God wants us to do does not make sense. It might even seem silly. For example, it made no sense for Joshua to lead his army around the heavily fortified city of Jericho seven times and blow horns as a military assault. It made no sense for Abraham to sacrifice his son, Isaac, on the altar when he was the only legitimate heir that could give birth to a nation. It didn't make sense for Ananias, a persecuted Christian, to visit his persecutor Saul. It made no sense for Peter to step out of the boat, expecting to walk on water. Faith, however, is not reliant on reason and understanding. Faith is essentially hearing the Word, doing it, and leaving the results up to God.

Freedom comes when we stop trying to figure out what is possible and simply do what God says. Jeremiah 1:12 declares the Lord watches over His Word and is careful to perform it. Ephesians 3:20 declares that God is able to do immeasurably more than all we ask or imagine.

Freedom Requires Putting the Gospel into Action

Many Christians claim to have faith in God, but their lives do not give evidence of it. They are spiritually lethargic. Faith without action is lifeless. Without some kind of works, faith is dead and meaningless (James 2:17-18). Faith and action are inseparable. If we don't surrender control to God and do what He says, we don't really believe in Him.

On the other hand, when you are obedient to the Word, you put faith into action. Freedom is realized and blessings follow. The Apostle James makes the point in James 1:22-25, *"Do not merely listen to the word and so deceive yourselves. Do what it says.... The man who looks into the perfect law that gives freedom, and continues to do this, not forgetting what he has heard, but doing it – he will be blessed in what he does."* The perfect law that gives freedom is not referring to the moral law.

Subscribing to a list of do's and don'ts does not set you free from the power of sin. It only makes you aware of how much you fall short of God's standards. The perfect law that James is referring to is the gospel. The gospel includes the teachings, the redeeming works, the faith, the character, the practices, the prophecies, the power, the promises, and the Spirit of Jesus Christ. When these things are worked into a person's life, freedom is realized. The Bible identifies these blessings in such terms as salvation, abundant life, eternal life, the kingdom of heaven, bearing fruit, fruit of the Spirit, new creation, walking in the light, walking in the Spirit, righteousness, glory, and much more.

Freedom Requires Teaching on How to Put the Gospel into Action

Certainly, when we do kind deeds and help meet the needs of others, we are putting the gospel into action. By doing these things, blessings flow. However, the gospel is not limited to social activism. Even atheists and pagans do these things. Putting the gospel into action is not restricted to filling stomachs. Ultimately the goal is to set people free from sin and evil by changing hearts. This requires communicating the gospel in both word and deed.

The Word of God is living and active. It can perform heart surgery. It cuts between soul and spirit (Hebrews 4:12). However, proper communication of the Word requires training. Just as a toddler needs to be trained to use the toilet without getting soiled, Christians need to learn to use the Word of God to relieve themselves from the defilements of sin and evil. 2 Corinthians 7:1 says: *"Therefore, since we have these promises, dear friends, let us purify ourselves from everything that contaminates body and spirit, perfecting holiness out of reverence for God."* John declares, *"All who have this hope in him purify themselves, just as he is pure"* (I John 3:3). Similarly, Ephesians 4:17-24 says, *"So I tell you this, and insist on it in the Lord, that you no longer live as the Gentiles do, in the futility of their thinking.... You were **taught**, with regard to your former way of life, to put off your old self, which is being corrupted by its deceitful desires; to be made new in the attitude of your minds; and to put on the new self, created to be like God in true righteousness and holiness"* (emphasis mine).

The Christian lifestyle is different from the lifestyle of the world. It is a way of life that goes all the way back to the book of Acts. Those early Christians were labeled people of the Way (Acts 9:2). They were a chosen people, a royal priesthood, a holy nation belonging to God (1 Peter 2:9). Christians need to be taught who they are in Christ and how to live life in a way that keeps them free from the negative effects of spiritual toxins.

To clean ourselves from defilements, to put off the old and put on the new, to be made new in the attitudes of our minds, to pursue holiness and function as holy priests, we need to be trained in how to live the gospel. We need to be trained in how to hear the Word of God and walk it out. We need to be trained in hearing the voice of God over the voice of Satan and the world. We need to be taught how to renew our minds. We need to be schooled in how to cast our cares upon the Lord and not take them back. We need to be instructed in how to speak the truth in love. We need to be taught to value of the gift of repentance. We need to be shown how to utilize spiritual gifts. We need to be taught how to pray. We need to be taught how to be refreshed in the Spirit. We need to be taught how to take down strongholds, overcome offenses, combat forces of darkness, and walk in righteousness in a way that bears witness to the presence, power, and love of Jesus.

The Scriptures say God sends forth His Word, and it does not return to Him empty but accomplishes what He desires (Isaiah 55:11). God's Word comes to us most perfectly through Jesus Christ. He is the Creator of the world. We learn truth indirectly through His creation and directly through the Scriptures (*logos*) and by revelation (*rhema*). The Bible uses both of these terms in referring to the Word of God. *Logos* refers to the mind or thoughts of God recorded in the Scriptures. *Rhema* refers to the utterance of God, spoken directly to us by the Spirit. Jesus said, *"The words I speak to you are spirit and are life"* (John 6:63). How do we hear Jesus speaking?

Jesus speaks to us through the Scriptures (*logos*). Most Christians can read the Scriptures for themselves but need training in how to interpret texts properly. This involves sound biblical exegesis that draws upon disciplined scholarship. Pastors and teachers specialize in this. However, Christians must not be overly dependent on the professionals. They need to engage in the disciplines of reading, listening, studying, memorizing, and meditating on Scripture for themselves.

Similarly, Christians can hear God speak to them through revelations (*rhema*). This includes dreams, visions, impressions, an inner voice, prophecy, hearing Scripture read, testimonies, signs, and physical manifestations (Acts 2:17-18). Here, too, people need training in how to discern and test whether these subjective revelations are coming from God or from another source (1 John 4:1). Prophets and apostles excel in this discernment. Teaching believers to trust revelation as much as reasoning can be a challenge, but it pays big dividends. We need both the Word and Spirit to put the gospel into action.

We can hear the word of God either by *logos* or *rhema,* but we need to act on that word to attain freedom. Faith apart from acts of courage results in bondage due to self-deception (James 1:22-25). Let me illustrate.

A tightwire artist stretched a wire across Niagara Falls. He shouted to a crowd of people who were watching, "Do you believe I can walk to the other side and back?" They responded back, "We believe you can." He then walked over and back. Upon his return he shouted to the crowd again, "Do you believe I can take this wheelbarrow across to the other side and back?" The crowd, excited to see this death-defying feat, shouted back, "Yes we believe." Then he replied, "Okay! If you really believe, which one of you will get in the barrow?" True belief is demonstrated by the courage to act. If it is not followed by action, we can deceive ourselves into thinking we believe when we really do not. This self-deception can have devastating consequences.

If I am hungry and there is set before me a banquet of abundance, I will remain starved until I pick up a fork and dig into the nourishment. I will die of malnutrition until I digest the life-giving properties of food. Similarly, we can have access to plenty of spiritual food, yet remain starved. We deceive ourselves into thinking we have enough. We say, "I am good, I don't need any more Bible study." Or "I am good, I am familiar the Bible stories and understand biblical doctrines." We could be dying in our delusion, not for lack for information, but lack of transformation. Until we make the effort to take in the Word of God and fully digest its life-giving properties, we slowly die.

Faith that produces a transformed life necessitates more than mental ascent. It requires a passion to act. We must dig deep into the truth to realize freedom. We must be willing to uncover the offensive ways that lay within our hearts (Psalm 139:24) and then apply the power of the gospel to purge them out. We must have courage to face down those giants of shame, abuse, addiction, low self-esteem, self-pity, pride, jealousy, abandonment, rejection, control, loneliness, and anger, believing God for deliverance. Freedom comes when we no longer settle for just talking the talk like Saul's soldiers. Freedom comes as we act like David, fighting the fight of faith, taking down giants.

Faith Sets Us Free from Fear

Faith and fear are incompatible. They are the antithesis of one another. They cannot exist together. Faith is described in Hebrews 11:1 as having a certainty that we cannot see. It is having confident assurance that God is behind the scenes working for our good according to His grace, mercy, and love. God's perfect love casts out fear (1 John 4:16, 18). In contrast, unbelief is rooted in fear that comes with worry, anxiety, and dread. Faith and fear are like a seesaw. When one is up the other is down. When we allow fear to rise, faith will decline. Alternatively, when we let faith rise, fear diminishes.

Our deliverance from fear and worry comes through the faith that God gives to us by the Holy Spirit. Faith is not something we can produce ourselves. It is a gift from God. Faith comes from a confident assurance that God the Father loves us, knows our needs, and is at work on our behalf. The more we come to know God's loving presence, the more we trust Him to help us overcome threats. Faith gives rise to boldness in the face of hostile opposition (Acts 4:31).

God does not want us to live in a state of fear. Isaiah wrote, *"Fear not, for I have redeemed you; I have called you by name, you are mine"* (Isaiah 43:1-2). The Psalmist said *"I sought the LORD, and he answered me. He delivered me from all my fears"* (Psalm 34:4). Jesus said, *"Peace I leave with you; my peace I give you. I do not give to you as the world gives. Do not let your hearts be troubled and do not be afraid"* (John 14:27). Paul wrote to Timothy, *"For God has not given us a spirit of fear and timidity, but of power and love and self-control"* (2 Timothy 1:7 NLT). Paul wrote to the church at Rome, *"The Spirit you received does not make you slaves, so that you live in fear again; rather, the Spirit you received brought about your adoption to sonship. And by him we cry, 'Abba Father'"* (Romans 8:15).

Anxiety is fear without a known cause. It is the accumulation of pain and unease that stems from concerns that remain uncertain or unfounded. Anxiety dominates modern life. Rapid change, information overload, distrust for authorities and government institutions, breakdown of the family, and instant media exposure to the crises around us are bound to produce anxiety. Symptoms of anxiety include insomnia, exhaustion, high blood pressure, upset stomach, depression, irritability, drug abuse, rage, eating disorders, and mental illness—to mention a few. Unresolved mental, emotional, relational, and spiritual issues lead to anxiety. Anxiety can be rooted in worry, guilt, resentment, spiritual confusion, generational curses, or spiritual attack. When anxiety drives you, the Spirit is not.

The Apostle Paul gives instructions on how to counter anxiety. He wrote, *"Rejoice in the Lord always…. Let your gentleness be evident to all. The Lord is near. Do not be anxious about anything, but in everything, by prayer and petition, with thanksgiving, present your requests to God. And the peace of God, which transcends all understanding, will guard your hearts and your minds in Christ Jesus"* (Philippians 4:4-7).

One of the most frequent commands of Jesus is "Fear not." Fear is the enemy of faith. It keeps us in bondage to the past and the future. Three ways God dispels our fears are helping us remember His promises, see from His perspective, and cast our cares on Him.

For example, when we are going through financial problems, we are promised in Philippians 4:19, *"And my God will supply all your needs according to His riches in glory in Christ Jesus."* When we have uncertainty about future decisions, Psalms 32:8 reminds us that God will *"instruct you and teach you in the way you should go; I will counsel you with my eye upon you."* These are a few of God's promises. There are hundreds of them in the Bible. Recalling and claiming God's promises brings freedom from fear. Proverbs 12:5 declares, *"Anxiety in a man's heart weights him down, but a good word makes him glad."*

We should remember that there are two kinds of fear. The good kind of fear protects us from real danger. Physically, it keeps us from walking in front of a car. Spiritually, it provides wisdom. The scriptures declare, *"The fear of the Lord is the beginning of wisdom and knowledge of the Holy one is understanding"* (Proverbs 9:10). The other kind of fear the Bible speaks of is detrimental. This kind of fear causes us to see things from the devil's perspective and keeps us from realizing God's purposes in our life. It precludes us from sharing our faith for fear of rejection and stops us from speaking the truth for fear of what man might think. Faith is having confidence to act on God's promptings and to see things from God's perspective. Pastor Harry Emerson Fosdick compared the difference between faith and fear with this quote. "Fear imprisons, faith liberates; fear paralyzes, faith empowers; fear disheartens, faith encourages; fear sickens, faith heals; fear makes useless, faith also makes serviceable."

Contrasts between the lies of the devil and the truth of God's Word.

Fear says: "I am afraid I will always be alone and unloved."
Faith says: "God loves me and draws me to Himself." (Jeremiah 31:3)

Fear says: "I can't help being overwhelmed by these feelings of fear."
Faith says: "These feelings are not valid. It is a bluff to my mind and body. It is not grounded in the truth." (Psalms 27:3)

Fear say: "I am afraid of failure."
Faith says: "I can do all things through Christ who strengthens me." (Philippians 4:13).

Fear says: "I have a sense of doom… I feel I am going to die."
Faith says: "The time of my death is up to God. I will choose to trust Him." (Job 14:5)

Fear says: "I have no hope of changing."
Faith says: "In Christ, I am a new person. All things are possible with Him." (2 Corinthians 5:17)

Fear says: "I must be in control to be safe."
Faith says: "God is in control of my life. He is with me each step of the way." (Deuteronomy 31:8)

Fear say: "I am afraid of what others think."
Faith says: "My peace comes from pleasing God, not from pleasing people." (2 Corinthians 5:9)

Fear says: "I am trapped. There is no way out of this mess."
Faith says: "God always makes a way." (1 Corinthians 10:13)

Finally, we gain freedom from fear through casting our cares on Christ. No one goes through life without experiencing some wounds that leave us with a residue of pain and fear. Fortunately, we can unburden ourselves of this emotional baggage. 1 Peter 5:7 says, *"Cast all your anxiety on Him because He cares for you."* To cast our cares on Christ is to transfer all emotional hurts to Him. Just as we transfer our sin to Him by faith, so do we transfer our emotional pain by faith. Isaiah 53:5 makes the point, *"But he was pierced for our transgressions, he was crushed for our iniquities; the punishment that brought us peace was on him, and by his wounds we are healed."* Jesus gives us peace when we give Him our fears. In this way, we make a divine exchange. We give Him our pain; He gives us healing and grace.

Other strategies to overcome fear include prayer, meditation, thanksgiving, worship, confession, prophetic words, and practicing the biblical one-another commands.

Freedom Comes Through Faith in the Form of Health

Chapter one makes the point that the average Christian is not very different from people in the world. Essentially, we try to control everything and live by our own strength. Even though we believe in God, we try to manage our own sin. This way of living requires so much inner resource that we grow weary and burn out. Without realizing it, we slowly drift from God's grace. Living a stressful lifestyle, we often make a mess of things. Peace eludes us. We become emotionally spent and physically ill. Medical research has shown that stress and anxiety increase physical ailments and are a threat to health.

In contrast to a self-defeating lifestyle, Jesus offers an alternative. He said, *"Come to me, all of you who are weary and carry heavy burdens, and I will give you rest. Take my yoke upon you. Let me teach you, because I am humble and gentle at heart, and you will find rest for your souls. For my yoke is easy to bear, and the burden I give you is light"* (Matthew 11:28-30).

God has a design for our well-being. He wants us to be reliant upon Him in all aspects of our life. This means surrendering control over to Him. Ironically, this results in more freedom, not less. Surrender does not mean the forfeiture of responsibility. On the contrary, it means taking responsibility for a new way of thinking and interacting. It means admitting that our attempts at meeting our most basic needs for love, significance, purpose, acceptance, worth, and security—apart from God—have not worked. When we stop trying to do things our way and let God direct our lives, we experience our desired fulfillment.

By engaging in activities that please and honor God, we experience joy, love, peace, trust, contentment, meaning, and belonging. This positive state of mind reduces tension and stress in the body, causing our glands to release chemicals that promote health.

Jeff Levin, PhD., in his book *God, Faith and Health* said, "The positive emotions resulting from religious worship can help us to negotiate and overcome the stresses of daily life."[2] The Psalmist makes the same point, only with more eloquence, *"You make known to me the path of life; you will fill me with joy in your presence, and eternal pleasures at your right hand"* (Psalms 16:11). Learning to live in an intimate relationship with God is the most life-giving thing a person can do. Warren Wiersbe, in his book *Five Secrets of Living* asserts the way to remain in God's presence is to obey His principles.[3] Through submission and obedience to God's principles, the Holy Spirit gives us power to make wise choices and behavioral changes that have a positive impact on our health, setting us free to enjoy life more.

Freedom Requires Faith Coupled with Patience

Exercising faith is critically important to experiencing freedom. But faith must be practiced over time if freedom is to remain strong. Folks tend to think of healing and deliverance as something that occurs instantaneously and in an isolated event. Many Bible stories reinforce this view, but other stories recognize healing as a process occurring over time (Luke 17:11-19, Mark 8:24). The blessings and freedom God wants us to have will not be accomplished with just one encounter. It happens over a lifetime of repeated healing and deliverance encounters. It occurs as a lifestyle of freedom is established. Hebrews 6:11-12 says, *"And we desire that each one of you show the same diligence so as to realize the full assurance of hope until the end, that you may not be sluggish, but imitators of those who through faith and patience inherit the promises."*

It takes faith to receive the good things God has promised, but waiting is equally important. Waiting in faith for God's promises to manifest requires patience. Without patience, frustration, anger, blame, fear, disappointment, discouragement, or bitterness can take over. Negativity left unchecked can lead to unbelief and unbelief short circuits the flow of God's promises. It prevents God's blessings from reaching into the soul. James tells us that a man without faith, in the midst of adversity, is unstable and will not receive anything from the Lord (James 1:2-7). Without patience, it is easy to believe lies and become hopeless. This works against the one who desperately needs an outpouring of God's grace. True faith does not waiver over time. It fiercely holds to the truth amid all kinds of trials. It dares to believe that *"In all things God works for the good of those who love him, who have been called according to his purpose"* (Romans 8:28). True faith perseveres in the face of uncertainty and adversity. It remains consistent even when circumstances and physical conditions have not changed.

Hebrews 6:15 states, *"After waiting patiently, Abraham received what was promised."* God rewards those who wait in faith. Like an expectant father sitting in the waiting room for the birth of his child, people of faith must learn to wait. Hannah had to wait years before God answered her prayer for a baby. Joseph spent years in prison before his vision of being a ruler would come to pass. Moses wandered in the wilderness for forty years before the Israelites took possession of the promised land. David waited years after being anointed king before assuming the throne. Waiting, eventually results in blessing. Isaiah said, *"they that wait upon the Lord shall renew their strength"* (Isaiah 40:31).

A person may instantly receive a significant amount of grace from a healing and deliverance encounter. But, if they do not patiently maintain the practice of faith, and wait for strength from the Lord, they are likely to return to old patterns of dysfunction. Freedom, once gained, can be forfeited. This is most evident in drug addicts that relapse or ex-prisoners who become repeat offenders. Certainly, the one who initiated the healing is the one who sustains it, but if we fail to cooperate with the Spirit, our freedom will revert to bondage. Our faith is not in the healing itself, but in God, the Healer. He deserves our continued trust, obedience, worship, thanksgiving, and service.

In summary, freedom requires the exercise of faith, both in believing in Jesus Christ as Savior and by imitating the faith of Jesus Christ as Lord. That faith comes by hearing the Word of God both through the *logos* and the *rhema*. Appropriating the word requires illumination from the Holy Spirit. This faith needs to be taught and practiced over the course of time and results in health and freedom from fear. Placing faith in Jesus' teachings and in the writings of His disciples requires more than the acquisition of biblical knowledge. It demands acting on His commands and waiting on His promises.

The next chapter presents the need for a biblical worldview. Everyone reads and interprets the Bible through a filter of culture and personal experience. Knowing the content of the Bible and adhering to orthodox teaching is not sufficient to realize the freedom that the Scriptures depict. If one does not have a biblical worldview, certain truths contained in Scripture are not going to be understood or accepted as relevant. This is particularly true for those with a Western mindset. What does a biblical worldview look like?

Discussion Questions

1. What role does faith have in the acquisition of freedom?

2. What gets in the way of people having faith in God's forgiveness?

3. What does faith have to do with receiving the Spirit? What does faith have to do with the ministry of the Holy Spirit?

4. How would you describe the faith of Jesus? How does that compare to your faith? Do you think you can do the same things Jesus did? Why or why not?

5. How does a proper understanding of receiving a measure of faith contribute to humility? How does this promote unity within the body of Christ?

6. How does fear block our faith? How does faith set us free from fear? What impact does the intellect have on faith? What impact do emotions have on faith?

7. Faith without action is dead. Can you think of a scripture, Bible story or parable that makes this point?

8. How does sharing the gospel increase spiritual growth? (Philemon 6-7 NIV).

9. How has your faith increased? How has your faith been tested?

10. What is the connection between faith and a person's physical health?

Endnotes
1. http://publications.americanalpineclub.org/articles/13197703001/Rappel-Failure-Inade-quate-ProtectionMissouri-Mark-Twain-South-County-Bank
2. Jeff Levin, *God, Faith and Health: Exploring the Spirituality-Health Connection,* (John Wiley & Sons, Hoboken, NJ, 2007).
3. Warren Wiersbe, *Five Secrets of Living,* (Tyndale House Publishers, Carol Stream, IL, 1978).

7

Acquiring a Perspective for Freedom

Needing a Biblical Worldview

In 1990 I left my first church in Virginia to become Senior Pastor of Swamp United Church of Christ in Reinholds, Pennsylvania. Swamp is one of the oldest Reformed churches in the area, dating back to 1749. For fifteen years we slowly implemented programs designed to make disciples. Things went relatively well, and we built a new addition in 2000. However, in 2005, my Christian worldview radically changed.

I grew up in conservative evangelical churches in which the Bible was considered the infallible Word of God, sufficient for all faith and practice. I believed the Bible was true. I enrolled in Lancaster Theological Seminary to equip me for pastoral ministry. In addition to learning pastoral skills, I was introduced to Reformed Theology, Liberation Theology, Neoorthodoxy and Roman Catholicism along with a host of liberal social stands including abortion and homosexuality. I learned to question a literal interpretation of the Bible and to replace it with a more sophisticated approach. This more scholarly approach viewed supernatural acts recorded in the Bible as symbolic narrative. This meant stories of crossing the Red Sea and a large fish swallowing Jonah were interpreted as nice entertaining stories that did not really happen. Still, they contained a greater spiritual truth worthy of our attention. Along with this demythologizing the Bible, hermeneutics and higher forms of biblical criticism were part of my education. All these disciplines forced me to clarify my beliefs. Admittedly, sometimes this intellectualism left me a bit confused. If it were not for my personal relationship with Jesus and the leading of the Holy Spirit, I don't know where my theology and ministry would be today. By the grace of God, I graduated from seminary stronger than when I went in.

During my early years in the pastorate, I labored intensely to prepare sermons that were doctrinally sound, intellectually sharp and filled with practical application. Drawing on my education and relying on the Bible and the Holy Spirit, I sought to lead the church by employing good organizational leadership principles and introducing programs that 'scratched where people itched.' Consequently, the churches I served grew. By the common standard of measurements of budgets, baptisms, and buildings, I did okay. Along the way, I encountered a few people caught up in the occult, reporting some supernatural experiences. However, in 2005, things took an unanticipated turn, causing me to re-evaluate my ministry.

I had a personal encounter with evil and it changed my worldview. Up until that time, evil was more or less an intellectual concept that explained why bad things happen. It was something Hollywood dramatized in horror films. The devil was more of a fictional character invented by primitive cultures to give credence to their superstitious beliefs. Even though the Bible was a depository of ancient myths, at some level I believed in the existence of a devil. After all, I had met people who told stories of being impacted by dark forces, but how demons impacted every day human life remained an enigma to me. I saw evil at work in global wars, political systems, criminal activity, and personal addictions. But to know first-hand how the power of the gospel could set ordinary people free from demonic bondage remained a mystery. For me, such freedom was more of a promise and a hope than an everyday common occurrence depicted in the New Testament.

In my ministry, I saw people grow in faith. I saw the Lord do great and wonderful things like miraculous physical healings. But I was blind to the schemes of the devil. I have since learned that the devil will let you engage in all kinds of religious activities and humanitarian work, as long as, you don't bring healing and deliverance to the soul. If you do, be prepared for all hell to break loose.

In the Spring of 2005, I met John and Leslie Kindler at a HarvestNet meeting. John and Leslie were friends with the founders of Restoring the Foundations, Chester and Betsy Kylstra. They served on the Board of Directors with the Kylstras and were trained to do the ministry. They gave me an application and asked to come back for a three-hour session. After explaining to me the components of the ministry, they led me in a prayer in which I renounced the sins of my ancestors. Near the end of the prayer, I experienced something that felt like an electrical current that began at the top of my head and traveled to my feet. I began to weep as the Kindlers prayed for me. When I gathered my composure, I felt lighter and the room was brighter. Something changed within me. I was different. I had been delivered from a demonic presence I did not know was within me.

Several months later, I asked a couple of friends who had prophetic giftings to come to my church to do a spiritual mapping in which they would identify certain things they saw in the spirit realm. After walking through the various buildings and sharing what they were seeing and hearing, we entered the fellowship hall. This was where Wayne, one of the prophets, ran into an intimating spirit that nearly knocked him over. He shared with me the vision of what he saw. He described the face of a man with a beard, dressed in clothes from a different era. The description of the man's face was vaguely familiar to me.

Several days later, I was looking through some the historical records of the church and found a photograph of a previous pastor whose tenure dated back to 1900. His facial features resembled what the prophet described in his vision. A few weeks later, I took the photograph to the prophet and asked, "Is this the guy you saw in the vision?" Wayne confirmed, "Yes, he is the one." I made it a project to go through church records and to ask some of the older senior members about the misdeeds of former pastors that had been swept under the rug. I felt that I needed to publicly repent of their sins as Daniel and Nehemiah did on behalf of Israel.

After several weeks of gathering the history of former pastors, I invited the elders of the church to come to the social hall. I read Exodus 20 regarding the passing down of generational sins, then we had a time of worship. I began to pray out loud, confessing and repenting of the sins of the previous pastors. To my utter surprise, the same electrical current passed through my body, but this time it was more forceful. My stomach began to react as though I had the dry heaves. I bent over and began to weep and moan profusely due to the pain in my gut. I cried out in agony for a solid thirty minutes without pause. I could not stop even when I tried. My sides ached and I was drained of my strength.

Finally, I gained my composure. When I looked up to those gathered around the table, their faces were as white as a ghost and their eyes as big as saucers. I did not know what had happened, and neither did they. We sat in disbelief. Then quietly and somberly, I closed the meeting.

For the next several days, I wondered what had happened. I prayed about it and asked the Lord for help. About a week later, I was reading in the Book of James, and suddenly I received an explanation:

You adulterous people, don't you know that friendship with the world means enmity against God? Therefore, anyone who chooses to be a friend of the world becomes an enemy of God. Or do you think Scripture says without reason that he jealously longs for the spirit he has caused to dwell in us? But he gives more grace. That is why Scripture says: 'God opposes the proud but shows favor to the humble.' Submit yourselves, then, to God. Resist the devil, and he will flee from you. Come near to God and he will come near to you. Wash your hands, you sinners, and purify your hearts, you double-minded. Grieve, mourn, and wail. Change your laughter to mourning and your joy to gloom. Humble yourselves before the Lord, and he will lift you up (James 4:4-10).

You would think that after having such a powerful cleansing experience, life would get better and blessings would flow. However, just the opposite happened. Members of the church began seeing apparitions and ghosts, while some saw dark shadows following people. Others observed objects flying across the room. People were hearing sounds of footsteps and knocking but no one was there. The leadership in the church became conflicted. Some leaders were caught in adulterous affairs. A key leader on the worship team was tragically killed in a car accident. Grief overwhelmed the congregation, draining our joy. We could not maintain two Sunday services and had to revert to only one. Among the congregation, harmony faded, personalities clashed, and gradually people drifted away. My leadership was challenged. Crisis after crisis severely tested my own family. I developed arrhythmia symptoms that required ablation surgery.

Through all of this, I sought to learn all I could about the spirit world. My understanding of the Bible took on meaning and significance that was previously lacking. I realized how important the fivefold ministry gifts are when wrestling with powers and principalities that Paul talks about in Ephesians six. I began to see that the gifts of apostle, prophet and evangelist were as necessary for the health of the church as the gifts of teacher and pastor. I did not have a lot of experience with revelatory gifts, out of which the apostolic and prophetic function, but I desired to learn. I received training in healing and deliverance and began to employ biblical principles that I learned from Restoring the Foundations and other sources. Sue, my secretary, joined me in this journey. We saw the Lord do a work in our own lives and in the lives of the people we ministered to.

Unfortunately, whereas my biblical worldview changed dramatically, much of my congregation did not. Some did grasp the change and encouraged me to press forward into uncharted territory. Now, some fourteen years later, I am convinced more than ever before that if a congregation is to experience the kind of freedom the New Testament speaks about, its DNA needs to reflect a biblical worldview that incorporates freedom from personal dimensions of evil.

Western verses Eastern Worldview

Dr. Neil Anderson makes the case as to why most Americans do not relate to personal dimensions of evil. He asserts the Western world sees reality in two tiers. The upper tier is invisible. It is the sphere in which God and spiritual beings exist and is understood through religion and mysticism. The lower tier is the empirical world. It is understood through science and the physical senses. For the most part, Westerners have adopted a secular worldview in which the spiritual world has no bearing on the physical world. Furthermore, where there is any attempt at integrating theology with psychology, the subject is restricted to God and humanity. The activity of Satan and demons is excluded.

The worldview of the West is in stark contrast to two-thirds of the world's inhabitants who hold to an Eastern worldview. An Eastern worldview readily believes and operates in the spiritual realm as an everyday reality. They make peace offerings and perform rituals to appease evil spirits. Many Westerners dismiss this kind of thinking as the ignorant perspective of the uneducated and superstitious. Neither of these two systems reflects a biblical worldview. The East seeks to appease evil and the West tries to ignore it.

Two Worlds Two Kingdoms

The Bible frames reality in terms of a spiritual world and a physical world that interact. Paul states in Ephesians 6:12 KJV, *"For we do not wrestle against flesh and blood, but against principalities, against powers, against the rulers of darkness of this world, against spiritual wickedness in high places."* The Bible frames reality as a conflict between the kingdom of light, governed by God and the kingdom of darkness, governed by Satan (Colossians 1:13). God's kingdom is superior and will one day totally eradicate evil from the earth (Revelation 20:10). But during the interim, humans must choose which kingdom they want to be part of—the kingdom of light or the kingdom of darkness. They must learn to contend for the faith that has been shown to them in Jesus Christ (Jude 3-4). They must learn from God's Word how to rely on the Holy Spirit to be an overcomer in this spiritual conflict.

When Christians exclude the supernatural from their worldview, they consign to live life apart from the gospel's power. They try to live a good, moral life in their own strength. When their human efforts fail, they feel frustrated and discouraged. Some will drift from the faith, put blame on others, put up façades, or try to explain reality in terms of psychological or natural causes. Further still, some will use all their resources and power to define their own reality. Apart from recognizing the personal dimensions of evil, they will remain in bondage or possibly even join the ranks of evil.

This manifestation of evil is what happened to Germany in the 1930s and early 1940s. Did you ever stop to think how a nation could rise to such a level of scientific and technological advancement and yet have leaders who murder millions of people? Humanistic education without morality leads to morality without religion. Religion without a comprehensive biblical worldview leads to a benign view of evil. A benign view of evil opens the door for the depravity of man. The depravity of man left unchecked leads to the captivity of man.

God wants to bring freedom to humanity. He sent His Son Jesus to proclaim the kingdom of heaven (Matthew 4;17), freedom for prisoners, and the release of the oppressed. (Luke 4:18). Jesus came to destroy the works of the devil (1 John 3:8).

Genuine Christianity Requires a Biblical Worldview

Chuck Colson says, "Genuine Christianity is more than a relationship with Jesus, as expressed in personal piety, church attendance, Bible study and works of charity. It is more than discipleship, more than believing a system of doctrines about God. Genuine Christianity is a way of seeing and comprehending all reality. It is a worldview."[1]

In the following pages we will consider the significance of a worldview and the importance of having a biblical worldview.

Dr. Del Tackett, President of Focus on the Family Institute, defines worldview as "a framework from which we view reality and make sense of life and the world."[2]

David Noebel, author of *Understanding the Times*, defines worldview as "any ideology, philosophy, theology, movement or religion that provides an overarching approach to understanding God, the world and man's relations to God and the world."[3]

James Sire, author of *The Universe Next Door*, defines a worldview as "a commitment, a fundamental orientation of the heart, that can be expressed as a story or in a set of presuppositions (assumptions which may be true, partially true or entirely false) which we hold (consciously or subconsciously, consistently or inconsistently) about the basic constitution of reality, and that provides the foundation on which we live and move and have our being."[4]

Basically, a worldview is the way we make sense of life in the world.

Worldviews are shaped by some fundamental questions. Most people wonder about the following:

- Where did we come from?
- What happens after we die?
- Why are we here?
- Did we evolve or were we created?
- Is there a God?
- If there is a God, what does He expect of us?
- What is my purpose?
- Is morality absolute or relative?

Answers to such questions form the building blocks of our worldview. Once these questions have been answered, we are ready for the next set of questions centering around our place in the world. How we see the world shapes how we see ourselves in it.

A word picture can help us understand how a worldview operates. Imagine you are standing in front of a window looking outside. You don't usually think much about the window, do you? That is because the window is clear. It allows you to see what is outside as it truly is. Suppose someone taped a piece of red plastic wrap over the window. Things would look different, wouldn't they? The grass might look brown instead of green and the sky look purple instead of blue. That wouldn't be the real colors of the sky and the grass, would it? No. Your ability to see the colors accurately depends on the clearness of the window. If the window is tinted, then the assumptions and beliefs we have about life become distorted.

What is a biblical worldview?

A biblical worldview is a framework for understanding reality through the lens of the infallible Word of God. Someone who has a biblical worldview is one who believes absolute moral truth exists and that its source is the Bible. They believe the Bible is accurate in the principles it teaches and it can be trusted. Although the Bible was originally written in three different languages, in different styles by forty authors over several centuries, Christians believe it is inspired by the Holy Spirit and that the Holy Spirit is needed to explain its meaning and application properly. Christians who have a biblical worldview point to Jesus

Christ as the central figure of human history. He is the Creator, Sustainer and Redeemer of all human life. They believe that He is the way, the truth, and the life (John 14:6). Those who place their faith in Him receive the gift of the Holy Spirit and eternal life with God (Acts 2:38). They will receive rewards according to their works (1 Corinthians 3:11-15; 2 Corinthians 5:10). Those who rebel against God will be judged fairly and sent to hell along with Satan (Matthew 25: 31-46; Revelation 20:3, 21:8). Is it not sin that sends a person to hell. Even Christians sin. It is unbelief that sends a person to hell (John 3:17-18).

Why does a biblical worldview matter?

The Bible presents a clear view of God, man, Satan, and the world. All worldviews are not created equal. Some distort the truth, some have partial truth, and some have reliable truth. Most people are unaware that the world around them affects their worldview. Media, entertainment, science, politics, and secular education all influence us. Without realizing it, we are taken *"captive through hollow and deceptive philosophy, which depends on human tradition and elemental spiritual forces of this world rather than Christ"* (Colossians 2:8). We are encouraged to become spiritually mature so as not to be *"blown here and there by every wind of teaching and by the cunning and craftiness of people in their deceitful scheming"* (Ephesians 4:14). Additionally, in Romans 12:2, Paul tells us, *"Do not be conformed any longer to the pattern of this world, but be transformed by the renewing of your mind."*

There are more than six thousand distinct religions in the world as well as numerous philosophies and social constructs. Each one has its own window through which to define truth. These worldviews can be broken into six broad categories as follows.

Naturalism

Naturalism holds that there is no God. The material universe is all that exists. Atheism, Agnosticism, Existentialism, Materialism, and Humanism fit into this category.

Pantheism

Pantheism holds to the belief everything is God. A force governs the universe. Everything is spiritual; all else is an illusion. Hinduism, Taoism, Buddhism, and much New Age Consciousness fall into this category.

Theism

Theism holds to the belief that a personal infinite God exists and He created and governs the universe. Christianity, Judaism, and Islam fit into this category.

Spiritualism and Polytheism

Spiritualism and Polytheism hold to the belief the world is populated and governed by spirits. Gods and demons are the real reason behind what happens. Animist fits into this category. Witchdoctors and shamans communicate with these spirits.

Postmodernism

Postmodernism holds to the belief that reality is interpreted through language and culture. Reality is socially constructed. In other words, humans create their own reality. Progressive liberal thought, secular humanism, situational ethics, political correctness, moral relativism, and tolerance fit into this category.

Critical Theory

Critical Theory is now emerging in America. It seeks to answer the question "who are we?" in terms of oppression. It divides the world into two factions: the oppressed and the oppressor. It seeks to dismantle current cultural structures in order to liberate oppressed groups in an effort to achieve a state of equality. It often uses the language of social justice to communicate its message.[5]

The world is filled with people holding different worldviews by which they determine truth. Christians define truth through the person of Jesus Christ. They rely on several sources of authority that bear witness to Jesus Christ. These sources include Scripture, experience, tradition, reason, culture, and revelation.[2] Although all Christians agree Jesus is the Son of God and provides for mankind, there is much on which they differ. They have different opinions about God, man, the purpose of life, and moral codes. According to Pew Research Center, in 2005, 75% of all Americans claimed to be Christian and 62% claimed to be a member of a church organization.[6] Why is there such disparity in the way American Christians define their faith?

According to Barna Research Group, only 9% of all Americans have a biblical worldview. Among those Christians who were identified as born-again believers, only one out of every five (19%) had a biblical worldview.[7]

For the purposes of Barna's research, a "biblical worldview" was defined as believing that:

- Absolute moral truth exists.
- The Bible is completely accurate and reliable in all the principles it teaches.
- Satan is a real being or force, not symbolic.
- A person cannot earn their way into heaven by trying to be good or by doing good works.
- Jesus Christ lived a sinless life on earth.
- God is the all-knowing, all-powerful creator who rules the universe.

As stated earlier, only 19% of American Christians meet the criteria for a biblical worldview. In providing a partial explanation as to why this number is so low, Barna Research Group and Summit Ministries conducted a study on how other competing worldviews like secularism, new spirituality, postmodernism, Islam, and Marxism influence Christians in America.[8]

Here are some notable findings among practicing Christians:
- 61% agree with ideas rooted in New Spirituality
- 54% resonate with postmodernist views
- 36% accepted ideas associated with Marxism
- 29% believed in ideas based on secularism
- 38% were sympathetic to some Muslim teachings

Clearly, alternative worldviews are influencing Christians. The church today needs to do a much better job of teaching a Christian worldview and how it differs from other competing worldviews. Believers need to understand that not all worldviews are created equal. They need to examine their own belief system to see where they may have compromised. For example, you have heard it said, "Beauty is in the eyes of the beholder." On the surface this seems to be an innocuous statement, but it actually reflects a secular, relativistic assumption. It is the antithesis of the absolute truth found in the Bible. Biblical truth holds that God's purity and creativity define beauty. Every person is uniquely beautiful because he or she is created in the image of God.

The problem in the church is the lack of a comprehensive biblical worldview. People in America are a product of Western culture. We hear the gospel through a secular humanistic filter, therefore, many biblical truths are not understood and applied. Parallel to that, every culture in the world hears the gospel through their unique cultural values and experience. Consequently, they incorporate portions of the gospel that we do not. They have adopted certain biblical truths into their lives that we fail to acknowledge. For example, in Africa, the reality of demons in the spirit world is commonly accepted. Western culture dismisses the existence of demons.

It is important that we learn how people from different cultures have incorporated various dimensions of the gospel into their collective lives. By learning from each other, we can all embrace a more comprehensive picture of the kingdom of God.

Because we don't have a comprehensive biblical worldview, people interpret Scripture in a way that absolutizes portions of Scripture to the exclusion of others. This varying interpretation results in different denominations with differing belief systems. Ultimately, this fragments the body of Christ. Treating part of the gospel, as though it were the whole, creates conflict and divisiveness.

Next we will look at beliefs found in the Bible that are relevant for freedom.

Discussion Questions

1. What is your view of evil? How does the problem of evil inform your understanding of God?

2. Have you ever had a personal encounter with demons? Do you know anyone who has? If you were to have a personal encounter with an evil spirit, how do you think it would influence your approach to life?

3. What worldview has had the most influence on you? How do you view the Bible? How does having a mix of worldviews affect your faith?

4. Why is it important to have a biblical world view that takes the presence of evil spirits literally?

5. How do you go about interpreting the Bible?

6. What authority do you give the Bible in shaping your life?

Endnotes

1. 1Charles Colson and Nancy Pearcey, *How Shall We Live?* (Tyndale House, Carol Stream, IL, 1999), pp. 14-15.
2. https://www.focusonthefamily.com/faith/whats-a-christian-worldview/
3. Ibid
4. https://www.shorter.edu/wp-content/uploads/1-Christian-Worldview-1.pdf
5. John Macquarie, *Principles of Christian Theology*, (Charles Scribner's Sons, New York, Second Edition, 1977).
6. "*America's Changing Religious Landscape*" Pew Research Center: Religion and Public Life. May 12, 2015.
7. https://www.christianitytoday.com/edstetzer/2009/march/barna-how-many-have-biblical-worldview.htm
8. https://www.barna.com/research/competing-worldviews-influence-todays-christians/

8

A Biblical Perspective Promotes Freedom

Key Biblical Concepts

Conceivably, there are over one hundred beliefs found in the Bible that constitute a biblical worldview.[1] However, a few are highly relevant to the acquisition and living out of freedom. These key truths form a framework for understanding the deliverance and healing that are vital for freedom. They include the following concepts.

The Bible speaks of God as the Creator of the world.

There are at least sixty-four Scriptures that ascribe God as the Creator of the heavens and of the earth. All three persons of the Godhead were involved in creation (Genesis 1:2; John 1:1-4; Acts 17:24; Hebrews 1:2; Colossians 1:15-16). The world did not randomly evolve as taught by some evolutionists. It was created by a Creator God. The world bears testimony to His handiwork (Psalm 19:1; Romans 1:18-20).

The Bible speaks of man as both a physical and a spiritual creature.

We have a spirit and soul living within a physical body. The spirit and soul are infinite and intangible. The body is finite and tangible. According to 1 Thessalonians 5:23, God sanctifies us in spirit, soul, and body. Some theologians see this division as a trichotomy and others a dichotomy. Those in the trichotomy camp, see man as having three distinct parts: body, spirit, and soul. Those in the dichotomy camp, see man as having two parts: the body and the inner man composed of spirit and soul. The spirit and soul are often used interchangeably to refer to the heart of man.

- **The soul consists of the intellect, will, emotions, attitudes, values, beliefs, conscience, and so forth**. These qualities make one's personality. These immaterial characteristics exist beyond the life span of the human body and are eternal. The Hebrew word for "soul" is *nephesh*. The Greek word is *psyche*.

- **The body is the physical house in which we live.** It relies on the five senses to interact with the world. It is temporary. One day it will die and go back to basic elements. In Genesis 1:27, 31; 2:7; 2:22, God created man with a physical body and declared it very good. The Old Testament does not have one exclusive word for body. Instead, it draws upon many terms referring to the physical nature. It includes such terms as bone, belly, flesh, and others. The New Testament uses one exclusive Greek word, *soma*.

- **The spirit is the life-giving force that animates the body.** Unlike the physical body, it never dies. The human spirit enables us to connect with God. When a person is born-again, their spirit fuses with the Holy Spirit. Their spirit becomes regenerated and receives eternal life with God. They have a connection with God that is personal and life-giving. They can hear the voice of God. The word "spirit" in *ruach* Hebrew and *pneuma* in Greek.

- **It takes the Word of God to discern the difference between the spirit, soul, and body.** Hebrews 4:12 says, *"For the word of God is alive and active. Sharper than a double-edged sword, it penetrates even to dividing soul, spirit, joints and marrow; it judges the thoughts and attitudes of the heart."*

When it comes to healing and deliverance, the Bible refers to cleansing the soul/spirit and body from defilements. According to 1 Corinthians 7:1, *"Therefore, since we have these promises, dear friends, let us purify ourselves from everything that contaminates body and spirit, perfecting holiness out of reverence for God."* This scripture instructs us to purify ourselves from sin, lies, strongholds, and demonic oppression. In this way, we pursue holiness in reverence to God and give Him glory.

The Bible identifies two realms.

I previously stated that the Bible conceives of reality as both the spiritual realm and physical realm. Because man is both physical and spiritual, he can relate to both realms. The physical world is material and tangible. It includes the earth with all its biological creatures and plants. Man interacts with the physical world through his five senses. Spiritual creatures like angels and demons comprise the spirit world and are generally invisible and undetected. Occasionally, they manifest. Man interacts with the spiritual world through revelation, imagination, dreams, visions, meditation, and prayer. People in the occult connect with spirit guides and demons. Christians connect with the Holy Spirit and angels.

There are two kingdoms.

The Bible sees humanity caught up in a cosmic conflict between two kingdoms: the kingdom of light ruled by God and the kingdom of darkness ruled by Satan. Jesus came to earth to resolve this conflict through His redemptive work. He came proclaiming the superiority of the kingdom of God (Matthew 4:17). He was anointed by the Spirit to preach this good news of salvation and set captives free (Luke 4:18). In the Sermon on the Mount and parables, Jesus reveals the kingdom of God and demonstrates its power through miracles, healing, casting out demons, and transforming lives. Through His death on the cross and subsequent resurrection, He disarmed Satan and made a public spectacle of his power and authority (Colossians 2:15).

The devil's purpose is to kill, steal and destroy. However, Jesus' mission is to give abundant life. He does this by giving His church the Holy Spirit, who leads them into truth, comforts them with peace and equips them with power (John 14:16,17,27; Luke 24:49). He promises He will never leave nor forsake His disciples, but will help them further establish the kingdom of God on earth (Matthew 28:20). The kingdom on earth will be fully restored upon His return when Satan is cast into hell forever. Meanwhile, His followers are instructed to seek the kingdom of God (Matthew 6:33). They are to be His witnesses (Acts 1:8), going into all the world to make disciples (Matthew 28:19).

The Bible identifies three heavens.

The first heaven

The first heaven is the atmosphere around the earth. It includes the air we breathe, clouds, and the birds of the air. It extends about twenty miles above Earth. The Bible refers to this heaven in Deuteronomy 11:17, Deuteronomy 28:12, Judges 5:4, and Acts 14:17. The first heaven is where humanity dwells and where demons and angels contend for the souls of men (Ephesians 6:12; Hebrews 13:2; Acts 12:15; Matthew 18:10).

The second heaven

The second heaven is where the moon, stars, and planets are in outer space (Isaiah 13:10). This is the celestial heaven, where celestial beings dwell. Satan and his demons are headquartered here. Demons and angels fight spiritual battles in this second heaven. The angel Michael, in Daniel 10:12-13, was delayed twenty-one days because he was in a conflict with the Prince of Persia. The great cosmic battle of Revelation 12:7-12 takes place in this celestial heaven. Angels pass through this region to bring messages to earth (Genesis 28:12).

The third heaven

The third heaven is where God dwells from His throne (Psalm 103:19). It is the highest heaven. God sits on His throne and sovereignly rules the universe with power, justice, wisdom, grace, honor, and love (Matthew 5:34; 2 Chronicles 18:18; Psalm 11:4; Proverbs 8:8; Hebrews 4:16; Hebrews 12:2; Revelation 1:4, 3:21, 4:2; 1 John 4:8). It is referred to as paradise (Revelation 2:7). Paul speaks of having been taken to the third heaven in 2 Corinthians 12:2-4.

People who are followers of Christ are not citizens of the earth. They are citizens of heaven. They sit with Jesus at the right hand of God (Ephesians 2:6). Even though believers may live on the earth, their true residence is with God in the third heaven (Philippians 3:20). For the present, they are God's ambassadors representing His kingdom here on earth (2 Corinthians 5:20).

What happens in the third heaven and the second heaven impacts what happens on earth (Job 1:6; 2 Chronicles 18:18-21; 2 Chronicles 16:9). God sends forth His Word. It does not return to Him void, but accomplishes what He sent it to do (Isaiah 55:11). He dispatches angels with messages and orders them to help men to accomplish His will (Psalm 103:20-21).

Within both the second heaven and third heaven are spiritual realms or places. Ephesians 1:20 says Jesus is seated in heavenly places (plural). Ephesians 6:12 says we wrestle against evil forces in heavenly places (plural). Just as there are different regions on earth, so too, there are different regions within the heavens.

The Bible speaks about the courts of heaven.

The courts of heaven are composed of divine council members. They hear cases, render verdicts, and carry out judgments. Much of this legal activity involves the opening of the Books of Heaven. There is intense activity, including martyred saints, who petition the Father for judgment (Revelation 6:9-10), deliberations concerning earthly matters (1 Kings 22:19-22; Psalm 89:7), angelic messengers (Revelation 8:2-6), prophetic visitors (Isaiah 6:1-4, 8-10; Revelation 4:1-2), and multitudes of heavenly hosts worshipping God (Revelation 5:11-13). Jesus is there interceding for the saints.

Daniel 7:21-26 presents us with a picture of a courtroom in which the Ancient of Days pronounces judgment in favor of the saints of the Most High. In teaching about prayer, Jesus draws upon a court setting to describe how God, as Judge, goes about answering prayer (Luke 18:1-18).

The Bible speaks about the Books of Heaven

Daniel 7:21-22; 26 and Revelation 20:12 refer to the Books of Heaven. These books were written by the council of the Lord (Jeremiah 23:18), a company that consults and settles on matters of the Kingdom. They allow God's purposes to be done. Psalm 139:16 tells us that every person has a book in heaven. This book contains the destiny and purpose for each person's life. In other words, it chronicles the plan God has for us. A battle in the heavenlies determines how much of each person's destiny is fulfilled here on earth. Hebrews 10:57 tells us that Jesus had a book written about His purpose in coming to Earth. Just as Satan tried to keep Jesus from fulfilling His destiny, so does he seek to keep God's people from fulfilling theirs.

Anything God has ordained for the earth has first been written in a book. Ephesians 2:10 tells us that we are Christ's workmanship and that our purpose is to do the good works that God prepared for us. The Greek word for "workmanship" is *poem.* In other words, a poem was written about us in one of heaven's books. It describes the work we are to do. In 2 Timothy 1:9, Paul exhorts Timothy to fulfill what was planned for him before time began. Once decisions are made in heaven regarding each person's destiny, each person on earth must decide whether they are going to obey what heaven has determined. When we agree with that determination, powerful things can happen to advance the kingdom of God. For more information on the Books of Heaven, see Robert Henderson's book, *Operating in the Courts of Heaven.*

The Bible identifies four kinds of men.

Natural Man

The natural man is not saved. He is lost and does not have the Spirit of God within. He can have many admirable qualities but is separate from God. He relies on human wisdom. The things of God are foolishness to him. Self-centered, fleshly appetites drive him. These folks are sinners who live in the world and are being blinded, deceived, and destroyed by Satan (1 Corinthians 2:13-16; Ephesians 2:1-3).

Carnal Man

These folks believe and are saved. Their sins are forgiven. The Spirit is within them. They are called saints who live in God's kingdom but are held back by their sinful nature and are influenced by Satan. They still behave and think much like the natural man. They live by their own mind, will, and emotions. They are plagued by doubt, fear, and unbelief. They are dominated by the desires and appetites of the flesh. They are still attracted to the things of the world and are often disobedient. They are baby Christians whose diet consists of milk. They have received the basic knowledge of the gospel of salvation but are not able to apply the deeper truths of Christ. Not knowing who they are and whose they are, their identity in Christ has not been fully established. They often feel defeated and discouraged. They are distracted, disturbed, and deceived by the devil. They may have knowledge of Scriptures, be able to preach, and have spiritual gifts, but they lack spiritual power (1 Corinthians 3:1-4; Hebrews 5:12-14; Galatians 5:16-18; Romans 7:14-20 NKJV).

Spiritual Man

The spiritual man does not live from his soul but by the Spirit. He has the mind of Christ, enabling him to examine and discern the world. Unlike the natural man, he knows good from evil. Unlike the carnal Christian, he crucifies the flesh by relying on the Word and Spirit. More than his own comfort, he longs for constant intimacy with God. He has moved beyond a soft diet of basic teachings about salvation. He is hungry for more substantial food and desires to digest and appropriate teachings on righteousness. He seeks to glorify God in all that he does. Being humble and relying on God's grace, he lives a lifestyle of repentance. He can combat Satan's schemes. He can restore sinners gently. He abides in Christ bearing the fruit of soul winning, holy living, Christ-like character, sacrificial giving, service to others, sensitivity to the Spirit's presence, spiritual giftings, and celebratory worship. He is an overcomer, turning away from temptation and persevering through hardship. Faith, hope, and love characterize his life (1 Corinthians 2:15; John 15:5; Galatians 6:1; 1 Corinthians 13:13).

Glorified Man

The redemptive work of God in the life of man is made complete (Romans 8:30). This redemption occurs after death. Man is pure and undefiled; God has removed all sin (Romans 8:17-18; 2 Corinthians 4:17). His life reflects the Holy Spirit (1 John 3:2). He receives a new body like Jesus; not a physical but a spiritual one, imperishable, honorable, and powerful (I Corinthians 15: 42-53). He is clothed in white garments (Revelation 3:4-5) and suited for heaven. He has received the fullness of Christ, the hope of glory (Colossians 1:27).

The Bible attributes four identities to believers.

- A created being made in the image of God (Genesis 1:27).
- A sinner who has rebelled against God (Romans 3:23).
- A sufferer who lives in a broken world full of trouble (John 16:33).
- A saint who by faith has received Christ as Savior and Lord and is His disciple (Ephesians 1:1; 2 Corinthians 1:1; Act 9:32).

The Bible speaks of strongholds.

Paul wrote, *"The weapons we fight with are not the weapons of the world. On the contrary, they have divine power to demolish strongholds"* (2 Corinthians 10:4).

Ed Silvoso defines a spiritual stronghold as "a mindset impregnated with hopelessness that causes us to accept as unchangeable, situations that we know are contrary to the will of God."[2]

Strongholds are fortified patterns of thought within the mind. They are arguments or reasonings that occur on a subconscious level. They contradict the truths and power of God and are based on lies. These thought patterns are deeply rooted and are often thought of as part of one's personality. They take the form of such things such as low self-esteem, anxiety, victimization, anger, control, performance, rejection, and many more. Strongholds are hindrances that keep us from living in the freedom God intends for us. These strongholds are dismantled with the truth of God's Word through the power of the Holy Spirit.

The following is an example of how a stronghold works. Imagine someone who is afraid or angry with God. He does not feel close to God and has difficulty experiencing His love, peace, and presence. Pastor Kyle had this problem as explained in chapter one. The murder of his Christian professor caused Kyle to lose faith in God's goodness. He could not trust the future of his two sons into God's care. Deep down, Kyle didn't believe God was a good Father. When we feel hurt and disappointed with God, we can't believe He is good and kind. We don't trust Him. Think of it this way. If your spouse is cruel and rude to you, would you be disposed to snuggling up to him or her? When you have judged someone as mean or untrustworthy, you are not likely to be open or allow yourself to be cared for by that person. Similarly, if your perception of God is that of a harsh dictator, it will hinder your ability to feel His love and presence. A stronghold is built on a lie concerning God. It is important that we have a correct perception of God to be able to experience the freedom that is in Christ.

The Bible speaks of different categories of sin: sin, transgression, and iniquity. There are also sins of omission and commission.

Psalm 32:5 says, *"I acknowledged my **sin** to You, and my **iniquity** I have not hidden. I said, 'I will confess my **transgressions** to the LORD,' and you forgave the **iniquity** of my **sin**"* (NKJV, emphasis mine).

This verse contains all three words related to sin. The Hebrew word for "sin" is *chattaath*. Sin means to "miss the mark." It means doing something against God or another person. It is a failure to do what is right in thought, word, or deed. It is trespassing across a line that should not be crossed. It can be intentional or unintentional. You may try your best and still miss the mark. Exodus 10:16 says, *"Pharaoh quickly summoned Moses and Aaron and said, 'I have sinned against the LORD your God and against you.'"*

The Hebrew word for "transgression" is *pesha*. Transgression means "to choose to intentionally disobey; a willful trespass." It has to do with wrongful conduct in which a person knowingly and intentionally engages. Psalm 32:1 says, *"Blessed is the one whose transgressions are forgiven, whose sins are covered."*

Iniquity means "to engage in a premeditated choice, continuing without repentance." It is more entrenched as a habit than a transgression. Left unchecked, it leads to a state of willful sin. It is not so much a particular action but more the character behind the action. It has to do with the inner state of a person, which is deformed. It has to do with an inner weakness that predisposes one toward sinning. Micah 2:1 says, *"Woe to those who plan iniquity, to those who plot evil on their beds! At morning's light they carry it out because it is in their power to do so."*

The difference between transgression and iniquity is that transgression points to our conduct, whereas iniquity points to our condition before God. In the world, we commit transgression; before God, we commit iniquity.

What is generational iniquity? Generational iniquity is not a sin like that of an intentional transgression; rather, it is predisposition or inclination. One of the Hebrew words used for iniquity is *avon*. It means "a crooked or bent branch." Iniquity describes a crooked or perverse attitude passed down from the fathers to the children. It is not sin per se, but a weakness that serves as the root motivation for sin. It is a character flaw that shapes your tendencies. Just like we inherit physical traits from our parents, we also inherit spiritual traits.

An example of generational iniquity would be the predisposition for alcoholism that can be passed down from one generation to the next. The following biblical reference illustrates this concept:

The LORD is slow to anger and abundant in lovingkindness, forgiving iniquity and transgression; but He will by no means clear the guilty, visiting the iniquity of the fathers on the children to the third and the fourth generation (Numbers 14:18 NASB).

If they confess their iniquity and the iniquity of their forefathers, in their faithfulness which they committed against Me, and also in their acting with hostility against Me—I also was acting with hostility against them, to bring them into the land of their enemies or if their uncircumcised heart becomes humbled so that they then make amends for their iniquity—then I will remember My covenant with Jacob, and I will remember also My covenant with Isaac, and My covenant with Abraham as well, and I will remember the land (Leviticus 26:40-42 NASB).

According to God's law, when a person sins, legal right is given to Satan to torment him. Until one repents of that sin, the legal right remains in effect through future generations. By breaking the binding power of generational sin, we cancel the right of the enemy to torment us in that area of our lives. When we confess generational sin, we do not take responsibility for that sin. We simply reduce the pressure on us to repeat that pattern of sin. God holds us accountable for only our own sin and our own iniquity. We are merely acknowledging this area of struggle in our family line and nullifying Satan's power over us. An example of confessing and repenting of generational iniquity is found in the story of Saul's family and the Gibeonites, recounted in 2 Samuel 21:1-14.

Sins of commission are committed when we do something we should not do. They can be intentional or unintentional. Foreknowledge is not a consideration. For example, you may go to a foreign country and break a traffic law. Even though you were ignorant of the law, you still committed a traffic violation, which would be a sin of commission. The Old Testament Law prescribed certain sacrifices for such unintentional sins. Unaware of God's standards, people continue to commit unintentional sins. Intentional sins of commission are those done with full knowledge of what is forbidden. These are the most familiar type of sins. For example, if a man robs a store or a man cheats on his wife, we would all recognize this as sin. Paul gives a short list of sins of commission in 1 Corinthians 6:10 and Jesus lists sins of commission in Matthew 15:18-19. These include adultery, murder, theft, drunkenness, slander, and false witness.

A sin of omission is not doing something right that we should be doing. James 4:17, a key verse, states, *"So whoever knows the right thing to do and fails to do it, for him it is sin."* In Luke 10:30-37, Jesus gives a good example of a sin of omission in the account of the Good Samaritan. All those who failed to help the injured man were guilty of the sin of omission.

It is not easy to get away with sins of commission because they are public and involve others. On the other hand, sins of omission are relatively easy to commit without others knowing. These are more insidious and dangerous. Some examples of these kinds of sins are: failing to pray regularly (1 Samuel 12:23); failing to tithe or be faithful financial stewards (Malachi 3:8); failing to help another when we have the capacity to do so (James 4:17); failing to help our own family members in time of need (1 Timothy 5:8); failing to fellowship with other Christians (Hebrews 10:25); failure to worship God and to keep the Sabbath (Exodus 20:8). Paul lists at least twenty things we should be doing in Romans 12:9-21). Some of these include demonstrating sincere love, honoring others above oneself, showing hospitality, and living in peace with everyone.

Christians, who know the full range and power of sin, ought to live with a sense of humility and dependence on God's grace. They need to be on high alert knowing that sin hinders their prayers (1 Peter 3:7) and can lead to chastisement (Jeremiah 40:3), demonic torment (Matthew 18:23-35), and death (Romans 6:23).

The Bible speaks of infirmities.

The Greek word for infirmities is *astheneia*. It means lack of strength or a weakness as found within the body and soul. In Matthew 8:14-17 Jesus heals the infirmities of those afflicted with illness and demons. Healing infirmities is a reference from Isaiah 53:4 in which the Messiah would be one who takes upon himself the people's weakness' including grief, sickness, sorrow and pain, that is either physical or mental.

The Bible speaks of angels and demons.

Angels are spiritual beings that serve God. They worship Him and serve as His messengers to people on the earth. They also minister to people, helping them accomplish God's purposes. They can appear in human form on earth. Demons are fallen angels who serve Satan. One-third of the heavenly angels rebelled against God (Revelation12:3-9). They form a hierarchy in Satan's kingdom. They are given different assignments designed to harm man and oppose God. They can cause physical illnesses (Mark 9:25-27) and mental torment (Mark 5:1-17).

They seek to dwell in a host, whether human or animal (Luke 8:33). Demons cannot possess a Christian belonging to Christ, but they can oppress a Christian. This oppression usually happens when demons gain access to a person through a legal agreement. This agreement can happen when a person believes a lie, refuses to forgive, or commits a sin and remains unrepentant (Ephesians 4:26).

The Bible speaks of humanity having three enemies.

- **Satan** is our primary adversary who seeks to steal, kill, and destroy (John 10:10). He uses deception to lure people away from God. He enlists a host of demons to assist him in forming his kingdom of darkness.

- The **flesh** is our sinful nature inherited from Adam. The New Testament word for "flesh" is *sarx*. It refers to the physical body that is corrupted and dominated by the law of sin. The flesh is responsible for selfish desires that oppose and war against the Spirit of God (Galatians 5:17).

- The **world** refers to a world order or system of thinking that is contrary to the kingdom of God (Romans 12:2). Satan governs the social order or culture of nations (1 John 5:19). These social constructs are cosmetically beautiful. They place great significance on temporary and transitory pleasures that distract people from the love and values of God (1 John 2:16-17). Some of the world's values include accumulation of wealth, lust, pride, status, power, selfish ambition, human achievement, pursuit of pleasure, traditions and philosophies of men (1 John 2:15-17). The world looks to external appearances to access acceptance and wellbeing. God focuses on the inner man, being most interested in the condition of heart. However, the world hates Christ and His followers (John 15:18-19). For those caught up in the world, being a follower of Christ is a foolish waste of life (1 Corinthians 1:18, 23). Those who are committed to the world-system are unable to receive the Holy Spirit (John 14:17). To be friends with the world is to be an enemy of God (James 4:4). There is no middle ground or compromise. You cannot live by the world's standards and Christ's at the same time (Luke 11:23).

According to Barna Research, "About half of all adults (54%) claim that they make their moral choices on the basis of specific principles or standards in which they believe. Other common means of making moral choices include doing what feels right or comfortable (24%), doing whatever makes the most people happy or causes the least conflict (9%), and pursuing whatever produces the most positive outcomes for the person (7%)."[3] This kind of thinking is reflective of the world. It is rooted in the sinful nature and satanic influence.

The Bible speaks of defilements, vows, and curses.

A defilement is an uncleanness or blemish on a person or immoral conduct under Mosaic law. In the New Testament, defilement is an impure motive or an immoral state or condition. To be *defiled* means to be "polluted or infected." If you cut your hand and let it get dirty or contaminated, you become vulnerable to infection. The same is true in the spiritual realm. Instead of becoming infected by germs, you can be infected by sin, unclean spirits, or demons. A few key New Testament passages concerning defilement are:

- *"But the things that come out of a person's mouth come from the heart, and these defile them. For out of the heart come evil thoughts – murder, adultery, sexual immorality, theft, false testimony, and slander"* (Matthew 15:18-19).

- *"Since we have these promises, beloved, let us cleanse ourselves from every defilement of body and spirit, and make holiness perfect in the fear of God"* (2 Corinthians 7:1 RSV).

- *"Religion that is pure and undefiled before God and the Father is this: to visit orphans and widows in their affliction, and to keep oneself unstained from the world"* (James 1:27 RSV).

Examples of defilement include:
- **Seeking mediums or others with occult power** Leviticus 19:31
- **Idol worship** Ezekiel 20:7; Ezekiel 22:4
- **Unforgiveness** 2 Corinthians 2:10-11; Hebrews 12:14-15; Matthew 18:23-35)
- **Bestiality** Leviticus 18:23
- **Sex outside of marriage** Genesis 34:2; Matthew 15:19-20; 1 Timothy 1:10
- **Power of the tongue, unwholesome talk** Genesis 9:25; James 3:6; Matthew 15:11; Ephesians 4:29
- **Cursed objects** Deuteronomy 7:25

Curses generally involve a wish that evil may befall another or oneself. In the Bible, a curse was meant to protect the terms of a covenant by exacting penalties for a violation. When it comes to the covenant of God's law, a curse would be levied upon those who were disobedient and rebellious against God's law. Curses are also words spoken with some spiritual authority that can have consequences for generations. Curses can be spoken by God, by others, or oneself.

Consequences of a curse include:
- Incurable sickness

- Continual financial lack
- Mental or emotional distress (confusion and depression)
- Reproductive problems
- Marriage breakdown
- Family alienation
- Accident prone
- Family history of suicide and premature deaths

Things that can bring on a curse include:

- Anti-semitism – Genesis 1:2-3
- Robbing God – Malachi 3:8-9
- Disrespect toward parents – Deuteronomy 27:16
- Idolatry – Deuteronomy 27:15
- Breaking of covenants - 2 Samuel 21
- Stealing from man - Zechariah 5:1
- Severed relationships across generations - Malachi 4:5-6
- Idle words and self-cursing - Psalm 109:17-18

The Bible speaks of soul ties.

Souls ties are physical, emotional, and spiritual bonds with another person, organization, or thing. They have a covenantal nature, binding two entities together. They can be positive or negative, godly or ungodly. Godly soul ties are healthy emotional ties with friends, parents, and marriage partner. They add value to the quality of life. Ungodly soul ties are unhealthy emotional ties characterized by co-dependency, control, manipulation, humiliation, or intimidation in attempt to diminish a person's free will. Soul ties can also be formed by immoral sexual relationships.

- Examples of godly soul ties: *"Jonathan became one in spirit with David and he loved him as himself"* (1 Samuel 18:1). *"For this reason a man will leave his father and mother and be united to his wife, and the two will become one flesh"* (Mark 10:7-8).

- Examples of ungodly soul ties: *"Do you not know that your bodies are members of Christ himself? Shall I then take the members of Christ and unite them with a prostitute? Never! Do you not know that he who unites himself with a prostitute is one with her in body"* (1 Corinthians 6:15-16)? *"Do not be deceived: Bad company corrupts good character"* (1 Corinthians 15:33).

The Bible speaks of believers having the mind of Christ.

This is the ability to think like Christ. Because the Holy Spirit dwells within the believer, he has access to the thoughts of Christ. This access means he understands God's plan for the world: bringing glory to Himself, restoration of creation to its original state, the redeeming of sinners, and salvation of the lost (Luke 19:10). God also plans that we would honor others, (1 Peter 2:17-21), commit no sin (1 Peter 2:22), be humble and obedient to God (Philippians 2:5-8), be compassionate (Matthew 9:36), be prayerfully dependent on God (Luke 5:16), and serve others (Philippians 2:6-7).

These truths are identified in 1 Corinthians 2:16:

- It stands in sharp contrast to the wisdom of man (verses 5-6)
- It reflects God's wisdom, once hidden, now revealed (verse 7)
- It is given to believers through the Holy Spirit (verses 10-12)
- It cannot be understood by those without the Spirit (verse 14)
- It gives believers discernment in spiritual matters (verse 15)

The Bible speaks of God as three persons: Father, Son and Holy Spirit.

Although the Bible does not explicitly use the term Trinity, there are several references in which all three members of the Trinity are identified and present at the same time (John 14:16; John 14:26; John 15:26; Luke 3:22). This trinitarian mystery is identified as one divine entity functioning in three ways: The Father governing the world; the Son redeeming the world; the Holy Spirit interacting with the world.

God's very presence on earth is manifested through the Holy Spirit (Acts 5:3-4). The Holy Spirit enables believers to have a personal connection with "God the Father" and "Jesus the Son." Through the Holy Spirit, believers are able to hear the voice of God, experience the power of God, understand the teachings of God, trust the promises of God, take on the character of God, receive the grace of God and utilize the gifts of God. The Holy Spirit intercedes, convicts believers of sin, convinces them they are righteous and assures them that Satan has no authority over them. Unbelievers cannot understand or receive the Holy Spirit because they are blocked from this revelation by Satan. However, through the proclamation of the gospel, men can be brought to faith in Jesus Christ, and through the power of the Holy Spirit, the truth is revealed about God, themselves, and others.

The Bible speaks of two kinds of revelation.

1. *Logos* (**general revelation**): *Logos* is a Greek word meaning "derived from logic." General revelation refers to knowledge attained about God or spiritual matters through natural means. This knowledge comes through the observation of nature, the historical records (Scriptures), conscience, reason, and philosophical discourse. This kind of knowledge is readily available to all mankind. General revelation is understood in terms of concrete temporal human experience. Biblical references supporting this concept include Romans 1:20, Psalm 19:1-6, and Matthew 5:45. These Scriptures point to the work and existence of God in indirect ways. However, in John 1:14 it says, "*The Word* (logos) *became flesh and made his dwelling among us.*" In this instance, revelation of the *logos* was direct. It came in the form of the incarnate Jesus Christ. Currently, because Jesus is no longer physically present, we draw upon logic to understand the reality of His existence.

2. *Rhema* (**specific revelation**): This kind of knowledge comes through supernatural means or divine inspiration that is outside human reason. It is given directly to an individual or group. Biblical examples of this kind of communication include miracles, angelic visitations, signs and wonders, visions, dreams, trances, prophecy, hearing the voice of God, impressions, and guidance given by the Holy Spirit. The purpose of special revelation is to equip Jesus' disciples with divine power, enabling them to proclaim the gospel of salvation, not in terms of theological propositions but in giving witness to a living resurrected Christ.

Jesus said He would build His church on this kind of revelation. In Matthew 16:13-20, Jesus asked His disciples, "Who do men say that I am?" Peter responded by saying He was the Messiah. Jesus declared that this answer came to Peter not by reasoning of the flesh, but specifically from God the Father. Jesus went on to assert that Peter's revelation would be the rock or foundation upon which He would build His church. Indeed, Paul later states that this kind of revelation given by the Holy Spirit established the church through the apostles and prophets (Ephesians 2:18-20). They were to be examples of recipients of God's grace to future generations (Ephesians 2:7).

This kind of revelation was prophesied by the prophet Joel. He said this type of revelation would be characteristic of the church in the last days (Joel 2:28-29). Peter confirmed this prophecy on the day of Pentecost (Acts 2:16-18). According to the book of Acts, this kind of revelation guided the ministry of the early church and is frequently referenced in the Epistles. Revelations of this type are essential to walking in the Spirit and overcoming in spiritual warfare. Unfortunately, this kind of revelation is not well understood by much of the Church in the West today.

The Bible speaks of knowing God's ways.

In Exodus 33:12-13, Moses says to the Lord, *"You have told me, 'I know you by name, and I look favorably on you.' If it is true that you look favorably on me, let me know **your ways** so I may understand you more fully and continue to enjoy your favor..."* Psalm 103:3 says, *"He made known his ways to Moses, his acts to the people of Israel."* In Psalm 25:14 it says, *"**The secret council** of the LORD is for those who fear him, and he reveals his covenant to them."* These passages speak about knowing God's ways. What are God's ways?

There is a difference between observing God's actions and understanding His ways. Most Christians can observe God's external actions including healing, miracles, material blessings, deliverance from physical threats, and answers to prayer. Immature Christians tend to focus on God's actions. But mature Christians understand His ways. This has to do with the way God operates His kingdom. It implies having personal intimate knowledge of God. It involves such things as His purposes, promises, plans, preferences, and priorities. It involves knowing His manner, motivation, desires, and thoughts. We come to know God's ways as we spend time in His presence and listen to His Word. It is crucial to understand His ways so that we will not become discouraged and overwhelmed by the troubles of this world.

The Bible speaks of God as one who delivers his people from peril.

Psalm 34:17 declares, *"The righteous cry out, and the Lord hears them; he delivers them from all their troubles."* The following scriptures identify how God delivers His people.

God delivers His people from:

- temptation. 1 Corinthians 10:13
- the wrath to come. 1 Thessalonians 1:10
- Satan's reign. Colossians 1:13
- the power of sin. Romans 6:5-23; Titus 2:14
- the curse of the Law. Galatians 4:4-5
- creation from decay. Romans 8:20-21
- the iniquity of their ancestors. 1 Peter 1:18-19

- the fear of death. Hebrews 2:14-15
- the righteous wrath of God. Romans 5:1,8
- famine. Psalm 33:19
- this present evil age. Galatians 1:4
- the trials of life. 2 Peter 2:9
- their enemies. Psalm 18:17
- being killed. 1 Samuel 17:37
- the power of Sheol. Hosea 13:14

The Bible speaks of salvation occurring in three different tenses: past, present, and future.

- **Those who are in Christ have already been saved.** Ephesians 2:8-9 declares, *"For it is by grace you **have been saved**, through faith – and this not of yourselves, it is the gift of God – not of works, so that no one can boast."*

- **Those who are in Christ continue to experience salvation.** 1 Corinthians 1:18 declares, *"For the message of the cross is foolishness to those who are perishing, but to us who **are being saved**, it is the power of God."*

- Those who are in Christ will experience salvation in the future. Romans 5:9 declares, *"Since we have now been justified by his blood, how much more **shall we be saved** from God's wrath through him!"*

The Bible speaks of deliverance in three different tenses.

According to 2 Corinthians 1:10, *"He **has delivered** us from such deadly peril, and **will deliver** us again. On him we have set our hope that he will **continue to deliver** us..."* This scripture occurs in the context of God rescuing Paul from death in Asia. However, its truth can be applied to how God works deliverance in our salvation.

- When we have been justified by faith in Christ, our spirit is delivered from eternal death. We are saved.

- When we are being sanctified by the Holy Spirit, our soul is delivered from the effects of evil. We become more like Christ.

- When God glorifies us, our body is delivered from corruption and death. We receive a new spiritual body. We will see the glory of Christ in ourselves and in others.

The Significance of a Biblical Worldview
for Christians Living in The West

To understand how faith works to secure freedom, you need a biblical worldview. You must understand how the Bible frames reality. It is not enough to know what the Bible says about moral issues, theological matters, and historical events. You need to understand what the Bible says about how the world operates. If you lack this perspective, you will not be able to make sense of much of what the Bible teaches.

A biblical worldview stands in stark contrast to other worldviews. This is particularly true in America because of the way people in the West are taught to think. Most folks are educated in the public education system, which draws upon a secular humanistic worldview. This view holds to the belief that humanity is capable of morality and self-fulfillment without God. The spirit realm does not interact with the physical world. Secular humanism conditions people to think in terms of evolution, science, reason, individual rights, self-sufficiency, situational ethics, philosophical naturalism, and social justice, and to reject absolutes, religious dogma, and supernaturalism.

Christians who have been educated in the public school system tend to view biblical truths through a secular humanistic lens. They observe religious rituals, hear the Word preached, practice traditions, believe in Christ as Savior, try to live moral lives, do good works, and subscribe to orthodox doctrine. However, they have little personal knowledge of revelation or the supernatural. They tend to rely more on reason than revelation. They traffic more in information than transformation.

People can subscribe to the Bible but see it as only one source of authority among many others, from which to base their lives. People make their decisions based on what feels good, what is convenient, what produces the least conflict, or what brings positive and rewarding outcomes. Where the Bible does not fit into their beliefs or preferences, it is easily dismissed as a fallible piece of literature rather than the authoritative Word of God. A Christian must settle in his heart that the Word of God is true, trustworthy, and infallible to realize freedom fully. Adherence to the Word of God is what brings freedom. Jesus said in John 8:32, *"You will know the truth and the truth will make you free."* And in John 17:17 He said that God sanctifies His people by the truth and God's Word is truth.

If the church is going to produce mature disciples who live in freedom, a biblical worldview must be included as foundational teaching. Without such a foundation, people are prone to make choices based on worldly values rather than the Word of God. Basing church success on the amount of money collected or on the number of programs that are provided rather than conformity to the truth is a disservice to Christ. Gauging church effectiveness on popularity and congregant satisfaction rather than compliance with biblical values is to become complicit with the world.

A believer must have a biblical worldview to be able to represent God's kingdom. Imagine a water faucet with hot and cold water. A biblical worldview is like the hot tap and the world's worldview is like the cold tap. Mixing the two produces a lukewarm, double-minded believer. Jesus finds this offensive; it makes Him sick. It causes him to vomit us out of His mouth. He gives this very strong warning in Revelation: *"I know your works, that you are neither cold nor hot. I could wish you were cold or hot. 'So then, because you are lukewarm, and neither cold nor hot, I will vomit you out of My mouth'"* (Revelation 3:15-16).

Living from a 100% biblical worldview enables us to be His ambassadors (2 Corinthians 5:20). To live in His kingdom and be His ambassador requires holiness. You can't be Christ's representative when your life lacks holiness. Hebrews 12:14 says, *"without holiness, no one will see the Lord."* In other words, holiness is a prerequisite for power to witness. Only after you have personally experienced the transforming power of the Holy Spirit to set you free from bondages, thereby making you holy, do you have anything to say to someone caught up in worldly bondage. This transformation comes through faith in God, who is faithful to perform His Word.

To embrace any other worldview, other than a biblical worldview, is to make friends with the world. James warns us that to make friends with the world is to make ourselves enemies of God:

> *Adulterers and adulteresses! Do you not know that friendship with the world is enmity with God? Whoever therefore wants to be a friend of the world makes himself an enemy of God* (James 4:4).

Satan is the ruler of this world (John 12:31; 16:11; 1 John 5:19). To live free of the world's influence, we must make every effort to know what worldview we are living. Jesus prayed to the Father, *"I have given them your Word and the world has hated them, for they are not of the world any more than I am of the world. My prayer is not that you take them out of the world but that you protect them from the evil one"* (John 17:14-15). To live in the world and not be of the world requires a biblical worldview.

D.L. Moody, an outstanding evangelist and educator of the 19th century said, "The Bible was not given to increase our knowledge, but to change our lives."

Leo Tolstoy once said, "Everyone wants to change the world, but no one wants to change themselves." For Christians, changing oneself begins with a biblical worldview.

Fundamental to attaining a biblical worldview is believing the Bible is a credible source of truth. For a list of reasons why the Bible is a reliable source of truth, go to Appendix B.

For a more in-depth study into a biblical worldview you might consider the online course by N.T. Wright, "Worldviews, the Bible and the Believer" available at https://www.udemy.com/course/worldviews-the-bible-and-the-believer/

In the next chapter we will examine the importance of understanding the spiritual world in order to be set free from bondage to evil.

Discussion Questions

1. What did you learn about the Bible that you did not know before? How does what you learned help you make better sense of the Bible?

2. Why is it important that Christians have a biblical worldview? When it comes to interpreting Scripture, why is it important to have a biblical worldview?

3. How would you assess the impact a humanistic worldview has on society as opposed to a biblical worldview? What impact has it had on you?

4. Does having a biblical worldview make you a better follower of Jesus Christ? If so, how?

5. What are some of the objections people have in viewing the Bible as the Word of God? What are some of the reasons it is a credible source of truth?

6. How would you encourage a believer to acquire a biblical worldview? How would you challenge a non-believer to learn what a biblical worldview is?

Endnotes

1. Biblicalworldviewinstitute.org/wp-content/uploads/09/101 Biblical-Worldview-Truths-short-forms-sans-Scripture.pdf
2. http://www.heavensinvasion.com/tsot/week3/Strongholds.pdf
3. https://www.barna.com/.../most-adults-feel-accepted-by-god-but-lack-a-biblical-world

9

Understanding the Spiritual World Facilitates Freedom

An Angelic Visitation

"Craig, did you see them? Did you see them?" With amazement on her face and excitement in her voice, Nancy Hamill said again, "Did you see them?" Nancy is a member of my church, and she serves our community as a District Justice. Without question, she qualifies as a reliable witness. What happened was incredible. What she saw was something right out of the Bible.

It was late December in the year 2000. We had just completed a building project, and this was the first worship service to take place in the new multi-purpose building. The Sunday service featured a Christmas Cantata performed by our thirty-voice choir.

Steph Benne, our choir director, called me the night before in distress. She had been in a car accident and was in the hospital emergency room. Her arm was injured, and she could not move it. Everyone else was okay, even though the car was totaled. Regretfully, she did not think she could lead the choir the next morning because of the painful injury. Surprisingly, I didn't panic. With an inexplicable peace, I told her we will see what the morning brings.

By the grace of God, Steph was at worship the next morning with her right arm in a sling. Being the trooper that she is, she attempted to lead the choir with only one hand. As the cantata began, I was standing in the back, next to the sound room. Things were going along nicely until about the third song. That is when Steph did something shocking. She threw her arm out of the sling and began to direct the choir with great passion and energy, seemingly unaware of any pain. She shouted back to the sound room, "Turn it off! Turn it off!" She thought the sound track was playing in the background and was telling the sound crew to turn it off. But the sound track was not on. That is when something in the atmosphere changed. Suddenly the musical went from a performance into an act of worship. I could feel something rising inside my chest. It was joy. The entire congregation was impacted. A heaviness was lifted. After the cantata was over, I greeted people as they exited. Person after person remarked how uplifting the morning had been.

After most people had left Nancy asked, "Did you see them?" "Did you see them?"

"Did I see who?" I responded.

"The angels, the angels. They were in the back of the choir," she replied.

"No, I didn't see them, but I felt them," was my reply. For some unexplainable reason, angels joined our choir to sing God's praises that morning.

I have known many people who have seen angels, but I don't think I ever did, except maybe once. Many people believe that angels exist but have never seen an angel. It has been my experience that people who have seen angels are reluctant to talk about it in public. Consequently, some people believe angels are real but don't live their life with an awareness of their presence. That was true of me until one Sunday morning.

A Ministering Angel Appeared

It was a regular Sunday morning worship service, except that one of our members, Char, brought a guest to the service. The day before, Char had come across this desperate-looking woman while hiking in a nearby park. She started a conversion with her. As it turned out, this woman was severely depressed and suicidal. By the grace of God, Char was able to talk to her, preventing her from taking her life. Char invited her to come with her to church. After the service, Char introduced the woman to me. The woman asked me to pray for her. I asked if I could lay my hand on her shoulder. She gave me permission. As I was praying, she fell to the floor, totally unconscious. I continued to pray for her as she laid on the floor. Slowly she awakened after some time had passed. Finally, she stood up. I blessed her and sent her on her way.

Immediately after that, another person who was visiting that morning came to tell me that when I prayed for that lady, he saw an angel standing next to me. I was astonished, first by the lady falling to the floor and secondly to hear there was an angel with me as I prayed. Since then, I have made it a practice to call on Jesus to send angels to help me with ministry. I still have not seen any, but occasionally I feel their presence.

What the Bible Says About Angels

The Bible tells us that angels come to earth from heaven and return to heaven (Genesis 28:10-22). This descension and ascension is what Jacob experienced at a place he named Bethel. Angels bring messages from heaven that reveal God's intentions for earth (Luke 1:26-38). The angel Gabriel told Mary she would give birth to the Son of the Most High.

Angels minister to men, helping them to escape trouble and fulfill God's purposes (Acts 12:3-19; Psalm 34:7). They fight against demonic princes. They come as a means of answered prayer and give strength to the weak (Daniel 10:4-21). Their appearance is so dazzling they inspire men to worship them (Revelation 19:10). Their appearance is so awe-inspiring that men are often afraid (Luke 1:13). Though usually invisible, sometimes people are able to see angels (2 Kings 6:15-17). They are ministering spirits sent to serve those who inherit salvation (Hebrews 1:14). Angels are assigned to serve as guardians over people (Psalm 91:11-12). They cleanse people of guilt, preparing them for ministry (Isaiah 6:7-8). Angels release healing (John 5:2-4). There are thousands upon thousands of angels standing with God in the throne room of heaven (Daniel 7:10). Angels ministered to Jesus in times of need (Matthew 4:11; Luke 22:43). Jesus has at His command thousands of angels (Matthew 26:53). Angels will accompany Jesus when He returns to earth (Matthew 16:27). With more than three hundred references to angels in the Bible, angels generally do three things:

1. **They give service to God through worship** – (Psalm 148:2)
2. **They give service to people** – (Hebrews 1:7,13)
3. **They carry out God's word** – (Psalm 103:20-21)

Categories of Angels

There are two classifications of angels: fallen angels and unfallen angels. Fallen angels followed Satan in his rebellion against God. Unfallen angels remained holy and faithful to God.

St. Gregory the Great, known as one of the doctors of the church who died in 604 AD, identified nine categories of unfallen angels. St. Thomas Aquinas in the thirteenth century identified three hierarchies of angels. The first hierarchy included seraphim, cherubim, and thrones. The second included the dominions, virtues, and powers. The third includes archangels and angels, which are the highest level of angels.[1] It is not within the scope of this book to fully address the subject. However, the following are some of the categories of angels found in the Bible.

- **Archangels serve as covering angels.** They are over other angels. Their name means "chief-angel." They are of the third and highest order in the celestial order (1 Thessalonians 4:16; Jude 1:9).

- **Cherubim attend to the worship of God.** They have wings, hands, four faces, and move in all directions (Ezekiel 10:3-14).

- **Seraph means "burning ones."** Seraphim cry "holy, holy, holy" and bring purity to sinful man (Isaiah 6:1-7).

Other terms for angels include:

- **The angel of the Lord** – Isaiah 63:9

- **Guardian angels** – Matthew 18:2-3,10; Acts 12:13-15

- **Angels assigned to churches** – Revelation chapters 2 and 3

- **Angels of great authority** – Revelation 18:1-2

- **Strong angels** – Revelation 5:2; Revelation 10:1-3; Revelation 18:21

- **Heavenly hosts** – Luke 2:13

Angels have different offices, strengths, and purposes. We are encouraged to be sensitive to the presence of angels. Hebrews 13:2 says: *"Do not forget to show hospitality to strangers, for by so doing some people have shown hospitality to angels without knowing it."*

Angels Bring Answers to Prayers

The Greek word for "angel" is *aggelos,* meaning "messenger" (Luke 2:10-13). Angels are God's messengers. They are sent by God to accomplish His purposes and answer prayers. One example of this is found in Luke 1:13, *"But the angel said to him; 'Do not be afraid Zechariah; your prayer has been heard. Your wife Elizabeth will give you a son, and you are to name him John.'"* Prayer is the way we access the power of the unseen world and make manifest the will of God in the seen world. We are instructed to pray in the Spirit with all kinds of prayers (Ephesians 6:18) and to pray without ceasing (1 Thessalonians 5:17). In Luke 11:1-13, Jesus teaches persistence in prayer. James 5:16 states that the prayer of a righteous person is powerful and effective. In Revelation 5:8, it says the bowls of heaven store our prayers.

Learning to pray appropriately is critical to establishing the kingdom of God on earth. Jesus taught His disciples to pray. He said, *"Pray, 'Thy Kingdom come, Thy will be done on earth as it is in Heaven'"* (Matthew 6:10 KJV). There are many different kinds of prayers mentioned in the Bible, including prayers of consecration (Matthew 26:39), corporate agreement (Acts 2:42), supplication (Philippians 4:6), intercession (1 Timothy 2:1), thanksgiving (Philippians 4:6), prayer in the Spirit (Jude 20), faith (James 5:15), meditation (Psalm 19:14), release (1 Peter 5:7), imprecation (Psalms 7, 55, 69), adoration (Ephesians 1:3), and declaration (Romans 4:17).

All types of prayer are important in the struggle for freedom, but one of the least understood and minimally practiced is declarative prayer. Declarative prayer is a form of the "prayer of faith." Charles Capp refers to this kind of prayer as a spiritual principle of "Calling Things,"[2] The basis of this phrase is 1 Corinthians 1:26-28 and Romans 4:17, in which Abraham believed in God who *"calls into being things that were not."* God employed this principle when He called the earth into being with a spoken word, declared Abram to become Abraham, the father of many nations, and called a frightened Gideon to be a mighty warrior. We see it when the prophet Ezekiel spoke to dry bones (Ezekiel 37:4). This kind of prayer has a prophetic quality to it, in which the unseen realm impacts the seen. God has ordained that we call upon eternal forces to change the temporal (2 Corinthians 4:18; Mark 11:24).

Declarative prayer asserts that once you know God's heart on a matter, you boldly declare it to be so. Then you walk in faith as though it were already manifested—even when the answer is not yet visible. John gives us this assurance: *"This is the confidence we have in approaching God: that if we ask anything according to his will, he hears us. And if we know that he hears us – whatever we ask – we know that we have what we asked of him"* (1 John 5:14-15).

This type of prayer is not a "name it, claim it" prayer. It is not based on a wish or personal desire. It is based on God's Word, either *logos* or *rhema*. It is based on revelation. After hearing from God, you announce what you believe God has said according to the leading of the Holy Spirit. The idea is to be God's spokesman. As 1 Peter 4:11 says: *"If anyone speaks, they should do so as one who speaks the very words of God."* It is speaking not so much with our faith, but with God's faith, who calls forth what does not yet exist in the natural realm (Romans 4:17). Jesus teaches this kind of prayer in Mark 11:23-24. He says, *"Truly I tell you, if anyone says to this mountain, Go, throw yourself into the sea and does not doubt in their heart but believes that what they say will happen, it will be done for them. Therefore, I tell you, whatever you ask for in prayer, believe that you have received it, and it will be yours."*

Discernment Needed

This kind of prayer hinges on the ability to hear the voice of God. All Christians who have the Holy Spirit in them have the capacity to hear God's voice. Jesus said, *"My sheep listen to my voice; I know them and they follow me"* (John 10:27). However, not all Christians hear with the same degree of clarity. Because of sin, lack of discernment or demonic interference, we could receive partial, inaccurate, or false revelation.

Demons can make inward impressions upon our spirit, just like the Holy Spirit does. If we are not able to discern the difference, we are apt to take these impressions and inner voices as being from God. This can cause chaos and division among believers. For this reason, the spirits need to be tested, lest the spirits deceive us.

The Apostle John wrote: *"Beloved, do not believe every spirit, but test the spirits to see whether they are from God; because many false prophets have gone out into the world"* (1 John 4:1).

When I was twenty-five years old, I was living in Virginia on my grandmother's farm. One Monday evening, my mother called me from Baltimore, Maryland, and said my cousin, Gary, was in intensive care and was not expected to live. I went to a prayer meeting that night, and we prayed for Gary. This was my first experience with the gift of prophesy. We gathered in a circle and held hands. People prayed with passion. I prayed with all my strength, until I became so weak that I fell to the floor. Others prayed also. Finally, Jim Jinks began to pray and then he prophesied that Gary would get well. His message witnessed with my spirit. Later that night in the early morning hours, the Holy Spirit prompted me to call my mother and tell her what the Lord said. I told her, "Don't worry, Gary will be okay." She asked, "How do you know that?" She was shocked and in disbelief. I quickly said, "God told me" and hung up the phone.

The next day while working on the farm, I kept hearing a voice in my head saying, "You are stupid. You have embarrassed yourself. You are a fool. He is going to die." This occurred several times throughout the day. Each time, I spoke back to that voice, saying, "God said it, I believe it and that is the end of it." It was like a tug of war going on in my head, angels on one side and demons on the other. This conflict went on for two days. Finally, on the third day, my mom called me and reported that the morning after I had spoken with her, Gary was sitting up in bed. The doctors removed the tubes attached to him but had no explanation for his miraculous recovery. Satan had tried to undermine my faith with whispers of shame and accusations of stupidity in my head. He was not successful. However, more importantly through this experience, the Lord taught me to know the difference between His voice and the voice of Satan.

Testing the Spirits

There are several ways to test revelation received from the unseen world. The test determines whether it is of the flesh or God or of Satan. Here are some helpful questions.

1. **Is it consistent with Scripture?**
2. **Does it reflect God's character and nature?**
3. **Does it build on the foundation and direction God has already established?**
4. **Does it promote bondage or restoration, healing, and freedom?**
5. **Does it edify, build up, console, or exhort?**
6. **Does it require or even challenge your level of faith?**
7. **Is it contrary to the flesh?**
8. **Does it instill an identity consistent with that of Christ?**
9. **Does it glorify God and testify to Jesus as the Son of God?**
10. **Does it convict or condemn?**
11. **Does it call for courage?**
12. **Does it call for more than your knowledge? It may conflict with reason.**
13. **Does it require more than what you can do in your natural ability?**
14. **Does it promote good fruit, fruit of the Spirit, and holiness?**
15. **Does it instill hope?**
16. **Does it witness with the Spirit that is in you?**
17. **Does it turn people toward God and away from the world?**
18. **If it is a future prediction, does it come true?**
19. **What is the character and reputation of the one bringing the revelation?**

Satan is always trying to counterfeit the work of God's Spirit. The Scriptures provide ways to discern between true and false prophets. Texts such as Matthew 7:15-17; 2 Peter 2:1-22 and 1 John 4:1-6 give guidelines for distinguishing a false prophet from a true prophet.

Overcoming Fear

Fear prevents many Christians from engaging the supernatural. Because of not being familiar, they are afraid they may be embracing occult or New Age practices. Since some Christians do not have confidence to clearly hear the voice of God or discern good from evil, they resist or even call things evil that are of the Spirit of God. Because some manifestations seem weird or bizarre, they dismiss them as demonic. Due to fear, they miss God's blessings.

Christians need to trust in God's ability to protect and prosper them. They need to put more faith in God's ability to reveal the truth and less faith in Satan's ability to deceive. The Bible tells us that if you ask God the Father for anything, He will not give you something that will hurt you. *"If you then, though you are evil, know how to give good gifts to your children, how much more will your Father in heaven give the Holy Spirit to those who ask him"* (Matthew 7:13).

There is nothing to fear when it comes to hearing from God through dreams, visions, impressions, words of knowledge, or prophetic utterance. As Christians, we have the Scriptures, the Holy Spirit, and the body of Christ to help keep us from becoming deceived. We simply need to believe we can be free from demonic influences through the grace given us in Christ Jesus. We need to spend significant time in the Scriptures. If we do not, it is at our peril. The less time we spend with truth, the more likely we are to believe lies.

Some will say that you can become so heavenly minded that you are no earthly good. But the opposite is true. It is only when you have connected with heaven that you can be an ambassador for the kingdom of God on earth. This is what Jesus taught his disciples when He said, *"Very truly I tell you, the Son can do nothing by himself; he can do only what he sees his Father doing, because whatever the Father does the Son also does."* (John 5:19).

Declarative Prayer Overcomes Fear

For many years now I have been meeting with some Amish and Mennonite leaders for prayer. We greet each other with a handshake, a holy kiss, an embrace, and a blessing. Then, we share what we see the Lord doing. After celebrating the goodness of God, we identify issues, problems, possibilities, and personal concerns. We then fall to the floor and bring these things to the Lord in humility. After a time of prayer, we stand and begin to make declarations according to what we have heard in our hearts by faith. Finally, before we depart, we bless and embrace one another again. These meetings are always exhilarating. With our spirits emboldened, we leave with great resolve and expectation as to what the Lord is going to do. We are free of fear and full of boldness.

Unfortunately, this is the exception, not the rule. Typically, church prayer meetings are not well attended. There could be many reasons for this, but one is that Christians have become comfortable with the way things are. They don't see themselves challenging the world's system and are not used to confronting opposition. Consequently, they don't see a need for boldness that comes from declarative prayer. They are reluctant to speak or declare because they have little confidence they have heard from the Lord. They have not had sufficient experience in calling things that are not as though they were.

In Acts 4, Peter and John are arrested and threatened by the authorities not to preach or teach in the name of Jesus. However, because they had performed a miracle of healing, they were reluctantly released. When Peter and John returned to the other disciples, they prayed together, calling on the Lord for more boldness. The Scripture says they were filled with the Holy Spirit and began to declare the word of God boldly (Acts 4:31). When believers come together to call upon the unseen realm, hear from the Lord, and declare what they heard, power is released, and heaven invades earth.

Acknowledging Demons Are Real

In the church, it is a lot easier to talk about angels than to talk about demons. People like to hear about angels because they are an extension of God's goodness and mercy. But to talk about demons can be weird and fearful. Christians seem to have just enough Bible knowledge about demons to make them afraid, but not enough understanding to make them confident overcomers. They read Scriptures such as 2 Thessalonians 2:9-10, *"The coming of the lawless one will be in accordance with how Satan works. He will use all sorts of displays of power through signs and wonders that serve the lie, and all the ways that wickedness deceives those who are perishing"* and feel intimidated.

Passages like this can arouse fear, causing some people to attach suspicion to all supernatural activity. Believing it to be demonic, they automatically assume they will be deceived. Consequently, they dismiss spiritual gifts and want nothing to do with prophecy, words of knowledge, or speaking in tongues. They rationalize these gifts are no longer active, believing they died with the twelve apostles. Sadly, they confuse cooperation with the Holy Spirit with mindless surrender to demonic spirits. People who lack knowledge of the spiritual world tend to be afraid of what they do not understand. This ignorance breeds fear.

In addition to this fear, many Christians don't grasp the true goodness and love of God. They lack faith in God's promises, lack confidence in hearing the voice of God, and lack attentiveness to the presence of God. Is it any wonder why the church is impotent? Consider further that many Christians don't trust God because of past injustices and hurts or they are so prideful of their biblical knowledge they don't need spiritual gifts. It quickly becomes apparent why the church in the West is filled with unbelief and is preaching a social gospel.

Even among Evangelicals who focus on personal salvation, there is lack of understanding of the spiritual world. This is not due to a lack of Bible knowledge, but lack of a biblical worldview. Most Christians in the West are educated into a secular humanistic worldview. This explains the deficiency of a worldview based on the Bible. They can recite Bible stories, but the media, universities, science, and culture shape their beliefs. When you add all this up, you have a good explanation as to why the church lacks power and seems irrelevant to much of society.

To make up for such a lack of power and relevance, many churches develop social programs designed to meet unmet human needs. This is an expression of the gospel but fails to address deeper spiritual needs. Most churches preach and provide for salvation by way of conversion but neglect the need for freedom. Neglect of the supernatural leaves people defenseless from the power of the flesh and the torment of evil. The local church will use its resources for charitable outreach and missions, but has little impact on transforming the soul.

It is difficult for people educated in the West to believe that demons are real or that they have any influence on their lives. In this information age, drug therapy and psycho analysis are common. Such things as witchdoctors, voodoo, demons, and other occult realities are not on the minds of most people. Granted, there is a certain fascination with ghosts, aliens, and paranormal phenomenon particularly in the entertainment industry. But the idea of Satan influencing people in everyday affairs is not part of most people's consciousness.

This unbelief is true even in my own family. It was not until my sister experienced deliverance in her living room that she began to think in terms of a personal evil affecting her life. Similarly, my aunt was talking to me concerning her spiritual condition when suddenly a window shade flew up without any visible explanation. She was startled and fearful. I assured her there was no need to be afraid. After calming down, she received cleansing and deliverance from things that kept her in bondage. As a rule, people have difficulty believing in the presence of personal evil until they personally encounter it.

George Barna Research has found that only 24% of the general population and 52% of Christians believe Satan is a real being.[2] C. S. Lewis, author of *The Screwtape Letters* once said, "There are two mistakes the church makes when dealing with the devil; to blame everything on him or to blame nothing on him." Jack Hayford put it this way: "There are two groups of people that Satan absolutely loves and gets excited over: the skeptics and the superstitious."[3]

One of Satan's strategies is to fool people into thinking he does not exist so that he can keep them ignorant of his schemes. Skeptics don't believe Satan is real. They see Jesus as only pretending to cast out demons to accommodate the beliefs of a primitive culture. They hold to the belief that demons were just another way of identifying physical and mental problems.

On the other hand, the superstitious see every negative thing that happens as the work of demons. If a person has an accident, gets sick, or suffers misfortune, it is because of a demon. They are quick to blame everything on Satan. The truth is, some things happen because we live in an imperfect and broken world. Other happenings are a result of sin and bad decisions, resulting in bad consequences. James 1:13-14 indicates it is our own lustful desires that cause us to sin. Paul tells us in Romans 6:23 that the wages of sin is death.

Yes, Satan does deceive us and tempts us to sin, and sin does allow Satan to have influence in our lives, but we cannot say, "The devil made me do it." We must take responsibility for our own decisions. We must learn to renew our minds to the truth about the spiritual world in order to live in freedom. We must also learn to cleanse ourselves of unclean spirits (2 Corinthians 7:1). The term "unclean spirit" occurs twenty-one times in the New Testament and refers to demonic torment. Unclean spirits are to be cast out of a person (Luke 11:24). Jesus cast seven demons out of Mary Magdalene (Luke 8:2).

With that said, we must accept, as fact, that demons are real. They oppress and torment people. They do Satan's work for him. In Matthew 12:24, Satan is identified as *"the ruler of the demons"* (Matthew 12:24). The word "demon" appears eighty times or more in the Bible depending on which version you are reading. There is a high concentration occurrence of the word, sixty-one time, in the Gospels because it was part of Jesus mission to set the captives free (Luke 4:18) and destroy the works of the devil (1 John 3:8).

There are many names for the devil in the Bible: Lucifer, meaning "Morning Star" (Isaiah 14:12); Satan meaning "adversary" (1 Peter 5:8); *the accuser of the brethren* (Revelation 12:10); *the ruler of this world* (John 12:31); *the god of this age* (2 Corinthians 4:4); *the prince of the power of the air* (Ephesians 2:2); *the prince of demons* (Matthew 9:34), and *the father of lies* (John 8:44).

Lucifer led a rebellion against God and took a third of the angels with him (Isaiah 14:12; Hebrews 12:22). The whole world is Satan's domain (Matthew 4:8-9). He has his own kingdom (Matthew 12:26), power over illness (Luke 31:16), power over death (Hebrews 2:14), and can perform signs and wonders (2 Thessalonians 2:9). Satan's power is limited and under the control of God (Job 1:12) and is temporary (Romans 16:20). He seeks to enslave men to false gods that are really demons (Galatians 4:8-9) and aims to kill, steal, and destroy humanity (John 10:10). As humans, we wrestle and fight with demonic powers (Ephesians 6:12-13). Satan, however, has been disarmed and defeated by Jesus on the cross (Colossians 2:15). Christians overcome Satan by the blood of the Lamb and the word of their testimony (Revelation 12:11). Satan will eventually be destroyed and thrown into the lake of fire by Jesus (Revelation 20:10).

It is incumbent upon the church and particularly pastors to equip their people with an understanding and a defense against Satan. The following are some of the strategies and schemes the devil uses against humanity:

He lies and is the father of lies.

"There is no truth in him. When he lies, he speaks his native language, for he is a liar and the father of lies" (John 8:44).

Satan's very nature is one of a liar. From the beginning, Satan misrepresented God's words and told Adam and Eve falsehoods. He deceptively caused them to doubt God's goodness (Genesis 3).

He blinds the minds of unbelievers.

"The god of this age has blinded the minds of the unbelievers, to keep them from seeing the light of the gospel of the glory of Christ" (2 Corinthians 4:4).

He not only speaks what is false, but also hides what is true. He allows us to see the truth but keeps us from seeing its relevance to our life. We can see facts and hear proofs but not understand their value for us. Because of a lack of spiritual knowledge, people perish (Hosea 4:6).

He accuses believers before God.

"*Then I heard a loud voice in heaven say: 'Now have come the salvation and the power and the kingdom of our God and the authority of his Messiah. For the accuser of our brothers and sisters, who accuses them before our God day and night, has been hurled down*'" (Revelations 12:10-11).

Satan's complete defeat is certain. He will be thrown into hell. But for now, he continues to bring accusations in the court of heaven against Christians. In much the same way he accused Job of not being righteous, he looks for legal arguments to bring against Christians. Where there is a legal infraction due to sin, he invokes his right to torment believers. Fortunately, we have an advocate in the person of Jesus Christ to plead our case before the court of heaven (Hebrews 7:25). We can approach Jesus as our legal representative at any time. He gives us legal counsel on how to win our case against Satan's accusations. Following his advice, we can be set free from any demonic oppression.

He tempts people to sin.

"*But I am afraid that just as Eve was deceived by the serpent's cunning, your minds may somehow be led astray from your sincere and pure devotion to Christ*" (2 Corinthians 11:3).

In Matthew 4:1-11, Satan sought to get Jesus to reject His identity and abandon His earthly mission by tempting Him in three crucial areas: physical needs and desires (cravings of the flesh), possessions and power (lust of the eyes), and status and importance (boasting in what a man has and does). These temptations are found in I John 2:15-17 and are typically used against people today.

He seeks to steal, kill, and destroy.

"*The thief comes only to steal and kill and destroy; I have come that they may have life, and have it to the full*" (John 10:10).

Satan seeks to steal your money, rob your joy, and swipe your identity. He seeks to kill your destiny and destroy your family relationships.

He causes some sickness and disease.

"*When Jesus saw that the crowd of onlookers was growing, he rebuked the evil spirit. 'Listen, you spirit that makes the boy unable to hear and to speak,' he said, 'I command you to come out of this child and never enter him again.' Then the Spirit screamed and threw the boy into another violent convulsion and left him*" (Mark 9:25-26 NLT).

147

He wars against the righteous and obedient.

"And the dragon was enraged with the woman, and he went to make war with the rest of her offspring, who keep the commandments of God and have the testimony of Jesus Christ" (Revelation 12:17).

He disguises himself as an angel of light.

"But I am not surprised! Even Satan disguises himself as an angel of light" (2 Corinthians 11:14 NLT).

Characteristics of Demons

1. **Demons are identified according to their function.** An example is Abaddon meaning "Destroyer," who is the angel of the abyss. (Revelation 9:11)

2. **Demons speak to and communicate with humans.** (Luke 4:33-35, 41; Luke 8:28-30; Acts 19:13-17)

3. **Demons are intelligent.** (Luke 4:34, 8:28; Acts 19:13-17)

4. **Demons form their own doctrines.** (1 Timothy 4:1-3; 1 John 4:1)

5. **Demons experience emotions and have feelings.** (James 2:1; Luke 8:28)

6. **Demons have different amounts of strength and wickedness.** (Mark 9:29; Matthew 12:45)

7. **Demons can appear in both physical and spiritual form.** (Matthew 4; Revelation 9:7-10, 17; Revelation 16:13-16)

8. **Demons can give humans supernatural strength.** (Acts 19:16; Mark 5:3)

9. **Demons can move quickly through space.** (Daniel 9:21-23, 10:10-14)

10. **Demons can physically assault people and inflict disease.** (Luke 9:39; Matthew 17:15; Matthew 9:32-34)

11. **Demons influence the wisdom of the world.** (James 3:13-18)

12. **Demons animate non-Christian religions and all forms of idolatry.** (1 Corinthians 10:14-22; Galatians 4:8-9)

13. **Demons dwell in different places.** They are:
    - active on the earth,
    - restrained in the abyss/*tartarus* (Luke 8:31; Revelation 9:1-3, 11; 2 Peter 2:4; Jude 6; 1 Peter 3:18-20), and
    - are in heavenly realms (Ephesians 6:12), probably the second heaven.

14. **Demons engage in battle with holy angels.** (Revelation 12:1-12)

15. **Demons foster unbelief and doubt through blinding the mind to the truth.** (2 Corinthians 4:3-4)

Satan's Hierarchy of Demons

Just as there is a ranking within the kingdom of God, so is there a ranking within Satan's kingdom. The following is not a complete list based on current demonology; however, it is biblical and based on Greek terms found in the New Testament. The Apostle Paul identifies the following:

- **Principalities** (*arche*) Ephesians 6:12 – authority of a prince or chief ruler over a territory

- **Authorities** (*exousia*) Ephesians 6:12 – having power to influence legal rights in judicial affairs

- **World forces** (*kosmokrator*) Ephesians 6:12 – ruler demons lower in rank than principalities

- **Dominions** (*kyriotes*) Colossians 1:16 – dominion, power, lordship

- **Thrones** (*thronos*) Colossians 1:16 - a place for kings; Satan is king of his kingdom

- **Spiritual forces** (*pneumatikos*) Ephesians 6:12 – soul belonging to a spirit higher than man but lower than God

Differences Between Angels and Demons

1. Angels love and serve God. Demons reject God and follow Satan.

2. Angels appear as human. Demons seek to inhabit humans.

3. Angels herald the presence of Jesus. Demons scream and are afraid of Jesus.

4. Angels rejoice when a person is saved. Demons prevent a person's conversion.

5. Angels watch over and protect from enemy attack. Demons launch attacks.

6. Angels connect us to God. Demons separate us from God.

7. Angels inhabit the church to worship God. Demons enter the church to disrupt.

8. Angels direct us to God. Demons lead us away from God.

9. Angels cleanse and promote holiness. Demons deceive and appeal to the flesh.

The Need to Pray

We need to pray, as Paul did in Ephesians 1:18-19, that the eyes of believers may be enlightened to understand the spiritual power, authority, and protection that is ours as an inheritance in Christ. As long as Satan can keep us in the dark about our position and authority in Christ, he can keep us stunted in our growth and ineffectual in our witness. Every Christian needs to understand the authority they have to confront and defeat the demonic. We need to pray for each other to not be deceived by Satan's lies. We need to learn to both trust and test what is being revealed.

Looking to Things Above

The Apostle Paul instructed the Colossians, *"Therefore if you have been raised up with Christ, keep seeking the things above, where Christ is seated at the right hand of God. Set your mind on things above, not on the things that are on earth"* (Colossians 3:1-2 NASB).

People who advance the kingdom of God on earth do not rely on human effort but on heavenly vision and blessing. This is how the Apostle Paul lived his life. When he appeared before King Agrippa he said, *"I was not disobedient to the vision from heaven"* (Acts 26:19). Paul practiced what he preached.

How can we be obedient to the heavenly vision? How can we make the invisible, visible?

A pastor friend of mine, Deryl Hurst, tells of an experience he had while traveling to New Hampshire.

I recently went on a weekend backpacking trip to the White Mountains in northern New Hampshire. As we were traveling along, one of my hiking partners requested a bathroom stop. Shortly, we came upon a rest stop. I pulled in for a quick pit stop.

Now you need to know, when I am on a road trip, I have one goal in mind: arriving at the destination a soon as possible. With this mindset, I was marching into the bathroom at the rest stop, when for some reason, my eyes were drawn to a man standing outside the bathroom, presumably waiting for his wife to exit. I noticed his t-shirt. It had a picture of a drum set on the front of it, with the words under it: "I destroy silence."

I walked on by. But as I was in the bathroom, I sensed God was saying, "I have a word for you to deliver to that man." My first thought was "Oh great, and what might that word be?" I mean, this man was from north Jersey. There is no chance we would have anything in common. If I were to approach him, he would not want to hear from this Lancaster County farm boy.

But I asked God, "Well if I do get to talk to him, what is the word?" I felt like God said, "Tell him that his hands are anointed to lead people to worship me."

But the voice on my other shoulder, the deceiver, was saying "Oh boy, this going to be a train wreck. He probably has never been in a church in his life."

However, I decided to be obedient. I told myself, "If he is still out there when I go out, I will approach him."

When I walked back out, he wasn't there anymore. I felt a strange mixture of relief and disappointment. I reasoned that if I saw him in the parking lot, I would still approach him.

As I headed toward my vehicle, I noticed a pickup truck with Pennsylvania plates sitting in the first parking space I would walk by. I noticed that he had a New York Giants license plate holder, a New York Giants bumper sticker, and a big New York Giants logo in the back window. And sure enough, my guy was sitting in the driver's seat with his window open.

I walked up to him and said, "How are you doing?" He said, "Good." I then said, "I noticed your Pennsylvania plates. I am from Pennsylvania as well. But I am a bit concerned, if you are from Pennsylvania, what are all these New York Giants stickers doing on your vehicle?'"

He laughed and said "Oh, so that's what this is about?" I just laughed, but I was thinking, "Oh no, that's not what this is about at all."

He told me that he was a transit bus driver somewhere north of Philly and that his riders were always busting on him big time. He used some colorful language—not vulgar, but colorful—and I thought "This guy probably isn't a believer, what I have to share with him isn't going to make any sense at all." Nonetheless, I plowed on.

After some small talk about the Giants and the new quarterback they signed, I took the plunge. "I noticed your t-shirt earlier when I was walking into the bathroom. Do you play drums?" I asked.

He said, "Oh yeah, I play drums and bass, and other instruments. Me and my family play all kinds of music. We play blues, pop, even country sometimes. Look I have my two amps in the back seat, I am headed up to my family for the weekend and we are going to do some jamming."

I stuck my head slightly in his window and saw the back seat filled with amps and other musical instruments. I asked him, "Do you ever play gospel music?"

He said, "Yeah, sometimes."

Somewhat encouraged, I said, "Listen, I hope this doesn't sound weird, but I am a man who prays, and I feel like I hear God's voice as well. And earlier, as I walked by you and saw your t-shirt, I felt like I heard God say 'I have anointed that man's hands to lead people into worship of Me.' I just want you to know that there is an anointing on your hands to lead people into worship. And I would encourage you to walk in that anointing and to leverage the gift that God has placed within you."

To my surprise he said, "That is awesome, thank you!"

I asked, "Could I pray for you?" He said it would be okay, and I went to reach into the truck to place my hand on his shoulder to pray for him. But he was having none of that. He jumped out of the truck and extended both of his hands. So, I prayed, releasing Gods anointing and favor on him and increase in the gift that God had placed within him.

When I was finished, he said something like, "You have no idea how much this means to me. This is huge. I will remember this as long as I live. Let me give you a hug."

He gave me this big bear hug and asked me my name again and said that he will be praying for me.

In the meanwhile, his wife had come back and had a sheepish smile on her face, trying to figure out what in the world was going on.

I believe that I impacted that man's life in a very real and powerful way. Who knows what the impact of that little encounter may have on his life, the people he contacts, and the people he may perform before? Who knows the impact that one little act of obedience may have on culture that reverberates for generations?

Man cannot orchestrate this kind of encounter. It only happens when a man of God hears from heaven and is obedient to do what he hears.

God calls us to human responsibility that is beyond our ability. He calls us to a vision that is greater than what we can accomplish on our own. He calls us to do more than we can by ourselves. We must abide with Him. We must walk with him in the Spirit, being attentive to His voice.

When speaking about salvation, Jesus said, in Matthew 19:26, *"With man this is impossible but with God all things are possible."* Currently, Jesus sits at the right hand of the Father, making intercession for us (Hebrews 1:3). He told us that He would never leave nor forsake us (Hebrews 13:5) and that although we can do nothing without Him, with him all things are possible (John 15:5). Hebrews 12:2 tells us to fix our eyes on Jesus, who is seated at the right hand of God. When we keep our thoughts turned on Jesus, we begin to think like Him and do things like Him. In this way, the kingdom of God comes to earth through us.

For these reasons, Satan continually wants to instill us with doubt, fear, jealousy, and shame. He distracts the mind with worldly concerns and fleshly passions. His goal is to keep believers from focusing on God and His Kingdom.

Paul makes the point that the way a person thinks indicates both his salvation and fruitfulness. He said, *"Those who live according to the sinful nature have their minds set on what that nature desires; but those who live in accordance with the Spirit have their minds set on what the Spirit desires. The mind of sinful man is death, but the mind controlled by the Spirit is life and peace"* (Romans 8:5-6).

A person may believe in Christ and be saved, yet have a carnal mindset rather than one focused on the Spirit. Believing in God's goodness and grace, these Christians will pray, asking the Lord to do things for them and for others. But how many church meetings open with a perfunctory prayer and then get down to doing the business of the organization? Yes, things get done. Budgets are met. Buildings are built and positions are filled. But does the kingdom advance? Instead of seeking direction from heaven first, we make our plans and then ask the Lord to bless our plans. Church leaders must learn to seek first the kingdom of God and His righteousness (Matthew 6:33). They must first look to things above, hear from heaven, share and compare what is heard, discern, declare, and then act in faith. When this becomes a common practice, we will see much more of the kingdom manifested. People will be set free from bondages, especially those who are not conscious they are in bondage. And others will be encouraged.

I will address the need to be set free from demonic bondages more fully in chapter eleven. However, before that, it will be helpful to examine in the next chapter the role discipleship plays in setting people free.

Discussion Questions

1. The Bible speaks about angels who help people. Do you have any angel stories or know of someone who does?

2. How does belief in an unseen spiritual world influence the way we live in the physical world? It has been said, "People can be so heavenly minded that they are no earthly good." Others say, "It is those who are heavenly minded who make the most contribution to the present world." Which statement do you agree with more? Why?

3. What can you do to become more sensitive to the spirit world? What role do reason and revelation play in discerning spiritual truth?

4. What doubts, fears, or concerns do you have when it comes to engaging in the spirit world?

5. How do knowledge and understanding of the spirit world help you walk in freedom? What value do you place on spiritual knowledge?

6. In what ways have you encountered the demonic? Have you experienced the presence of angels?

7. How has this chapter impacted the way you interpret Scripture?

Endnotes

1. James W. and Michal Ann Goll, *Angelic Encounters: Engaging Help from Heaven,* (Charisma House, Lake Mary, FL, 2007), p. 52.
2. Charles Capps, *Calling Things That Are Not* (Capps Publishing, Broken Arrow, OK, 2015), pp. 2-4.
3. Barna Research, http://www.barna.org/faith-spirituality/260-most-american-christians-do-not-believe-that-satan-or-the-holy-spirit-exis?q=satan+realy 2009.
4. Robert Morris, *Truly Free,* (Thomas Nelson Publishers, Nashville, TN 2015), p. 11.

10

Discipleship Is Integral to Freedom

Discipleship More Than A Program

In the late 1990s, our church regularly participated in a church-wide Lenten campaign called "The Fifty Day Adventure" developed by David Maines. Before each campaign, an orientation session introduced the campaign topics to church leaders. When I attended an orientation session for this campaign with a church elder, the facilitator asked participants, "What is the goal of your church?" After several others responded, I raised my hand from where we were sitting in the back row and said, "The goal of our church is to become a disciple-making church." Someone near the front, in a sarcastic tone, shouted out, "You don't really think that will ever happen, do you?" The hair stood up on the back of my neck and I replied, "If I live long enough, it will!"

For years, our church developed a strategy for making disciples. We experienced some success as people began to grow spiritually, primarily through small groups, church-wide campaigns, contemporary worship, and identification of spiritual gifts. However, in subsequent years, I discovered we were only on the tip of the iceberg. There was much more required to make mature disciples.

My most significant learning came through events in my own life. This started in 2005 when I was personally delivered from demonic spirits. I was fifty-three years old and in my 26th year of ordained ministry. After giving voice to a series of cleansing prayers, I suddenly felt a powerful wave of energy move through my body. The room became brighter, and I felt lighter. It was that event that opened by eyes to a level of truth I had not known before. I came to the conviction that disciples do not become mature until they experience the freedom Jesus came to give. Jesus came not only to forgive us of sin and save us from death; He also came to set us free from the effects of evil (John 8:32-44).

In our society, malicious behaviors like murder, rape, abuse, and terrorism most readily identify evil. However, much evil goes unrecognized because it is subtle and hidden. It takes the form of what the Bible calls "strongholds." These are patterns of thinking and attitudes that are contrary to the kingdom of God. The Apostle Paul identified a number of these in Galatians 5:19-21. They include such things as jealousy, sexual immorality, witchcraft, selfish ambition, pride, strife, and many more. To be a disciple of Christ requires the tearing down of these strongholds. This purging of strongholds requires the implementation of all five of Christ's gifts given to the church (Ephesians 4:11). I will address the topic of strongholds more fully in a later chapter. For now, we will consider the connection between discipleship and the soul.

The Well-being of the Soul

The Bible teaches that every person has a body, a spirit, and a soul (I Thessalonians 5:23). God is concerned for the welfare of the entire person, especially the soul. The soul is the essence of a person. The Bible refers to it as the heart or inner man. The soul consists of the intellect, will, emotions, attitudes, values, beliefs, memories, and conscience. These qualities comprise one's personality. These immaterial characteristics exist beyond the life span of the human body and are eternal. Like the human spirit, the soul is the immaterial part of our being. Our soul gives us the ability to think, believe, choose, reason, imagine, remember, and feel. The Greek word for "soul" is *psyche*. Our English word "psychology" derives from *psyche*. The *psyche* is the embodiment of the mind. It is in the mind that demons contend against the truth. In this respect, the mind becomes a battlefield. War is waged between the kingdom of light and the kingdom of darkness. For this reason, we must be able to discern the source of our thoughts. Are they from God? Are they our own? Are they from the devil?

How the mind processes God's truth determines our response to temptation and deception. It is in the mind that we contend with lies, strongholds, and fleshly appetites. For this reason, the mind needs to be renewed by the Word of God (Romans 12:2). Our minds need to learn how to take every thought captive, making each one obedient to Christ (2 Corinthians 10:5). Our minds need to be regularly stimulated by the living Word (Matthew 4:4). Our minds need to be taught to think like Christ (Philippians 2:5).

The way we think affects every aspect of our life. It has an impact on the health of our bodies, the quality of our relationships, and the curses or blessings we receive from God (Deuteronomy 28). It is God's desire to bless and prosper us by disciplining our souls. In 3 John 1:2, we read: *"Dear friend, I pray that you may enjoy good health and that all may go well with you, even as your soul is getting along well."*

For the soul to get along well, it needs to commune with God in prayer (Luke 18:1). It needs to repent in order to be refreshed (Acts 3:19). It needs to feed on the Word (Matthew 4:4). Because the soul can become sick, it needs to be corrected, restored, instructed, strengthened, and comforted by wise counselors. These counselors must be led by the Holy Spirit and guided by the Word (John 14:26; 2 Timothy 3: 16-17; 1 Peter 5:10). Spirit-anointed counseling is vital to discipleship. Discipleship counseling cannot be the exclusive domain of pastors. From a biblical perspective, discipleship counseling is a function of the entire church (Ephesians 4:16-32). It is speaking the truth in love.

Every Christian is called to be a counselor. What? Yes, that is what I said. If you believe every Christian is called to live their life as Christ did, then you are a counselor. Isaiah 9:6 tells us that Christ is called a Wonderful Counselor. If you identify with Christ, then you, too, are a counselor. Furthermore, when Jesus gave the Holy Spirit to His followers, he named him the Counselor—the Spirit of Truth (John 14:16 RSV). When you receive the Holy Spirit, you receive an internal Counselor. You may not realize it, but when Jesus told His disciples to go and make disciples, He was calling His followers to be counselors. He told them to go and baptize and teach obedience to all His commands (Matthew 28:20). How could His disciples convince self-centered people to change their stubborn minds, submit, and obey Christ's commands unless they were equipped to be counselors?

The work of discipleship is all about counseling. The nurture and care of souls requires counseling. Discipleship is not simply learning about Christ; it is training the mind to think like Christ. It is adopting a Christlike identity. How is this to be accomplished?

According to Paul, the gifts Christ gave to His church are essential to acquire a Christlike identity. He has provided apostles, prophets, evangelist, pastors, and teachers who counsel and empower others to do the work of ministry (Ephesians 4:11-12). What is the work of ministry?

Most people think of ministry in terms of professional clergy standing behind a pulpit, preaching, and teaching from the Bible. Whereas this has its place, the personal counseling of the Word by the laity is the ministry modeled in the New Testament. It is the rank and file believer who ministers the Word. Ephesians 4 depicts believers ministering to each other in the body. In this way, the body *builds itself up in love* (Ephesians 4:16 KJV). In this way, infants in the faith are brought to spiritual maturity, unity, and full knowledge of Christ.

As each person is set free from the sinful nature, he becomes equipped to love the way Christ loved. Being set free involves taking off the old man and putting on the new. It is accomplished by believers who counsel each other, speaking the truth in love. This is what Jesus did for His disciples. He formed them into a small group. He counseled them on how to live in the kingdom of God. He gave them words that brought them life (John 6:68) and mentored them with grace and truth (John 1:14).

Jesus Made Disciples Who Made Disciples

The Scriptures record that Jesus came to earth proclaiming that the kingdom of God was near (Matthew 4:17). He said, *"The kingdom of God is within you"* Luke 17:21). In other words, the kingdom of God has much to do with the condition of the soul. It was Jesus' vision that the church be responsible for the nurture and care of souls, including the healing of wounded emotions, as well as, deliverance from evil.

Jesus stated, *"I will build my church and the gates of hell will not prevail against it"* (Matthew 16:18 ESV). He taught that the casting out of demons was evidence that the kingdom of God had arrived (Matthew 12:28). Jesus trained His disciples to proclaim the kingdom. To do this, He gave them authority to set people free from the influence of demons. Mark 3:14 says, *"He appointed twelve to be with him and that he might send them out to preach and to have authority to drive out demons."*

Jesus trained His disciples to live the way He lived and to do ministry the way He did ministry. He revealed to them what the Father had revealed to Him. As His apprentices, He showed them how to live in the kingdom of God. He said, *"I am the way, the truth and the life"* (John 14:6). He taught them abundant life (John 10:10). He not only taught them forgiveness of sins, but also schooled them in how to live victoriously through the power of the Holy Spirit (Matthew 5-7). He instructed them in prayer (Luke 11:1-4). He taught them to understand prophecy (Luke 24:32). He showed them how to live godly, righteous lives (Matthew 9:35). Before He ascended into Heaven, He commissioned them to go into the world. He said, *"As the Father has sent me, I am sending you."* (John 20:21). He did all this to equip them for a ministry that would set people free from the works of Satan. The bottom line is, you cannot be like Jesus or think like Jesus if the devil is influencing your mind.

Satan is at the heart of all sin. We learn this in 1 John 3:7-8 NLT: *"Dear children don't let anyone deceive you about this. When people do what is right, it shows that they are righteous, even as Christ is righteous. But when people keep on sinning, it shows that they belong to the devil, who has been sinning since the beginning. But the Son of God came to destroy the works of the devil."*

To be a disciple of Christ, every believer needs to be trained to keep the faith and live free from sin and evil.

Becoming an Overcomer

Jesus defeated Satan on the cross. But that did not remove Satan from the earth. Satan is still here tempting and tormenting people (1 Peter 5:8). He is deceiving people into believing lies and coaxing them to disobey God by yielding to their fleshly appetites (James 3:14-16). He traps them into arguing and quarreling (2 Timothy 2:23-26). However, Jesus has given every believer the means to overcome evil. He has given the Word and the Spirit. Every believer knows Satan is their enemy, and they are at war with him. They also know that Satan will not be permanently banished from the earth until Christ throws him into the pit of hell, fully establishing His kingdom on the earth at the end of the age. Until then, Jesus continues to defeat Satan by equipping His disciples with the truth. He said, *"You will know the truth and the truth will set you free"* (John 8:32).

The truth of the Word and the power of the Spirit set disciples free from the influences of sin and Satan. The Bible refers to these disciples as those who overcome. 1 John 4:4 says: *"You, dear children, are from God and have overcome them, because the one who is in you is greater than the one who is in the world."* Similarly, 1 John 5:4-5 says: *"For everyone born of God overcomes the world. This is the victory that overcomes the world, even our faith. Who is it that overcomes the world? Only those who believe that Jesus is the Son of God."*

Overcomers are mature disciples who have not only been personally set free from Satan's influence but are also equipped to set others free. Mature disciples know Jesus has given them authority over the devil. This does not mean we should go looking for demons behind every bush. However, it does mean disciples should be able to recognize Satan's schemes and be ready to drive him out. Christians in the West feel uncomfortable with this concept. However, this demonstration of power is necessary if we are to be true disciples of Christ.

Discipleship is about learning to live the way Jesus lived. Jesus did not expect life to be easy, comfortable, and convenient. He knew that for life to be purposeful and meaningful, it would involve adversity, sacrifice, and suffering. Jesus did the most challenging thing possible on behalf of humanity. He willingly layed down His own life that we might have abundant life. To be His disciple, we must be willing to follow through on hard things as well. We must be willing to embrace hard truths, love hard-hearted people, and break hard habits. We must be willing to follow through on hard to keep commitments and let go of things we hold dear. We must be willing to give grace to the undeserving and forgive the unforgivable. Readiness to die to the flesh is required. Christians are called to overcome many hard things. In short, to be a follower of Jesus, we must learn to become comfortable with the uncomfortable. Jesus put it this way: *"Whoever loves his life loses it, and whoever hates his life in this world will keep it for eternal life"* (John 12:25).

Overcomers Face Down Evil

One of the hardest things a disciple must learn to do is to overcome evil. Jesus showed us that before He was ready to do ministry, He had to face down evil. After His baptism, He was driven by the Holy Spirit into the desert to be tempted by the devil (Luke 4:1). There, in a desolate place, He was tested. He had to confront the powers of darkness and show that He knew the truth. He had to prove He trusted the Father and was totally committed to fulfilling His mission. He had to demonstrate He could be led by the Holy Spirit and appropriately use His power to overcome the enemy. After passing all these tests, He returned to Galilee in the power of the Holy Spirit (Luke 4:14). After forty days in the wilderness, He was ready to begin His public ministry.

In preparing His disciples for ministry, Jesus put them through a similar test. He sent them out two-by-two to face down evil, heal the sick, and proclaim the kingdom (Luke 10:1-9). They returned to Him excited, saying that even demons submitted in His name (Luke 10:17). Jesus' response was sobering. He warned them not to be overly impressed with their ability to cast out demons. He reminded them that He gave them authority over demons and emphasized that the recording of their names in the Book of Life is what they should celebrate. In other words, inclusion in the kingdom of God is what legitimates power over Satan and is the reason to rejoice. Jesus was teaching His disciples the nature of ministry. The goal of ministry is not commanding demons to submit. Rather it is demonstrating the presence of the kingdom by overcoming evil with good. Paul recognized this truth when he wrote, *"Do not be overcome by evil, but overcome evil with good"* (Romans 12:21). The goal of ministry is not to whip up on demons; instead, it is to demonstrate the love and goodness of God who delivers us from evil.

Stages of Discipleship

The question becomes, how do we equip believers to demonstrate the goodness of God? How do we empower them with the Word and the Spirit to overcome evil? How do we make disciples who are sober, alert, and able to overcome sin and Satan? The answer is to follow Jesus' example. Jesus made disciples in four stages.

The first stage revealed in Scripture is the *"Come and See"* stage (John 1:38-39). Two of John the Baptist's disciples asked Jesus, *"Where are you staying?"* Jesus responded, *"Come and see."* This stage is **invitational** in nature. People are invited to explore the Christian life for themselves. They examine the truths and are exposed to the practices of Christianity. This stage culminates in receiving forgiveness for sin and baptism into Christ. He becomes their Savior. They are born again, receiving the Holy Spirit. At this point, they are baby Christians.

The second stage is the *"Come and Follow"* stage (Mark 1:16-20). Peter and Andrew were fishing when Jesus said to them *"Come and follow me and I will make you fishers of men."* This stage is **educational** in nature. Believers learn doctrine, practice spiritual disciplines, and learn to live in community with one another. They realize how to relate to others in a way that reflects the kingdom of God. Although they have assurance of salvation, their behavior reflects that of those in the world. They are like little children, needing instruction in how to overcome their selfish desires.

The third stage is the *"Come and Be with Me"* stage. Jesus appointed twelve disciples to be with Him so they could be sent out to preach (Mark 3:13-14). This stage is **transformational** in nature. It is here that spiritual maturity begins. You move from elementary teachings to advanced teachings of righteousness (Hebrews 5:11-6:3). Living in the presence and submitting to the sanctifying work of the Holy Spirit empowers believers to live a holy life. The inner man is transformed through spiritual cleansing, inner healing, renewal of the mind, and deliverance. At this stage, believers begin to hear the voice of the Lord regularly, and clearly, and take on a Christlike way of life. They are set free from the lusts of the flesh to walk in the power of the Spirit. Because of their intimate relationship with Christ, they are equipped for battle and engage in life-giving ministry. They have learned to overcome the desires of the flesh and the schemes of the devil. They are young adults in the army of God (1 John 2:14).

The fourth stage is the *"Come and Remain in Me"* stage. This stage is **collaborative** in nature. Jesus told His disciples that He was like a vine, and they were like the branches. If they stayed connected to Him, they would bear good fruit (John 15:5-8). In this stage, the believer continues to collaborate with the Holy Spirit and other believers to maintain a kingdom lifestyle. They are spiritually mature, having vast knowledge of Scriptures and experience in following the Spirit. They reflect Christlike character and utilize spiritual gifts. They carry out Christ's mission to the world, proclaiming the gospel in Word and in deed. Whatever their vocation, they understand their ultimate purpose to be glorifying God. They can lead others to Christ and mentor them into maturity. With an ability to speak the truth in love, they counsel others in the personal ministry of the Word. These are the spiritual fathers and mothers of the faith. There are few of these in the church. Paul said, *"For though you might have ten thousand instructors in Christ, yet you do not have many fathers…"* (1 Corinthians 4:15). It is my belief that the more spiritual fathers and mothers are within a fellowship, the healthier and more effective the congregation will be.

To further understand the disciple-making process, see Appendix N.

Each stage of discipleship has unique characteristics, and these stages tend to be progressive and sequential. However, they are not absolute categories. For example, a person may have experienced deliverance from an addiction when first accepting Christ as Savior, but much of their life remains carnal. In addition, a person may have gaps in their spiritual development. They may exhibit a few qualities found in stage three but still have not achieved all the characteristics found in stage one or two. When a person wavers between elements in stages two and three, they are vacillating between being carnal and spiritually minded. James identifies this as being double-minded and warns against becoming friends with the world (James 4:4-8).

One question needs to be considered when making disciples: After a person is saved and they know they are going to heaven, what would make him want to stop living a carnal lifestyle? What would make them stop being friends with the world? What would motivate them to embrace doing hard things? Why would that person want to die to self to become holy? Why face down evil to endure the pain of rejection? Why would he pay so costly a price to follow Jesus? For me, the answer is in the life-giving promise of freedom. It is the joy of seeing the kingdom of God manifested in the lives of people who were once captive to evil but are now set free. It is the kind of joy Jesus experienced when he suffered the cross, so that those enslaved to sin and evil could know liberty (Hebrews 12:2).

Other Metaphors for the Four Stages

The Bible also speaks of four growth stages in terms of human development. For example, 1 Corinthians 3:1 speaks of *baby Christians*, 1 John 2:12 speaks of *little children*, 1 John 2:13-14 speaks of *young men* and 1 John 2:13-14 speaks of *fathers*. Each of these stages depict a level of spiritual maturity. Just as a person's physical body makes a shift into adulthood at puberty, the same is true in spiritual growth. Between the little children and young men stages comes a shift, marked by surrender and consecration to the Spirit. The person moves from living as a carnal Christian to being a Spirit-filled Christian. At this point, the person demonstrates he can overcome his personal battle with the evil one.

The Bible also speaks of spiritual growth in terms of the four kinds of men, as we explained in chapter 8: the natural man, carnal man, spiritual man, and glorified man. The glorified man (Romans 8:30) is pure and undefiled. This person's life reflects holiness and is consistently surrendered to the Holy Spirit. Ultimately, this is not fully accomplished until after death when the person receives a glorified body.

The Bible also speaks of spiritual growth using the metaphor of a farmer sowing seed into four kinds of soil. Each kind of soil depicts a different way the human heart receives the Word of God. There is the hard-packed soil along the path, the shallow rocky soil, the thorny soil, and good soil. The point of the parable is that spiritual growth is contingent upon a person's ability to assimilate the Word of God into the soul. With every opportunity to hear the Word of God, there also come hindrances. However, as a person learns to overcome those hindrances, much fruit can be harvested. Scriptural references depicting the four soils are in Matthew 13:1-23; Mark 4:1-20, and Luke 8:4-15.

People who believe in Jesus Christ as Lord and Savior, live out their faith at different levels. The Christian life advances from glory to glory as described in 2 Corinthians 3:18, *"And we all, who with unveiled faces contemplate the Lord's glory, are being transformed into his image with ever-increasing glory, which comes from the Lord, who is the Spirit."* A believer grows in Christ-like glory as he is set free from sin and Satan's grip. Galatians 5:13 declares: *"You, my brothers and sisters, were called to be free. But do not use your freedom to indulge the flesh..."* This freedom is accomplished as the person is delivered from generational curses, ungodly beliefs, painful trauma, and demonic oppression. Being set free from these bondages enables a person to reflect Christ's character. With each deliverance, a measure of spiritual authority is released empowering the person to be an effective ambassador for God.

Discussion Questions

1. What is your response to the statement that Christians cannot become mature disciples until they experience freedom in Christ? Does everyone need to be delivered from something? How do you know what you need to be delivered from?

2. How does your church disciple believers? Do you think that discipleship is about counseling the soul and is expected of every believer? In what ways have you been equipped to counsel others to become mature disciples? What would help you be a better counselor?

3. The Bible says Christ's disciples are called to be overcomers. How do they overcome the world? How do they overcome evil? In what ways have you overcome the world? In what ways have you overcome evil?

4. What are the four stages of discipleship that Jesus used? Why is it important to understand these stages? Where do you find yourself on the Discipleship Chart? In what areas are you carnal minded? In what areas are you spiritually minded?

5. The Bible uses several terms and metaphors to describe the various stages of a disciple's growth and maturity. What do these metaphors have in common? What makes them unique? Which one speaks to you the most?

11

Discipleship Keys

The Equipping Process

In the Great Commission found in Matthew 28, Jesus sends His followers into the world to make disciples. He gives them authority to baptize new believers in the name of the Father, the Son, and the Holy Spirit. He further commands them to teach these new believers to be obedient saying, *"Teach these new disciples to obey all the commands I have given you. And be sure of this: I am with you always even to the end of the age"* (Matthew 28:20 NLT). This process involves learning, unlearning, and re-learning. We must learn what Christ has commanded. We must unlearn what the world has taught us. We must re-learn how not to comply with the sinful nature, but to obey Christ who teaches kingdom living.

Teaching people to be obedient is not easy. It is more than instructing people to read their Bible and be good moral people. Telling people to stop sinning is like telling a toddler to be good and not to mess his diaper. A child cannot stop doing what comes to him naturally. Telling him to change his nature by altering his behavior is insufficient. He needs to learn how to cleanse himself from the messes that naturally occur in life. This requires unlearning and re-learning.

In the same manner, disciples must unlearn the ways of the world. They must learn to overcome their sinful nature by becoming new creations. They need to replace what is natural with what is supernatural, what is earthly with what is heavenly, and what is sinful with what is holy. To do this, they must be motivated to obey Jesus' teachings out of love for him not out of fear of judgment. He said, *"If you love me keep my commandments"* (John 14:15). Jesus promises that if we remain obedient to Him, we will stay within the parameters of God's law, and enjoy abundant life.

Obedience is needed to remain healthy and whole in a sick world. Teaching obedience involves more than didactic instruction. It requires something more than majoring on the do's and don'ts and the should's and should nots. It is about nurturing love relationships. Jesus said, *"By this all men will know that you are my disciples, if you love one another."* (John 13:35). Loving others involves investing your time and attention. It means making personal sacrifices and pouring out your life by giving time for prayer, coaching, modeling, correction, mentoring, encouragement, and accountability. Transference of intellectual knowledge, while needed, is no substitute for the impartation of grace and anointing through the laying on of hands. Believers must learn to rely not on their own strength but on the Holy Spirit. They must learn to hear from the Spirit and walk in His presence.

Most importantly, they must learn to mend the broken places in their own lives. All too often, I have seen people get excited about Christ and get involved in church life, but eventually their enthusiasm trails off. In the course of ministry, their feelings get hurt. Someone says something or does something that stirs up a deep wound from the past. They become offended, and the gossip begins. Before long, they either drop out or dig in for a fight. The Holy Spirit is grieved, and Satan moves in to oppress the church with stinky thinking.

Without healing and deliverance, the local church is held hostage. The people are not able do the things God wants them to do, nor are they able to become the people God designed them to be.

Discipleship is about helping people to realize and maintain their true identity in Christ by appropriating freedom.

Overview of the Equipping Process

This passage describes the equipping process.

And he gave the apostles, the prophets, the evangelists, the shepherds, and teachers, to equip the saints for the work of ministry, for building up the body of Christ, until we all attain to the unity of the faith and of the knowledge of the Son of God, to mature manhood, to the measure of the stature of the fullness of Christ, so that we may no longer be children, tossed to and fro by the waves and carried about by every wind of doctrine, by human cunning, by craftiness in deceitful schemes. Rather, speaking the truth in love, we are to grow up in every way into him who is the head, into Christ, from whom the whole body, joined and held together by every joint with which it is equipped, when each part is working properly, makes the body grow so that it builds itself up in love (Ephesians 4:11-16).

Besides identifying the apostles, prophets, evangelists, pastors, and teachers as the ones who do the equipping, the passage identifies the purposes of the equipping process, those being:

1. To equip the saints to do the work of Christ's ministry (vs. 12)
2. To build up the body of Christ (vs. 12)
3. To promote unity of the faith (vs. 13)
4. To advance the knowledge of the Son of God (vs. 13)
5. To bring the person to complete maturity in Jesus Christ (vs. 13)
6. To enable people to resist false teachers and deceitful schemes (vs. 14)
7. To grow in Christlikeness by speaking the truth in love (vs. 15)
8. To promote corporate effectiveness as each member does his part as God designed (vs. 16)
9. To enable the church to build itself up in love (vs. 16)

These nine purposes clearly depict the purpose of the church. But this alone is not adequate to set people free from sin, worldly influences and evil. More instruction is needed. Beginning with verse 17, Paul outlines how people are set free from darkened minds as they throw off the sinful nature. The following summarizes his instructions:

1. Renew your thoughts by surrendering to the Holy Spirit (vs. 23)
2. Put on your new nature that is righteous and holy (vs. 24)
3. Put off falsehood; remove lies you tell yourself and others (vs. 25)
4. Don't let anger become sin; deal with it immediately (vs. 26-27)
5. Set your hands to purposeful work and be generous (vs. 28)
6. Don't use abusive language; rather speak encouragement (vs. 29)
7. Don't grieve the Holy Spirit; instead, get rid of bitterness, slander and all kinds of evil (vs. 30-31).
8. Be kind, showing compassion and forgiving others (vs. 32)

For a parallel passage further describing this taking off and putting on process, see Colossians 3.

Based on the nine purposes and the eight instructions, we gain a good idea of how the church is to function. When the church implements the instructions to accomplish the nine purposes, people are set free from bondages and are empowered to live like Christ. This defines discipleship. People do not merely receive information; they undergo a transformation. Through the work of the Holy Spirit, the ministry of the Word and the utilization of Christ's gifts, the church builds herself up in love.

All five of Christ's gifts are needed to empower the church to achieve this vision. Failure to employ any one of them creates a handicap, rendering the church unable to make mature disciples. You cannot become fully mature in Christ if you cut yourself off from any of His giftings.

Whereas many people see these gifts as offices filled by individuals who have a special calling and anointing, I think there is something more. Yes, some individuals have an anointing and have developed a high level of expertise that qualifies them for a particular office. However, I am convinced every believer has access to all five of Christ's gifts by virtue of the Holy Spirit dwelling within. The Holy Spirit can activate these gifts at any time. However, it is the responsibility of office holders to model out and ensure the practice of these gifts throughout the congregation, equipping every believer to do ministry like Christ. In the words of Randy Clark, "everyone can play." These five gifts are not just for the spiritual elite, but for every disciple.

To illustrate the point, you may remember Ananias. At significant risk to himself, Ananias responded to the Lord's directive to lay hands on Paul, thereby allowing God to restore Paul's sight and fill him with the Holy Spirit. Ananias did not receive recognition as an apostle, prophet, or teacher. He was a believer who heard from God and was obedient (Acts 9:12-17).

These five gifts function as a whole, not in isolation from each other. They operate as a team. They do not compete; rather they complement one another. Moreover, the primary function of these gifts is to equip, not to rule. These gifts are not to be viewed as hierarchical positions of authority by which to govern a local congregation. According to the New Testament, the role of governance is assigned to ruling elders. Elders operate in these five gifts, but these gifts are not exclusively theirs. Christ's gifts are given to the household of God, the whole body, not just a few designated leaders.

Ephesians 4:8 declares, *"When He ascended on high, he led a host of captives and He gave gifts to men...."* The Greek word for "men" is *anthropos*. It refers to human beings, whether male or female. All members of the body, male and female, receive these gifts. They are given *"to equip the saints for the work of ministry"* (Ephesians 4:12). This is a pivotal phrase. The reason Christ gives His gifts to the *anthropos*, rather than church leaders only, is so that the body can implement the nine purposes necessary to set people free and to build herself up in love (Ephesians 4:16). Three words need to be unpacked to grasp the importance of this key phrase: equip, saints, and ministry.

"Equip" is translated from the original Greek word *katartismos*, which is derived from the verb *katartizo*. It means "to restore, mend or repair that which has been broken, to put in order, join together, to complete what one ought to be." In Matthew 4:21, *katartizo* is used to refer to the mending of broken fishing nets. In the classic Greek, *katartizo* is also used as a medical term that refers to the realigning of broken bones. The term infers a level of skill, knowledge, and care like that of a doctor who sets a fractured bone in place. Scripturally, it means "to make someone or something completely adequate or sufficient for a purpose." In 1 Peter 5:10, *katartizo* is what Jesus does to restore those who have suffered. In Galatians 6:1, *katartizo* is used as a means to make fit or to restore someone who has been caught in a sin. The idea is to put broken pieces back together. Restoring, mending, healing, and putting things in order as God initially designed is at the heart of Jesus' mission of salvation (Luke 4:18).

In Ephesians 4, Paul is saying that Christ has given His gifts of apostles, prophets, evangelists, pastors, and teachers to both men and women of the church to restore, mend, heal, and join back together that which has been broken. He does this to build up the church so that she may function in unity and bring believers to spiritual maturity in Christ. In this way, the church becomes an extension of Christ's ministry as His representative to the world, establishing His kingdom on the earth.

It is the role of church elders to recognize those who are proficient in the exercise of these gifts. They are to make sure that people who are anointed and called to function as apostles, prophets, evangelists, teachers, and pastors are not only setting members free of bondage but are also equipping members to use their gifts so that they too, can set others free. Indeed, Paul echoes this sentiment in 2 Corinthians 13:11. He says, *"Finally, brothers and sisters, rejoice! Strive for full restoration (katartizo), encourage one another, be of one mind, live in peace. And the God of love and peace will be with you."* When each member does his or her part to bring restoration and healing, they fulfill God's vision for the priesthood of all believers (Exodus 19:6; 1 Peter 2:9; Revelation 1:6).

As the church sets believers free from bondages, brokenness, and dysfunction, she equips members to be God's representatives to the world. Because they are delivered, they carry the message of deliverance. Because they are free to live in love and unity, they become a powerful witness. It is of utmost importance that the church come to see herself not only as a purveyor of faith but a practitioner of freedom.

When the church functions in this manner, she is aligned with the very purpose and proclamation Jesus made in Luke 4:18, declaring His mission. He quotes Prophet Isaiah, saying, *"The Spirit of the Lord is upon Me, because He has anointed Me to preach the gospel to the poor; He has sent me to heal the broken hearted, to proclaim liberty to the captives and recovery of sight to the blind, to set at liberty those who are oppressed; to proclaim the acceptable year of the Lord"* (Isaiah 61;1). This Scripture not only reveals Christ's mission but also how He was to do ministry.

The phrase, *"He has sent me to heal the broken hearted"* can be interpreted as making whole that which is broken into pieces. The Greek word for "broken-hearted" is *syntribo*. It means to break or shatter into pieces. In other words, Jesus was sent by God to mend, to restore, and to make whole shattered souls that are crushed into pieces by sin and Satan. This healing sets hurting people free from the oppressive schemes of the devil. To do this, those who are blind to Satan's schemes must have their sight restored by the truth. In John 14:6 Jesus declared, *"I am the way and the truth and life. No one comes to the Father except through me."* In this way, God shows His favor and good will toward man.

Other places in the New Testament where *katartizo* is found include Matthew 4:21; Matthew 21:16; Mark 1:19; Luke 6:40; Romans 9:22; 1 Corinthians 1:10; 2 Corinthians 13:11; Galatians 6:1; 1 Thessalonians 3:10; Hebrews 10:5; Hebrews 13:21; 1 Peter 5:10. These references also encapsulate the idea of preparing, completing, and restoring a person to the place where they can function as God intended.

The second word we will examine is "saints." The Greek word is *hagios*. It means holy but not perfect. It refers to those who are chosen to fulfill God's purposes. It means God's people who are set apart for godly character. The saints are those who belong to Christ. It is the role of the apostle, prophet, evangelist, teacher, and pastor to help restore God's people to complete godliness.

The third term is "ministry," or in other words, "works of service." The Greek term for work is *ergon*. It means "to act, to undertake, to do things." The Greek word for "service" is *diakonia*. It means "to execute the commands of another." As these terms are combined, the concept is to act on the commands of another. Through ministry or acts of service, one does what Christ commands rather than what the sinful nature desires.

Succinctly stated, Christ gave the church giftings that would restore people to wholeness or holiness, so they would be free to accomplish the things God commands them to do.

The Importance of the Five Gifts

In Ephesians 4:11, Paul explains that as Jesus ascended to heaven, He gave the gifts of apostles, prophets, evangelists, pastors, and teachers to the church so that she could function in a way worthy of her calling (Ephesians 4:1). Jesus Himself possessed these gifts. They reflected His anointing and identity. In the New Testament, Jesus is identified as "the apostle" (Hebrews 3:1), "the prophet" (Acts 3:22), the evangelist (Luke 19:10), "the good shepherd" (John 10:11), and the authoritative teacher (Matthew 7:29). Jesus utilized these gifts in His disciple-making ministry and the church presently needs these gifts to nurture believers to full spiritual maturity. They are all essential in preparing the bride of Christ for the Lord's return. Each of these gifts has a role in equipping the church to be without spot or wrinkle in advance of the bridegroom's return (Ephesians 5:25-27). Together these five gifts facilitate conversion, healing, deliverance, cleansing, freedom, and holiness within the body of Christ. They empower faith and love. The deployment of all these gifts in the church is a major factor in hastening the second coming of the Lord.

Not every person in the church is called to function at the five-fold level. Those who are called, not only practice these gifts, they also act as equippers. They enable others to put into practice the ministry of Jesus. Several things need to be operative to qualify as a five-fold minister. Ron Myer, in his book, *Fivefold Ministry Made Practical* has identifies five requirements:[1]

1. You have a discernable and operative gift.
2. You have the ability to identify that gift in others.
3. You have the ability to activate that gift in other individuals.
4. You have the heart to nurture others in that gift and bring it to maturity.
5. You have the ability to release others into ministry.

Unfortunately, in many churches today, only some of these gifts are being utilized. This leaves a void in the disciple-making process. Many churches rely on only three gifts: pastor, teacher, and evangelist; unfortunately, neglecting the gifts of apostle and prophet. These gifts are not understood, nor are they recognized as necessary for the disciple-making process. This tragic rejection of the gifts of apostle and prophet amounts to rebuffing two-fifths of Jesus' ministry, resulting in a vast number of Christians remaining at the carnal level. Although shocking, all is not lost. Even though there may not be a formal place for apostles and prophets at the leadership level, these gifts still exist within the body. However, they need to be discovered, cultivated, and recognized.

If leadership is lacking in these areas, many people will be underutilized and ill-equipped. They will feel they do not fit in and are likely to leave for other churches. Those who remain behind will become the status quo and miss out on an opportunity for spiritual growth. In resisting the gifts of the Spirit, they will remain ignorant and be content at their chosen level of maturity. Where the Spirit is resisted, there will be a lack of power in witnessing.

Casual and Captive Christians

In his book titled *The Seven Faith Tribes: Who They Are, What They Believe, and Why They Matter,* George Barna identifies America's seven major faith tribes.[1] The largest group is Casual Christians. They comprise 66% of all Americans and are characterized as having moderate faith. Their faith allows them to feel religious without making it a priority. They take a low-risk position on difficult public social issues. A pleasant and peaceful existence drives them. Casual Christians desire to please God while extracting as much enjoyment and comfort from the world as possible. They do not view matters of faith as central to their purpose in life.

The Bible identifies these believers as babies or carnal Christians. They believe but have not yet experienced the more profound aspects of the Spirit. They rely on their reasoning rather than revelation that engages the power of the Spirit. These Christians are in the "Come and See" and "Come and Follow Me" stages. They believe in Jesus, but their lifestyle mirrors that of the world. They desire what Jesus provides, but they have not yet sufficiently died to themselves. They see themselves as consumers rather than ambassadors for the kingdom. They are religious, but their testimony lacks power, therefore, they do not change the culture around them. Paul warned Timothy to be aware of such people (2 Timothy 3:5).

Today there are lots of wonderful Christians who do humanitarian work, but are not spiritually mature. They have no clue of the spiritual power and authority available to them. It is the power of the Spirit that makes us effective in witnessing to the world and overcoming the schemes of Satan. Paul wrote to the Corinthians, *"I did not come with eloquence of human wisdom as I proclaimed to you the testimony about God. For I resolved to know nothing while I was with you except Jesus Christ.... My message and preaching were not with wise and persuasive words, but with the demonstration of the Spirit's power, so that your faith might not rest on human wisdom, but on God's power"* (I Corinthians 2:1-5).

The next largest group in Barna's study is Captive Christians. They comprise 18% of all Americans. They are defined by their faith, their core spiritual beliefs, and resultant values on which their worldview is built. Captives define success in life as obedience to God. They carry out His commands and principles through adherence to both *logos* and *rhema*. The Bible describes these Christians as mature or Spirit-filled. These are Christians who are in the "Come and Be with Me" and "Come and Remain in Me" stages. For them, Jesus is more than an idea. He is a living presence. They hear His voice, follow His leading and carry out His mission. They pursue holiness and are quick to repent when convicted. These are the ones who boldly share the gospel in the power of the Spirit in spite of opposition. Because they live in the center of the will of God, they tend to disturb those living outside the will of God. They disturb the comfortable and bring comfort to the disturbed.

The Need for Apostles and Prophets

Evangelists, pastors, and teachers tend to be the ones who effectively minister to those in the first two stages. Their gifts are particularly suited for the ignorant and inexperienced. They focus on teaching the Word by helping people to accept the gospel, fit in, and feel loved. They help people understand biblical truths and principles that govern the kingdom. They excel in communicating the the Word. They introduce people to the faith. However, to transition from a carnal Christian to a spiritually mature-Christian, the gifts of apostle and prophet are needed. These gifts take believers into a deeper walk with Christ, focusing on life in the Spirit, as well as, the Word.

The prophetic gift helps believers to understand faith, not simply from the standpoint of reason but from revelation. It enables the believer to understand the kingdom of God, not from an earthly perspective but a heavenly perspective. It uncovers that which is hidden and helps believers to trust the *rhema*, as well as, the *logos*. The prophetic calls forth that which God desires to accomplish through and within a person. It speaks forth what God has revealed, activates spiritual gifts, and helps people hear the voice of the Lord. It strengthens, encourages, and comforts (I Corinthians 14:3). It calls believers to keep their covenant with God and, in so doing, empowers them to fulfill their heavenly destiny.

The apostolic gift helps the person delve into unfamiliar territory. It equips the person to not only know the truth but to live and speak the truth in love. It models out submission and obedience, enabling ministry to be done in the power of the Spirit, not the flesh. The apostolic gift helps people come to terms with hard things and engage their will with the Word, under the power of the Holy Spirit. This gift overcomes resistance and sets things in order. It brings correction, confronts evil, and casts it out. This gift walks in miracles and signs, pioneering new works and reproducing leaders for the kingdom, promoting holiness. It provides new vision and mobilizes people to overcome significant challenges. It helps people see how they can impact the world for the kingdom.

Both the prophetic and apostolic gifts tend to make people feel unsettled, as they call them out of their comfort zones and into greater levels of spiritual effectiveness. These higher levels of spirituality result in regular engagement with the supernatural realities such as spiritual gifts, signs and wonders, miracles, healing, deliverance, and the power of the cross. These things bear witness to the power of the gospel to set people free.

Prophetic and apostolic gifts were both needed for Paul and Barnabas to fulfill the mission of Christ. Before being sent out on their missionary journey, they spent a year at Antioch, where they joined teachers and prophets in the ministry of the gospel (Acts 13:1). Spending time in this equipping church, they were released into their apostolic ministry. Under the anointing of the Holy Spirit, the church laid hands on them and sent them out to fulfill their calling.

The Ministry of Prophets and Apostles is Foundational

The Apostle Paul wrote in Ephesians 2:20 that the church is built on the foundation of the apostles and prophets, with Christ Jesus Himself as the chief cornerstone. Some interpret this passage to infer that since a foundation is laid at the beginning of a building project, there is no need to lay the foundation over again. Therefore, the functions of apostles and prophets are not necessary today. They further postulate that since we have the Scriptures, there is no need for apostles and prophets. For this reason, miracles and other supernatural gifts have ceased as well. This doctrine has come to be known as Cessationism. This doctrine teaches that spiritual gifts manifesting revelatory or miraculous power ended when the New Testament was completed. To preserve the *Sola Scriptura* doctrine of the Reformation in which Scripture is the final authority, they argue against the revelatory and miraculous gifts. For them to allow prophetic utterance and other revelatory gifts would be to invite distortion, confusion, abuse, and corruption into the church.

Counter to Cessationism is the doctrine of Continuationism. This doctrine asserts that spiritual gifts, revelatory gifts (tongues, prophecy, etc.) and miracles still exist. Continuationists contend that the offices of apostle and prophet listed in Ephesians 4:11-12 are still functioning and are necessary for the church to be effective. I am a continuationist. Because of my ministerial experience with revelatory gifts and because there is nothing in the Bible that says these gifts have ceased, I believe the gifts of apostle and prophet are needed to bring disciples to maturity in Christ. In addition, I believe that the revelatory gifts listed in 1 Corinthians 12:7-10 are needed and are in operation today.

It is not the purpose of this book to debate this controversy. Suffice it to say, I hold the Scriptures as the supreme authority for faith and practice. I believe prophecy, as it was applied in the New Testament, is relevant for today and is essential for the edification of the church (I Corinthians 14:3). However, as the New Testament instructs, it needs to be tested for its veracity (1 Thessalonians 5:20-21). This belief does not put current day prophecy on the same level as canonical (biblical) prophecy. Canonical prophecy has been thoroughly tested by numerous church councils over the course of centuries and has been determined to be the infallible Word of God, even though all prophesies have not been fulfilled. Just as there were false prophesies in biblical times needing discernment, so there is false prophesy today needing discernment.

Because this gift is sometimes abused, it does not follow that all prophecies and revelatory gifts today are counterfeit. If this were true, the same could be said about the gift of teaching. However, we are warned that in the last days there will be false prophets and before Christ returns there will be false messiahs and prophets that could deceive the very elect (1 Timothy 4:1-2; Matthew 24:24). For this reason, the church needs to hold fast to the Scriptures and the Holy Spirit for discernment. A good barometer for testing a teaching or prophesy is the amount of honor and love given to brothers and sisters who may differ in opinions but are committed to preserving the unity of spirit through the bond of peace (Ephesians 4:3).

I hope that readers who are not familiar with how the gifts of apostle and prophets function within the church will keep an open mind, so that people can be set free from bondage and grow into the full stature of Christ, as Paul teaches in Ephesians 4.

A list of books that give arguments on both sides of the cessationist /continuationist debate is provided at the end of this chapter. This debate needs to be settled in the minds of believers so that freedom can be realized. I am convinced that the restoration of the apostolic and prophetic gifts to their proper place is necessary. They need to be accepted, validated, implemented, and given time to be refined just like the gifts of evangelist, pastor, and teacher. They need to be held accountable but not restricted. This will require much prayer, dialogue, and education.

A Historic Perspective

The New Testament indicates that the early Christians believed in signs and wonders and miracles, as evidence of the Holy Spirit's presence. They believed that these signs were a means of grace that validated the preaching of the Word (Mark 16:17, 20; Acts 14:3). The church continued to believe in the supernatural and revelatory gifts as means of God's grace right up to the time of the Reformation in the 1500s. During this period, Martin Luther and other reformers, emphasized the authority of Scripture to counter corrupt church leadership. They said apostolic succession no longer defined the church. They asserted the purpose for apostles and prophets was to provide Scripture as the foundation for the church. They determined that since the canon was complete, there was no need for fallible apostles and prophets. They reasoned that miracles in the Bible were given to attest to Jesus' deity and were given to the early apostles to validate what they said about Jesus, but are no longer needed. One of the leading voices promoting this cessation theology was Benjamin Warfield. He was a reformed theologian who wrote *Counterfeit Miracles* in 1918. Today, John MacArthur, is one of the leading advocates for Cessationism.

Some cessationists look to 1 Corinthians 13:10 as biblical evidence that revelatory gifts have ceased. The Scripture reads, *"But when that which is perfect is come, then that which is in part shall be done away."* They deduce from this verse that we no longer need fallible apostles, prophets, or miracles because Scripture alone is perfect, complete, and authoritative.

In an effort to keep the church from being misled and deceived by false prophets and apostles, the Reformers began to persecute those who held to different doctrines (anabaptists) and practiced spiritual gifts. These people were declared heretics and were hunted down and killed by the Reformers. Admittedly, some of their radical revelatory practices were heretical and needed correction. But to kill people and to judge the gifts as invalid was also heretical.

Think about this. If God gave the apostles and prophets revelation for the sole purpose of writing Scriptures, how many of them listed in the New Testament actually wrote scripture? Of the twenty-three apostles, only four of them; Matthew, John, Peter, and the Apostle Paul. Moreover, Luke was a medical doctor and not an apostle. This would mean there were nineteen apostles who did not write Scripture.

Obviously, apostles and prophets had functions other than writing Scripture. Their gifts contributed to the health and development of the church. Their revelatory and miraculous giftings provided leadership and inspired the power needed to take the gospel into pagan territory where they faced fierce opposition. Paul demonstrated the Holy Spirit's power not only at Corinth (1 Corinthians 2:4), but also at Philippi, where he cast out a demon from a girl who was a fortune-teller (Acts 16:16-18). Philip, the evangelist, performed signs and miracles in Samaria where he encountered Simon the sorcerer (Acts 8:4-40). In Acts 4, John and Peter were arrested by the religious authorities for healing a lame man and preaching the resurrection of Christ. After being threatened and warned not to talk about Jesus, they in turn prayed for more boldness, asking the Lord for more healings, signs, and wonders. With these gifts and the proclamation of the gospel, the apostles and prophets turned the world upside down (Acts 17:6).

These same conditions exist today. People need to be delivered. Lies of the world need to be corrected. More than talking theology, power is needed to help believers abandon their self-interest and develop a passion for the lost. Believers need to be empowered by the Holy Spirit to keep from becoming apathetic and discouraged. If you are going to preach a gospel of transformation, there needs to be evidence of change. Reason alone cannot achieve this kind of transformation. It requires the power of the Holy Spirit to release revelation, healing, and miraculous signs inherent in the gifts of the prophet and apostle.

The argument that prophets and apostles ceased with the completion of the canon may be motivated by a desire to protect the church from deceit and counterfeit miracles. However, the argument is inadequate. It leaves the church academically astute but spiritually powerless against the forces of darkness. The Bible itself declares in 1 Corinthians 4:20, *"For the kingdom of God is not a matter of talk but of power."* In fact, the Apostle Paul wrote, *"My message and my preaching were not with wise and persuasive words, but with a demonstration of the Spirit's power, so that your faith might not rest on human wisdom, but on God's power"* (1 Corinthians 2:4-5).

To dismiss the revelatory and manifestation gifts out of fear of being deceived is to foster unbelief in the power of God.

The Ministry Process

I said earlier that a believer who wants to be a mature disciple needs to be willing to do hard things. To do hard things requires courage. How do you get courage? Where does it come from? It comes from others in the form of encouragement. Encouragement is an act that gives someone support, confidence, or hope.

Many Christians are looking for encouragement. They desire to be built up and to grow into Christlikeness, but do not know how to do it. They hear sermons, study the Bible, and serve others, but that is not enough to correct the course of their life. The Apostle Paul recognizes that bringing a darkened mind and hardened heart into correct alignment with godliness is a hard thing (Ephesians 4:18). To meet this challenge requires equipping by apostles, prophets, evangelists, pastors, and teachers (Ephesians 4:11-12). It takes the speaking of truth in love (Ephesians 4:15). It requires "taking off the old self and putting on the new self" (Ephesians 4:22-24). In short, it takes both discipline and deliverance.

Each of us has blind spots. We get duped by lies. Our perceptions get distorted. Our attitudes go sour, and our beliefs become warped. Jeremiah 17:9 NLT says, *"The human heart is the most deceitful of all things, and desperately wicked. Who really knows how bad it is?"* We need someone we can trust who will love us and tell us the truth. Instead of being deceived by devils and seduced by philosophies of men, we need someone with spiritual authority who can deliver us from deception.

My late friend Frank Ferrari used to say, "When a person comes to church, they are asking two questions: Is there anyone here who will love me? Is there anyone here who will tell me the truth?" We all need someone who is willing to do the hard things, to love and to tell the truth, so that we might be set free from strongholds that keep us in bondage to sin and evil.

We need someone to do what the Bible says in Ephesians 4:15, *"Speaking the truth in love, we will grow to become in every respect the mature body of him who is the head, that is, Christ."* We all need to hear hard truths about ourselves, but we resist hearing it because it is painful. Hearing difficult things is easier when we feel loved and our defenses are not high. For this to happen, a safe, nonjudgmental, non-threatening atmosphere is needed. A community distinctly marked by love and acceptance, where people are willing to be vulnerable and accountable is optimal. The Bible calls the church to be this kind of community and provides instruction on how this can happen. There are over fifty "one another" commands in the Bible, including to teach, honor, forgive, pray for, encourage one another, and more. When these "one another's" are not practiced, spiritual stagnation sets in. (For a list, see https://compass1.org/the-one-anothers/).

Speaking the truth in love requires more than good intentions. It requires wisdom and skill. It requires a person who is kind, gentle, patient, humble, and who makes allowances for faults (Ephesians 4:2). It requires a person who has been set free by the truth. Jesus referred to the Holy Spirit as the Spirit of Truth (John 14:17). The person filled with the Spirit can set others free. Just like Jesus, he is filled with both truth and grace (John 1:14). Because he has already been set free from strongholds of his own, he can empathize with the person still in bondage. Through the power of the Holy Spirit, he can set others free.

However, speaking the truth alone is not enough. Simply stating a fact, calling out a fault, quoting a Scripture, or recounting a testimony is not adequate. It must be done in the spirit of love. This kind love is referred to in Ephesians 4:15 as *agape_love*. It is a self-sacrificial love that works for the benefit of another. This kind of love is not motivated by personal gain or by the satisfaction of being right. This kind of love is motivated by the joy of seeing another person set free for the well-being of their soul.

Speaking the truth in love is necessary for freedom, but its work is not complete until we take off the old man and put on the new man. For this to happen, a divine exchange needs to take place and the renewing of the mind must occur. Paul speaks of this process in Ephesians 4:21-24, saying *"Surely you heard of him and were taught in him in accordance with the truth that is in Jesus. You were taught, with regard to your former way of life, to put off your old self, which is being corrupted by deceitful desires; to be made new in the attitude of your minds; and to put on the new self, created to be like God in true righteousness and holiness."*

What is involved in this process? First, we must connect with the living presence of Jesus, surrender control, and consecrate our will to Him. We must be open to revelation without compromising the intellect. At this point, the prophetic gift comes into play. Knowledge of the Scriptures and oneness with the Spirit will provide guidance and discernment. Being honest with ourselves and others will reveal the areas that need healing.

Being willing to forgive offensives and receiving forgiveness will cancel bitter root judgments. Getting rid of generational curses, renouncing lies, and breaking agreements with demons will dismantle strongholds. Nullifying word curses, vows, and severing negative soul ties will set you free from bondage. Casting your cares unto Jesus will facilitate the divine exchange of pain and sorrow for God's healing and grace. Confessing and repenting of sin will bring hope and strength for a renewed life. Exercising authority that commands defiling spirits to leave you will allow the Holy Spirit to plant greater measures of righteousness within you. Discipline and encouragement will be needed to maintain your freedom. Constant praise and thanksgiving will help resist the ongoing attacks of the devil.

This healing and deliverance process is a lifestyle that includes the following practices: Recognize, Respond, Repent, Renounce, Remove, Receive, Rejoice, Resist, Restore, and Repeat. For a complete explanation with Bible references, see Appendix C.

Along with these practices are some key components necessary for building Christ-like character into a disciple. I call these the 7 D's of discipleship. They include sound **doctrine**; personal **discipline**; **dependence** on the Holy Spirit; habits of **devotion**; **dying** to self; the appropriation of **discernment**; and **deliverance**. These 7 D's do not focus on changing behavior. They focus on developing the inner life. For a more complete explanation of these terms go to Appendix D.

Cultivating the Spiritual Life

It is widely recognized that spiritual gifts are given at the discretion of the Spirit for building up of the church. However, some people have interpreted this to mean that they are to passively wait until the Spirit supernaturally showers them with this mysterious grace. Instead, we are instructed to pursue love earnestly and to desire spiritual gifts (I Corinthians 14:1). Yes, the Spirit gives gifts, but like everything else given to us from God, we receive it by faith. James 4:2 says, *"You have not because you ask not."* God wants to give good gifts to those who ask him (Matthew 7:11). We must have faith to ask.

Spiritual gifts like prophecy, words knowledge, and healing need to be cultivated and nurtured. We must put into practice what God's Word declares. Just as gifts like teaching and pastoring need to be taught, exercised, and fine-tuned, so do the supernatural gifts. Learning to prophesy accurately is as important as learning to teach accurately. Only as we practice using spiritual gifts do we grow in confidence in their proper use. Paul told Timothy to fan into flame the gift that was deposited in him through the laying on of hands (2 Timothy 1:6-7). We fan into flame spiritual gifts by putting faith into action. The same is true for the fruit of the Spirit. These are given by the Spirit, so that our character reflects the character of Jesus (Romans 5:5). They, too, need to be cultivated and refined through encouragement and practice.

Believers need to realize the Spirit's life has already been placed in them at conversion. We have received all we need for salvation. We have received every spiritual blessing from heaven (Ephesians 1:3). It is in us, but it needs to come out of us. Paul said we are to work out our salvation with fear and trembling (Philippians 2:12). This means acting in faith, as Jesus did, in the fear of the Lord (Isaiah 11:2-3). We are to cut away that part of ourselves that is dead and not bearing fruit (John 15:1-4). We need to remain connected to the Spirit, so that Christ's life continues to flow into us and through us.

To do this we need to first examine ourselves regularly to see if we are still in the faith (2 Corinthians 13:15; 2 Peter 1:10-11). This does not mean continual self-doubt, but a regular check to ensure our lives truly reflect what we believe. Are we bearing all the fruit we possibly can? Are we using gifts to advance the kingdom? What areas need more transformation?

Secondly, we must die to our sinful nature by cutting away dead works. Tearing down strongholds built on lies, generational curses, judgments, vows, and trauma allows us to empty ourselves of ourselves. This includes releasing negative emotions, renouncing all agreements and false beliefs. It requires that we take authority and command all defiling spirits to leave.

Thirdly, once sin and evil have been renounced and released, we are ready to receive empowerment. The Holy Spirit fills us with more truth and grace. In this way, we are equipped to be Christ's ambassadors to take His ministry of reconciliation to the world.

To successfully take Christ's ministry to the world, we must grow from being a believer, to a disciple, to a son of God. In the next chapter we will look at what it means to be a son of God.

Discussion Questions

1. How do you teach people to stop doing what comes natural to them? How do you motivate people to be obedient to Christ?

2. Do you agree that without the healing and deliverance ministry the church is held hostage to the devil? Why or why not?

3. According to Ephesians 4, what are the nine purposes of the church? How are those purposes accomplished? What are the eight things a church can do to build herself up in love? What does it take to speak the truth in love?

4. Why are all five of Christ's gifts needed to equip the church for ministry? What happens when some of them are absent? What role do the prophetic and apostolic gifts play in the equipping process?

5. What is the difference between a cessationist and a continuationist? How does this ongoing debate affect the church's witness?

6. What does it take to speak the truth in love?

7. On a scale of one to ten, how would you rate yourself at living out the "one another's"? Which ones could you improve on?

8. The author outlines the healing and deliverance process with "10 R's". What questions do you have about this process?

9. The author identifies seven things are needed if a church is going to make mature disciples. Which ones does your church do well? Which ones need improvement?

8. What role do spiritual gifts play in making mature disciples?

Suggested readings on the Cessationism verses the Continuationism debate:

> *On the Cessation of the Charismata* by Jon Mark Ruthven
>
> *Holy Fire* by R.T. Kendall
>
> *Strange Fire* by John MacArthur
>
> *Authentic Fire: A Response to John MacArthur's Strange Fire*

Endnotes

1. Ron Myer, *Fivefold Ministry Made Practical*, (House to House Publications, Lititz, PA, 2006), p. 87.

12

Freedom Reveals God's Glory in His Sons and Daughters

Eagerly Waiting

My wife, Yvonne and I were married in May of 1979. We tried to have children without success. After seven years, Yvonne was diagnosed with a disease called Endometriosis, a condition that prohibited her from becoming pregnant. She underwent several surgeries to mitigate the condition, but to no avail. After seven years, we went to a specialist at the University of Virginia Hospital. He performed exploratory surgery using an endoscopic procedure. He found Yvonne had no left ovary and only one-third of an ovary on the right side. The remaining piece of ovary was so covered over by scar tissue, he could not see it.

He did not give us any hope of having children, but he did refer us to an infertility clinic in Washington D.C. We made an appointment. Meanwhile, we went to a seminar put on by the Virginia Department of Social Services in hopes of adopting a child. We were greatly discouraged when we learned not one healthy Caucasian baby had been placed for adoption in the entire State of Virginia since Rowe vs. Wade passed in 1973.

Not giving up hope, we went through several cycles of infertility treatment. Each time Yvonne needed to take hormone shots for weeks in advance in hope of producing an egg. At $3,000 per cycle, we went through three cycles without any success. We were crushed and about ready to give up. Then in the summer of 1986 my church, St. Andrews UCC, granted me a sabbatical leave. As part of my leave, I went on an eight-day silent retreat at the Jesuit Center in Wernersville, Pennsylvania. Toward the end of that week, I was in a time of deep meditation when the Lord gave me a vision of a child inside a womb. He said we were going to have a baby. I was so excited I could hardly contain myself. As soon as saw I my wife, I told her we were going to have a baby and explained what had happened. She was stunned. Although a bit apprehensive, she agreed to give invitro fertilization one more-try.

We had been on an emotional rollercoaster but decided to wait it out a little longer. We went back to the clinic in the fall. This time we saw a new doctor named Maria. We followed her instructions, and in April of 1987, she was able to harvest three eggs from Yvonne. Maria put the fertilized eggs into a petri dish and instructed us to wait a couple of days for a phone call. We went to my mother's house in Baltimore to wait for the call. That night, I had a dream in which I was standing under a streetlight when a man walked up to me and handed me two babies. He put one baby in a knap sack on my back and the other into my arms. The man said, "I am giving you these babies to steward, but you must give them back to me when they are grown." I agreed. The next day we received the phone call. The technician said that one of the eggs died over night, but the other two were still alive. I said, "That's it; we are going to have twins." We went to the clinic the next day to have the fertilized eggs implanted in Yvonne's womb. I was not prepared for what was about to happen.

When we arrived the next day, we were told that one of the two eggs had died overnight. I was totally bewildered and confused. The Lord said He was giving me two babies, yet only one egg survived. While still trying to collect my thoughts, the doctor invited me to be present as she implanted the living egg into Yvonne's womb. As Maria was going through the procedure, I saw a glowing white light over Yvonne's stomach. It lasted for several minutes. I was in awe.

Yvonne had to lay flat on her back for several hours, so she laid down in the back seat of the car as we made the two-and-a-half-hour trip back home. We arrived home about 1:00 a.m. Yvonne went straight to bed. I went to my office to check my answering machine for any calls.

I was shocked when the recorded voice on the answering machine said, "Reverend Snow, I am calling on behalf of the Department of Social Services. We have a baby boy for you." I fell to my knees and cried. That was the second child from the dream. Adam was born on March 5, 1987, and nine months later Yvonne gave birth to our second child, Rachel. She was born on December 11, 1987. After waiting for better than six years, we went from having no babies to having two babies in less than one year. As Verna, a lady from my seminary days, used to say, "All good things come to those who wait."

Waiting for sons and daughters to be born is a struggle. It can be painful, stressful, and emotionally exhausting. It can be confusing and not make any sense. Yet, for those who eagerly wait in hope for what the Lord has said, it is glorious.

Waiting for God's Sons and Daughters

Chapter 8 in the book of Romans is perhaps the most profound chapter in the Bible concerning freedom. It speaks of freedom in cosmic terms. It talks about creation waiting to share the same freedom and glory as the Sons of God.

The creation waits eagerly for the sons of God to be revealed; for the creation was made subject to frustration—not willingly, but because of the one who subjected it. But it was given a reliable hope that it too would be set free from its bondage to decay and would enjoy the freedom accompanying the glory that God's children will have. We know that until now, the whole creation has been groaning as with the pains of childbirth; and not only it, but we ourselves, who have the first fruits of the Spirit, groan inwardly as we continue waiting eagerly to be made sons—that is, to have our whole bodies redeemed and set free (Romans 8:19-23 CJB).

To put this scripture in context, we need to look at the preceding verses found in Romans 8:9-17. Before stating that creation eagerly waits for the sons of God to be revealed, Paul describes what the sons of God look like. He identifies them as people who have the Spirit of God living in them. They have been made right with God. They follow the leading of the Sprit. They are no longer slaves to fear. They understand God as a Father, and they cry "Abba." They are heirs with Christ. They share in His sufferings, as well as, in His glory. These are some of the attributes of the sons of God.

If you are a disciple of Jesus Christ, you should know you are being called to be a son of God. This is the highest level of spiritual maturity. The term "son of God" in the Bible refers to both men and women. We are all called to realize our union with Jesus Christ and share in the same kind of relationship Jesus has with the Father.

Since the time of Enoch, there has always been a remnant of believers who have learned to walk with God in a special way. Jesus showed His followers that way. He said, *"I am the way and the truth and the life"* (John 14:6). It is this kind of life His followers exemplified in the book of Acts. They were identified as "people of the Way" in Acts 9:1-2.

Paul says creation longs to see this kind of believer inhabit the earth. Why? As believers live their lives the way Jesus lived His, creation itself will be set free from the bondage of decay, corruption, and futility it was subjected to when Adam sinned.

Most people are waiting for the world to become a perfect place so that they have no worries, hardships, or struggles. They are looking for a world where there is no suffering, pain, or injustice. But Paul is saying the reverse. It is by suffering and overcoming the corruption of this broken world that God's sons appear. And when they appear, creation is restored to its original state of perfection. As believers become complete in Christ, they receive God's glory. That is when the world returns to its perfect condition. Until that happens, creation is groaning in pains of childbirth, waiting for the children of God to be revealed through the redeeming work of Christ.

How God's Glory Is Revealed

The Bible teaches that God has ultimately revealed His glory in Jesus Christ (John 14:9). Those who turn toward the light of Jesus see His glory with increasing brightness. *"For God, who said, 'Light shall shine out of darkness,' is the One who has shone in our hearts to give the Light of the knowledge of the glory of God in the face of Christ"* (2 Corinthians 4:6 NSB). And Galatians 4:6 states, *"Because you are his sons, God sent the Spirit of his Son into our hearts, the Spirit who calls out, 'Abba, Father'"*.

In the heart of man, the light of the knowledge of the glory of God is revealed in the face of Christ. Those who have Christ's Spirit in their hearts cry out to God as Daddy, saying "Abba." Simply put, it is the light of Jesus shining in our hearts that reveals the glory of God. Those who turn away from the light of Christ, even in little things, turn away from God. They choose to live in the darkness of this world. They deceive themselves. They fool themselves even to the point of calling good evil and evil good (Isaiah 5:20-21). The Apostle John speaks of this turning away in John 3:19, *"This is the verdict: Light has come into the world, but people loved darkness instead of light because their deeds were evil."*

Believers Resist Without Realizing It

The truth is even believers resist Christ as the light because they have become comfortable with the sinful practices of this dark world. Titus 1:16 says, *"Such people claim to know God, but they deny him by the way they live"* (NLT). The world is full of offense and injustice, and believers have become accustomed to living that way too. Paul put it this way, *"All have sinned and fallen short of the glory of God"* (Romans 3:23). Without realizing it, Christians absorb the lies and faulty practices of their culture into their hearts, which in turn fosters further offense and injustice. The evil one is constantly baiting believers to take up offenses. Christians need to realize this. We must acknowledge the reality we are living in. We are in constant spiritual warfare. There is a continual battle going in our hearts between righteousness and the spirit of injustice.

In Psalm 139, David recognizes this inner conflict. He prayerfully asks God to search his heart and to test him to see if there is any offensiveness or wickedness within him. This self-reflection is something sons and daughters of God must do regularly. To be sanctified, we must come to terms with defilements buried deep within. The reality is, we are not always aware of the poison the world has deposited into our hearts. Consequently, we are not always conscious of what is happening inside us. We think we have things under control, but we are not in touch with the forces that are controlling us. We need God to make us aware of that which has been hidden, so that we may live an offense-free life.

Because the world constantly contaminates the soul, we must be careful as to where we obtain our news and information. We need to guard our hearts because deception causes darkness, confusion, anger, fear, and despair. It is important to remember that the news behind the news is always spiritual. We must learn to discern light from darkness and good from evil. Recognizing this difference is not as easy as it may seem. Jesus warned that in the last days, even the elect could be deceived (Matthew 24:24). How can this be? Despite having the Bible and the Holy Spirit, how is it we are still prone to being deceived?

The prophet Jeremiah warned that the human heart is altogether deceitful and too sick to be cured (Jeremiah 17:9). In other words, we must acknowledge that our own hearts can deceive us. Our own beliefs can deceive us. On the other hand, it is the objective truth that exposes darkness and sets men free from deception and evil. Being willing and humble enough to admit you have been wrong in your former beliefs is the starting point for maturity.

However, what to do about that deception requires discernment. Such discernment comes not from earthly wisdom but from wisdom from above (James 3:13-17). We need to filter what we hear and what we watch through the living Word of God. Hebrews 4:12 states, *"For the word of God is alive and active. Sharper than any double-edged sword, it penetrates even to dividing soul and spirit, joints and marrow; it judges the thoughts and attitudes of the heart."* We need to pay attention to what the Holy Spirit is saying about the attitudes lodged in our hearts. If you ask the Holy Spirit, He will reveal what is going on inside of you. You can expect that as your God-consciousness increases, so will your discernment. The more sensitive you become to the Holy Spirit, the more you will know what is and what is not truth.

Maturity Requires Cooperation

Spiritual maturity is not something you can achieve by your work, although it does require your willingness and assistance. Becoming spiritually mature is about allowing God to do his transforming work in you. It is about surrendering to His presence and submitting to His power. Through the Holy Spirit, Jesus leads you to maturity and freedom. Romans 8:1-2 declares, *"There is now no condemnation for those who are in Christ Jesus, because through Christ Jesus, the law of the Spirit who gives life has set you free from the law of sin and death."* The more you are set free from the law of sin the more mature you become.

This process of being set free is what brings new life. It is like childbirth. Although the process happens naturally, it is not easy! It is labor intensive. It requires cooperation. This cooperation takes the form of trusting and obeying the Holy Spirit. Romans 8:14 NKJV declares: *"For as many as are led by the Spirit of God, these are sons of God."* And John 16:12-15 says: *"But when He, the Spirit of truth comes, He will guide you into all truth. He will not speak of his own; He will speak only what He hears, and He will tell you what is yet to come."* Following the leading of the Holy Spirit fosters the maturity that reflects being a son of God.

Spiritual maturity is also achieved through partnership with other believers. Christians need each other for encouragement, correction, protection, and provision. Being a Christian is all about loving God and loving others, forming a community that is distinct from the world. Hebrews 10:24-25 says, *"And let us consider how we may spur one another on toward love and good deed, not giving up meeting together, as some are in the habit of doing, but encouraging one another -- and all the more as you see the Day approaching."* Speaking the truth in love to each other is what makes us mature. *"As iron sharpens iron, so one person sharpens another"* (Proverbs 27:17).

The Holy Spirit Perfects Love

Some people put faith in love, only to be disappointed and disillusioned. Betrayal and rejection leave them broken hearted. In contrast, Christians put faith in Christ, whose love never disappoints. Galatians 5:5 asserts, *"For through the Spirit we eagerly await by faith the righteousness for which we hope."*

Your relationship with the Holy Spirit is critical for life as a son of God. The Spirit operates as the voice of God, the presence of God, and the power of God in us (Ephesians 3:16). He convicts and directs us in the ways of God. He makes us righteous (1 John 1:9). Being filled with the Spirit repeatedly, we function more and more in the love of God. Romans 5:5 says, *"God's love has been poured out into our hearts through the Holy Spirit, who has been given to us."* In this way, God's love is perfected in us. The Father's love is *agape*—a selfless love that makes sacrifices for others. This kind of love is revealed in Christ Jesus.

God works His love into our lives in many ways. Primarily it happens in our daily relationships as we try to obey God's command to love our neighbors as we love ourselves (Matthew 22:39). This is a challenge because the people God puts around are not always easy to love. We need God's grace to overcome our human weakness and inability to love.

Learning to submit to God's love requires dying to self. Because the sinful nature always seeks to make itself superior; it needs to be crucified. Our natural inclination is to judge people as being unworthy of our love and even God's love. When we withhold love from others, we stifle the Holy Spirit. Consequently, the light of God within us grows dim. Unable to see the way God sees, we judge falsely. When someone shares about an offense and we become angry and bitter, we become unconscious of God's love within. If offenses go unforgiven and unhealed, our hearts become cold. Withholding love because of an offense steals our joy, fosters loneliness, and keeps us from glorifying our Father in Heaven.

The Bible prophesies that in the last days, there will be increased wickedness causing the love of many to grow cold (Matthew 24:12). During this tumultuous time in which political correctness and offenses abound, we must be careful to guard our hearts, less our mouths contribute to the problem. We must be careful not to join Satan in accusing the brethren (Revelation 12:10). In an atmosphere saturated with suspicion and animosity, it is most difficult to survive emotionally unless our relationship with the Holy Spirit is cultivated. Our inner joy and peace are directly linked to being led by the Holy Spirit. For this reason, sons and daughters are very protective of their relationship with the Spirit.

Two Kinds of Love

Jesus told His disciples that the love they shared would be an indication of being His disciples. *"A new commandment I give to you, that you love one another; as I have loved you, that you also love one another. By this all will know that you are My disciples, if you have love for one another"* (John 13:34-35). Loving people who believe what you believe and value what you value is one way of fulfilling this commandment. However, Jesus taught an even higher form of love.

Whereas the world will know we are Jesus' disciples by our love for each other, they will know we are sons of God by our love for our enemies. Jesus said in Matthew 5:43-48 (emphasis mine):

*You have heard it said, 'You shall love your neighbor and hate your enemy.' But I say to you, love your enemies, bless those who curse you, do good to those who hate you, and pray for those who spitefully use you and persecute you; that you may **be sons of your Father** in heaven; for he makes his sun rise on the evil and on the good, and sends rain on the just and on the unjust. For if you love those who love you, what reward have you? Do not even tax collectors do the same? And if you greet your brethren only, what do you do more than others? Do not even the tax collectors do so? Therefore, you shall be **perfect**, just as your Father in heaven is **perfect*** (NKJV).

The word, *perfect* means "to be complete" or "to come into full maturity." Believers reach full maturity not when they love their neighbors, but when they love their enemies like God loves sinners.

Romans 5:8,10 declares, *"But God demonstrates his own love for us in this: While we were still sinners, Christ died for us…. For if, while we were God's enemies, we were reconciled to him through the death of his Son, how much more, having been reconciled, shall we be saved through his life!"* In other words, to become fully mature like Christ, we must love our enemies in such a way as to seek their salvation through reconciliation. In extreme cases, this may mean martyrdom. Loving your enemy is a path to spiritual maturity.

In a speech Abraham Lincoln delivered at the height of the Civil War, he referred to the Southerners as fellow human beings who were in error. An elderly lady chastised him for not calling them irreconcilable enemies who must be destroyed. 'Why, madam,' Lincoln replied, 'do I not destroy my enemies when I make them my friends?'" [1]

Abraham Lincoln was truly one of the sons of God who appeared at a critical time in our nation's history. He was assassinated at Ford's Theater. Another one of God's sons appeared in the 1960s in the person of Martin Luther King Jr. He called the nation to repent of the sin of racism. In the interest of freedom and in the spirit of peace, he led protest marches that were met with attack dogs, tear gas, clubs and lynching. In the end, he, too, was martyred in the pursuit of justice and righteousness.

Today in the face of social unrest, political upheaval, cultural conflict, and economic distress, the sons of God need to appear once again. There needs to be an awakening in which an army of men and women no longer tolerate sin. There needs to be a movement of courageous believers who live for freedom and fight for righteousness. These believers will no longer be content with carnal Christianity. They will be committed to the glory of God shining through them in increasing radiance. Having come out of the darkness of fear and self-protection, they stand firm in faith and hope. They are set free from the fear of dying because Christ, through his death has broken the devil's power over death (Hebrews 2: 14-15). As sons and daughters, they see themselves as God sees them, not as the problem but as the solution to the ills of society. They are the light of the world (Matthew 5:14). Like Jesus, they love justice and hate evil (Hebrew 1:9). Because of their love for Jesus, they keep His commands even when it costs them everything.

The Way to Be Happy

I remember singing the hymn "Trust and Obey" as a child. John H. Sammis wrote it in 1887. It heralds the rewards of trusting God's Word and obeying God's will. It was one of the favorite hymns of the congregation.

Trust and Obey

When we walk with the Lord in the light of his word, what a glory he sheds on our way!
While we do his good will, he abides with us still,
and with all who will trust and obey.

Refrain:
Trust and obey, for there's no other way
to be happy in Jesus, but to trust and obey.

Not a burden we bear, not a sorrow we share, but our toil he doth richly repay;
not a grief or a loss, not a frown or a cross, but is blest if we trust and obey.

But we never can prove the delights of his love until all on the altar we lay;
for the favor he shows, for the joy he bestows,
are for them who will trust and obey.

Then in fellowship sweet we will sit at his feet, or we'll walk by his side in the way;
what he says we will do, where he sends we will go; never fear,
only trust and obey.

Trusting and obeying is the real test of faith. Many may talk the talk, but it is only those who walk the walk who will find the happiness Jesus promises. In Matthew 5, Jesus warns of those who perform great acts of ministry, but in their hearts, they are doing their own thing rather than following the will of God.

Not everyone who says to me, "Lord, Lord" will enter the kingdom of heaven, but only the one who does the will of my Father who is in heaven. Many will say to me on that day, "Lord, Lord, did we not prophesy in your name and in your name drive out demons and in your name perform many miracles?" Then I will tell them plainly, "I never knew you. Away from me, you evildoers!" (Matthew 7: 21-27).

After speaking, Jesus expounded on what He meant by telling the parable of a wise man who built his house on the firm foundation of a rock and of the unwise man who built his house on the sand. The wise man is he who hears Jesus' words and puts them into practice, while the unwise man is he who hears His words and fails to put them into practice.

It is important to note that Jesus is not saying that prophesying, casting out demons, or doing miracles is wrong. In fact, the Bible speaks of His disciples being instructed to do these things in His name. What Jesus is saying is that one should not put ministry ahead of obedience. It is easy to become so enamored and passionate about ministry that it becomes an idol. You can become so excited about using your talent, knowledge, and skills that ministry becomes more about you than about God. One can become so consumed with the importance of what you are doing that your relationship with God becomes secondary. Doing good things in Jesus name can easily slide over into the flesh rather than out of obedience to the Spirit.

The way Jesus brings God's children to glory is the way He Himself received glory—through obedience (John 17:4-10). Obedience is more than service. Obedience is what sets God's children apart from the world. Ungodly people will do charitable things to serve people, but they fail to submit to the will of the Father. They will religiously commit themselves to doing good things but fail to address their sinful nature, follow the leading of the Spirit, bring others to faith, or develop Christ-like character.

The Bible is clear that God is not interested in religious sacrifices; He is interested in obedience. He promises to honor those who honor Him (1 Samuel 2:30). He desires that we listen and obey His voice, rather than practice religious rituals or do what we think is good. In 1 Samuel 15:22, it says: *But Samuel replied: "Does the Lord delight in burnt offerings and sacrifices as much as in obeying the Lord? To obey is better than sacrifice, and to heed is better than the fat of rams."*

Many other scriptures state this same truth. The mere frequency indicates it's importance. The list includes: 1 Samuel 15:22; Hosea 6:6; Psalm 51:16-17; Proverbs 21:3; Amos 5:21-24; Mark 12:33; Matthew 9:13; Jeremiah 7:22-23; Psalm 40:6-8; Ecclesiastes 5:1; Matthew 12:7; Isaiah 1:11-17; Hebrews 10:4-10; Matthew 23:23; Psalm 50:8-9; Matthew 5:24; Jeremiah 26:13; Jeremiah 11:7; Exodus 19:5; Jeremiah 11:4. Obedience out of love is what brings God glory.

God is Most Interested in the Heart

Many Christians have a "life verse" that serves as an anchor or guiding star throughout every season of life. If I were to choose one verse that does this for me, it would be Proverbs 3:5-6, *"Trust in the LORD with all your heart and lean not on your own understanding, in all your ways submit to Him, and he will make your paths straight."* This verse, along with Proverbs 23:7, has taught me to keep watch over my heart. Proverbs 23:7 says, *"For as a man thinketh in his heart so is he"* (KJV).

God is concerned with what goes on in the human heart. Humans are disposed to making judgments and decisions based on outward appearances, physical features, performance, status, giftedness, ethnicity, gender, and the like. In contrast, God is most interested with the inner life. 1 Samuel 16:7 declares, *"But the LORD said to Samuel, 'Do not consider his appearance or his height, for I have rejected him. The LORD does not look at the things people look at. People look at the outward appearance but the LORD looks at the heart.'"* Freedom is not merely a political consideration or a state of mind; it is primarily a condition of the heart. God is most concerned that the heart of man be set free of all deceit and corruption. God desires that our hearts be pure. That is why He gives us the Holy Spirit. Genuine human freedom is realized by internal self-control. It comes from moral self-government enabled by the Holy Spirit.

What the Church Needs Now

In past centuries, since the Protestant Reformation, the church has focused mostly on justification. She has emphasized bringing people to salvation by grace through faith. In an effort to bring people to faith, we have written creeds, published multiple versions of the Bible, educated clergy, sent out missionaries, conducted crusades, planted new churches, built megachurches, and developed denominations. Despite all these activities, we have not been very intentional about sanctification. Purifying the hearts and souls of believers has not received a lot of attention despite Jesus' teaching that it is the pure in heart that shall see God (Matthew 5: 8). At best, the church has participated in periodic revivals that seek to reconnect believers to the Spirit. Admittedly, there have been some holiness movements, but they have been short lived, and in some cases, misguided. In this season, it is time for the church to become resolute enough to not only preach justification but to also practice sanctification.

The practice of sanctification is not optional. It is a necessity if we are to make mature disciples. With the culture growing increasingly secular and even hostile toward Christianity, we can no longer afford to do business as usual. We must become galvanized in the fight against hypocrisy, apostasy, passivity, and irrelevance. The Apostle Paul warned Timothy that in the last days, *"People will love only themselves and their money. They will be boastful and proud, scoffing at God, disobedient to parents, and ungrateful. They will consider nothing sacred. They will be unloving and unforgiving; they will slander others and have no self-control. They will be cruel and hate what is good. They will betray their friends, be reckless, be puffed up with pride, and love pleasure rather than God. They will act religious, but they will reject the power that could make them godly"* (2 Timothy 3: 2-5 NLT). As long as people reject the power to make them free, the sons of glory cannot appear.

Creation is waiting for the sons of God to appear. It is time for the church to be more intentional in raising up sons and daughters to glory. Church leaders need to be more concerned with what is happening in the hearts of their people. They need to teach their people how to seek God's face, listen to His voice, abide in His presence, feel His love, obey His word, experience His power, follow His Spirit, die to the flesh, be cleansed from defilements, discern Satan's schemes, test the spirits, be set free from sin and evil, and be clothed in righteousness. Church leaders must be committed to helping their people to first seek the kingdom of God and His righteousness, believing all other things will then fall in place (Matthew 6:33). Church leaders need to teach their people how to pray effectively. After all, it is the effectual fervent prayer of a righteous man that avails much (James 5:16 KJV). They will need to teach people how to take on a new identity that will enable them to fulfill their destiny and to live free in Christ. Doing these things, fulfills the two Great Commandments; to love God with all your heart, mind, and soul, and to love your neighbor as yourself. Doing these things allows the sons and daughters of God to appear.

The following pages provide key concepts and practical applications that can help equip a local church to join Christ in raising up many sons and daughters to glory. The goal is to help local church leaders be set people free from strongholds constructed of generational curses, ungodly belief systems, trauma, and demonic oppression. This release from strongholds will involve examining the need to die to self, renew the mind, and establish a new identity in Christ. Lastly, consideration is given to what it takes to establish and maintain a culture of freedom.

In order to realize more and more freedom, we need to learn how to conduct a funeral for the flesh. In the next chapter, we will examine in more detail the need to die to self to live in the Spirit.

Discussion Questions

1. Why do you think Paul believes creation is in labor pains waiting for the sons of God to appear? How would this motivate a believer to become a son or daughter?

2. What are the qualities that define a son or daughter of God? Make a list of those qualities based on Romans 8. Can you think of other qualities found elsewhere in the Bible?

3. What can a believer expect if he trusts the Word of God and remains obedient to the will of God? What does it look like to honor God?

4. Why do you think loving your enemies sets you apart as one of God's sons?

5. Why do you think God is most interested in the human heart? How does it make you feel knowing that God is concerned about the condition of your heart?

6. Do you agree the church has focused on justification at the expense of sanctification? Why or why not? What is the consequence of focusing mostly on justification?

7. What will it take to galvanize your church to fight against hypocrisy, apostasy, passivity, and irrelevance?

Endnotes
1. Robert Greene, *The 48 Laws of Power*, www.goodreads.com

13

Dying to Be Free

More Than a Movie

In the fall of 2005, Rick, Patti, Sue, and I boarded a plan headed for an adventure in Chicago, Illinois. We were looking forward to attending a conference sponsored by the Willow Creek Association. After getting settled into our hotel, we traveled to the site of the conference. We listened to a few speakers and explored the campus. During the last session of the afternoon, it was announced we would be given free tickets to preview a new movie, soon to be released around the country. The film was "The End of the Spear." It recounted the true story of Jim Elliot and fellow missionaries. They were martyred in 1956 while attempting to share the gospel with the Waodoni people in a tropical rainforest in eastern Ecuador.

The movie was a gripping account of how the very people they were trying to save killed these missionaries. At the end of the film, with the house lights turned up while the credits were running, a person asked the crowd what they thought of the movie. I was seated half-way back in the theater. Suddenly, I heard a voice that seemed to come from the upper front right corner near the ceiling of the theater. It was the voice of the Lord. It was clear and understandable as though someone next to me were speaking. The voice said, "Craig, if you want to change your culture, you must be willing to die."

I was startled and wondered if this meant I, too, must be martyred like those in the film. For weeks, months and even years, I pondered what this message meant for me. Slowly, it became clear. If I were to change the culture of my church, my family, my community, I had to die to myself. I had to die to my sinful nature. But how would I do that? I had no idea. I knew Jesus died to forgive my sins, but how to die to my own sin was not something I had considered. I had studied Scripture and preached sermons for twenty-nine years, but I had not given much thought to how to be free from my sinful nature. I had not yet fully emptied my heart in the way D.L. Moody describes:

> I firmly believe that the moment our hearts are emptied of self-ishness and ambition and self-seeking and everything that is contrary to God's law, the Holy Spirit will come and fill every corner of our hearts; but if we are full of pride and conceit, ambition and self-seeking, pleasure and the world, there is no room for the Spirit of God. I also believe that many a man is praying to God to fill him, when he is full already with something else. Before we pray that God would fill us, I believe we ought to pray that He would empty us. There must be an emptying before there can be a filling; and when the heart is turned upside down, and everything that is contrary to God is turned out, then the Spirit will come...[1]

Learning to empty yourself of yourself is essential if you are going to be a mature follower of Christ. Jesus had to do this. If He were to fulfill His purpose in coming to the earth, He needed to become nothing. Philippians 2: 6-7 says, *"Being in very nature God, did not consider equality with God something to be used to his own advantage; rather he made himself nothing by taking the very nature of a servant, being made in human likeness."*

The Greek term for "made himself nothing" is *kenoo,* derived from *kenos.* It means "to empty" or "to make void." Jesus emptied Himself of His divine privileges to fulfill God's plan. Secondly, He emptied Himself of His human will in order to do the Father's divine will.

Selfish Ambition in The Heart

In the years following the experience in the theater, the Lord began to teach me about dying to self. It has been a slow process. I read a book entitled *The Political Spirit* by Faisal Malick. It gave me insight into how blind I was to my self-centered condition. The author pointed to James 3:14-15, which said, *"If you have bitter envy and selfish ambition in your heart do not boast about it or deny the truth. Such 'wisdom' does not come down from heaven but is earthly, unspiritual, demonic."* The scriptural definition for *self-ambition* is "self-seeking." It has the connotation of putting oneself forward, as a candidate in an election. It is the desire to get your own agenda accomplished in a partisan fashion. Selfish ambition includes anything that is contrary to the will, the Word, the purposes, and the character of God. It lacks humility.

Up until that point, I never thought of myself as prideful or arrogant, at least not any more than anyone else. That was the problem! I was comparing myself to others rather than to Christ, the only true standard. Comparing yourself with others is always a losing proposition because you either judge yourself above someone else or below someone else. In both instances, the focus is on yourself. You make the big "I" the standard by which you judge everyone else.

The big "I" is located right smack in the middle of PR I DE. Pride always seeks to assert itself. It is inherent in the sinful nature. Whether we acknowledge it or not, pride is at the very core of our flesh. It is deadly. Pride destroys loving relationships. Song writer, Rodger Miller, in his song, "Husband and Wives," puts it this way: "Two broken hearts lonely, looking like houses where nobody lives, two people each having so much pride inside, neither side forgives, the angry words spoken in haste, such a waste of two lives, it's my belief pride is the chief cause and decline…" Pastor and author Tim Keller says, "Pride is the carbon-monoxide of sin. It silently and slowly kills you without you even knowing it."[2] Scripture explains: *"There is a way that seems right to a man, but its end is the way to destruction"* (Proverbs 14:12 ESV).

Biblically speaking, the flesh is marked by affections, thoughts, behaviors, and desires that are contrary to God's will, Word and nature. Pride is one of the three ways Satan appeals to the flesh in order to get man to sin against God. (1 John 2:16). It was pride that made Satan rebel against God. He put himself above the authority of God (Jude 1:6).

The Prophet Isaiah records how Satan asserted himself against God with the big "I." Five times He said, *"I will ascend to the heavens…," "I will raise my throne…," "I will sit enthroned…," "I will ascend above….," and "I will make myself like the Most High"* (Isaiah 14: 13-14). Satan would like nothing more than for you to join him in his pride, enticing you to assert yourself as he did. This is what Satan did with Peter. After God had given Peter the revelation that Jesus was the Messiah, Peter immediately became a mouthpiece for Satan, trying to prevent Jesus from going to the cross. Jesus rebuked him, saying, *"'Get behind me, Satan! You are a stumbling block to me; you do not have in mind the concerns of God, but merely human concerns.' Then Jesus said to his disciples, 'Whoever wants to be my disciple must deny themselves and take up their cross and follow me'"* (Matthew 16:23-24).

During a recent ministry session, a forty-year-old man learned what it meant to deny himself and to take up his identity as a Christ-follower. He was a successful businessman. However, he was dealing with some internal conflicts that left him feeling lonely. Even though he was married, his life lacked intimacy. The Holy Spirit revealed to us what was going on his heart. When he was in his early 20s, he made a vow to himself, "I will not base my identity in what I do. I am not going to base my life on pleasing others. I will do my own thing." It was good for him to realize that people-pleasing was not the answer. But what he chose to base his life on equally was not the answer. The vow he made led him to base his life on self-sufficiency, an action that took him down the trail of self-imposed isolation and loneliness. He came to understand that true identity is not based on what others expect of him or even what he expects of himself. His true identity is based on what God says about him. He confessed his sin of self-sufficiency, and as he did, the Spirit showed him that his self-sufficiency was rooted in unbelief. He confessed the sin of unbelief and received forgiveness and inner peace flooded into his heart that was not there before.

A Helpful Lesson

During the years immediately following my experience in the movie theater, the Lord began to impress upon me the relationship between dying to myself and the acquisition of spiritual authority. My father died in 1998. He left me some jewelry that I turned into a lapel pin. It featured a gold crown laced with small diamonds that encircled a red cross. I wore it on my coat on Sunday mornings as a reminder that the more I died to myself, the more I would live in the Spirit. The more I lived in the Spirit, the more I would rule in the kingdom of God.

Interestingly, I later learned of a quote by William Penn, a Quaker, who founded the State of Pennsylvania. He said, "No cross, no crown." He wrote this while a prisoner in the Tower of London in 1668-1669. The full quote reads, "No pain, no palm; no thorns, no throne; no gall, no glory; no cross, no crown."[3] What the Lord impressed upon me was the realization that dying to self is necessary if I am going to reign with him as a priestly king (Revelation 5:10). In the kingdom of God, you must lower yourself before you are raised up. This is true in our relationships as well, especially marriage.

Dying to Self Requires Crucifying the Flesh

The Christian life involves dying to self or, as the Apostle Paul put it, crucifying the flesh. As a pastor and teacher, I was familiar with how Paul struggled with his flesh. He said, "*So I find this law at work: Although I want to do good, evil is right there with me. For in my inner being I delight in God's law; but I see another law at work in me, waging war against the law of my mind and making me a prisoner of the law of sin at work within me. What a wretched man I am! Who will rescue me from this body that is subject to death? Thanks be to God who delivers me through Jesus Christ our Lord! So then, I myself in my mind am a slave to God's law, but in my sinful nature a slave to the law of sin"* (Romans 7:21-25).

Also, I was familiar with how he sought to die daily to his sinful nature. He wrote in 1 Corinthians 15:31, *"I face death every day, Yes, just as surely as I boast about you in Christ Jesus our Lord."* I was acquainted with what he wrote in Galatians 2:20: *"I have been crucified with Christ and I no longer live, but Christ lives in me. The life I now live in the body, I live by faith in the Son of God, who loved me and gave himself for me."* And I had read what he said in Romans 6:6, *"We know that our old sinful selves were crucified with Christ so that sin might lose its power in our lives. We are no longer slaves to sin"* (NLT).

Although I was familiar with all the things Paul said about dying to sin and crucifying the flesh, I did not have a clue what that meant in practical terms. In looking back, I must admit that I heard many sermons on how to live as a Christian, but I never connected those teachings with dying to self. For example, I heard messages on prayer and fasting, but I never saw that as means to dying to self. I knew what James said, *"Be quick to listen, slow to speak, and slow to get angry"* (James 1:19), but I never connected that with dying to self. I knew Christians were supposed to be humble (James 4:10), but I never saw that as a way to die to self.

I knew what the Bible said about being crucified with Christ, but I grew up in a culture that glorified the self rather than humility. No one taught me how to die to self. In fact, all the TV preachers glorified success, with big buildings, big budgets, and big crowds. I was aware of the works of the flesh that Paul listed in Galatians 5:19-21, including jealousy, sexual immorality, selfish-ambition, sorcery, idolatry, and others. However, I didn't identify with those things. They seemed far removed from my efforts to be a "good church-going Christian."

The truth is, works of the flesh are not always as obvious as those listed in Galatians. We can have private sins and even hidden sins rooted in the carnal nature of which we are not conscious. There are things hidden within our hearts. A good way to conceptualize this is through a diagram developed by Joseph Luft and Harrington Ingham called "The Johari Window." It helps us better understand our relationship with self and others. Most of us do not recognize the hindrances to our Christian walk as attitudes, beliefs, and hidden sins residing deep within the heart. See Appendix E for the diagram.

The Bible identifies these internal unconscious thoughts, attitudes, and motives as strongholds. Lies, vows, judgments, curses, trauma, and generational iniquity fortify these strongholds. We can be doing ministry with mixed motives and not know it. We can be serving Christ from a sense of call and obedience and, at the same time, have self-centered motives. Ministry can be a platform for gaining status, popularity, approval, significance, or self-worth. In 3 John 1:9, Diotrephes was rebuked for trying to please God from self-centered motives.

In my case, I was in bondage to a stronghold of addiction. It was not an addiction to alcohol, pornography. or drugs. It was far more insidious and justifiable. I knew I was a workaholic, but I was not aware of the sin that was driving me to work all the time. I justified my workaholism by convincing myself that I was doing the Lord's work. In reality, my sin was putting my own self forward in doing ministry. The accolades I received were intoxicating. Coupled with the fear of man and generational patterns, I was a prisoner to performance mentality. I did not realize the link to the sin of selfish ambition lodged in the flesh.

Different Dimensions of Self Ambition

In reading the *The Political Spirit* by Faisal Malick, I discovered that selfish ambition prevents a person from receiving heavenly wisdom (James 3:15-16). My inability to resolve personal conflicts due to a lack of wisdom motivated me to take an in-depth look at myself. I began to understand the many forms selfish ambition can take. I started to see that self-centeredness, self-promotion, self-gratification, self-indulgence, self-pity, self-protection, self-interest, self-achievement, self-reliance, self-determination, self-serving, self-doubt, self-limiting, self-sabotage, self-excusing, self-assertion, self-pity, self-disqualification, self-blame, self-condemnation, self-consciousness, self-sufficiency, self-righteousness, self-fulfillment, self-glorification, self-justification, self-preservation of reputation, self-deception, and self-will are all rooted in the flesh. Wow! I suddenly came to an awareness of how deeply infected I was with sin. Charles Spurgeon put it this way, "You cannot slander human nature; it is worse than words can paint it."[4]

Incidentally, we can behave in socially acceptable ways and even find enjoyment in serving others, yet remain self-centered. Trying to please God from self-centered motivation is having a desire to do God's will, but on our own terms and in our own way. King Saul offered sacrifices in his own way instead of waiting for the Prophet Samuel, for example. His sacrifice did not have the blessing of the Lord.

Performing ministry with self-centered motives not only lacks the Lord's blessing, but it can lead to unhealthy competition, comparison, jealously, gossip, strife, slander, bitterness, burnout, and disappointment. I believe these insidious sins are what cause relationships to implode more than anything else. These sins are the reason why many organizations are mired in conflict, remain stagnant, or are in decline. In failing to crucify the flesh, one can easily become disillusioned with ministry. After putting in so much work doing good, blessings do not materialize because nothing has changed in the inner man.

What pleases God is not simply doing good humanitarian works, per se. Pagans do altruistic work in the flesh. What God is most interested in is the godly fruit that is produced in us through continual surrender to the Holy Spirit. God's idea of pure religion is not simply meeting the needs of the less fortunate but also the pursuit of righteousness (James 1:27). The more we release control of our life to the Spirit, the more godly we become. In this way, we comply with God's desire to become holy as He is holy (1 Peter 1:16). By dying to our sinful nature, we can avoid doing God's work in the flesh.

Freedom Requires Vigilance

As servants of the Lord, we must not become complacent in our struggle against the sinful nature. We must be vigilant to remain free. The Apostle Paul makes it clear that we are to consider ourselves dead to sin (Romans 6:6; Colossians 3:3; Galatians 5:24). Indeed, Jesus has already paid the penalty for our sin and has broken its power. But the truth is, sin still exists.

In 1 John 1:8 we read, *"If we claim to be without sin, we deceive ourselves and the truth is not in us."* We are in a constant battle with the sinful nature. Paul explains in Galatians 5:17 that the flesh wars against the Spirit and the Spirit against the flesh. He warns us, *"If you live according to the flesh you will die, but if by the Spirit you put to death the deeds of the body, you will live…. Put to death therefore what is earthly in you"* (Romans 8:13; Colossians 3:5). When it comes to achieving freedom, we must earnestly draw upon the power of the Holy Spirit to put to death the sinful nature. When it comes to achieving freedom through the ministry of deliverance, about 90% is devoted to dying to the flesh. You can easily cast out demons with an authoritative command, but you cannot cast out the flesh. You have to die to the flesh. You must crucify the flesh. The vast amount of work involved in freedom is learning to die to self. With this said, the question remains: what does "dying to the flesh" look like in practical terms?

Remembering the Price Paid for Freedom

Dying to the flesh begins with a commitment to living a holy life, desiring God more than anything else. It means living your life without blemish. Being holy is not a choice. It is a command. Peter says, *"But just as he who called you is holy, so be holy in all you do; for it is written: 'Be holy, because I am holy'"* (1 Peter 1:15-16). Being holy is not just an optional idea. It is a directive from the Lord.

Yet, even when we are committed to becoming holy as God is holy, we sometimes forget how deadly sin is. We forget how offensive our sin is to God. For this reason, we must never lose sight of the immense price God paid for our freedom. It was through the suffering and death of His only begotten Son on the cross that we can be free of sin. Every time we take Holy Communion, we need to be reminded that we are not only forgiven of particular sins but are also set free from the depravity of our sinful nature. Because of the resurrectuion, we have new life. We have been given power through the Holy Spirit to live holy lives.

Many Christians recognize that Christ died to forgive them of their many sins but do not believe Christ died so that they can live free from sin. It has not occurred to them that such freedom is possible. They are so accustomed to deferring to their sinful nature, they do not consider that God has an alternative. They identify more with their sinful nature than they do with their new life in Christ. Although they are saved, they remain in bondage. They may think they are okay, but in truth, they are living far beneath their spiritual inheritance. They have learned to say, "I am a sinner saved by grace." Whereas this statement is true, it is not helpful. Such a statement brands a person with a sinful identity rather than an identity of freedom. It is much better to say, "I am a saint who sometimes sins." Such a statement acknowledges the possibility of sin but embraces a more positive identity of a saint who enjoys freedom.

Biblically speaking, a saint is not someone who has achieved moral perfection. Rather, a saint is someone who has consecrated himself to living a holy life of worship and obedience to God. Saints are made righteous not by their moral perfection, but by the righteousness Christ imputes to them. It is not their righteousness, but Christ's righteousness, that qualifies them for salvation. In this way, they are set apart from the corruption of the world to live a holy life.

However, there is more. Even though we are God's children, we are still living in a corrupt world. To not be influenced by that corruption, we need to grow into maturity. As we grow spiritually, we receive greater measures of righteousness imparted to us as we surrender to, and cooperate with the Spirit.

There Is an Internal War Being Fought

Part of growing into maturity is learning to fight against the enemy who tempts us to sin. When we are converted, the Holy Spirit enters our body and makes it possible to live a holy life. As we learn to surrender more control over to the leadership of the Holy Spirit, sin loses its grip. Eventually, it loses its appeal, allowing us to grow in holiness. However, this is not easily accomplished.

There is a hard-fought war going on between the Spirit and the flesh. The sinful nature wants to do evil, which is the opposite of what the Spirit wants. The Spirit and the flesh have conflicting desires. This is why we cannot always carry out our good intentions. We are like the Apostle Paul who said, *"I don't really understand myself, for I want to do what is right, but I don't do it. Instead, I do what I hate…. Oh, what a miserable person I am! Who will free me from this life that is dominated by sin and death? Thank God! The answer is in Jesus Christ our Lord"* (Romans 7:15, 23-25 NLT*)*. When we are in this conflicted state, fighting these contradictory desires, we are miserable. We feel helpless, as though we are pinned down, unable to free ourselves. We need someone stronger than ourselves to set us free. We need Jesus to not only forgive our sins but to take our sin away. To do this, we need to go to the cross and give Him our sins. In this way, our sinful nature dies with Him. If you struggle with self-sufficiency or self-righteousness or self-pity, you need to take them to the cross and let them die there with Jesus.

The Sinful Nature and Satan

Every war has casualties. Usually, this is not good news. But in this war with Satan, it is good news because you are victorious when you die to self. Paul speaks of this as crucifying the flesh (Galatians 5:24). The degree to which a person is successful in crucifying the flesh will determine whether they remain as a carnal Christian or become a mature Christian who is led by the Spirit. A person who fails to crucify the flesh will be prone to conceit and jealousy (Galatians 5:26), which opens him up to torment from demons. If he is successful in crucifying the flesh, his life will take on the life of the Spirit, which is characterized by the fruit of love, joy, peace, patience, kindness, goodness, faithfulness, gentleness and self-control (Galatians 5:22-23).

Self-interest or desires of the flesh dominate the world. The world proliferates a "me first" approach to life. It is always about me getting what I want, when I want it, and always wanting more. Satan uses this to keep people in bondage. He deceives people into thinking they are serving themselves or even serving

God when they are actually serving the devil. The devil loves it when he can get you to focus on yourself.

This strategy was on full display in Jesus' conversation with Peter, *"...He asked his disciples, 'Who do people say the Son of Man is?' They replied, 'Some say John the Baptist; others say Elijah; and still others, Jeremiah or one of the prophets. 'But what about you?' he asked. 'Who do you say I am?' Simon Peter answered, 'You are the Messiah, the Son of the Living God'"* (Matthew 16:13-16). Jesus immediately recognizes this revelation is from God, rather than from Peter himself. A few verses later, Jesus tells his disciples He must go to Jerusalem to be killed and Peter erupts in protest. He rebukes Jesus, *"Never Lord! he said. This shall never happen to you"* (Matthew 16:22). Jesus responds by saying, *"Get behind me. Satan! You are a stumbling block to me; you do not have in mind the concerns of God, but merely human concerns"* (Matthew 16:23).

Peter's reprimand of Jesus was initiated out of self-interest. He did not want to see Jesus die. That would mean he would not only lose a friend, but his vision for a future kingdom would be in jeopardy. His objection was rooted in a satanic scheme. Satan's chief strategy is to get people to make self-interest their primary goal. If he can do that, he will get them to rebel against God. Peter fell into this trap when he made his own desires the standard for serving Christ. Because he thought he knew what was best for Jesus, he put himself in opposition to the will of God. In essence, whenever we believe we are serving God by seeking our own desired agenda, we are deceived. In ignorance, we resist the Spirit and do the devil's bidding.

Because Peter did not recognize the depravity of his own flesh, he was vulnerable to the devil's schemes. Jesus knew this and later warned Peter that Satan was going to sift him as wheat. Jesus was not distressed by this. Instead, he saw it as an opportunity for Peter to learn a valuable lesson. It would be a lesson that would enable him to encourage his brothers once he repented (Luke 22:31-32).

The test came when the rooster crowed three times and Peter denied knowing Christ three times. Peter had previously boasted that he would go to prison or even die for Christ, but when push came to shove, he chose to protect himself. Fortunately, Jesus reinstated Peter into His service by helping him get in touch with the love that was in his heart rather than deferring to his self-centeredness. Three times Jesus asked Peter, "Do you love me?" Three times Peter affirmed his love for Him (John 21:15). Calling people to love God and love others is an effective way to help people get free of themselves.

Learning to die to the desires of the flesh requires the practice of disciplines that demonstrate love for Christ. Several strategies need to be applied to transition from a childish carnal Christian to a mature Spirit-led Christian.

Strategies to Overcome the Flesh

Acknowledge that our human nature is utterly sinful and selfish.

In doing so, we establish our need for God (Romans 7:14-24). Such an acknowledgement produces humility that recognizes the need for grace (James 4:10). Embracing such poverty of spirit opens the way for God's blessing (Luke 6:20). Blessings come through the power of God that puts to death the deeds of the sinful nature (Romans 8:13).

Recognize that our sinful nature is part of the world and is antithetical to the love of the Father.

The Bible identifies worldliness as not only immoral behavior, but also internal attitudes. In 1 John 2:16, three things are identified connecting to the sinful nature: the lust of the flesh (physical cravings), the lust of the eyes (cravings for material things), and the boastful pride of life (obsession with status and importance). It is in these three areas that Satan tempts us to sin against God. Satan tempted Jesus this way in the wilderness (Matthew 4:3-10).

Take responsibility to purify ourselves of sinful desires.

By confessing our sin, we position ourselves to receive grace and healing (2 Corinthians 7:1; 1 John 1:9; James 5:16). The Greek word *iaomai* translated as "healed" in James 5:16 can refer to either a physical cure or being set free from error or sin in order to bring about salvation. Those who have the hope of becoming like Christ purify themselves just as He is pure (1 John 3:3).

Take off the old nature and put on the new man.

In this way, we become righteous and holy (Ephesians 4:22-24; Colossians 3:9-11). This taking off and putting on enables us to take on a new identity as a child of God in the likeness of Christ (Ephesians 1:5). Romans 13:14 says, *"Rather, clothe yourselves with the Lord Jesus Christ, and do not think about how to gratify the desires of the flesh."*

Cooperate with the Holy Spirit.

The Holy Spirit is the Spirit of **truth**, who reveals our hidden sins, convicting us to confess our sin and to receive power to overcome the flesh (Ephesians 1:16-23; I Corinthians 10:13; 1 John 1:9)). Good intentions alone do not bring about transformation. It only happens through the power of God, like that which raised Jesus from the dead (Ephesians 1:18-20).

Be careful not to slip back into old ways.

Be aware of how easy it is to revert into worldly patterns of thought. Be obedient to what the Spirit says. He will guide you into all truth. Cry out for a pure spiritual life so that you may have a full experience of salvation (1 Peter 1:14; John 14:17; 1 Peter 2:2).

Take care of yourself.

This may seem contradictory, but it is not. All of us have needs. Matthew 6:8 says that the Father knows our needs even before we ask. Jesus teaches us to ask for what we need (Matthew 6:11, 7:7-12). James 4:2 says, *"You do not have because you do not ask God."* It is our responsibility to ask God to fill us with his Spirit. It is when we allow our cup to be made full that we have something to pour into others. Jesus commands us to love our neighbors as we love ourselves (Matthew 22:39). We can only give to others what we have first received. We all need to be loved. Having our need for love met enables us to love others the way God loves us. For a brief description of love needs, see Appendix F.

Be willing to submit to others out of reverence for Christ (Ephesians 5:21).

This is the opposite of what the world teaches. It teaches self-assertion, self-protection, and demanding your rights without regard to how it impacts others. It is making yourself and your agenda first. The Bible teaches us to love and serve others, looking out for their welfare. We are to consider their best interest ahead of our own (Philippians 2:3-4).

Remain humble in a world that rewards pride.

We are used to asserting ourselves, not humbling ourselves. Do not allow knowledge, status, spiritual experiences, or revelation to create spiritual pride (Romans 11:18, 20, 25; 12:16, 14:4). Choose to make yourself humble. Rather than defaulting to harsh circumstances, pain, or tragedy to humble you, voluntarily choose humility (Luke 18:13-14; 1 Peter 5:5-6; James 4:6-7; Matthew

23:12). Recognize that all your accomplishments are made possible by the grace of God. Paul, said, "*I am what I am by the grace of God*" (1 Corinthians 15:10).

Practical Steps for Dying to Self

1. **Believe the truth that your old sinful nature is already dead** (Romans 6:6; Colossians 3:3; Galatians 5:24). It died when Christ was crucified on the cross. You are set free to choose righteousness.

2. **Seek to live in the freedom Christ has provided** (Romans 6:11; 2 Corinthians 7:1; 1 John 3:2-3). Confess and surrender your self-centeredness, self-ambition, self-consciousness, etc. Receive the grace of God (John 12:24). It is in an environment of grace that new life in Christ flourishes.

3. **Develop a genuine hate for sin.** Sin destroys our souls (Proverbs 8:36; 1 Peter 2:11) and separates us from God. For this reason, God hates sin (Isaiah 59:1-2), and so should we. Sin is the antithesis of God's holy nature (Psalm 5:4).

4. **Keep in mind sin's empty promises.** Sin may offer short term gratification, but it only lasts for season, then leaves you unsatisfied and unfulfilled (Hebrews 11:25).

5. **Know that sin cannot be kept secret.** It will be exposed. Its destructive nature will become apparent (Numbers 32:23). If you attempt to hide your sin, you will not be successful (Proverbs 28:13).

6. **Be confident that whenever you are tempted to sin,** you do not need to comply. There is a way out of it (1 Corinthians 10:13-16). Don't be bullied by sin's deceitful lusts, half-truths and lies (Romans 6:12; Ephesians 4:22). Surrender to truth, not your feelings.

7. **Commit yourself to submitting to God daily.** Decide to live in right relationship with Him and be an instrument for righteousness (Romans 6:13; 12:1). God's blessings of protection and provision cannot flow if you are not surrendered to His rule. Submit all hurt from offenses to God (1 Peter 5:7). Submit to Christ's Lordship by taking up your cross daily (Matthew 16:24-26).

8. **Do not put yourself in a place where sin can access your soul.** Guard your heart and eyes (Proverbs 4:23; Romans 13:14).

9. **Be careful of the company you keep.** You are prone to pick up habits like those of the people you associate with (1 Corinthians 15:33).

10. **Admit failures and confess all known sin daily** (1 John 1:9). Ask God for forgiveness (Matthew 6:12). Admit your faults to others and be healed (James 5:16).

11. **Discipline your mind to think on things of God.** Learn to renew your mind (Romans 12:2) by thinking on things of the Spirit, things above, and things that are positive (Romans 8:5; Colossians 3:2; Philippians 4:8). Feed your spirit, not your flesh. Worship joyfully and give thanks daily (Ephesians 5:19-20). Take every thought captive to Christ (2 Corinthians 10:5). Pray continually, without ceasing (1 Thessalonians 5:16).

12. **Recognize the spirit of the age.** Be aware of what the world is trying to get you to believe and do (Romans 12:2) In our time, the spirit of the age is entitlement and self-indulgence. "If it feels good, do it" is the world's slogan. Truth is relevant, not absolute. Repent! Turn away from these.

13. **Expect to be tested. Jesus was tested by Satan and by men.** Don't let negative circumstances create unbelief or offenses create bitterness (John 16:33, Ephesians 4:26; Luke 17:1-4; Matthew 18:23-35). Be willing to forgive. Understand trials as a refining process (1 Peter 1:6-7; James 1:2-4).

14. **Ask the Holy Spirit to help you to overcome the flesh by imparting the fruit of the Spirit and the gifts of the Spirit.** Put on the armor of God (Romans 8:13; Galatians 5:22; 1 Corinthians 14:1; Ephesians 6:11-18). Speak in tongues. In this way, you die to your own way of thinking and build yourself up in the Spirit (Jude 1:20).

15. **Be part of a local fellowship that will hold you accountable** by speaking the truth in love and instructs you to be cautious of the deceitfulness of sin (Hebrews 3:13; Ephesians 4:15).

16. **Recognize that sin encumbers your ability to hear God's voice.** It quenches the spirit and reduces your ability to receive divine wisdom (Hebrews 5:11; 1 Thessalonians 5:19-22; James 3:13-17).

17. **Resist the impulse to sin with the determination of an athlete** who fights to win a boxing match or a runner who fights fatigue in a marathon (1 Corinthians 9:27; 2 Timothy 4:7). Overcome temptation with Scripture and prayer (Psalm 119:11,67; Matthew 26:41).

18. **Know that sin damages your testimony, weakens your evangelism, and prevents others from seeing God** (Hebrews 12:14).

19. **Be aware how easy it is to let yourself slip into "works of the law"** forgetting that "works of faith" are the basis of your warfare (Galatians 3:2-3, 5; 1 Thessalonians 1:10-11). Trust God's promises rather than your own efforts.

20. **Be alert to double-mindedness and deceitfulness.** Be willing to mourn and grieve your self-deception. It is possible to entertain sinful thoughts and worldly motives, all the while thinking you doing God's will (James 4:8-9, Jeremiah 17:9). Avoid pretense, giving the appearance of being kind to others, while your motive is to promote your own enterprise (Colossians 3:9). Be sensitive to false humility, particularly if you find yourself talking a lot about "your" ministry or deflecting the praise of others.

21. **Ask the Lord for wisdom and revelation, so that you may know the hope that God gives His holy people** (Ephesians 1:18). Pay attention to the sin to which the Holy Spirit is convicting (John 16:8). Confess it, ask forgiveness, receive grace, and repent of it (James 1:5; Jeremiah 33:3; Daniel 2:22).

22. **Make declarations that align with the Word of God.** Replace lies with the truth. Hold fast to the promises of God. Affirm your identity in Christ. Words have power (Proverbs 18:21). They impart grace (Ephesians 4:29). They can unlock your destiny (Judges 6:12).

23. **Recognize you have a built-in tendency to be confident in your own ability,** knowledge, toughness, and righteousness. You have a bent toward comparing, judging, criticizing, blaming, and looking down on others. This is the opposite of being Christ-like (Luke 18:10-14; Proverbs 16:18).

24. **Remember it is humility that moves the heart of God.** It is not your own knowledge, talent, skill, or ambition that impresses God to bestow His grace. Being humble moves the hand of God (James 4:6). Pride goes before destruction (Proverbs 16:18).

25. **Know that you cannot crucify yourself alone.** You may be able to nail one hand to the cross but you can't nail the second without help. Rely on others to speak the truth in love into your life. Others can see your blind spots and help you die to them (John 5:16).

26. **Ask the Lord what Satan is accusing you of.** After hearing the Lord's reply confess it, ask forgiveness, receive forgiveness, renounce it, break all connections with it, and receive God's grace (Revelations 12:10; James 1:5).

27. **Spend extended time alone with the Lord.** Go into your prayer closet to commune privately with the Lord (Matthew 6:6). Worship the Lord daily

(1 Chronicles 16:23). Worship is an act of an abandoned heart devoted to God. Go on spiritual retreats (Mark 6:31).

28. **Periodically fast as an act of self-denial, an expression of humbling oneself before God** (1 Kings 21:27-29). Fasting reveals a surrendered and consecrated heart. It demonstrates a reverence and need for God. It denies the flesh in order to engage the Spirit.

29. **Ask God to reveal any area of offensiveness in your heart to which you may be blind.** Listen for the Lord's answer. Ask the Lord what you should do with what He reveals (Psalm 139:23-24). Confess your faults to others and pray for others that you may be healed (James 5:16).

30. **Ask the Lord to teach you how to be content in all things** (Philippians 4:11-13). Let the peace of God rule your heart through the practice of thanksgiving and prayer (Philippians 4:5-7). Ask the Lord to help you wait on Him (Isaiah 40:31). Believe God causes all things to work out for the ultimate good for those who give themselves to the purposes of God (Romans 8:28). Trust in the Lord with all your heart and do not lean on your own understanding (Proverbs 3:5).

31. **Remember a cloud of witnesses surrounds you.** Be willing to cast off that which weighs you down and causes you to stumble (Hebrews 12:1-2). Be aware of wrong beliefs and unbelief. Remember, what is not of faith is sin (Romans 14:23).

32. **Ask yourself if you can take delight in honoring others above yourself.** Ask those close to you how well you are at doing this. If this is a problem, you may be more self-centered than you realize (Romans 12:9-10; Philippians 2:3-4). Can you rejoice with those who rejoice (Romans 12:15)? Can you celebrate the achievements of others without competing, comparing, or coveting (1 Corinthians 3:3; Galatians 5:26)?

33. **Be aware of how you make others feel.** Do they feel what they have to say is valued or do you dominate the conversation? Do you always have to be right or have the last word? Do you intimidate with your knowledge and expertise? Romans 12:3 says, *"Do not think of yourself more highly than you ought, but rather think of yourself with sober judgment."*

34. **Take an inventory of your language in response to those who resist and oppose you.** Ask the Lord to forgive you for speaking negative words, gossip, or curses against anyone. Receive forgiveness and repent from such behavior (Romans 12:14). Ask the Lord to annul all curses and negative judgments

you have spoken. Never take revenge (Romans 12:19). Do good to those who oppose you (Romans 12:20). Ask the Lord to give you a gentle tongue that speaks the truth in love (Ephesians 4:15) and an instructed tongue to comfort the weary (Isaiah 50:4). Declare: *"The words of my mouth and the meditations of my heart will be pleasing to the Lord"* (Psalm 19:14).

35. **Take your hurts, disappointments, unmet expectations, and anxiety to the Lord. Cast your cares upon the Lord** (1 Peter 5:7). With thanksgiving make your request to God (Philippians 4:6). Don't let your heart be troubled or afraid. Take comfort in the Holy Spirit, who is your Advocate (John 14:1, 16). Don't process your pain alone. Seek the help and encouragement of others (1 Thessalonians 5:11; 2 Corinthians. 1:3-4; Hebrews 10:25).

36. **Ask your spouse if they feel that you put his or her welfare, ideas, and opinions ahead of your own.** If he or she does not feel honored, determine if you are being self-centered and decide what can be done to make the relationship mutually fulfilling (Ephesians 5:21-33). Be willing to submit to each other out of reverence for Christ (Ephesians 5:21).

37. **Bring a tithe to God: 10% of your income.** This act of faith demonstrates that you put the worship of God rather than of yourself first (Malachi 3:10).

38. **Remember your need and give thanks for God's mercy.** We have all sinned and fallen short of the glory of God (Romans 3:23). We need God's continual mercy and forgiveness (Psalm 86:5 LB). Because of our weaknesses, we need to continually go into the throne room of our merciful God to receive grace (Hebrews 4:15-16 CEV).

39. **Remain keenly aware of the order of things.** God is a God of order, not confusion (Genesis 1; 1 Corinthians 11:1-6; 1 Corinthians 14:33, 40). Dying to self involves honoring God's order. You can be doing good by worldly standards but miss God's blessings because your good does not align with God's best (Luke 10:38-42).

Principles of Order in the Kingdom

God has established spiritual laws by which His kingdom operates. These laws have to do with the way things work. Psalm 103:7 says, *"He made known His ways to Moses, His deeds to the people of Israel."* God prescribes the order in which things are done to realize the kingdom of righteousness.

It is the responsibility of every Christian to manifest the kingdom of righteousness here on earth. This is accomplished through obedience to God in the power of the Spirit. If believers do godly things in their own way instead of God's way, some good things may happen—but without following the leading of the Spirit, they will not receive the full blessings of God. By observing God's order, you die to the flesh and live in the Spirit. Following are some examples of the way things are done according to God's Word.

- **Presence precedes purpose** John 15:5

- **Repentance precedes refreshment of Holy Spirit** Acts 2:38, 3:19-20

- **Giving precedes receiving** Luke 6:38; Galatians 6:7

- **Giving forgiveness precedes receiving forgiveness** Matthew 6:14-15

- **Passion precedes power** Romans 1:16; 1 Thessalonians 1:5

- **Surrender precedes freedom** James 4:7

- **Confession, forgiveness, and cleansing precedes righteousness** 1 John 1:9

- **Righteousness precedes provision** Matthew 6:33; Proverbs 10:3; Deuteronomy 28:1-14

- **Submission precedes leadership** Matthew 8:8-10; Matthew 20:26; Ephesians 5:21-33

- **Relationship precedes revelation** Deuteronomy 29:29; Psalm 25:14; Amos 3:7; Proverbs 3:5

- **Heavenly transaction precedes human achievement** John 5:19; Matthew 3 & 4

- **Hearing God's voice precedes doing God's work** Matthew 7:24-27; John 10:27; Romans 10:17

- **Discernment precedes direction** 1 Thessalonians 5:20-21; Acts 21:10-14

- **Love precedes knowledge** 1 Corinthians 8:3; 1 Corinthians 13:2

- **Being precedes doing** Ephesians 2:10; 2 Corinthians 5:17; Proverbs 23:7

- **Identity precedes destiny** Romans 12:2, John 3:21

- **Grieving precedes comfort** Matthew 5:4

- **Humility precedes honor** 1 Peter 5:6; Philippians 2:3; James 4:10; Proverbs 15:33

- **Honor precedes unity** 1 Corinthians 12:12-27

- **Unity precedes blessing** Psalm 133

- **Hope precedes purification** 1 John 3:3

- **Justification and sanctification precede glorification** Romans 8:30; Hebrews 12:14

- **Faith in God's promises precedes the fulfilment of God's promises** Romans 4: 13; Hebrews 4:2

If these get out of order, you are likely operating in the flesh and not in the Spirit.

In the next chapter, we will see that humility is the best way to die to self.

Discussion Questions

1. If you heard God say, "If you want to change your culture, you must be willing to die," how might you respond?

2. Why do you think D. L. Moody says you must pray that God will empty you before God will fill you up?

3. What keeps a person from receiving wisdom from heaven? What do you think about Tim Keller's comments about pride?

4. What do you think Paul meant when he referred to crucifying the flesh? What does selfish ambition look like? How would you describe your sinful nature?

5. What can you expect if you do ministry from self-centered motives? How can taking Holy Communion help you die to the flesh?

6. How do you experience the war between the flesh and the Spirit? How did Satan take advantage of Peter's sinful nature? How does he do it to you?

7. Of the nine strategies given for combating the sinful nature which one's appeal to you the most? Of the thirty-eight practical things you can do to die to the flesh, which ones do you think you will most likely implement?

8. How important is it to get things in order when trying to avoid serving God in the flesh? Can you think of more things that need to be added to the list?

Endnotes

1. https://www.goodreads.com/quotes/4474-i-firmly-believe-that-the-moment-our-hearts-are-emptied2. https://quotefancy.com/quote/921449/Timothy-Keller-Pride-is-the-carbon-monoxide-of-Sin-It-silently-and-slowly-kills-you
3. https://www.goodreads.com/quotes/183754-no-pain-no-palm-no-thorns-no-throne-no-gall
4. https://www.azquotes.com/quote/353566

14

Living Free

Humility is Key to Dying to the Flesh

I already stated that humility plays a key role in the acquisition of freedom. Humility is what justifies us before God. It is something we must choose to do with the conviction of the Holy Spirit.

In Luke 18:13, Jesus told the story of the Pharisee and tax collector praying in the temple. The Pharisee extolled his own virtues in terms of gratitude. He gave thanks for his self-acquired righteousness, comparing himself to other men. On the other hand, the tax collector chose to acknowledge his sin while beating his chest. He made no excuse or comparison. He simply expressed his sorrow. Jesus concluded the story saying: *"I tell you, this sinner, not the Pharisee, returned home justified before God. For those who exalt themselves will be humbled, and **those who humble themselves** will be exalted"* (Luke 18:14 NLT, emphasis mine). Choosing to acknowledge your sinful nature is the first step toward freedom.

Humility recognizes that there is nothing good about our human nature. When we come to Christ, we come in humility. The Greek word for *humility* means 'lowliness of mind." Humility admits to absolute bankruptcy of moral and spiritual worth inherent to oneself. Jesus said, *"Blessed are the poor in spirit, for theirs is the kingdom of heaven"* (Matthew 5:3). The way we receive salvation is by admitting our spiritual poverty and our need for Christ. The way to remain in Christ is choosing to die daily to pride through the practice of humility. God has promised to give grace to the humble, but He opposes the proud (Proverbs 3:34; 1 Peter 5:5).

In John 12:24-25, Jesus says, *"Very truly I tell you, unless a kernel of wheat falls to the ground and dies, it remains only a single seed. But if it dies, it produces many seeds. Anyone who loves their life will lose it, while anyone who hates their life in this world will keep it for eternal life."* To die to self requires a hate for yourself. This hate is not self-condemnation in which you grovel, telling yourself what a terrible person you are. Instead, the kind of self-hate Jesus is referring to is not thinking of yourself at all. It is ignoring the lustful desires of the flesh in order to turn your full attention on God. It is treating your lustful desires as though they were dead in order to concentrate on the God's presence. This is what it means to delight in the fear of the Lord (Isaiah 11:3). Humility focuses on the worship of God rather than preoccupation with self. True humility is rooted in a desire to die to pride, in order to obey and glorify God.

Paul spoke of this kind of godly humility when writing to the Philippians. He told them they should have the same attitude that Jesus had. He said of Jesus, *"Though he was God, he did not think of equality with God as something to cling to. Instead, he gave up his divine privileges, he took the humble position of a slave and was born as a human being. When he appeared in human form, he humbled himself in obedience to God"* (Philippians 2:6-8 NLT). Humility always chooses obedience to God over the desires of the flesh. It desires intimacy or closeness to God rather than godlike privileges or credit. Humility is a choice we make in order to be like Jesus.

Choosing to Be a Servant

Jesus' attitude was like that of a servant. He did not come to be served, but to serve and give his life for many (Matthew 20:28). One way to die to selfish ambition is to cultivate an attitude of sacrificial service.

Recently, I read that the world renown tightrope walker, Nik Wallenda, is a Christian. He has performed incredible death-defying acts by walking across Niagara Falls in 2012 and walking across the Grand Canyon in 2013. Knowing that he is the best in the world at performing his craft, someone asked him how he keeps from becoming prideful. His response was a bit surprising. Instead of getting in a limousine after his performance, he would spend hours cleaning up the trash that his fans left behind. He said:

> "Three hours of cleaning debris is good for my soul. Humility does not come naturally to me. So, if I have to force myself into situations that are humbling, so be it.… I do it… because it's a way to keep from tripping. As a follower of Jesus, I see Him washing the feet of others. I do it because if I don't serve others, I'll be serving nothing but my ego."[1]

The ultimate solution for the pride problem is to choose to be humble. Humility involves more than doing good deeds, since one can be prideful when rendering service to others. Humility is an inner attitude that keeps the ego in check. The Scriptures offer several ways to humble yourself:

1. **By confessing your sin to others** (Luke 18:10-14)

2. **By serving others** (Matthew 23:11-12)

3. **By honoring others,** valuing them above yourself (Philippians 2:3-4)

4. **By submitting** to others (1 Peter 5:5-6)

5. **By asking for help** (2 Chronicles 7:14; Proverbs 12:15)

6. **By not looking to please men,** rather seek God's approval (Matthew 6:3-6; Galatians 1:10)

7. **By changing the way you think** by renewing your mind with the truth (Romans 12:2)

8. **By not thinking highly of yourself,** but thinking with sober judgment (Romans 12:3)

9. **By not trusting in your own knowledge,** but trusting God to show the way (Proverbs 3:5).

10. **By recognizing that knowledge makes you feel important,** but love strengthens the church (1 Corinthians 8:1-30); get in touch with the love in your heart; take an interest in the well-being of others (Philippians 2:4).

11. **By being honest about your weaknesses,** believing God uses broken vessels to accomplish His purposes through His power (2 Corinthians 4:7 CEV)

12. **By living for a higher purpose than self,** rather the message and ministry of Jesus Christ (Ephesians 2:10 LB; 2 Corinthians 4:5 GW)

Eyes Opened to the Truth Fosters Humility

Through most of my years of ministry, I thought I had an obligation to make sure that what I was teaching and preaching was doctrinally correct. I studied in depth, making sure my points were correct and defendable. I was vigilant not to succumb to any false doctrine while remaining open to revelation from the Spirit. That was well and good, but sometimes the quest to be right overshadowed the need to be humble. It was then I crossed the line. I stepped out of humility into self-ambition, out of the Spirit and into the flesh. I rationalized this need to be always right by telling myself that the salvation of others depended on it.

Fortunately, my understanding was enlightened after reading an article that encouraged the reader to ask God: "What is Satan accusing you of?" That opened my eyes. In prayer, I asked the question, "Lord, what is Satan accusing me of?" What I heard back was sobering and humbling. I heard the words pugnacious, belligerent, and patronizing. I had only a vague sense of what these words meant, so I went to the dictionary to get a clear definition. I was appalled at what I read. *Pugnacious* means "combative, quick to argue or dispute." *Belligerent* means "aggressive and contentious." *Patronizing* means "kind and helpful but feeling superior." These definitions were hard for me to swallow, but deep down, I knew the accusations were true. They were not only true of me but also for generations before me. They were family traits. I repented of these sins and gradually began to see a difference in the way I responded to grievances and offenses. My visceral reactions were more relaxed. I became less defensive. I sensed a growing gentleness in my spirit.

Sometimes we get stuck in patterns of behavior for which we need to repent but fail to do so because we are blind to our own sin. It is at such times that God uses circumstances of life to get our attention. We could be presented with questions we cannot answer, relationships we cannot fix, problems we cannot solve, diseases we cannot cure, or events we cannot control. God uses these things to expose the condition of our hearts.

Once we realize the depth of our sin, we can either humble ourselves and repent or remain prideful and hard hearted. This was true in my case. It was only after going through several years of family crisis and turmoil in ministry that I slowly began to understand what Jesus was telling me in the movie theater. If you want to change your culture, your life must demonstrate humility. Along the way, I learned that humility goes along with transparency. It is one thing to say, "I am a sinner." It is quite another to say, "this is my sin."

Our fallen human nature is completely and utterly selfish. We are born wanting all our needs met immediately. We demand to be fed, to be cleaned up, and to be held. If we are not taught differently, we will continue to live as self-centered, immature children. We will remain blind to the influence the sinful nature has on us. But as Christians, there is a higher call to die to self (1 Corinthians 15:31), to put off our old nature and put on the "new man" (Ephesians 4:22-24; Colossians 3:3-11).

Humility Hates Sin

Humility teaches a healthy hate for sin. The Scriptures indicate that sin destroys the soul of a person (Proverbs 6:16-19). Sin damages people's minds, emotions, and relationships. Eventually, it is so destructive that it brings death. In contrast, God is about creating, sustaining, and restoring life. God is grieved and provoked by sin because it separates man from Himself. Due to this separation, He sent Jesus as a sacrificial lamb who takes away the sin of the world. Jesus took on our sin, enduring the shame of the cross so that we could be set free from the power of sin. God hates sin, and so should we. Sin is the antithesis of God's holy nature. God does not condemn a believer when they commit a sin. However, He becomes sufficiently angry to do something about it. He disciplines those He loves (Hebrews 12:26), showing them the way of truth through the Holy Spirit (John 16:13).

If you truly appreciate what God has done for you through Jesus Christ, you will not want to allow any sin, no matter how small it may be, to get in the way of your relationship with God. You will confess and repent of it immediately. You will joyfully ask others to point out any sin in your life, especially those you may not be aware of. You will turn to the Holy Spirit for restoration, healing, and freedom.

One of the deceitful sins of the flesh that often escapes our attention is coveting (Mark 7:21-23; Romans 13:9; James 4:1-2). It is a hidden sin located in the heart. Coveting is desiring something that does not belong to you. It is a form of pride, thinking more of yourself in relation to others. If you are truly humble, you will have died to the desire to possess what others have and will not lust after their status, influence, talents, or possessions. Instead, you will be content with what God has provided and called you to. A humble person is not jealous, nor does he compete or compare himself with another (John 21). Such competing and comparison leads to quarreling (James 4:2).

A humble person is secure in the love, identity, and calling that Christ has given him. On the other hand, coveting is rooted in anxiety and insecurity. It obsesses over what it does not have and is consumed by thoughts of what it thinks it deserves. A person struggling with pride will have difficulty sincerely honoring others. They may flatter others, but deep down, they are more concerned about advancing their own agendas. The Apostle Paul told the Philippians, *"Do nothing out of selfish-ambition or vein conceit. Rather, in humility value others above yourselves, not looking to own interests but each of you to the interest of others"* (Philippians 2:3-4). The ability to honor others stems from a humble heart that has emptied itself of pride.

Humility versus False Humility

Humility involves having a humble opinion of yourself and your importance, having an accurate self-awareness, and seeing yourself the way God sees you. Being humble does not mean being inferior. Humble people appreciate their abilities but do not esteem themselves above others. Humility is not thinking less of yourself; it is not thinking of yourself at all. It gives space for others to shine. Paul wrote in Philippians 2:3, *"Do nothing from selfish or empty conceit [through factional motives or strife], but with [an attitude of] humility [being neither arrogant nor self-righteous], regard others as more important than yourselves"* (AMP).

On the other hand, false humility is pride in disguise. Attempting to appear humble, a person will discount their contribution or devalue themselves. For example, a person may deflect praise, appear to be helpless or powerless, refuse credit, or engage in self-deprecating humor. A person may fish for unwanted compliments by telling glowing stories of themselves while verbally giving credit to God or others. Ironically, in trying to look humble, they attempt to draw attention to themselves.

The best way to avoid false humility is to maintain an attitude of gratitude. Hold power and position very loosely. Do not let your abilities or good deeds define your personal significance. Graciously accept the praise of others with a simple "thank you." Concentrate on serving others without regard to what others think of you. Take your identity not from what you do but from who you are.

Believers are taught about the value of humility but live in a world that endorses self-promotion. This conflict is a constant source of tension. How do we remain humble and avoid false humility? By relying on the Holy Spirit and avoiding personal judgments based on performance, we can evade this conflict.

When I judge my works of service as the measurement of my worth to the Lord and to others, I become subject to false humility and religious spirits. Even when I deflect compliments, the focus remains on my talents and accomplishments. When my focus remains on me rather than on what God is doing through me, false humility embroils me.

It is better to recognize the truth, as did the Apostle Paul. He saw himself as both a sinner and a saint and recognized both his unworthiness and his righteousness. He said, *"I am what I am by the grace of God"* (1 Corinthians 15:10). True humility acknowledges that I am who I am in Christ because of the grace of God. Like Paul, I can be both the chief of sinners (1 Timothy 1:15) and at the same time be an apostle worthy to be imitated (1 Corinthians 11:1). True humility is reflected not in devaluing my good deeds but in dying to self.

Humility Gives Way to Love

The way to realize the depth and width of God's love is to recognize the full extent of our sin. In Luke 7, Jesus was visiting a pharisee named Simon.

A woman in that town who lived a sinful life learned that Jesus was eating at the Pharisee's house, so she came there with an alabaster jar of perfume. As she stood behind him at his feet weeping, she began to wet his feet with her tears. Then she wiped them with her hair, kissed them and poured perfume on them (Luke 7:37-38).

When Jesus saw Simon's contempt for the woman and recognized all the degradation she had suffered over the years, He told a parable about the payment of debts. A man owed a lender 500 denarii. Another man owed the same lender 50 denarii. The money lender nullified each man's debt. Jesus then asked Simon which of the debtors loved the moneylender the most. Simon said it was the man who owed the most debt. Jesus told Simon he had answered correctly, then pointed out to Simon how he had not provided water to wash Jesus' feet, but that the woman washed them with her tears. He then said, *"Therefore, I tell you, her many sins have been forgiven—as her great love has shown. But whoever has been forgiven little loves little"* (Luke 7:47).

This story illustrates that the more we are in touch with our sinfulness, the more we appreciate the depth of God's forgiveness, grace, and love. It only follows that the more we realize the full depravity of our flesh, the more apt we are to demonstrate gratitude to God and compassion for people. Besides, the more we get in touch with our sinful nature and recognize our need for God's grace, the more likely we are to grow in humility.

Paul Grows in Humility

This was certainly true of the Apostle Paul. The longer he walked with Jesus, the more aware he became of his own sinfulness. This awareness produced in him a growing sense of humility. Prior to his conversion, he was a pharisee among pharisees. In his self-righteousness, he religiously persecuted Christians. Five years into his faith walk, he was given a special revelation of heaven. By his own admission, he believed the Lord gave him a thorn in the flesh in order to keep him spiritually humble (2 Corinthians 12:7). Over the years Paul grew in humility, evidenced in what he said about himself in his letters. Notice the progression in his life. Prior to establishing a relationship with Jesus, he was a proud and zealous man. Sometime after his conversion, he joined up with Barnabas, who connected him with other believers in Jerusalem. Barnabas mentored him until they went their separate ways over a disagreement concerning John Mark. Notice what he says about himself nearly twenty years after his conversion in writing to the Corinthians (emphasis mine):

- In AD 55, he wrote in 1 Corinthians 15:9, *"I am the **least of the apostles** and do not even deserve to be called an apostle, because I persecuted the church of God."*

- In AD 57, he wrote in Romans 7: 14, 18 NLT, *"I am all too human, a slave to sin…. I know **nothing good lives in me,** that is my sinful nature."*

- In AD 60, he wrote in Ephesians 3:8, *"I am **less than the least** of the Lord's people."*

- In AD 64, he wrote in 1 Timothy 1:15, *"Christ Jesus came into the world to save sinner – of **whom I am the worst."***

Shortly after writing to Timothy, Paul was martyred in Rome. In thinking about himself, Paul went from being the least of the apostles to the worst sinner that ever lived.

Despite his great gifts, knowledge, overcoming of trials, and receiving incredible revelations, Paul grew in humility. The more intimate he became in his relationship with Christ, the more he walked in humility. Like Paul, the truly humble will grow in humility. They will increasingly depend on and celebrate God's grace. Emptying oneself of pride requires a daily effort. It has a cumulative effect. Over the course of many years of practice, a spirit of humility sews itself into one's character.

This poem by a young pastor friend of mine, Christopher J. Tangert, speaks about his transformation as he has learned to die to himself.

The person you now see
Is not who I used to be

I'm waving bye,
And I ain't gonna cry,

That kid was shy,
I surrendered him to Christ, and said,
it's time for him to die

The person I used to be
Is not who you now see

Formerly addicted to porn
A heart filled with hate and scorn

Formerly playing the blame game
I was always walking in shame,

I used to think that life was fun
But, now I understand,
what it's like to be a son.

Like I said, the person you now see
Is not who I used to be

From the last time I spoke
I'm a bit more woke
That sweet amazing Grace
Removed the blinders, so I can now run the race

Like I've said in the past, The king of Glory
HE came to rewrite my story
HE's here to rewrite your story

Now I'll keep pursuing HIS Glory
I'll keep swimming after HIM,
like my friend named Dory

He's not a fake king like Mufasa
He's a Real King, my king, Jehovah Rapha

Like an elf on a shelf
That's where I put my old self

Now all I am
Is for the great I Am
Like I've said

The person you now see
Is not who I used to be
The person you now see
Is Christ in me

Charles Spurgeon eloquently asserted, "Beware of no man more than of yourself; we carry our worst enemies within us."[2]

Similarly, Dr. Paul David Tripp explains, "What's inside of us is far more dangerous to us than what's outside of us. You can live beyond your history, you can run from a bad situation, you can escape a destructive relationship, but you simply cannot run away from yourself."

In Summary, You Experience Freedom When You:

1. **Acknowledge how utterly sinful** you are by nature.

2. **Recognize the three ways Satan appeals to your sinful nature** to tempt you.

3. **Take responsibility to purify yourself** from all defilements, especially pride.

4. **Take off the old identity and put on the new.**

5. **Cooperate with the Holy Spirit,** who gives revelation and power to overcome the sinful flesh.

6. **Avoid slipping back into old patterns** by asking God for a pure heart.

7. **Develop a love for God and a hate for sin** by being attentive to your need for continual forgiveness.

8. **Consistently choose do things that foster humility** over time.

9. **Be part of a community of believers** that are committed to your spiritual growth and freedom that they will earnestly hold you accountable by speaking the truth in love. They will hear your confession without judging you.

By learning to die to yourself and by crucifying the flesh, you will not only grow in humility but also in the Holy Spirit. God is pleased by your desire to become holy through humility and wants to bless you. James 4:6 states: *"God opposes the proud but shows favor to the humble."* Part of His favor involves receiving His authority and power that enables you to live free of demonic oppression. The next chapter will address freedom from demonic spirits.

Discussion Questions

1. Why do you suppose it is an attitude of humility that justifies us before God?

2. God has promised to give grace to the humble. What does that mean to you? How does Jesus' instruction to hate your life fit in with His command to love your neighbor as you love yourself?

3. Nik Wallenda intentionally puts himself into a humbling situation to develop humility in his character. Can you identify some situations where you could do that?

4. Ask God what Satan is accusing you of. Listen for what God says. Be ready to repent. Share with someone what you are led to confess.

5. God hates sin, and so should we. Why should we hate sin? Is it valid to say that coveting is a sin that we don't think much about? Why or why not?

6. What is the difference between humility and false humility? How does getting in touch with our sin help us grow in gratitude and compassion?

7. Paul's life shows that he grew in his capacity to be humble. What do suppose were some of the things that contributed to this?

8. Charles Spurgeon said, "Beware of no man more than of yourself; we carry our worst enemies within us." How can we be aware of our worst self yet not succumb to poor self-esteem?

8. Dr. Paul David Tripp says, "What's inside of us is far more dangerous to us than what's outside of us." Do you believe that? Why or why not?

Endnotes

1. Kyle Idleman, *The End of Me: Where Real Life in the Upside-down Ways of Jesus Begins,* (David C. Cook, Colorado Springs, CO, 2015), p. 84.

2. Charles Spurgeon, "According to Promise: Or, The Lord's Method of Dealing with His Chosen People," A companion volume to *All of Grace,* p. 69

3. Bob Kellemen and Kevin Carson, *Biblical Counseling and the Church: God's Care through God's People* (Zondervan, Grand Rapids, MI, 2015), p. 14.

15

Freedom Through Deliverance

First Time Experience

One of my earliest experiences with the ministry of demonic deliverance occurred in my office. A young Christian woman had come to our church with two children. She was a single mom who worked hard to take care of her family. Even though she was a creative and resourceful person, given the many challenges she had stacked against her, she was constantly in a state of crisis. Many people in the congregation reached out to help her, and by the grace of God she was able to get through some very difficult days. On more than one occasion, she struggled with suicidal thoughts and self-harm. Over a period of years, she eventually trusted me with a deep dark secret. She was having flashbacks of traumatic events from her childhood. The more we explored those memories, the more it became clear that she had suffered satanic ritual abuse.

All of this was new to me. It was clearly over my head, so I went searching for some help. I found someone who had some experience with inner healing. I attended several counseling sessions with the young woman, and she began to experience some relief. However, it was not until an intervention in my office that a significant breakthrough occurred. She agreed to meet for prayer.

At that time, I was very ignorant regarding demonic oppression. It took tremendous courage on her part to face those horrifying memoires. The panic and pain she experienced were overwhelming. To help her feel safe, she came with a married couple, trusted friends of hers, who showered her with love and comfort throughout the evening. Sue was in the next room interceding in prayer. I had no idea what I was doing, but forged ahead, relying on the Holy Spirit to lead me to ask questions and requesting that He minister to her.

Three times, she became nauseated and had to run out of the office. After several hours of intense interaction, she finally reached a place of calm. She achieved deliverance but was emotionally and physically exhausted. She went home with the couple to recuperate overnight. A supposed one-night stay turned into a week-long recovery.

All of this left me bewildered and amazed at the same time. What proved to be most remarkable is what followed. This young woman previously had attempted to enter a two-year college program. To be accepted she needed to take an academic readiness test. Before the deliverance session, she scored in the low 30th percentile. After the deliverance session, she retested and scored in the mid-80th percentile. It became apparent that demons had been interfering in her thought processes, creating a state of confusion. However, free from these demons, she was able to focus, concentrate and think clearly. Now walking in her full potential, she went on to a successful career with secure employment in several responsible positions.

To the average person, this may seem to be an extreme case. However, I can assure you that I have ministered to countless people who experienced demonic interference at various levels. Most had only mild disruptions—things like anxiety, depression, and anger—that hindered their spiritual life. Others struggled with addiction and suicidal thoughts, a much more severe disruption. They appeared to be functioning okay on the surface, but on a deeper level, their life was fraught with pain and irritation resulting in disruptive relationships. Only after being set free did they realize the magnitude of their captivity.

I had no idea how negatively demons influenced me until I experienced deliverance personally. I knew I was a workaholic, but I did not know why. I knew I was driven to perform, but I didn't know how to stop. I rationalized my behavior as "doing good for the Lord." I didn't realize the negative impact this had on those closest to me. I loved my family, but our emotional connection suffered. I felt I had it under control. But, in truth, I was helpless to do anything about it until John and Leslie Kindler led me through a prayer of deliverance. That was the beginning of a new way of thinking and the start of a new chapter in my life.

Clearly, Jesus came to earth to deliver mankind from sin, disease, death, and evil. Most Christians in the West have a good grasp of Jesus forgiving them of their sin and giving them eternal life. Deliverance from personal evil, however, is not well understood. In many cases, it arouses fear. The very word "deliverance" causes some people to freak out. My family was in that category until something happened that changed everything.

Deliverance Comes to My Family

I was visiting my sister Brenda who lives in Parkton, Maryland. My mother, my Aunt Evelyn and I were talking with Brenda in her sitting room. Brenda began to tell us about how frustrated she was. Various Christian women's organizations would ask her to speak at their sponsored events, but never allowed her into the inner circles of leadership. This happened several times. She did not understand the constant rejection. The more she talked about it the more stressed she became. Her concern turned into complaining. I was becoming uncomfortable and my patience was running thin. Then suddenly, I developed a pain close to my heart. The more Brenda talked, the greater became my pain. I asked the Lord what was going on. I heard him whisper into my ear in a small voice, "It is a demon."

Without thinking, as if in an automatic response, I immediately jumped to my feet. I felt a power and confidence as I commanded the demon to come out of my sister. With a shocked look on her face, my sister grabbed her chest and then her throat and began choking. I continued to command the demon to come out. Meanwhile, my mother, full of fear, started screaming, "Oh my God! Craig, what is happening?" I momentarily turned to my mom and told her everything was okay. She stopped screaming but was still in panic.

As I turned back to my sister, she looked to the ceiling, raised her hands, and said, "It is gone." At that point my Aunt Evelyn chimed in with a loud voice, "I saw it leave." I asked my sister if she was alright.

"I felt pressure on my chest and began to choke. Then I felt it leave out my mouth," she said. I fell to my knees to thank the Lord for His goodness and grace. After things settled down, I explained to my mother what had taken place. My sister had opened herself up to a demon because of the hurt and resentment she was holding in her heart. The pain I was feeling in my heart mirrored the pain in Brenda's heart.

Many Christians mistakenly believe that demonic influence is only evident in extreme or violent behavior or terrible sin. But demonic activity is present in people living normal lives who experience interpersonal problems.

The Number One Question

The subject of deliverance from demonic spirits sparks both interest and controversy. People have many questions about it. The number one question is: "Can a Christian be possessed by a demon?" The short answer is "no," but that answer is not sufficient to address the need for deliverance among Christians. Christians need deliverance just like they need healing when they become sick.

The Scriptures teach that we live in a fallen world system that is under Satan's rule (Ephesians 2:1-3). Most Christians have no trouble believing it is Satan who tempts them to sin. Satan tempted Jesus in the wilderness, but people have difficulty believing that demons are dwelling in them. They reason that because Christ's Spirit is in them, demons cannot reside there. They may think demons could negatively impact a person from the outside but not from the inside.

So the next question is: "Can the Holy Spirit and an evil spirit occupy the same space within a human being?" The answer is "yes," just like the Holy Spirit and evil spirits occupy the same space within the atmosphere. Two different substances can exist within the same container and not mix, just like oil separates from water when they are in the same container.

To understand how this works spiritually, we need a biblical perspective of our human selves. The Bible sees man as a tripartite being composed of three parts, a physical body, a soul, and a spirit (1 Thessalonians 5:23). Paul says it is God's desire to make all three parts holy. It is God's will that all three parts be free from bondage. At conversion, the Holy Spirit sets the human spirit free, but the body and the soul remain subject to demonic influence. It is intrinsic to the sanctification process to set free the body and the soul.

When a person accepts Jesus as Savior, their spirit is regenerated. The Holy Spirit enters their spirit and they become spiritually alive. They belong to God. He owns them, and therefore, the devil cannot possess them. However, the soul and the body are not yet redeemed. The sinful nature is still part of the soul and physical body. The soul is comprised of the emotions, intellect, and will, all residing temporarily in the physical body. Although the Holy Spirit protects the spirit, the soul and body remain vulnerable to demonic influence.

Demons are always looking for bodies to dwell in, whether human or animal. The story of the man who lived naked among the tombs, unable to be restrained and continually cutting himself, graphicly portrays this search for a host body in which to dwell. When Jesus delivered the man of thousands of demons, the demons begged permission to go into a herd of pigs grazing nearby (Mark 5:1-13; Matthew 8:28-32; Luke 8:26-33).

To have a proper understanding of how demons can attach themselves to people, we need to realize that the term "demon possessed" in English is not the same term used in the original Greek language in the Bible. In the New Testament, there are two terms used for "demon possessed." The first is *daimonion echei* which translates, "has a devil" (Luke 8:27). The second term, *daimonizomenou,* means "demonized" (John 10:21). The term *daimonion echei* indicates that man has the demon, rather than the demon has the man. The inference is that demons do not have ultimate control. They influence but do not own. The point here is that demons cannot enter a person unless the person allows it, either by intentional agreement as in the case of occult activity, by passively agreeing to lies, by committing habitual sin without repentance, or through generational iniquity. These methods of agreement represent open doors or legal access.

Ways Demons Gain Legal Access

Demons can gain access to a person in a variety of ways including:

Practicing sin – Any ongoing practice or agreement made with the devil that opposes God's will, Word, or way. These can be intentional or unintentional thoughts and behaviors rooted in lies, fear, or unbelief, that in effect are a form of rebellion against God.

Traumatic experiences – Severe painful events that leave a person emotionally wounded and suffering mental dysfunction.

Believing lies – Believing things that are not true regarding self, others, and God.

Offenses – Transactions that dishonor or hurt another person.

Unforgiveness – An unwillingness to forgive someone who has trespassed against you.

Contact with unholy objects – Demons attach themselves to objects, particularly those used in spiritual ceremonies.

Involvement in the occult – Engaging in practices that look to powers of darkness to exert control or influence.

Subscribing to false doctrines - Adherence to false teaching, false prophets, false philosophies, or false religions.

Word curses – Identifying with negative statements said about oneself.

Generational iniquity – Having a predisposition or natural bent toward sin passed down through family lines.

Ungodly soul ties – Negative unhealthy emotional connections that have a detrimental effect.

Listening to unholy music – This opens the soul to ideas that promote a sinful lifestyle.

Although the term "demon possessed" does not occur in Scripture, the Bible clearly portrays demons dwelling inside the body of a person. The terms used when demons are removed from a person are *ap autou* meaning, "off" or "out of the self" (Matthew 17:18); *ekbleethentos,* meaning "plucked out and expelled from within" (Matthew 9:33); and *exelthontos* meaning "to issue from" (Luke 11:14). These terms infer an internal position from which demons infect a person, much like a bacterial infection in the body. The cure for such infection is removal by way of deliverance in the name of Jesus Christ (Luke 10:17-19).

Demons seek to dwell in a host, whether human or animal (Luke 8:32-33). They can attack a person from within the physical body or from without. There are several ways Satan launches his attacks.

Four Kinds of Demonic Attacks

There are four ways demons take advantage of a person. The first way is without any legal right. They come at a person from outside the body. The person has not sinned and has not made any agreements or believed any lies of Satan. The demons simply seek to deceive the person into disobeying God. They tempt the person with half-truths, false promises, getting the person to question what God has said. Jesus himself had to face this kind of attack. When He was in the wilderness forty days and nights, the devil tempted Him three times. Jesus countered the temptations with the Word of God, and upon the last one He commanded the devil to leave Him. Notably, the devil left.

The second way Satan attacks is through gaining legal right to do so. In this instance, the Christian gives legal right for the demons to attach themselves by entering into agreements with Satan. Agreements are characterized by participating in the occult or by engaging in sin. The word *occult* means "secret or hidden," as in secret knowledge in the supernatural realm of Satan.

The third way Satan attacks is through the evil acts of another person or natural tragedy. In this instance, someone is offended, violated, abused, or harmed in a brutal way. In reaction to such injustice, the violated person responds sinfully against God or the trespasser, opening the door for demons to gain legal access.

The fourth way Satan attacks is through generational sins and curses. In this case, Satan harasses and torments a person through dysfunctional family relationships. Because of unrepented iniquity, sinful patterns of belief and behavior plague future generations.

Becoming Informed About Demons

We do not need to be paranoid or spooked into thinking that demons are lurking behind every bush. Nor should we take the other extreme position of ignoring them as if they don't exist. Instead, we should heed the Scriptures. We should familiarize ourselves with Satan's schemes (2 Corinthians 2:11) and engage him in battle as a good soldier (2 Timothy 2:3-5). Indeed, learning to overcome the enemy is essential in growing to spiritual maturity (1 John 2:13-14). Jesus has potentially equipped every believer with spiritual authority and power to defeat Satan.

Freedom comes as a matter of learning how to apply the authority and power Jesus has already given. There is nothing to fear. Demons have no more control over you than sin or the flesh. The only power they have over you is what you give them through disobedience or by agreeing with their lies. We need to remember that the devil and his demons are already defeated. Jesus defeated Satan on the cross (2 Colossians 2:15). He has set us free by revealing truth (John 8:32). Christians simply need to enforce the victory that is already theirs in Christ. Here are some Scriptures indicating we have power to be free from demons (emphasis mine):

*He said to them, "Go into all the world and preach the gospel to all creation. Whoever believes and is baptized will be saved, but whoever does not believe will be condemned. And these signs will accompany those who believe: **In my name they will cast out demons;** they will speak with new tongues; they will pick up snakes with their hands; and when they drink deadly poison, it will not hurt them at all; they will place their hands on sick people, and they will get well"* (Mark 16:15-18).

*Jesus returned to Galilee in the power of the Spirit …. "the Spirit of the Lord is on me, because he has anointed me to proclaim good news to the poor. He has sent me to **proclaim freedom for the prisoners** and recovery of sight for the blind, to **set the oppressed free"** (Luke 4:14-18).*

*I have given you **authority to trample on snakes and scorpions** and to overcome all the power of the enemy; nothing will harm you (Luke 10:19).*

*When Jesus had called the Twelve together, **he gave them power and authority to drive out all demons** and to cure diseases, and he sent them out to proclaim the kingdom of God and to heal the sick (Luke 9:1-2).*

*Calling the Twelve to him, he began to send them out two by two and **gave them authority over impure spirits.... They drove out many demons** and anointed many sick people with oil and healed them* (Mark 6:7, 13).

*Jesus called his twelve disciples to him and **gave them authority to drive out impure spirits** and to heal every disease and sickness* (Matthew 10:1).

*Go rather to the lost sheep of Israel. As you go, proclaim this message: 'The kingdom of heaven has come near.' Heal the sick, raise the dead, cleanse those who have leprosy, **drive out demons**. Freely you have received; freely give* (Matthew 10: 6-8).

*The one who does what is sinful is of the devil, because the devil has been sinning from the beginning. The reason the Son of God appeared was to **destroy the devil's work*** (1 John 3:8).

In these scriptures, Jesus specifically told the apostles to cast out demons. He commissioned them to go out to save, heal, teach, and proclaim the kingdom. He modeled deliverance as part of His own mission, and it remains part of the church's mission today.

Deliverance Is Needed to Accomplish God's Plan

From ancient times, different religions and cultures have believed in demon possession and have practiced various forms of deliverance. Assyrian tablets refer to incantations and prayers as a direct challenge to demons. Babylonian priests performed exorcisms, as did Zoroaster of ancient Persia. References are made in the Hindu Vedas of evil beings interfering into the affairs of the living.[1] In many parts of the world, especially in the Middle East and Northern Africa, Mexico, Central and South America, demonic possession is a common belief.[2]

The Western church in modern times has not embraced deliverance as a viable component of its ministry. Rare is the occasion to find a church that practices this ministry. However, God has made deliverance an important part of His plan. Jesus practiced deliverance and the church needs to rediscover it.

From the time of the fall, God has had a plan to restore sinful humanity to a right relationship with Himself. In the broadest of terms, this plan follows a process laid out in Obadiah 17, *"But on Mount Zion will be deliverance; it will be holy, and Jacob will possess his inheritance."* This shows the progression God uses to make good on His promises. In the Old Testament, He sent Moses to deliver His people from bondage in Egypt. He then gave them the law that they might become holy, then led them into the Land of Promise to "possess their possessions." In this way, He fulfilled His promise to Abraham.

233

Similarly, in the New Testament, God sent Jesus to deliver humanity from bondage to sin and evil so that man could become holy and possess eternal life. Deliverance is not the goal in itself but is a necessary step toward restoring man to an intimate relationship with God. Apart from deliverance, holiness is not possible. Jesus not only taught His disciples to cast out demons, but also taught them to pray that God would deliver them from evil. When a person receives deliverance from demonic influence, they are free to grow in the Spirit and walk in God's presence. No amount of Bible study, correct doctrine, or counseling can cast out demons. Deliverance is a critical component of God's plan for freedom.

On the other hand, deliverance is not a panacea. There is a real need for spiritual disciplines including, Bible study, prayer, worship, obedience to Word and Spirit, repentance, forgiveness, giving, and fellowship. All of these are needed to cultivate a relationship with the Lord and to bring disciples to spiritual maturity.

Deliverance Is A Birthright of Every Christian

Deliverance is part of the birthright given to everyone who is in covenant with God. In Mark 7:24-30, a Syrophoenician woman asks Jesus to deliver her daughter from an unclean spirit. Being a Canaanite rather than a Jew, she was not entitled to the blessings connected to Israel's covenant with God. Jesus responds to her request in a negative tone. He says, *"Let the children be filled first, for it is not good to take the children's bread and throw it to the little dogs"* (Matthew 7:27). The children's bread refers to the blessings that belong to God's covenant people. In this case, the blessing was deliverance from demon possession. Those people outside of the covenant were not entitled to this blessing. However, they could receive a miracle based on God's mercy through faith. It was because of the women's faith that Jesus decided to show her mercy and deliver her daughter from demons. As Christians, we are in covenant with God through Jesus Christ. Therefore, we are entitled the benefits of deliverance.

In Luke 1:71-75, Zechariah prophesied that God had redeemed His people. He says that Jesus came *"that we should be saved from our enemies, and from the hand of all who hate us; to perform the mercy promised to our fathers and to remember his holy covenant, the oath which He swore to our father Abraham, to grant us that we, being delivered from the hand our enemies might serve Him without fear, in holiness and righteousness before Him all the days of our life."* We see in this passage that the descendants of Abraham are in covenant with God. As Christians, we too are in covenant with God. This is made possible through faith in Jesus Christ. Through Him we have received the promise of salvation, including deliverance from our enemy, Satan.

In other words, through the covenant we have with God, made possible through Jesus' work on the cross, He not only delivers us from sin and death but also provides deliverance from demons. This, too, is part of our salvation. It sets us free from evil so that we can live our lives in holiness and righteousness.

Practicing Deliverance Is Part of Working Out Our Salvation

Philippians 2:12-15 conveys the concept of deliverance being part of salvation:

Therefore, my beloved, as you have always obeyed, not in my presence only, but now much more in my absence, work out your own salvation with fear and trembling: for it is God who works in you both to will and to do His good pleasure. Do all things without murmuring and disputing, that you may become blameless and harmless, children of God without fault in the midst of a crooked and perverse generation, among whom you shine as lights in the world.

Some people believe Jesus' work on the cross ultimately delivers us and all we have to do is believe in His sacrificial act. But the verses from Philippians indicate there is something more we humans must do for salvation to be actualized. We must be participants in our own deliverance.

I like to think of it this way. Imagine a parakeet locked in a cage for years. He has grown content sitting on his swing in captivity, eating the same old food and water provided for him. Someone sees this little bird living in a state of bondage and pities him. He opens the door of the cage, freeing the little critter. But the bird remains imprisoned until he decides to leave his perch and fly out the open door.

In much the same way, Jesus has acquired our salvation from sin, evil and death through His crucifixion and resurrection. He has opened the door, setting us free. But our freedom is not actualized until we decide to act on what we believe Jesus has done. We have a role to play in our own deliverance.

In verse 12, the term for "salvation" is the Greek word *soteria*. It means "deliverance from harm, danger and bondage to acquire safety, health and well-being." According to this verse, each believer is to work out the freedom Christ has acquired for them by looking to God for the motivation and ability to do His good pleasure. When we are unencumbered by demonic influence, we are free to do what pleases God.

All Christians Are Expected to Purify Their Soul from Unclean Spirits

In order to understand how we are to work out our deliverance, it is necessary to understand our human makeup. As explained previously, we are composed of three parts: spirit, soul, and body (1 Thessalonians 5:23). While the Holy Spirit fuses with the believer's spirit at the time of conversion, the soul and body are yet to be purified. Through the sanctifying work of the Holy Spirit and with cooperation from the person, the believer is made clean of sin and demonic influence. In 1 Thessalonians 5:22-23, Paul instructs his readers to reject every kind of evil by looking to the God of peace to sanctify them in body, soul, and spirit. Paul writes in 2 Corinthians 6 that believers are to have no fellowship with Belial (the devil). He further states, they need to give attention to the condition of their body and soul. He said in 2 Corinthians 7:1, *"Therefore, since we have these promises, dear friends, let us purify ourselves from everything that contaminates body and spirit, perfecting holiness out of reverence for God."*

Cleansing oneself from evil spirits is something Jesus fully expected His followers to do. He taught them to ask the Father for deliverance from evil, as seen in the prayer He taught (Matthew 6:13). Jesus knew that His disciples would have to overcome the evil one just as He had to do in the wilderness.

The Early Church Carries Out Jesus' Mission of Deliverance

Central to Christ's mission and purpose is the deliverance of those held captive by the devil (Luke 4:18 RSV). Jesus identified His mission this way in John 10:10, *"The thief comes only to steal, and kill and destroy; I have come that they may have life, and have it to the full."* If believers are to carry out the ministry of Jesus and experience freedom, they, too, need to do battle with the demonic.

In Acts 5, Peter identified Satan as the one who caused Ananias and Sapphira to lie to the Holy Spirit. Because they were complicit with the devil, they were struck dead. Later in verse 16, Peter healed those who were tormented by impure spirits. In Acts 8:7, Philip cast out demons among the people in Samaria. In Acts 13:8-11, Paul opposes the sorcerer Elymas, declaring him to become temporarily blind. In Acts 16:18, Paul cast out an evil spirit from a slave girl who told fortunes. In Acts 19:19, because of Paul's preaching and delivering people of evil spirits, many who practiced sorcery burned their books.

Throughout the Epistles, the biblical writers warned and advised their readers about the schemes of the devil. In 2 Corinthians 2:10-11, Paul emphasizes the importance of forgiveness so that the devil would not outwit them. Paul further instructs the believers at Ephesus concerning anger. They are not to let the sun go down on their anger, lest they give the devil a foothold (Ephesians 4:27). In Ephesians 6:12, he reminds them of the inevitable conflict they are in with the devil. He says, *"For our struggle is not against flesh and blood, but against rulers, against the authorities, against the powers of this dark world and against the spiritual forces of evil in the heavenly realms."* Paul instructs Timothy, *"Be humble when you correct people who oppose you.... They have been trapped by the devil, and he makes them obey him, but God may help them escape"* (2 Timothy 2:25-26 CEV). Peter warns, in 1 Peter 5:8-9, *"Be alert and of sober mind. Your enemy the devil prowls around like a roaring lion looking for someone to devour. Resist him standing firm in the faith."* Peter learned this lesson first-hand as Jesus warned him that the devil was going to sift him as wheat, but when he returned, he was to strengthen his brothers (Luke 22:32). James tells his readers in James 4:7, *"Submit yourselves, then to God. Resist the devil, and he will flee from you."*

In 1 John 2:12-13, John identifies three levels of spiritual maturity: children, young men, and fathers. It is the young men who have learned to overcome the evil one. To become spiritually mature and effective in proclaiming the kingdom, every believer must learn to overcome the evil one in their own life.

Jesus Trained His Disciples in The Ministry of Deliverance

Many Bible scholars point out that almost one third of Jesus' miracles recorded in the Gospels had to do with the demonic. Clearly, Jesus recognized the need to confront and overcome the powers of darkness in order to establish His kingdom here on earth. He not only taught His disciples to pray for deliverance from evil, He also taught them to deliver others. His expectation of them was not only that they would personally overcome the devil, but that they would also help others gain freedom. As part of their training, Jesus sent out His twelve disciples to minister to the people of Israel. He gave them authority to drive out impure spirits and to heal every disease (Matthew 10:1). They were to proclaim the kingdom of God, heal the sick, raise the dead, cleanse those with leprosy, and drive out demons (Matthew 10:7-8).

It was not Jesus' intention to limit this ministry to the inner circle of twelve apostles. No, He wanted to include as many followers as He could. In Luke 10, He recognized that the harvest was great and the laborers were few. He then sends out seventy disciples in teams of two and gives them instructions similar to those He gave the twelve. He tells them, *"Heal the sick who are there and tell them, 'The kingdom of God has come near to you'"* (Luke 10:9). As a result of their obedience, verse 17 says they returned with joy saying, *"Lord, even the demons submit to us in your name."* Jesus then makes it clear as to the reason for their joy. He says, *"I have given you authority to trample on snakes and scorpions and to overcome all the power of the enemy; nothing will harm you"* (Luke 10:19). Then, Jesus celebrates their success. Verse 21 reports that Jesus was full of joy because the Father has revealed these things to His young-in-faith followers even though they were hidden from those who were wise and learned.

Jesus not only sent His disciples out on mission trips to learn about deliverance, but He also mentored them as situations presented themselves. In Mark 9, Jesus' disciples try to drive out a demonic spirit from a young boy but are unable to. They took the boy to Jesus, who after talking to the his father, cast out the spirit. Later the disciples wanted to know why they could not drive out the demon. Jesus told them they needed to do more work in the area of prayer and fasting.

He Educated His Disciples to Recognize Satan's Activities

Jesus taught His disciples to recognize Satan's activity among themselves. He pointed out where the devil was operating in their lives. When Peter refused to accept the fact that Jesus had to suffer, Jesus rebuked him saying, *"Get behind me Satan"* (Matthew 16:23) and explained to Peter that Satan was seeking to sift him as wheat (Luke 22:31.) In John 6:70, Jesus identifies one of His disciples as a devil. It was Judas. At the last supper, He pointed out that the devil had entered Judas causing him to betray Him (John 13:21-27).

Jesus taught His disciples to identify Satan's activity among the teachers of the law and Pharisees. In John 8:43-47, He points out they are unable to hear the truth about Him because they do not belong to God and that their malicious motives were the result of believing Satan, the father of lies.

Jesus used parables to teach about the activities of Satan. In the parable of the four soils, he spoke of Satan taking away the Word that was sown in a heart, causing a person not to believe (Matthew 13:3-8). In the parable of the wheat and tares, a man sows good seed in his field. In the night, the enemy secretly sowed weeds among the wheat (Matthew 13:24-30). Here Jesus teaches that on the day of judgment, evil planted by Satan will be uprooted and burned. The good seed that is planted by the Lord will be harvested into the kingdom of God.

Jesus taught His disciples how Satan tempts people, keeping them from fulfilling their God-given purposes. He shared with them how Satan tried to tempt Him in the wildness, twisting Scripture and appealing to His human weakness (Matthew 4:1-10). By His example, He taught His disciples that the way to counter Satan is with the Word of God. It causes him to flee.

Jesus Commissioned His Followers to Make Disciples Utilizing the Ministry of Deliverance

On several occasions, Jesus commissioned His disciples to go into the world to perform the ministry in which He had trained them. The most notable commission occurred just before He ascended into heaven, known as the "Great Commission." There are at least four references in the New Testament in which Jesus commissions His disciples just before He ascended to heaven. They include Matthew 28:18-20; Acts 1:8; Luke 24:46-47; Mark 16:15-20.

Each of these references emphasizes different components. The one most clearly identifying the ministry of deliverance is found in Mark 16. It says, *"He said to them 'Go into all the world and preach the gospel to all creation. Whoever believes and is baptized will be saved, but whoever does not believe will be condemned. And these signs will accompany those who believe: In my name they will drive out demons; they will speak in new tongues; they will pick up snakes with their hands; and when they drink deadly poison, it will not hurt them at all; they will place their hands on sick people, and they will get well'"* (emphasis mine).

This emphasizes the supernatural components involved in carrying out His commission. It identifies "driving out demons" as part of Christ's ongoing ministry.

Historical Records Show that Exorcisms were Common Before Baptism

To the modern Christian, the idea of being delivered from evil spirits or driving demons out of others is a bit foreign. But historical records show that this was quite common among Christians up through the 3rd century. It is recorded in the church order of Hippolytus (ca. AD 210) that there was a pre-baptismal order for exorcism in which a candidate for baptism underwent several exorcisms before baptism. Also, on the day of baptism, the bishop conducted another exorcism to make sure the baptizand was clean. In other ancient documents, "Apostolic Tradition" the "Epistle of Barnabas" (ca. AD 130) and *"Excerpta ex Theodoto"* by Clement of Alexandria, references are made to pre-baptismal deliverance.[3] Even today, in many church liturgies of baptism, renunciation of evil is included. This renunciation, however, is largely ritualistic and is not understood to be a cleansing from demons.

Historical Records Show Ordinary Christians Casting Out Demons

When it came to driving out demons, ancient historian Tertullian, in his Apologeticum to the rulers of the Roman Empire (Defense, written 197 A.D.), said: "… Let a person be brought before your tribunals who is plainly under demoniacal possession. The wicked spirit, bidden to speak by a follower of Christ, will readily make the truthful confession that he is a demon, as elsewhere he has falsely asserted that he is a god. Or, if you will, let there be produced one of the god-possessed, as they supposed – if they do not confess, in their fear of lying to a Christian, that they are demons, then and there shed the blood of the most impudent follower of Christ… all authority and power we have over them is from our naming the name of Christ, and recalling to their memory the woes with which God threatens them at the hands of Christ, as judge."

Justin Martyr, in his second Apology addressed to the Roman Senate, said: "For numberless demoniacs throughout the whole world, and in your city, many of our Christian men exorcising them in the name of Jesus Christ, who was crucified under Pontius Pilate, have healed and do heal, rendering helpless and driving the possessing demon out of the men, though they could not be cured by all the other exorcists, and those who use incantations and drugs."

Cyprian wrote that after saying evil spirits inspired false prophets of the Gentiles he added, "Nevertheless these evil spirits adjured by the living God immediately obey us, submit to us, own our power and are forced to come out of the bodies they possess."[4]

Origen (ca. AD 235) wrote in *Contra Celsum*, VII 4, that Christians prevailed over evil spirits not by incantations or with magic but by the name of Jesus. He said, "… for the most part it is unlettered persons who perform this work; thus making manifest the grace which is in the word of Christ, and the despicable weakness of demons, which in order to be overcome and driven out of the bodies and souls of men, do not require the power and wisdom of those who are mighty in argument, and most learned matters of faith."[5]

The Schemes of The Devil Are Revealed in Scripture

Paul tells the Corinthians that he also forgives those they have forgiven *"in order that Satan might not outwit us. For we are not unaware of his schemes"* (2 Corinthians 2:11). The devil uses certain tactics to kill, steal and destroy humanity. As Christians, we are not ignorant of his tactics and can combat them. The Scriptures reveal his schemes.

The Bible attributes different names to Satan indicating his mode of operation. Each name reveals how he functions.

Satan means "adversary" (Job 1:6-7; 1 Thessalonians 2:18; John 8:42-45; Revelation 12:9). Satan opposes God and God's people through deception. He works against the Kingdom of God in order to establish his own kingdom.

Lucifer means "shining one," "morning star," or "bearer of light" (Isaiah 14:12). He appears bright and beautiful rather than ugly and horrible. He comes to you as attractive and alluring. He hides his evil nature in order to seduce you.

Devil means "slanderer" (1 Peter 5:8). One of the ways he operates is to say false things about people, in order to destroy their reputation. He stirs up gossip and generates false witnesses against God's representatives.

Belial means "false god who is worthless" (2 Corinthians 6:15). Satan tries to divert worship from the true God onto himself. The false gods of Greek mythology are an example. Any idol that diverts worship from the true God indicates demonic influence.

Beelzebub means "lord of the flies" (Matthew 12:24). The Hebrews understood Beelzebub to be "god of filth and dung." Flies swarm around garbage in order to feed themselves. Wherever there is corruption or defilement, we can expect demons to be hanging around.

The Tempter (Matthew 4:3; 1 Thessalonians 3:5). Satan takes advantage of legitimate human needs and desires by enticing people to meet those needs and desires in illegitimate ways. Cravings for food, sex, security, and significance are distorted and twisted in a way that is opposed to the will of God. Satan invites you to focus on yourself. He did this with Adam and Eve. He twists the truth and plants seeds of doubt and unbelief to incite disobedience. He tells you that all your selfish desires should be met (Matthew 4:11-11; I John 2:16-17).

The evil one (Matthew 6:13; 1 John 5:19). Satan is wicked. He causes pain and trouble. He kills, steals, and destroys. His motives are malicious and corrupt. He is the enemy of all that which is good and godly.

The prince of this world (John 12:31; 2 Cor. 4:4; Ephesians 2:2). Satan rules the world through false systems of religion, government, education, philosophies, commerce, and false doctrines. This does not mean he has absolute authority. It simply means he uses deception to get people to do what he wants, often appealing to their pride.

The accuser of the brethren (Revelation 12:10; Job 1:6; Zechariah 3:1). Satan condemns you and blames you, pointing out your sins to make you feel worthless. He is continually charging people of sin before God to discredit them and weaken their influence.

Satan Influences People in Many Ways

- He tempts people to sin, enticing them to disobey God (Genesis 3:4; Matthew 4:3).

- He puts people into bondage, enslaving them into compulsive and addictive behavior (Hebrews 2:14-15; 2 Timothy 2:24-26).

- He oppresses people, exercising harsh control over them, shattering their souls into pieces (Luke 4:18; Acts 10:38).

- He torments people with troubling, disturbing, and harassing thoughts, including irrational fears, unbelief, self-hatred, self-harm, suicidal thoughts, guilt, and shame (Luke 6:18; Acts 5:16).

- He afflicts people with illness, sickness, and disease (Luke 13:10-11; Matthew 17:18).

- He deceives people through lies, false teaching, and false prophecy (1 Timothy 4:1; Matthew 7:15; 2 Corinthians 11:14; 1 Kings 22:22).

- He counterfeits prophetic revelations, miracles, signs, and wonders through the occult (Acts 16:16).

- He indwells humans and animals (Mark 5:1-16).

- He encourages idolatry (Deuteronomy 32:17; Psalm 106:37).

- He draws people into false worship (1 Corinthians 10:20-21).

- He blinds the mind so that people cannot receive truth (2 Corinthians 4:4).

- He influences people through divination (Acts 16:16, 1 Samuel 28).

- He fights against missionary plans (1 Thessalonians 2:17-18).

- He uses people to murder others (1 John 3:12).

- He chokes off faith in those who have heard the Word (Mark 4:1-9,15).

- He fools people with partial truth (2 Corinthians 11:13-15; Matt. 4:6).

- He accuses people before God (Revelation 12:10).

Satan Is A Powerful Foe, But Is No Match for God

- He is subordinate to God (Job 1:6).
- He cannot tempt without God's permission (Job 1:12; Matthew 4:1; Luke 22:31).
- He cannot physically harm without God's permission (Job 2:2-6).
- He cannot use the forces of nature without God's permission (Job 1:12,16,19).
- He cannot kill without God's permission (Job 2:6; Hebrews 2:14).
- He cannot touch you without God's permission (Job 1:10; 1 John 5:18).
- He cannot force believers to sin against their will (James 1:13-15; 1 Corinthians 13:10).
- Jesus defeated Satan on the cross (Colossians 2:15).
- God has given Jesus all authority over Satan (Matthew 28:18; Philippians 2:9-11).
- Jesus has delegated His authority to believers (Mark 3:15; Matthew 10:1; Matthew 28:18; Ephesians 2:6).
- Satan can be resisted by believers (James 4:7).
- Satan cannot separate believers in Christ from God's love (Romans 8:38).
- Satan cannot snatch the redeemed away from God (Hebrews 6:17-20; John 10:27-29).
- Satan cannot touch the "new self" given by God (1 Peter 1:23; Ephesians 1:13-14).
- Satan cannot offer any eternal positive rewards (John 10:9-10; Revelation 20:10).
- Satan is overcome by the blood of the Lamb and the testimony of the saints (Revelation 12:11).
- Satan's destiny is already determined. God will eventually cast him into hell forever (Revelation 20:10).

Ghost and Demons

Haunted houses, mediums, and psychics have one thing in common. They all point to disembodied earth-bound spirits that are still hanging around in this dimension for one reason or another. Supposedly, these are spirits of people who have died but have not crossed over to the other side where the source of all energy resides. According to one psychic who has written various articles on the internet, these spirits have their own reasons for staying. They include:

- They are attached to things such as jewelry, cars, houses, furniture, or places where they lived, found comfort, or died.
- They are meddlers who don't want to leave.
- They are seeking revenge or pursuing justice.
- They fear judgment or punishment on the other side.
- They want to protect the living.

People have sought to communicate with the dead for centuries. In 1 Samuel 28:3-25, Saul goes to the witch of Endor to conjure up the spirit of the prophet Samuel. Saul had fallen into such a depraved state of mind that he turned to an unlawful means of supernatural guidance. The Scriptures forbid involvement in this kind of occult activity. Mosaic law says clearly that believers are not to consult with mediums and necromancers in order to talk with the dead (Deuteronomy 18:10-13; Leviticus 19:31; Leviticus 20:27). This is called divination. The New Testament also warns of such practices (1 John 4:1; 2 Corinthians 11:14; 1 Timothy 4:1; Galatians 5:19-21).

Historically within the church, there has been an ongoing debate as to whether these disembodied spirits are actually the spirits of dead people or whether they are demons disguising themselves as dead people.

The early Christian historian, Tertullian wrote on this topic, saying:

Some people say that those who are cut off by an early death wander about hither and yon until they complete the number of years they would have lived, had they not died untimely... But it is demons that operate under the fiction of being dead souls... Sometimes an evil spirit disguises itself as the share[*persona*] of a dead person... as when in exorcisms the spirit sometimes affirms that it is one of the person's relatives (Tertullian 1841-66:746-48).[6]

Demons and Mental Illness

One of the biggest challenges facing deliverance ministry in this modern era is the lack of understanding concerning mental illness. Deliverance ministries need to be very cautious not to label all mental illness as demonic. Let me state very clearly: having a mental illness does not mean a person is afflicted by demons any more than a person suffering with physical illness is afflicted by a demon. There is much to be learned about the interplay between mental illness and demonic activity.

Modern science and medicine have made recent discoveries that show previous assumptions of how the brain works to be wrong. It was once thought that brain cells do not regenerate. Now it is widely understood that they do.[7] New neuro pathways can be formed in the brain enabling a change in behavior.[8] This is good news for those seeking freedom through the renewing of the mind (Romans 12:2).

Even among professionals, there is often a lack of clarity between what constitutes mental illness and what is demonic activity. Both can generate similar symptoms. Some of those symptoms include:

Feelings of sadness, helplessness, worthlessness, or emptiness, overeating or loss of appetite, insomnia or sleeping too much, restlessness, irritability, a feeling of impending doom or danger, lack of energy, distancing yourself from others, feeling numbness or lacking empathy, extreme mood swings, inability to concentrate, thoughts of hurting yourself and others, being unable to carry out day-to-day activities, hearing voices in your head, alcohol or drug misuse.[9]

Both modern science and practitioners of deliverance have made miscalculations. The medical field has made misdiagnoses and has over-prescribed drugs resulting in addiction and suicide. In addition, there is much controversy concerning neurochemical imbalances and their impact on such illnesses as bi-polar disorder, OCD, ADHD, PANS disorder, DID and other psychological conditions. Mental illness is complex and not fully understood. Seunggu Han M.D., Assistant Professor of Neurological Surgery School of Medicine, concurs that chemical imbalances simply do not cause mental disorders in the brain. There is a lot more involved.[10]

Similarly, there is much to be learned concerning the interplay of mental illness and the work of demons. Much needs to be done to correct the misconceptions and abuses in deliverance ministry. Admittedly, there has been extreme malfeasance in which people have been harmed and a few people have died.[11] However, in the majority of malpractice cases, people have been unnecessarily inflicted with fear, confusion, despair, or hopelessness.

Despite these shortcomings, both disciplines have a role to play in restoring health and freedom to those who are suffering. With that said, it is important to recognize that not everyone who displays symptoms of mental illness has a demon and not everyone who has a demon displays symptoms of mental illness. The majority of people influenced by demons are normal and function in society as regular citizens. For that reason, it is helpful to identify some characteristics of demonic activity.

Indicators of Possible Demonic Activity

1. **Strained social interaction** – an aversion to being around people; prefer isolation, suffer from loneliness and often feel rejected; tend to be passive, easily offended and have little desire to change; strife, jealousy and gossip follows them.

2. **Violent mood swings** – outbursts of uncontrollable anger; feel victimized and will lash out at others in bitterness and resentment; can be argumentative over trivial matters and hold grudges.

3. **Personality changes** – sometimes they seem one way and at other times they come across completely different; can be pleasant in one breath but vile and attacking in the next; are double-minded; shifts can be extreme or mild; compulsive reactions and impatience are frequently displayed.

4. **Restlessness and insomnia** – because of a lack of sleep there can be mental fatigue; unable to cope and subject to constant irritability.

5. **Emotional pain** – sense of constant inner turmoil; grief, fear, anger, depression persist and will not leave after receiving counseling, therapies, encouragement, and prayer.

6. **Self-inflicted harm** – includes self-imposed pain through cutting, burning, and beatings; often, there are suicidal thoughts and attempts.

7. **Addictions** – a variety of forms include drugs, alcohol, work, sexual, financial, and food; serve as a means to find relief from inner pain.

8. **Identity issues** – this can include poor self-esteem, body image, gender struggles, and orphan mentality.

9. **Unexplained illness** – with no obvious medical cause these are often referred to as psychosomatic illnesses; can be connected to the effect of stress on the autoimmune system causing pain, rashes, fatigue, digestion, headaches, and other symptoms.

10. **Sexual perversion** – could include adultery, fornication, prostitution, homosexuality, pedophilia, masturbation, bestiality, rape, fantasy, and lust.

11. **Occult involvement** – could include witchcraft, sorcery, divination, spiritism, satanism, new age, horoscopes, Ouija boards, and secret societies.

12. **Doctrinal error** – can include false teaching, false prophecies, half-truths, false religions.

13. **Defeated Christian life** – a sense of not being fulfilled, or lacking purpose; a constant sense of failure, discouragement, discontent, and depression.

14. **Religious legalism** – includes bondage to tradition, rules, policies, perfectionism, outward appearances and performance; can include a desire to be intellectually and morally superior; a propensity to be critical and controlling of others; feels threatened by the prophetic.

15. **Compulsive sinning** – pornography addictions, gambling, masturbation, eating disorders, and lying.

16. **Double-mindedness** – a person of two minds or souls who wavers back and forth and is unstable; is conflicted within himself, holding two opposing views at the same time; trying to serve two masters.

17. **Racing compulsive thoughts and torment** – a person's thought life is troubled, harassed or tormented by an evil spirit; the Bible calls this "vexed with a devil" (Matthew 15:2 2 KJV); like sharing your mind with another person or spirit in which you experience irrational thoughts, or having impulses to say and do things you would not ordinarily do; King David describes this kind of experience in Psalm 143:3-4, 11-12.

A clear example of the final example occurred with one of my church members. An elderly couple, Jerry and Ellen came to visit me. Ellen was very distraught. Her husband had been arrested for pilfering at a grocery store. I asked him what happened. He said he was walking down an isle when he saw something that caught his eye. He heard a voice say, "Pick it up and put it into your pocket." So that is what he did. I asked him if he had money to pay for the item. He said the item was cheap and he had money to pay for it. It cost only a few dollars. He knew what he did was wrong, but just listened to the voice in his head. We prayed. He asked the Lord for forgiveness and I explained that he should not listen to every voice in his head because demons plant thoughts that make people do wrong things.

When Conducting Deliverance Ministry Demons Will Manifest in Different Ways

One of the most bizarre manifestations of the demonic I have witnessed occurred when I was preaching a crusade in Ngoliba, Kenya. After the message, people were coming forward to receive prayer. One woman lingered longer than the others. Pastors Peter and Ruben were praying for her. She began to flail her arms, roll her head and her whole body began to wobble. More astonishing, her stomach became inflated, matching the size of a basketball. I had never seen such a contortion. Both pastors were calmly commanding demons to come out of her, but they were met with much resistance. The women's stomach began to protrude to the left and to the right, then up and down, but they were unable to deliver her. Because she was holding up the crusade meeting, we decided to take her to the back of the platform to further minister to her. Once again, the demon was stubborn and would not obey commands to release her. Finally, I asked the Lord what was keeping her from being delivered. The Lord gave me a word of knowledge. I heard the word "jealousy." So, I whispered into the ear of one of the pastors, "Ask her if she is jealous of anyone." The pastor asked her in Swahili, "Are you jealous of someone?" Suddenly she became excited. Speaking in Swahili, she revealed that she had gone to a witchdoctor to put a curse on a woman of whom she was jealous. After she repented for being jealous and going to the witchdoctor, she was delivered of the demon. She walked out from behind the platform in peace. The next Sunday, she attended church where she received more love and care.

Demons will manifest in different ways. Some manifestations include vomiting or nausea, choking, change of voice, hurling threats, gnashing of teeth, change in countenance, snarling, trembling and shaking, making sexual gestures, falling to the floor, pain in the body or head, dizziness, sudden sleepiness, eyes becoming black, turning their back, running away, rage, feats of great strength, levitation, speaking foreign languages not learned, or moving objects. I have personally witnessed most of these manifestations. A few of these manifestations were witnessed by friends and other pastors who shared them with me.

When engaging in deliverance ministry, it is best to minimize manifestations by taking authority in prayer at the beginning of the session. By commanding the demons not to distract or interfere in anyway, you can avoid a lot of unnecessary drama. In many cases, there are no manifestations at all. The demons simply leave without putting up a fight. Evidence of their departure comes later as the person finds themselves reacting differently to life challenges.

There Is No One Formula to Deliverance Ministry

Every person and situation in deliverance ministry is unique. There is no single formula. One must fully rely on the wisdom and guidance of the Holy Spirit. Some deliverance sessions are quick and easy. Others are prolonged and struggle for a breakthrough. Some demons are stronger and more wicked than others (Luke 11:26). Progress comes a little at a time. One area of life at a time gradually achieves freedom. There is a parallel to this in Israel's history. The Lord told them they would drive out enemy nations from the Promised Land one at a time. Exodus 23:29-30 states, *"But I will not drive them out in a single year, because the land would become desolate and wild animals too numerous for you."*

In much the same way, a person is set free in one area of their life at a time and increasingly experiences freedom.

Seven Factors That Impact Freedom

In deliverance ministry, at least seven factors influence how a session might unfold.

1. The **"God Factor."** This has to do with God's timing, plan, and purposes. Ultimately, God is sovereign.

2. The **"Person Factor."** This has to with readiness to receive and the depth and level of demonic infestation due to severity of damage to a person's soul.

3. The **"Minister Factor."** This has to do with the giftings, anointing, experience, knowledge, and authority of those doing the ministry.

4. The **"Resistance Factor."** This has to do with many obstacles that work against healing, including demonic interference, sin, fear, unbelief, ignorance, emotional pain, misconceptions, unforgiveness, inability to hear God's voice, strongholds and much more.

5. The **"Support Factor."** This has to do with the support network the person has to encourage and hold them accountable to maintain freedom. This is a small group of people the person deeply trusts.

6. The **"Intercessory Factor."** This has to do with any number of people who are earnestly praying for the person's healing and deliverance.

7. The **"Discipling Factor."** This has to do with the faith community in which the person is a member. This is a body of believers who under the anointing of the Holy Spirit apply the Word. They teach, reinforce, and provide opportunities for the person to express what they have learned.

Two Approaches to Deliverance Ministry

There are two distinct approaches to deliverance. One is a direct confrontational approach, also known as a power encounter. This is usually unplanned and spontaneous. In this instance, demons manifest or are called forward, and the minister casts them out drawing upon the spiritual authority given him in the name of Jesus. An example of this is found in Mark 1:21-25 in which Jesus is teaching in the synagogue. Suddenly, a man becomes disruptive, shouting out objections to Jesus as the Holy One of God. Jesus commands the demon to be silent and to come out of the man.

A second approach is one which is planned and intentional. An example of this is found in Mark 1:32-34. Jesus is in a house whose owners are open to receiving hurting and damaged people. The entire town intentionally goes to Jesus for the expressed purpose of receiving healing and deliverance. In this instance, Jesus did not allow the demons to speak. He spends the entire evening doing ministry.

Another example of the intentional approach is seen when a man brings his son to Jesus' disciple to be delivered, but they could not do it. The disciples took the man and his son to Jesus. Jesus engages the man in a conversation. He listens as the man describes the boy's condition. Jesus then asks the man some questions about his faith and how long the boy had been suffering (Mark 9:17-29). Jesus delivers the boy from a deaf and dumb spirit. On this occasion, Jesus took the diagnostic approach. He gathered the history, assessed the symptoms, made a diagnosis, identified the spirit, and drove it out.

While there is a need for both approaches, I prefer the intentional, planned, diagnostic approach. I draw upon a diagnostic questionnaire, interviews, spiritual gifts, discernment, and the leading of the Holy Spirit. This approach is more in keeping with the discipleship model found in Ephesians chapter four. In this model, church leaders draw upon Christ's gifts to equip believers to do the work of ministry and build up the body so that unity is achieved and all become mature in Christ. By speaking the truth in love, believers take off the old sinful self and are made new in the attitude of their minds. They are taught not to grieve the Holy Spirit and are set free to love and be tenderhearted. This kind of deliverance requires a long-term relationship in which people are empowered to live a holy life. Ideally, this approach works best in churches with small groups practicing intercessory prayer, encouragement, and accountability.

This systematic approach to deliverance makes a strong contribution to the disciple-making process. It is a vital ingredient to church life and is needed to equip the church to engage the culture. The following is a list of key components:

Key Components

Recognize

First, recognize God's presence. Second, recognize what has you in bondage and ask for God's help. This can be done with use of questionnaires, interviews, revelation, and a prayer of consecration (Isaiah 5: 13; Hosea 4:9; Hebrews 5:14; Psalm 139: 23; James 1:5; Matthew 6:33).

Responsibility

Take responsibility for what you understand your bondage to be. Submit yourself to God. This can be done through a prayer of surrender (Psalm 51:3-4; Proverbs 28:13; Psalm 32:5; James 4:7-10). See Appendix I for a sample prayer.

Repent

Begin to change the way you think. This is accomplished through several transactional steps. First, forgive those who have sinned against you and offended you (Matthew 6:15). Secondly, confess your sin, ask for forgiveness, and receive cleansing (Acts 3:19; 1 John 1:9). To receive total cleansing, you may need to make a divine exchange in which you give Jesus your emotional hurt and pain and He gives you much-needed grace to heal your wounded heart (1 Peter 5:7; Philippians 4:6-7). Thirdly, renew your mind by renouncing the lies you have believed and exchange them with the truth of God's Word (Romans 12:2; John 8:32). Meditate on these positive thoughts (Philippians 4:8).

Renounce

Renounce all word curses, vows, judgments, ungodly soul ties, and all defiling spirits connected to the flesh. Treat them as your enemy. Hate them (Psalm 97:10; Psalm 119:4, 28; Proverbs 8:13; Proverbs 13:5; Amos 5:15; Romans 12:9; Ephesians 4:26-27, 1 Peter 1:14-15; Jude 1:23).

Remove

Get rid of all unclean spirits by commanding them to leave and not return (Acts 16:16-18; Mark 16:17; 2 Corinthians 7:1; Mark 9:25).

Receive

By faith, receive the Father's blessing. Receive the grace God imparts into you so that you can reflect the glory of God (James 1:17; Romans 8:32; I Corinthians 2:12; Ephesians 2:8; Ephesians 5:18-19; Hebrews 11:6; Romans 5:5).

Rejoice

Give God praise and thanks for setting you free and blessing you (Psalm 54:6; Psalm 34:1-4; Philippians 4:4).

Resist

When demons try to come back, assert your authority, reject, and rebuke them. Praise God for having been set free (Matthew 12:44; Luke 11:25,26; John 5:14; James 4:7; 1 Peter 5:8-9; Ephesians 6:11-19; Psalm 8).

Restore

Testify to what God has done for you and help others find freedom (Matthew 28:20; 2 Timothy 2:2; Acts 3:6; Matthew. 10:8).

Repeat

Continue to practice this process until it becomes a lifestyle (John 8:31-32; Philippians 1:6, 2:12, 4:9; 1 Peter 1:15-16; 2 Corinthians 7:1).

Characteristics of One Who Has Been Delivered

Whether freedom comes in a moment or whether it is worked out over a period of time, there are indicators that change has occurred. If deliverance has done its work, there will be evidence of spiritual transformation. This transformation will be manifested in different ways.

The following are some of the characteristics of what freedom looks like:

- **Initially, the person may experience a weight being lifted off or the room may seem brighter.** There is a clarity of thought which the person did not have before. They feel like they have a choice rather than being driven by overpowering thoughts.

- **There is a surprising ability to move past previous sticking points**. What was once a preoccupation and single focus has lost its grip. What used to consume the person is no longer there.

- **There is a new desire to bring every area of life into submission** to righteousness.

- **There is a sense of having a new lease on life.** Hope has entered the heart.

- **There is a conviction that God has answered prayers.**

- **The person feels supported by the Lord** and is strengthened to resist temptation.

- **There is a restoration of personhood.** The person is free to be their true self.

- **There is a hunger for more revelation and truth.**

- There is a renewed sense of being led by the Spirit.
- There is an increased desire to celebrate and praise God.
- There is a desire to see others experience freedom.
- There is gratitude for what God has done.

Maintaining Freedom from Demons

The Bible teaches that once demons are cast out of a person they will attempt to come back and therefore need to be resisted.

In Matthew 12:43-45, Jesus gives insight into the importance of remaining vigilant, not giving demons an opportunity to return, less they come back even stronger.

When an unclean spirit goes out of a man, he goes through dry places, seeking rest, and finds none. Then he says, 'I will return to my house from which I came.' And when he comes, he finds it empty, swept clean, and put in order. Then he goes and takes with him seven other spirits more wicked than himself, and they enter and dwell there; and the last state of that man is worse than the first (Matthew 12:43-45).

The Apostle Peter makes this same warning. He writes, *"Be alert and sober minded. Your enemy the devil prowls around like a roaring lion looking for someone to devour. Resist him standing firm in the faith..."* (1 Peter 5:8).

The Apostle James also speaks of resisting Satan. He wrote, *"Submit yourselves, then to God. **Resist the devil**, and he will flee from you. Come near to God and he will come near to you. Wash your hands, you sinners and purify your hearts, you double-minded. Grieve, mourn and wail. Change your laughter to mourning and your joy to gloom. Humble yourselves before the Lord, and he will lift you up. Brothers and sisters, do not slander one another. Anyone who speaks against a brother or sister, or judges them, speaks against the law and judges it. When you judge the law, you are not keeping it, but sitting in judgment on it. There is only one Lawgiver and Judge, the one who is able to save and destroy.... Instead you ought to say 'if it is the Lord's will, we will live and do this or that'.... If anyone, then, knows the good they ought to do and doesn't do it, it is sin for them"* (James 4:7-17).

Ways to Maintain Freedom

In the passage above, James not only gives instruction to resist the devil, he also provides concrete ways to do it, summarized as follows.

- **Submit** – Subject yourself to the control of God. This is achieved by consecrating and surrendering yourself to the leadership of the Holy Spirit daily. At a minimum, this requires that you do not quench the Spirit.

- **Resist** – Actively oppose Satan by putting on the armor of God. This includes applying the truth, righteousness, salvation, the Word, faith, and peace to your circumstances and situation.

- **Draw near to God** – Enter the manifest presence of God through prayer and worship.

- **Grieve and mourn** – Feel sorrow for your complicity with fleshly desires, sin, and Satan's lies. Do not deny or rationalize your sinful nature. Instead, acknowledge you have either grieved or quenched the Spirit.

- **Wash and purify** - Get rid of impure thoughts and beliefs that come with being double-minded. These thoughts contaminate you and need to be cleansed.

- **Humble yourself** – Admit your inadequacy and to acknowledge your dependency on God.

- **Do not speak evil** – Refrain from criticizing or judging others. We are to leave judgment up to God. This is especially true in dealing with offenses. Do not return evil for evil, but overturn evil with good. Speak blessings.

- **Make plans according to the Lord's will** – Do not presume upon tomorrow by making your own plans. Ask the Lord for His plans instead of simply asking Him to bless yours.

- **Remember** – Be cognizant of what you ought to do in accordance with God's Word and then do it by faith. Love God's law. Put it in your heart that you might not sin.

- **Quickly forgive** – Whenever you are offended, forgive that person from your heart immediately. Recognize that even the slightest irritation or frustration indicates you have been offended. By practicing this, you do not let any bitterness build up in your heart.

- **Remain teachable** – Remain open to what others may tell you regarding what they are seeing in you that is not godly. Invite others to show you where you are blind. Do not let anything separate you from the Father.

- **Don't give in to unbelief** – Persevere. At times life presents harsh, unjust, or impossible circumstances. The temptation becomes to doubt, waver, compromise, or give up. The child of God achieves victory over the evil in the world by faith.

Trends in Deliverance Strategies

Over the centuries, the practice of demonic deliverance in the church has wavered between a high-profile ministry to almost obscurity. Over the past fifty-plus years, ministries with different approaches and styles have emerged. Some of the more notable spiritual warfare movements include the early charismatics of the 1970s featuring people like Don Basham, Bob Mumford, and Derek Prince. Secondly, there are the Dispensationalists. These are non- charismatics arising out of Dallas Theological Seminary and Moody Bible Institute. Leading influencers include Mark Bubeck, Merrill Unger, and C. Fred Dickason. Thirdly, there is a movement identified as the "third wave of the Holy Spirit." This movement is centered around Fuller Theological Seminary and the Vineyard movement. At the forefront of this movement are people like John Wimber, C. Peter Wagner, Charles Craft, John White, and Wayne Grudem. Fourthly, there is what might be broadly identified as the evangelicals. Persons leading this effort include Neil Anderson, Timothy Warner, Tom White, Ed Murphy, and Ray Beeson.[12] A fifth category is a group of exorcists trained by the Roman Catholic Church. This approach draws upon psychological evaluations and a manual called the Rite of Exorcism. One of the leaders in the Unites States is Adam Blai, theological advisor for the Diocese of Pittsburgh. He is also a member of the International Association of Exorcists.[13]

Spiritual warfare is a topic worthy of much investigation. However, it is not the purpose of this book to provide a treatise on spiritual warfare. Neither is it intended to be a manual on deliverance. I simply want to give legitimacy to the practice of deliverance in helping people develop their faith in the quest for freedom.

In the next chapter we look at the need to break free of strongholds that keep people in bondage.

Discussion Questions

1. What has been your experience when the subject of deliverance from demons comes up? How do people react? Why do many become afraid?

2. How would you answer the question whether a demon can possess a Christian? What are some of the way demons gain access to Christian believers?

3. What are the four ways demons attack people?

4. How do you respond to the idea that deliverance is needed for salvation and is the birthright of every Christian? How does practicing deliverance contribute to the believer working out his salvation? What is your reaction to the historical record regarding ordinary Christians casting out demons?

5. What are some of the various names given to Satan? What are some of his schemes? What power do believers have over demons?

6. What should be the Christian response to ghosts?

7. What is your view of the demonic and mental illness? What are some indicators a demon may be influencing a person? What are some ways demons manifest?

8. What are the two approaches to deliverance? What are some of the components of deliverance ministry? What are some indicators that a person has been delivered?

9. How important is it to you to maintain freedom? What are some of the ways you can do that?

Endnotes

1. April Holloway, Demonic Possession and the Ancient Practice of Exorcism, https://www.ancient-origins.net/news-mysterious-phenomena-unexplained-phenomena/ancient-practice-exorcism-rise-again-001211

2. Timothy C. Thomason, Possession, Exorcism and Psychotherapy, https://www.shsu.edu/~piic/winter2008/Thomason.html

3. Dr. Oscar Skarsaunel, htts://www.lausanne.org/content/historical-overview-

4. Jessie Penn-Lewis with Evan Roberts, War on the Saints, (Diggory Press, UK, 2005), p. 223

5. Dr. Oscar Skarsaunel, htts://www.lausanne.org/content/historical-overview-

6. Nancy Mandeville Caciola, The Wicked and the Damned: Demons, the dead, and spirit possession in medieval Italy, https://doi.org/10.4000/terrain.16630

7. Regina Bailey, "Regeneration of Brain Cells Brave New World of Adult Neurogenesis" https://www.thoughtco.com/regeneration-of-brain-cells-373181

8. The Neuroscience of Behavior Change https://healthtransformer.co/the-neuroscience-of-behavior-change-bcb567fa83c1

9. Seunggo Han M.D. https://www.healthline.com/health/chemical-imbalance-in-the-brain

10. Ibid

11. Timothy C. Thomason, Possession, Exorcism, and Psychotherapy, https://www.shsu.edu/~piic/winter2008/Thomason.html

12. David Powlison, https://www.equip.org/articles/deliverance-ministry-in-historical-perspective/

13. Earle Cornelius, Lancaster News Paper (LNP), March 9, 2019

16

Breaking Free
of Strongholds

What is a Stronghold?

The Apostle Paul wrote to the Corinthian church concerning the way Christians are to deal with conflict within relationships. He told them the weapons Christians fight with are not the weapons of the world. He says:

On the contrary, they have divine power to demolish strongholds. We demolish arguments and every pretension that sets itself up against the knowledge of God, and we take captive every thought to make it obedient to Christ (2 Corinthians 10:4-5).

In effect, Paul says Christians have access to divine power to demolish strong arguments or fortified patterns of thought that keep people in conflict with each other, themselves, and God.

A stronghold is a composite of beliefs, attitudes, feelings and thought patterns lodged within the heart. In contemporary language, these thought patterns are located in the subconscious. They act as a fortress built upon lies, curses, judgments, unforgiveness, vows, generational iniquities, worldly beliefs, expectations, and emotional trauma. These strongholds are in opposition to the ways and the Word of God. Strongholds that remain in place keep a person in bondage. On the other hand, when God's counsel deconstructs these strongholds, the heart is strengthened and the person is free to live a glorious destiny (Psalm 73:24-26 NLT). In tearing down strongholds, the person seeks the way of righteousness and is positioned to receive the promises of God (Matthew 6:33). When a person learns to live this way, they have joined the ranks of the few who have found the small gate and narrow road that leads to life (Matthew 7:14). They are essentially walking in the favor of God (Hebrews 11:6 KJV).

Identifying Strongholds

Strongholds can be constructed around an incorrect perception of God, an incorrect perception of self, or an incorrect perception of others.

Symptoms associated with an incorrect view of God include:

- Lack of desire to have an intimate relationship with God.
- Lack of love and passion in your heart for the ways of God.
- Feeling unwanted and uncared for by God.
- Irrational fears of God that produce compulsive thoughts and behaviors.
- Feeling condemned and finding it hard to trust God.
- Feeling obligated to organize life around performance, rules and regulations in order to please God.

Symptoms associated with an incorrect view of self include:

- Low self-esteem.
- Feeling unworthy and condemned.
- Seeing self as a failure; a shame-based identity.
- A guilty conscience that hinders faith.
- Comparison of self to others.
- Seeing self as a victim.

Symptoms associated with an incorrect view of others include:

- Accepting the opinion of others as if it were God's opinion of them.
- Projecting on to others what is true for them.
- Blaming others for their own short-comings and disappointments.
- Taking responsibility that belongs to others.
- Difficulty trusting others because of past hurts.
- Judgment of others in order to protect themselves from rejection.

By virtue of living in a broken, sinful world, all of us have faulty thought patterns and are subject to strongholds. Jeremiah 17:9 declares, *"The heart is deceitful above all things, and desperately wicked and beyond cure. Who can understand it?"* Similarly, Proverbs 14:12 says, *"There is a way that seems right to a man, but its end is destruction."* The truth is we all have deceitful thoughts and feelings that need to be reworked to fall in line with the mind of Christ.

Paul tells us in Romans 12:2, *"Do not be conformed to the pattern of this world, but be transformed by the renewing of your mind. Then you will be able to test and approve what God's will is – his good, pleasing and perfect will."* To discern the Lord's will, we need to replace lies and wrong attitudes with the truth found in the Word and character of God. By taking every thought captive to Christ, strongholds are demolished and we begin to realize the freedom Jesus came to give us. Jesus makes it clear that believers can remain in bondage to sin and evil even after they have claimed God to be their Father due to ignorance of the truth of God's Word (John 8:31-36). Indeed, strongholds are usually formed early in life when we are ignorant and easily deceived. Hosea 4:6 says, *"My people are destroyed for lack of knowledge."*

Some common examples of lies and faulty beliefs that keep people in bondage are listed below. Typically, these lies cluster together to form themes in a person's life story. For example, a person may continually struggle with fear, rejection, jealousy, control, anger, shame, or addictions. Generally, people are aware of these life themes as they experience them over and over again, but are not conscious of the lies that give rise to them since they are hidden. They are buried deep within the heart (subconscious) until they are exposed. It is the work of the Holy Spirit to reveal them and to replace them with the truth. If undetected, these lies have a detrimental impact on the way we relate to others, ourselves, and God.

Lies that affect the way we relate to ourselves include:

- I don't belong. I will always be left out.
- I am not worthy to receive anything from God.
- I am a failure if I don't get things done.
- I am unattractive.
- I must plan every day of my life.
- I am not good enough.
- I have wasted the best time in my life, and it will never be recovered.

Lies that affect the way we relate to others include:

- I can't let anyone have the satisfaction of knowing they hurt me.
- I will never be recognized, understood, or appreciated by those close to me.
- If I let anyone get close to me, my heart will be broken again.
- I must strive to please others in order to feel accepted.
- I have made such a mess of my life there is no reason to go on.
- I must never show emotion. To do so is to be weak.
- I must never inconvenience or be a bother to others.
- I can't be honest for fear of being judged, criticized, or rejected.

Lies that affect our relationship with God include:

- God loves others more than He loves me.
- God will judge me as lazy if I do not always stay busy.
- I am so messed up God could never use me.
- Because people suffer unjustly, God cannot be trusted.
- God doesn't care about me. If He did, He would answer my prayers the way I want.
- God has disappointed me before. He will do it again.
- God abandoned me when I was troubled. I can't believe His promises.

Satan tries to get you to believe two things. First, that you are not good enough for God to love and second, God is not good enough for you to trust fully. In either case, the lie will disrupt your relationship with God.

The Scriptures teach, *"As a man thinketh in his heart so is he"* (Proverbs 23:7 KJV). If you think of yourself as a failure, you will feel like a failure and set yourself up to be a failure. If you think of yourself as a new creation, delivered from your past, you will feel clean, hopeful, and alive in Christ. Strongholds are patterns of thought and feeling that give shape to who you are. You cannot live contrary to what you believe about yourself. When you know the truth of what God says about you, and believe it, then you can live free of strongholds that keep you in bondage.

Tearing Down Strongholds

Before dismantling a stronghold, it is helpful to understand how they form. Each person develops a belief system based on their life experience. In response to life situations, events, traumas, and cultural expectations, each person constructs a belief system. From those beliefs, they make judgments and decisions that result in behaviors. Chester and Betsy Kylstra capture how beliefs impact a person's life in this short mantra written by an anonymous author whose thoughts are similar to those of Ralph Waldo Emerson. I have taken the liberty to add one more line. It goes like this:

- If you accept a Belief, you reap a Thought.
- If you sow a Thought, you reap an Attitude.
- If you sow an Attitude, you reap an Action.
- If you sow an Action, you reap a Habit.
- If you sow a Habit, you reap a Character.
- If you sow a Character, you reap a Destiny." [1]
- If you sow a Destiny, you reap a Reckoning.

In effect, the things we experience, the things people say to us, the things we hear from the media and our education, establish our belief systems. In this way, the world impacts us through external influences. How a person assimilates these influences into what he accepts as true determines his belief system. If a person accepts something as true, when it is actually false, the prince of this world has deceived him. It is the Spirit of truth that sets a person free from the devil's lies. In addition, the Holy Spirit renews the mind, rebuilding a godly stronghold through acceptance of the Word of God as truth. Tearing down strongholds is a relatively easy process.

A Four-Step Process

The way to tear down a stronghold is to follow the four-step process laid out in the Word of God. This involves confession, renouncing, breaking off, and repenting (changing your thinking).

Confession

First identify the lie and confess it. Forgive those who contributed to your forming the lie. Ak God to forgive you for allowing the lie to define you. Forgive yourself for having agreed with the lie (Ephesians 4:32).

Renounce

Renounce the lie by abandoning any right to possess it (Ephesians 5:11).

Break off

Break all agreements with demons attached to the lie. Command demons to leave by the authority given to you in Jesus Christ (James 4:7).

Repent

Change your way of thinking by replacing the lie with the truth based on God's Word. Then spend thirty to sixty days meditating on the truth until it sinks deep into your soul and you automatically respond with the truth when faced with people and circumstances that want to dredge up the old lie. Be aware: Satan will always test you to see if you believe the truth. Resist the devil by putting on the girdle of truth daily and stand firm (Acts 3:19; Ephesians 6:14).

Tearing Down Strongholds Saves a Marriage

Joe and Trish were married over 25 years. Looking from the outside, they had a perfect marriage, but that was far from the truth. Their marriage was approaching the breaking point.

Everyone knew Joe as Pastor Joe, who ran an outreach mission in the City of Reading and a local church pastor. Trish was his dutiful wife but secretly she was disconnected from God. She carried the burden of having had an abortion. She understood God had forgiven her, but she still felt unshakeable shame.

Trish was in desperate need of inner healing and deliverance. She received healing through a ministry called, Deeper Still but recognized she needed more healing. She was introduced to Faith to Freedom Ministry and received deliverance in the area of abandonment. She broke off generational curses, core lies and soul wounds that held her captive her entire life. She was thrilled to be set free.

Joe got a brand-new wife, but he was not thrilled. He was intimidated by her radical change. In fact, he was jealous. Trish's transformation challenged Joe to begin to look at his own life. Reluctantly, he went to Faith to Freedom to deal with their marriage issues. His first session was an angry one. He was skeptical of this deliverance stuff. He thought it best to leave things from the past in the past.

It took several sessions until Joe began to receive the same freedom that Trish enjoyed. He dealt with inadequacy and with several layers of unforgiveness. His pain seemed to melt away under the power of the Holy Spirit. He was no longer a skeptic. He experienced a beautiful sense of freedom.

The best part to all of this was their marriage was transformed. They dealt with inner vows, wounds and resentments in their marriage. They began to love each other again. For their 30th wedding anniversary they renewed their vows and are now living their lives together!

Pastor Joe Sclafani is the Executive Director of City Light Ministry, Reading, Pennsylvania. Trish is the Executive Director, Deep Still, Eastern Pennsylvania.

Discussion Questions

1. What is a stronghold? What three things construct a stronghold?

2. What are some lies and faulty beliefs with which you identify?

3. How are strongholds constructed? What are its components?

4. How do you deconstruct a stronghold?

5. Why should Christians give their attention to tearing down strongholds?

6. Can you identify a possible stronghold in your life?

7. What does it take to build back a stronghold based on godly beliefs?

Endnotes

1. Chester and Betsy Kylstra, *Belief System*, (Proclaiming His Word Ministries, Mount Juliet, TN, 1999)

17

Three Prominent Strongholds to Consider

Travis' Story

Travis is a bright, energetic young man in his thirties. He works as a manager of a Friendly's restaurant. Through his vital leadership role in church, he helps newcomers assimilate into the congregation. Sometime ago, Travis went through a life crisis that led him into deep soul searching. For several years, I have been serving as a mentor for Travis. He writes about the transformation that took place in his life.

Over the course of the last two years, the Lord has laid on my heart what it really means to find peace, contentment, and true identity. I feel like many people can identify with me as I struggle to gain freedom from a life-long bondage. I had fallen into a trap in which my identity was linked to my accomplishments and perfectionism.

This started in high school when grades became the most important thing in my life. I believed that grades determined my future. I let them shape my identity. I would get a test back with one point off and stew over the one point I missed. I had determined that my identity rested on a performance-based scoring system. If I scored high, then I could feel good about myself. If I scored low, then I didn't feel good about myself. Depending on the score, I felt my identity was either protected or threatened.

Keeping score continued in other areas of my life. When I mowed yards, I would subtract a point for every skipper I left standing in the yard. This need for self-validation through performance followed me into being the president of my class. I sought to make everyone happy. When I could not please everyone, the way I viewed myself suffered. As a young adult, I managed several restaurants, albeit at the lowest level of the totem pole. I knew that to advance in the restaurant business, I had to perform at a very high level. This meant submitting to the pressures of out-producing all the other managers. The problem with this was that once I achieved a particular objective for a work week, I would have to set an even higher goal the following week. To feel good about myself, I would have to work harder and harder.

The best way to describe this way of life is to compare it to the game of golf. You get a hole in one on the first green, and you feel wonderful. But as soon as that hole is over, it is time to play hole number two. To feel good about yourself, you need to get another hole in one. To maintain your performance, you need to get a hole in one on every hole that follows. How realistic is that? I didn't realize it, but I was keeping a scorecard in life. I bought into lies that my identity was solely tied to my performance. This was true in my spiritual life, as well. I viewed God as the ultimate scorekeeper.

All of this changed when I went through a crisis in which my girlfriend ended our long-term relationship. This breakup caused me to examine my life to see where I went wrong, what I really valued, and what was most significant and meaningful. In all of this, I looked to Jesus for answers. He showed me that I had to reorder my priorities. I had invested so much of myself in work, accumulating things, and seeking success that I had lost sight of who I really was.

The truth is that my identity is found in Jesus and His sacrifice on the cross. I cannot work for my salvation. It is a gift from God that is received by faith. I was recently reminded of that liberating truth when I was preparing for the busiest day of the year at one of our restaurants. I had broken all the sales records for six straight years. On this particular day, I was poised to do it again. But about mid-day, a heavy storm threatened to wreck the outdoor event. I was feverishly working at a pace that surpassed record sales when the clouds came rolling in. I felt a little discouraged, but unlike in the past when I would stew over missing the one point on a test or the one skipper in the yard, the Lord reminded me that my identity was settled on the cross. My sense of well-being no longer depended on possessions or career accomplishments. Neither is my worth found in other people's assessment of my value. My worth and identity is found only in Him!

I am not suggesting that we should not aspire to accomplish things while we are in this world. But we must understand that we are built for eternity. As Christians, we find true meaning, purpose, and happiness in accomplishing the good things God planned for us long ago. These are the things that last for eternity.

Our task is to seek clarity between what is eternal and what is temporary. There is no short-term worldly accomplishment that can fill the need for eternity. Only Jesus can fill that empty hole in our heart. He provides for our salvation, and His Holy Spirit enables us to experience eternity now, here on earth. The only firm ground we can place our identity on is Jesus! He is the same today, tomorrow, and forever!

Using the world's performance system created a trap that held me in bondage. It set up happiness as a moving target, one that changed every day. Living life based on performance mentality prevents you from finding true peace and freedom.

I fell victim to this trap for about two decades before I fully realized the cost. Basing my identity on performance led to broken relationships, heartbreak, fatigue, and anxiety. When I realized the root cause of this pain, I knew I had to re-order my life around Jesus. I found rest in Him and began to care for others the way He calls us to. My measuring stick for success was replaced with a new perspective. I now approach each day believing no matter what I accomplish or do not accomplish, my identity is secure in Jesus Christ and what He did for me on the cross.

1. Performance Stronghold

Like many people living in our success-driven society, Travis was caught up in a performance or perfectionist stronghold, allowing his performance in everything he did to determine his identity. The trouble was, he could never be content. Continually comparing himself to others, he had to always out-perform others and surpass even himself to feel good about himself.

One of the schemes Satan uses in the life of a Christian is to make him base his self-value on the type and the quality of work he does. This is called "performance-based acceptance." A person with a performance-based identity can feel good about himself as long as he has a good job and is doing that job well. But that is a "slippery slope." The moment he loses his job or cannot perform it well, he easily slips into an identity crisis. Timothy Keller puts it this way, "If our identity is in our work, rather than Christ, success will go to our heads, and failure will go to our hearts." [1]

The Apostle Paul had a job failure that went to his heart. On the road to Damascus, he had an encounter with the living Christ that propelled him into a crisis. With his job performance drastically questioned, his identity as a Pharisee seriously shaken, and his faith profoundly challenged, Paul had to re-evaluate his life purpose. Later he would write that what he did before his conversion was the root of his identity, based on human effort and self-righteousness. But now his identity came from faith in Jesus Christ (Philippians 3:2-9).

It is a good to focus on self-improvement to upgrade our performance, but that is not a sufficient foundation on which to build a positive self-identity. Perfectionism can only lead to narcissism, strained relationships, depression, and anxiety. On the other-hand, grace received through faith leads to self-acceptance, harmony, contentment, and fulfillment.

For several years when I was a pastor, my former secretary, Sue, and I sought to free ourselves from our perfectionistic tendencies. Even though we did not fully recognize we were functioning out of a performance-based identity, we knew we were not operating in the Spirit. It was only after admitting that our perfectionism was tied up with our sinful nature that we began to repent. One day, Sue casually remarked, "When I was perfect, everyone else was stupid." I laughed. From then on, we would catch ourselves saying and doing stupid stuff. We would gently remind each other of our perfectionism by saying, "When I was perfect, _____. Over several years, we developed quite a list.

Here are a few examples:

- When I was perfect, there was no authority but me.

- When I was perfect, everyone else was the problem, not me. I was the only one who was right.

- When I was perfect, I felt it my job to straighten out everyone else. Now I leave the straightening out to God.

- When I was perfect, I had no issue with pride.

- When I was perfect, I was never convicted of sin.

- When I was perfect, my looking good was more important than being honest. I feared man's judgment more than God's.

- When I was perfect, I was extremely aggressive to do things on my time. Now I wait for God to tell me what to do, and when and what to say.

- When I was perfect, I saw everyone's faults. Now I see their pain.

For a more complete list see Appendix G.

By keeping a running list of these things, we helped each other chip away at our narcissism. Without realizing it, we were putting into practice Hebrews 10:24, *"And let us consider how we may spur (motivate) one another toward love and good works."* In a light-hearted way, we reminded ourselves of how destructive our perfectionism and performance mentality had been.

Living life based on outward appearances, accomplishments, status, titles, and recognition does not produce internal peace, significance, or maturity. What brings contentment is not conformity to the world's false promises; rather, freedom comes from realizing our identity in Christ. In Romans 13:14, Paul says: *"Rather clothe yourselves with the Lord Jesus Christ, and do not think about how to gratify the desires of the flesh."* The desires of the flesh are fleeting. Real happiness is found in truth.

Once the lies and worldly beliefs are exposed and renounced, it is imperative that we clothe ourselves with the truth of who we are in Christ. How do we do this? First, we need to discover what the Bible says about who we are in Christ. Here are a few examples of what the Scriptures reveal:

- **I am a son of God and one in Christ** (Galatians 3:26,28).
- **I am a child of God** (John 1:12).
- **I am a slave of righteousness** (Romans 6:22).
- **I am a saint** (1 Corinthians 1:2; Ephesians 1:1; Philippians 1:1; Colossians 1:2).
- **I am a citizen of heaven, seated in heaven right now** (Ephesians 2:6; Philippians 3:20).
- **I am a new creation** (2 Corinthians 5:17).
- **I am reconciled to God and am a minister of reconciliation** (2 Corinthians 5:18-19).

For a more complete list go to http//vintagelawreance.com/wp-content/uploads/2013/01/ANDERSON-WhoIAmInchrist.pdf.

Being a Christian is not simply about receiving forgiveness for sin, having a hope of going to heaven, or receiving the Holy Spirit. Being a Christian involves transformation. You become someone that did not exist before, taking on a new identity. Understanding who you are in Christ is essential in living out your God-given purpose and destiny. As you take on this new identity, you begin to live in victory and freedom that Christ Himself lived in.

To take on this new identity, we need to ponder, reflect, and meditate on these truths of who we are in Christ. We need to let them sink deep into our souls until they become the way we naturally think. In this way, we retrain our minds to think the thoughts of Christ. By exchanging lies for the truth, we renew our minds (Romans 12:2). Gradually, with practice and reinforcement, we come to see ourselves the way Jesus saw Himself. He believed He was favored and loved by God (Matthew 3:17). Convinced that the Father loved Him, He was secure in who He was.

Consequently, He desired to please the Father in everything He did. He carried Himself with humility and authority and was without anxiety or fear. Although tempted in every way, He was without guilt, shame, fear, rejection, pride, jealousy, or self-centeredness (Hebrews 4:15). Neither man nor Satan deceived Him. He was full of truth and grace. God the Father was with Him. He and the Father were one. As we learn to identify more and more with Jesus, we also enjoy the Father's love. Sin and Satan lose their grip on us. We are set free to live as conquerors (Romans 8:36,37) and overcomers (1 John 5:4-5). Our life increasingly takes on the character of the Holy Spirit (Galatians 5:22-23).

2. Rejection Stronghold

Due to the excommunication of Adam and Eve from the garden, mankind has struggled with rejection. It is a consequence of living in a sinful world. Children unwanted by their parents, a student refused admittance into college, the worker who fails to achieve promotion, the borrower who gets turned down for a loan, the suitor whose romantic gestures are rebuffed, and a once-married divorcee all suffer rejection. In the Bible, Joseph, Moses, David, Jeremiah, Paul, and many more heroes of the faith suffered great rejection. Yet, because of their faith in God's goodness, they overcame adversity. Jesus Himself suffered horrific rejection, yet He overcame and conquered because He knew the love of the Father.

When people have little understanding of the Father's love, they are less resilient when they suffer rejection. They tend to become disappointed, angry, and bitter. It tests their faith in God and severely shakes their confidence in themselves. They find it hard to trust anyone. They become captive to fear. One hurting person put it this way, "I can never be honest without being afraid of being judged." The fear of being judged keeps you from being yourself. On the other hand, when you connect with the Father's love, you can be yourself. No longer shackled by fear, guilt, and shame that come with rejection, you are free to love. You have freedom to be a son or daughter of God.

A Revealing Parable

Leif Hetland has written a wonderful book entitled *Healing the Orphan Spirit*. He addresses the subject of rejection by drawing upon Jesus' "Parable of the Prodigal Son." Hetland makes a compelling argument that the parable should be re-titled the "Parable of the Loving Father."[2] With great insight into the human condition, he points out that both sons carried a spirit of rejection, failing to connect with their father's love. The younger son, impatient with his father's generosity, demanded his inheritance so that he could live a rebellious, immoral life. The older son was disappointed with the father. He had lived a dutiful, religious life, and because of his loyalty, he expected his father's favor. When it did not come, he became angry and resentful. Both brothers demonstrated a mentality of a slave rather than that of a son. Neither one enjoyed intimacy with the father or connected with his heart.

The overarching point in the parable is that God wants his sons and daughters to know the fullness of His love. He wants them to know His heart. He wants to share a deep intimacy with them. Jesus said, *"Anyone who has seen me has seen the Father"* (John 14:9). He makes it clear that He came to the world to reveal the Father's love. John 3:17 declares, *"God did not send his Son into the world to condemn the world, but to save the world through him."*

We have experienced so much judgment, rejection, and emotional pain that it is difficult for us to connect with God's love. Even when we believe it intellectually, we have trouble feeling it in our hearts. It is only through the power of the Holy Spirit that our hearts can be healed and made to feel the Father's love (Romans 5:5). Having our emotions healed by the Holy Spirit is as essential as having lies replaced with the truth. Jesus was full of both truth and grace. We can talk about love, but until we feel love, it remains an enigma or, at best, an intellectual concept. When it comes to tearing down strongholds, we need to recognize that Christ's truth dismantles lies and Christ's grace heals wounded emotions. Both truth and grace are necessary to realize healing and freedom fully.

Practicing Truth and Grace

Sue and I learned to extend both truth and grace to each other in a simple way. One year for Christmas, she gave me two hand-made cards. One was a grace card that I could use when she poured out more truth than I could handle. When I pulled out the grace card, she knew to back off and give me some space. The other was a truth card. When I pulled out the truth card, she knew I was going to tell her some things that would be tough to hear. Well, that worked fine but it was a bit one-sided, so Sue equipped herself with a ruler. When the ruler was in her hand, she became known as "The Humbler." Every pastor needs a "Humbler." She marked one end of the ruler with the word "grace" and the other was marked by the word "truth." When she pulled out the ruler, I knew it was time for me to sit down and listen to "The Humbler." Most of the time, I didn't know which one I was going to get, truth or grace. Only after she turned the ruler, enabling me to read the word, did I know what was in store.

This process was our way of learning to deal with the fear of rejection. Challenging topics and difficult conversations have a way of uncovering painful wounds of rejection, and we want to avoid them. However, they are necessary if we are going to grow into full maturity in Christ. Slowly we became comfortable speaking the truth in love to each other and the fear of rejection subsided.

Rejection is one of the severest emotional wounds a person can suffer. It attacks the very essence of who we are and demolishes our self-esteem. This could be why rejection is a favorite tool of Satan which he uses to destroy human life. "Nothing impacts the human heart more than rejection."[3] It hardens the heart, steals hope and joy, impairs relationships, and stunts spiritual growth. Rejection is really the absence of love. To reject someone is to deny them love. Satan loves to make you feel unloved with the offense of rejection.

When someone experiences the pain of rejection, their first tendency is to respond out of the flesh. They become defensive, build up walls, or withdraw. When expectations are not met, people become rebellious. They exercise their self-centered will, becoming independent. There is a proclivity toward unforgiveness, anger, bitterness, resentment, and revenge. Because of their disappointment, they will blame others and God. Where pain is intense, they will choose not to believe God's Word. They may continue to believe God exists but no longer believe in His goodness. Life becomes joyless, characterized by hopelessness, shame, ridicule, sarcasm, insult, perfectionism, compulsivity, obsessiveness, jealousy, and judgment. Loneliness sets in. People who suffer from severe rejection develop a fear of rejection. They carry a sense of failure and anxiety that can lead to eating disorders, addictions, sexual promiscuity, self-mutilation, isolation, depression, and suicidal thoughts.

People who have experienced rejection and abuse as a child grow up with deep emotional wounds. If these wounds are not healed, Satan will take advantage of their injury, infecting their souls with torment. They will develop habits and hang ups that keep them from realizing their God-given purpose and potential. Some of the symptoms that accompany rejection include:

- Pretending to be someone you are not
- Rebellion against established norms
- A tendency to reject others before they reject you
- Always questioning if someone is accepting or rejecting you
- Needing to be involved in everything to feel accepted
- Full of self-pity; feeling bad because you think you are all alone
- Resists correction and unable to receive constructive criticism
- Needing to always be right
- Having an emotional deficit characterized by being starved for love and attention
- Blaming God for not making you ideal – physically attractive
- Having a propensity for pride; "How dare you reject me!"
- Being consumed with feelings of worthlessness, anxiety, and hopelessness
- Being afraid of what others think of you
- Being driven by perfectionism and performance
- Fear of confrontation because the opinion of others impacts your identity
- Comparing and competing with others for influence
- Being prone to addictive behavior: workaholism, porn, alcoholism, cigarettes
- Being a people pleaser – always looking for approval
- Allowing envy and jealousy to be the roots of rejection
- Expecting to be in control even when lacking expertise and authority
- Withdrawing from conflicted relationships
- Perceiving others rejecting you even when they are not; easily offended

Anytime we base our identity on what others think of us, we entrust that person with our identity. We erroneously give them the power that belongs to God. On the other hand, when we allow God to define us, we spare ourselves a lot of pain. Man's rejection may hurt, but it does not cripple. God's grace and acceptance is more than sufficient. His love fills our greatest need.

God created us to be in a loving relationship with Himself and others, designing us to receive and give love. The withholding of love threatens our very existence, draining the life out of us. The devil uses rejection to make us feel unloved and thereby undermines our relationship with God. Jesus came to earth with a mission to restore intimacy. His assignment was to reconcile men to God (2 Corinthians 5: 18-19). By demonstrating God's love on the cross, Jesus disarmed Satan and made a spectacle of him (Colossians 2:15). Through His death and resurrection, He poured out God's mercy and grace. He sent the

Holy Spirit to be our Comforter and Guide. The Spirit's indwelling presence reconnects us to the Father's love.

Having faith restored in God's goodness, we are empowered to love others who see things differently than we do. Galatians 5:6 says: *"For when we place our faith in Christ Jesus, it makes no difference whether we are circumcised or not circumcised. What is important is faith expressing itself in love."* In other words, when we are reconciled to God, we are empowered to overcome rejection with love. Our love for God sets us on a path toward loving ourselves and our neighbor (Matthew 22:39) even when we disagree. *"We love because He first loved us"* (1 John 4:19).

Taking every thought captive to Christ's love, the stronghold of rejection is dismantled, tearing down a false identity and replacing it with a true identity. The old self is replaced with a new self. The new self reflects the identity of a son and daughter of God rather than a servant or orphan identity.

In his book, *Spiritual Slavery to Spiritual Sonship*, Jack Frost provides a chart that reflects this change in identity.[4]

Contrasting the Orphan Heart with the Heart of Sonship

ORPHAN HEART		HEART OF SONSHIP
See God as Master	Image of God	See God as a Loving Father
Independent/Self-reliant	Dependency	Interdependent/ Acknowledges Need
Live by the Love of the Law	Theology	Live by the Law of Love
Insecure/Lack Peace	Security	Rest and Peace
Strive for Praise, approval, and acceptance of people.	Need of Approval	Totally accepted in God's love and justified by grace.
A need for personal achievement as you seek to impress God and others, or no motivation to serve at all.	Motive for Service	Service that is motivated by a deep gratitude for being unconditionally loved by God.
Duty and earning God's favor or no motivation at all.	Motive behind Christian Disciplines	Pleasure and Delight
"Must" be holy to have God's favor, thus increasing a sense of shame and guilt.	Motivation for Purity	"Want to" be holy; do not want anything to hinder intimate relationship with God.
Self-rejection from comparing yourself to others	Self-Image	Positive and affirmed because you know you have such value to God.
Seek comfort in counterfeit affections; addictions, compulsions, escapism, busyness, hyper-religious activity	Sourse of Comfort	Seeks times of quietness and solitude to rest in the Father's presence and love.

Competition, rivalry, and jealousy toward others' success and position.	**Peer Relationships**	Humility and unity as you value others and are able to rejoice in their blessings and success.
Accusation and exposure in order to make yourself look good by making others look bad.	**Handling Other's Faults**	Love covers as you seek to restore others in a spirit of love and gentleness
See authority as a source of pain; distrustful toward them and lack a heart attitude of submission.	**View of Authority**	Respectful, honoring: you see them as ministers of God for good in your life.
Difficulty receiving admonition; you must be right so you easily get your feelings hurt and close your spirit to discipline.	**View of Admonition**	See the receiving of admonition as a blessing and need in your life so that your faults and weaknesses are exposed and put to death.
Guarded and conditional; based upon others' performance as you seek to get your own needs met.	**Expression of Love**	Open, patient, and affectionate as you lay your life and agendas down in order to meet the needs of others.
Conditional and Distant	**Sense of God's Presence**	Close and Intimate
Bondage	**Condition**	Liberty
Feel like a Servant/Slave	**Position**	Feel like a Son or Daughter
Spiritual ambition; the earnest desire for some spiritual and distinction and the willingness to strive for it; a desire to be seen and counted among the mature.	**Vision**	To daily experience the Father's unconditional love and acceptance and then to be sent as a representative of His love to family and others.
Fight for what you get!	**Future**	Sonship releases your inheritance!

A person who suffers from rejection will exhibit at least some of the characteristics of an orphan heart. The process of transforming your identity from an orphan to a son requires the discipline of renewing the mind as explained in Romans 12:2.

Renewing the mind involves reconstructing your belief system. This is more than correcting faulty theological beliefs. You can have the right doctrine, recite the Apostles' Creed and subscribe to orthodox beliefs yet still be functioning out of lies. These lies obtain their power in how you have learned to frame reality. For example, if you have experienced hypocrisy from church leaders and are hurt, you are likely to form a belief system that says, "All spiritual leaders cannot be trusted." It will be through that filter that you will determine if you will engage in church involvement. Whereas some church leaders cannot be trusted, it is not true that all church leaders cannot be trusted. Identifying ungodly beliefs born out of painful experience or the lies that the world has indoctrinated you to believe is the first step toward renewing your mind.

Once faulty beliefs have been identified, you need to ask and receive God's forgiveness for accepting those lies as the truth. Next, you need to renounce the lies and break all agreements with demons attached to those lies. After that, you need to replace the lie with the truth of God's Word. For example, the lie might be, "I will always be lonely." To transform that lie into the truth, you would say, "I am never alone because Christ is always with me" (Hebrews 13:5-6). Finally, you need to meditate on these truths until they become automatic patterns of thought. Just like when you learned the multiplication tables as a child, through repetition, you automatically responded with the right answer. The more you think about the truth, the more it becomes a part of you.

In addition to renewing the mind, the Apostle Paul instructs that we need to develop a heavenly mindset. In Colossians 3:1-2, he writes, *"Since you have been raised to new life with Christ, set your sights on the realities of heaven, where Christ sits in the place of honor at God's right hand. Think about the things of heaven, not the things of earth"* (NLT). You may have heard it said, "You can be so heavenly minded that you are no earthly good." But according the Bible, just the opposite is true. Having a heavenly mindset is important in advancing the kingdom of God on earth. Satan is always trying to flood our minds with fears, doubts, unbelief, temptations, and worldly concerns to prevent us from focusing on our relationship with God and our place in the kingdom.

In contrast, Jesus instructs us to pray by keeping our thoughts on praising God and bringing His kingdom to earth. Similarly, in Isaiah 26:3, we are reassured that right thinking brings us peace. The Scripture promises, *"You will keep in perfect peace all who trust in you, all whose thoughts are fixed on you!"* (Isaiah 26:3 NLT). When our thoughts are focused on God, we are free of anxiety, worry, and fear. Indeed, Psalm 34:4 declares, *"I sought the LORD, and he heard me, and delivered me from all my fears"* (KJV). Keeping our thoughts focused on God in praise and in prayer makes us mindful of His presence. In His presence, there is joy and eternal pleasure (Psalm 16:11).

A heavenly mindset is developed by desiring what the Spirit of God desires. Paul says in Romans 8:6, *"So letting your sinful nature control your mind leads to death. But letting the Spirit control your mind leads to life and peace"* (NLT). One of the ways we allow the Spirit to control our thoughts is to remember our resurrected position in Christ. Paul stated, *"Since, then, you have been raised with Christ, set your hearts on things above"* (Colossians 3:1). In other words, believers who understand their resurrected position also understand the authority they have in Christ. Paul puts it this way in Ephesians 2:6, *"And God raised us up with Christ and seated us with him in heavenly realms in Christ Jesus."* When Paul speaks about being seated with Christ in heavenly places, he references "authority" and "rulership." God has given Christ supremacy that is above all authority, power, and dominion (Matthew 28:18). Furthermore, that same power and authority is available to those who believe.

In Ephesians 1:17-20, Paul prays that the Ephesians' hearts would be open to receive wisdom and revelation, so they know the hope that is theirs. This revelation knowledge is what gives them hope of their glorious inheritance and the incredible power that is available to those who believe. This power bestowed on believers is the same power that raised Jesus from the dead. Succinctly stated, those who believe in Jesus, who surrender and align themselves with His Spirit, not only have hope for a rich inheritance but will share in the power to rule and reign with Him. They become power brokers who share in His glory both now and in eternity.

Paul wants us to see that by renewing our minds and by thinking on things above, we surrender to and align ourselves with the Spirit of Christ. Christ gives us His authority and power to overcome the things of the earth. In this way, we live in freedom despite the troubles of living in this world.

Judging Self - Is Most Destructive

When we judge ourselves, we negate the grace of God. We do not allow God to show us His love. In essence, and unknowingly, we align ourselves to Satan's biggest lies—that the cross has no effect in salvation, Christ's blood has no power to cleanse, and Christ's death cannot atone for our sin. Satan has convinced us that our sin is so bad that God cannot forgive us; we are unworthy of His love and grace.

When we have a bad thought or act sinfully, we condemn ourselves and feel shame and unworthiness. We think God is angry with us, but that is not the case. The good news of the gospel is Jesus took away God's wrath, judgment, and condemnation when he died on the cross. Jesus paid our sin debt for us. He also took our guilt and shame on to Himself, becoming our scapegoat in exchange for His righteousness (Isaiah 53:1-12). When we receive this truth and believe that Christ has made us righteous, there is no need to judge ourselves.

When we do make a mistake, we simply ask forgiveness, receive forgiveness and ask God to give us more grace to help us overcome our sinful nature through the power of the Holy Spirit (1 John 1:9). In doing so, we become like Christ by faith, not trying harder to be on good behavior. Being on good behavior in our own strength is what religion is all about. Living in a love relationship with Jesus is the essence of true faith and freedom.

In the Sermon on the Mount, Jesus warns, *"Do not judge, or you too will be judged. For in the same way you judge others, you will be judged, and with the measure you use, it will be measured to you"* (Matthew 7:1-2). The truth is that you cannot show love to those you judge, including yourself. When you judge yourself, you cannot show love to yourself. You cannot act any differently than what you believe about yourself.

In judging yourself, you cannot fulfill the second great commandment: to love your neighbor. In Matthew 22:37-38, Jesus replied to the experts in the law as to the most important part of living out faith. He said, *"Love the Lord your God with all your heart and with all your soul and with all your mind. This is the first and greatest commandment. And the second is like it: Love your neighbor as yourself."* When you judge or curse yourself, you lose your capacity to show love to others. This loss of demonstratable love creates all kinds of problems in maintaining healthy, life-giving relationships.

Furthermore, Paul teaches us by his example the importance of not allowing others to judge us nor judge ourselves. Judgment belongs only to God (James 4:12). Believers have the added assurance that God's mercy rises new every morning (Lamentations 3:23) and *"The Lord God is waiting to show you how kind He is and to have mercy on you. The Lord always does what's right and He blesses those who trust Him"* (Isaiah 30:18 CEV)! Anxiety decreases when you understand the mercy of God. Fear, shame, self-pity, unworthiness, anger, blame, comparison, and jealousy lose their grip when God's mercy is fully embraced.

Paul wrote in 2 Corinthians 4:3-5 NLT, *"As for me, it matters very little how I might be evaluated by you or by human authority. I don't even trust my own judgment on this point. My conscience is clear, but that doesn't prove I'm right. It is the Lord himself who will examine me and decide. So, don't make judgments about anyone ahead of time – before the Lord returns. For he will bring our darkest secrets to light and will reveal our private motives. Then God will give to each one whatever praise is due."*

Christians who enjoy freedom, live life in a judgment-free zone. They do not judge themselves nor do they judge others. They are not afraid of how others judge them. They remain confident in God's love even when they commit a transgression. Christians have the assurance that in God's economy, mercy triumphs over judgment (James 2:12-13). This does not make them cavalier in sinning. Instead, they are humble knowing it is the mercy and kindness of the Lord that leads to repentance (Romans 2:4). Therefore, they are free to confess their sins to one another and thereby receive healing (James 5:16). God's mercy keeps them from condemning themselves. It keeps them from believing the accusing lies of Satan. Acts 2:21 says, *"Anyone who asks for mercy from the Lord shall have it and shall be saved"* (LB).

One of the most dangerous things we can do is to think of ourselves differently than the way God thinks of us. If we do, we will miss the destiny that God has for us. We will not be able to receive the grace needed to fulfill our God-given purpose. Learning to see ourselves the way God sees us establishes our identity as sons and daughters of God. In this way, we bring God's kingdom to earth. We are assured in 2 Corinthians 3:5-6, *"The capacity we have comes from God. It is he who made us capable of serving the new covenant"* (TEV).

We live in a world that continually criticizes, compares, abuses, abandons, bullies, and blames. We are reminded daily of how inadequate, unacceptable, and deficient we are. This barrage of negative messaging brings on discouragement, despair, and hopelessness. To counter all this negativity, we need to learn how to give ourselves the same grace that is given to us in Christ Jesus. Otherwise, we have no hope. Christ is our hope of glory (Colossians 1:27). Christ lives in us and gives us hope in all situations. In our weakness, His power is made perfect and His grace is sufficient (2 Corinthians 12:9).

There are at least two things we can do to live a life filled with grace. First, we can be humble, relying on the Holy Spirit to sustain us in times of insult, suffering, and pain. As in 1 Peter 5:6-7, *"Humble yourselves, therefore, under the mighty hand of God, that he might exalt you in proper time, casting all your anxiety upon Him, because He cares for you."* Learning to give Jesus our pain, regrets, fears, lies, injustices, judgments, curses, and negative self-talk is vitally important for experiencing freedom. I will address this topic in the next chapter.

Second, we must learn to discern the difference between conviction and condemnation. Believers often hear negative thoughts in their head and think it is God condemning them. But this is not true. God never tells us that we are worthless or a "lost cause." The Bible tells us that Jesus came into the world not to condemn the world but to save it (John 12:47).

What is condemnation?

Condemnation is from Satan. He desires to tear you down. He comes to rob, kill, and destroy you of life (John 10:10). He points out where you have failed and where you are the problem. He points out inadequacy and never provides the solution. Condemnation says: "Look at what a terrible person you are." The Bible assures us, *"There is now no condemnation for those who are in Christ Jesus"* (Romans 8:1). Satan, on the other hand, is known as the accuser of the brethren (Revelation 12:10). You will never hear Jesus tell you that you are a loser, a failure, or a reject. Jesus said, *"I came not to judge the world, but to save the world"* (John 12:47). I make it a point to tell the people I minister to they are not the problem. They may "have a problem," but they are not "the problem." Jesus did not die for a problem. He died to help people to get free of their problems.

What is conviction?

Conviction is godly sorrow. The Bible tells us that godly sorrow is what leads to repentance—a change in thinking (Romans 1:4). Conviction says, "Come to me and I will forgive, and give you a hope and a future" (Jeremiah 29:11). Conviction is where you feel sorrow because of your sin, but you also feel hope that there is a way out of your situation. Hebrews 4:15-16 says, *"Jesus understands every weakness of ours, because He was tempted in every way that we are. But He did not sin. So, whenever we are in need, we should come bravely before the throne of our merciful God. There we will receive mercy and find grace to help us in our time of need."* (CEV). And as declared in 1 John 1:9, *"If we confess our sins, He is faithful and just to forgive us our sins, and to cleanse us from all unrighteousness."* Conviction always gives hope. It provides us a way to answer the problem.

The difference

Condemnation makes you believe you are irredeemable. It makes you feel like a failure who will always be stuck in past sins. The devil is an accusing spirit that tells you how your heart will never be right with God. This is false guilt and makes you feel worthless. It conveys that you don't read your Bible enough, are not good enough to be loved by God and are an embarrassment to God.

Conviction, on the other hand, says the blood of Christ washes away your sin and forgives you. It makes you feel there is hope and enables you to believe that you can be set free from your problem.

Discerning which voice you are listening to will make the difference between living in bondage and walking in freedom. This chart summarizes the differences.

278

REAL GUILT	FALSE GUILT
You feel sorrow for your sin	You feel worthless and inadequate
The Spirit of Truth reveals what is wrong	Your identity is attacked; you are a bad, shameful person
The Spirit provides understanding and perspective	The devil accuses and blames
The specific infraction is clarified	A vague sense of failure overshadows you
Shows the way to resolution	Obscures and darkens the way to resolution
Brings you to repentance (change in thinking)	Keeps you stuck in a state of confusion
Experiences freedom in which you feel lighter, righteousness and at peace	Continue to feel heaviness, dread and hopelessness
You may agree with the truth but experience some internal resistance to repenting, but with persistence you eventually overcome	You may be willing to confess to any sin but cannot attain freedom because of unrecognized hindrances
You are being drawn closer to God	You remain distant and disappointed with God
You are able to proclaim the goodness of God for yourself	You have doubt and unbelief in the goodness of God

When you judge yourself, you set yourself up to judge others by that same judgment. You will even judge God the same way. The result is that you have little grace in your life to share with others. Judging the faults of others as a means of justifying yourself keeps others and God at arms-length. People who are hard on themselves are also hard on the people around them. The truth is when you poison the well with judgment, you can't drink from it. You can't receive anything from those whom you have judged. You cut yourself off from the blessings they can bring into your life. This is especially true when it comes from receiving from God.

3. Religious Stronghold

You will never get totally free as long as you are held captive to spirits of religion. The spirit of religion, or dead religion, portrays God as distant, cold, and impersonal. Religious spirits focus on the law and seek to discredit the power of the cross. They emphasize what you should or should not do, making it difficult to comprehend and accept God's grace. The spirit of religion depends on *human effort* to achieve righteousness, striving for holiness rather than resting in the Holy Spirit. Religious spirits emphasize sweat and toil, instead of trust and obedience. They drain the life out of you. Dead religion is interested in knowing about Jesus rather than the way of Jesus. It desires position and honor (Matthew 23:7) to assert its own credibility rather than following God-honoring leadership.

In the Bible, the Pharisees and Sadducees are the best example of people who practiced a dead religion. They demanded conformity to Jewish traditions and condemned anyone who did not subscribe to their standards. Being more interested in judgment than forgiveness, they governed by rules and regulations. They were motivated by the love for the law than the law of love.

Most Christians today do not come close to exhibiting the behavior of the Pharisees and Sadducees but are nonetheless impacted by religious spirits. Not recognizing their insidious nature, believers do not recognize their bent for destruction. They fail to see how they interrupt their intimacy with the heavenly Father, stunting their spiritual growth. They do not understand how these spirits hold them captive.

Believers who are committed, to doing what the Bible says, want to do things right. They look to older Christians and church leaders to show them how to "do" life. It is common for them to want to earn the approval of spiritual leaders as a way to assure themselves they are in good standing. Unfortunately, this puts the focus on pleasing people rather than their relationship with God. Any time the devil can keep you focused on pleasing people or your own self-effort rather than the presence of God, he has won. Without the help from someone who knows the difference between religion and true spiritual freedom, you will remain in a performance mentality. Entire churches can stay stuck in this religious mindset rather than depend on the Spirit to direct them.

Churches mired in religion will emphasize sound organizational and managerial principles rather than hearing the voice of God. Meetings take on a business flavor rather than prayerful discernment. These churches can grow numerically but have limited impact in advancing the kingdom. They tend to become program-based rather than presence-led, task driven rather than relationship focused. Success is measured by corporate numbers, (baptisms, budgets, buildings) rather than by heart transformation. These churches tend to foster a Greek approach rather than a Hebrew approach to living out faith. Greek culture seeks to live out faith through the exercise of intellect, knowledge, talents, and education. The Hebrew approach emphasizes participation, experience, relationship, and wisdom.

Religious churches will often excel in offering humanitarian aid but lack spiritual intimacy with the Father. In effect, they are like the church at Ephesus that lost sight of its first love. Having experienced the manifest presence of the resurrected Jesus at salvation, they no longer exhibited love toward God and people with the same passion they had at first. Churches that are alive in the Spirit want to have an intimate knowledge of Christ to experience the power of his resurrection (Philippians 3:10). Alternatively, churches caught up in dead religion seek to know about Christ and to do good works, by human effort. Spiritually alive churches learn to abide in His presence rather than strive to do His work apart from His presence.

In spiritually alive churches, the work gets done and the church gets built, but it is Jesus who does it, through souls surrendered to the Holy Spirit. There is a sense of light-hearted joy and thankfulness rather than a sense of duty.

Perhaps the number one reason why churches get caught up in dead religion is because they do not understand the importance of prayer. They do not recognize that prayer is the key factor in building the church and changing the world (1 Timothy 2:1-4). Based on self-confidence and self-sufficiency, people attempt to do things for God in their own strength. Of course, believers acknowledge God has a role to play and will tack on a little prayer asking God to bless their efforts, but for the most part, prayer is neglected. The church of North America needs to return to a lifestyle of fervent, constant, powerful prayer if she will experience revival.

Religious Spirits

Religious spirits can manifest in different ways. They tend to be subtle and hidden. You do not have to have all the symptoms to be in bondage; only a few can create a negative impact. If a person is plagued with the feeling that they will never be good enough for God, they live with a sense of guilt, shame, fear, and rejection. On the other hand, someone corrupted with pride may be permeated with self-righteousness and false humility. Some may have a bent toward earning their status with God. Others may find it easy to criticize and judge their fellow man. Still others are subject to legalism, requiring strict adherence to rules and policies. Being perfectionistic, they are prone to unforgiveness, unbelief, and intolerance of others.

What are the symptoms of dead religion?

The religious spirit is the work of the devil. It nullifies the importance of faith and grace. It substitutes religious principles for kingdom principles. It causes a person to feel religious while loading down the next person with guilt, shame, and condemnation. A religious spirit is a form of pride and self-righteousness that judges and condemns others according to a man-made standard. It prefers rules over relationship, retribution over restoration. It is prone to gossip, replacing honor with criticism, cynicism, and accusation. Eager to hold others accountable while overlooking or denying its own shortcomings, it is full of hypocrisy.

Religion cries out for justice. Relationship cries for mercy.

If you feel like people should pay the penalty for their wrongs rather than receive grace and mercy, you may have a religious spirit. If you want people to receive justice rather than repent of their sin, you may have a religious spirit. Love seeks the well-being of another through forgiveness and repentance. Religion wants people to pay the consequences for their actions. Pharisees wanted to stone the woman caught in adultery. Jesus did not condemn her. He encouraged her to change (John 8:1-11).

Religion is the opposite of agape love.

Religion requires you to prove to be faithful, so that it can acknowledge and accept you. In contrast, God's *agape* love says, "I love you for who you are, and I will help you remove those sins that act as barriers between us." God's love clothes us in His righteousness and provides salvation. Religion requires you to earn salvation, so that you can be loved.

Religion does not like instant forgiveness.

Religions wants you to feel bad before forgiving your sin. It wants you to wallow in regret. It wants you to believe you must suffer before acquiring forgiveness or favor. If you believe you have to beat yourself up for a time before you can experience forgiveness, you may have a religious spirit. The devil accuses you and makes you feel guilt and shame (Revelation 12:10).

Religion attempts to dismisses the severity of sin.

If you deny or have difficulty admitting when you are wrong, you may have a religious spirit. You may temporarily feel better by discounting the seriousness of sin, but ultimately such rationalization ruins your spiritual relationships.

Self-righteous pride keeps you in bondage to sin instead of granting freedom through repentance (Luke 18:9-14).

Religion does not embrace grace.

If you feel you are on good terms with God because you have kept the rules and have earned His approval, you may have a religious spirit. Grace is humble, admitting weakness and failure. Religion justifies its actions. Grace recognizes its failures and need for mercy. Religion avoids the need to repent and dismisses mercy. Grace is eager to receive mercy and to change to glorify God. Religion talks about righteousness; grace practices it. The Pharisees rejected grace because it embarrassed them. It threatened their religious stature (Matthew 21:32).

Religion is judgmental and despises others.

Religion criticizes and sees the worst in others. It is quick to point to the negative. Love sees the best in people and calls it out. The Greek word for *despise* means "to esteem others less than yourself." Religious people base their identity and status with God on the good works they do. When others do not measure up to their level, they despise and look down on them (Luke 18:9-14). If you judge others based on your standard of doing good and then despise them because they are not as committed as you, you may have a religious spirit.

Religion is legalistic. Religion keeps a record of wrongs. Love does not.

Religions holds to a strict set of laws. It is rigid and inflexible, requiring conformity and subjugation. It rejects or punishes those who do not comply to cultural norms (John 8:1-11). It will keep score, holding things against others. It retains grudges out of spite and unforgiveness. It seeks to get even: an eye for an eye. If you keep track of the times others have hurt or disappointed you and remain bitter, you may have a religious spirit. Love does not keep a record of wrongs (I Corinthians 13:5).

Religion makes demands and has high expectations of others and self.

Religion requires performance, focusing on doing rather than being. It expects others to adhere to certain predetermined standards and requires this compliance from oneself as well. It is best friends with perfectionism. If you need things to be "just so" in the pettiest of matters, you may have a religious spirit. If you are your own worst critic, you may have a religious spirit (Matthew 23:25). In contrast, the person governed by the Spirit does what is right not because he has to but because he wants to (Philippians 2:13).

Religion shuts up and kills the prophetic spirit.

Religion relies on rules, regulations, traditions, policies, and programs. It is suspicious and easily dismisses revelation from prophetic-type people, labelling them as weird or false. Religion seeks to control and intimidate through intellectualism. It claims to have a superior knowledge of the Scriptures and doctrine. If it cannot disprove the prophetic voice, it will seek to eliminate it through political or devious means. Religious spirits resisted and murdered Jesus. If you have a dislike for, suspicion of, or fear of someone who speaks of receiving personal revelation through the Holy Spirit, you might have a religious spirit (Matthew 23:31-35; Luke 11:47; Acts 7:52; 1 Thessalonians 2:15). There is a need to test and discern false prophecy, but that does not negate godly revelation (1 John 4:1-6; I Thessalonians 5:20-21). Religion is a false gospel. It is powerless to save (1 Corinthians 2:5).

Religion teaches unbelief.

Avoiding or treating as irrelevant some Scriptures results in an attitude of unbelief. Minimizing the power of God's Word in such a way as to dismiss, distract, divide, and confuse God's people teaches unbelief. God's Word never changes. It is the same yesterday, today, and forever. Religion focuses on what it sees and knows. It depends on human reasoning to understand spiritual matters and judges those who operate by faith and revelation. It demands proof (Matthew 12:38,39; Matthew 16:1). It promotes the lie: "If it doesn't make sense, it cannot be true." Religion fails to apply Proverbs 3:5, *"Trust in the lord with all your heart and lean not to your own understanding."*

Religion appears good but denies the power of God.

On the outside, religion looks good, but on the inside the heart is corrupt (Matthew 23:27-28). A person can talk the talk, fall in line with the customs, and play the part of a good person but deny the power of God to forgive, save, and transform (2 Timothy 3:2-5). Religion does not know the power of God to change a hard, self-centered, dying heart into a life-giving organ. If you find yourself saying, "I will always be this way. It is the way I am. I will never change," or, "My sins are not so bad. God will love me the way I am," you may have a religious spirit. You have believed a lie that God, who is righteous and holy, accepts and tolerates sin.

Religion likes to act as a policeman.

Religion takes it upon itself the false responsibility of straightening out someone else under the guise of accountability. It criticizes others, thinking it is doing them a favor by condemning their appearance, relationships, and behavior. Religious people readily point out the faults of others, thinking they can make other persons conform to their expectations. There is a place for admonishment and correction in the church (I Thessalonians 5:14; 2 Timothy 3:16-17); however, it is to be done out of mercy, love, and the desire to heal—not self-righteousness. If you are prone to tell others what they should or should not be doing, how they should do things, how they should spend their time or who they should befriend, you may have a religious spirit (Matthew 11:19).

Religion likes to discredit the ministries of others.

Religion is critical of other people's walk with God. It will overlook all the good fruit of a ministry and focus on a few areas of weakness. It concentrates on negatives and flaws, rather than celebrating positive contributions of another person or ministry to the kingdom. A good example of this is how the Pharisees criticized Jesus for healing on the Sabbath (John 5:1-18). If you tend to focus on negative technicalities and overlook the good others are doing, you may have a religious spirit.

Religion resents correction. It must always be right.

Religion has to prove that it is right and everyone else is wrong. It is argumentative. It cannot stand being shown where it is wrong. It hates correction. It takes pride in its superior knowledge and sees its opinion as above reproach (Mark 8:11). If you resist correction and like to argue in order to prove yourself right, you may have a religious spirit.

Religion is given to hypocrisy and iniquity.

Religion likes to point out the flaws in others while ignoring those same flaws in oneself. It will condemn others for the very same things it is doing (Matthew 23:13). It will pretend to be righteous on the outside, but on the inside, the heart is corrupt. If you think yourself to be a good person because of all the good things you do, yet in your heart, you are bitter, jealous, lustful, hostile, covetous, or unforgiving, you may have a religious spirit.

Religion will falsely accuse others of nefarious motives.

Religion will seek to leverage its opinion against others, accusing them of wrong motives. It has a strong propensity for labeling good as evil and evil as good. The Pharisees falsely accused Jesus of driving out demons by the power of Beelzebub (Matthew 12:24). They accused him of blasphemy because He claimed He was one with God and that His good works came from the Father (John 10:30-33). If you tend to ascribe wrong motives to others who are engaged in doing miraculous works of God without spiritual discernment, you may have a religious spirit.

Religion will always question and doubt the validity of a person's salvation.

Religion will cause people to fear they have lost their salvation. It will cause them to believe they are condemned because they have sinned (John 8:1-11). This fear will trigger people to think they have to do something to earn back their salvation. Religion creates an unhealthy fear of God. It instills such deception that people forget God is loving, merciful, and kind. They forget that sincere confession and repentance reinforce the work of the cross in restoring a strained relationship (I John 1:9). If you feel condemned rather than forgiven even after sincere repentance, you may have a religious spirit.

Religion is arrogant.

Religion compares itself to others and determines itself as being is more righteous. It sees others as less worthy than itself. It will engage in false humility. It says things like, "I am not perfect, but at least I am not as bad as so-and-so." It points to its own attributes as the reason for having favor with God (Luke 18:9-14). If you think your charitable giving, morality, or going to church earns you favor with God, you may have a religious spirit.

Religion is Prideful.

Religion appeals to the intellect and thinks it has superior knowledge. Knowledge puffs up with pride (1 Corinthians 8:1). It says, "I know so much; you can't tell me anything I don't already know." It is open to change in methods, practices, and programs that maintain or advance the institution, but closed to any ideas that move you forward when the Holy Spirit begins to speak. If you reject any revelation that calls for spiritual change, you may have a religious spirit.

Religion operates out of its own agenda.

Religion devises its own plans for ministry. It relies on human wisdom and methods to accomplish its goals. It is selective in the religious teachings it seeks to enforce while neglecting the more important principles (Matthew 23:3). It lacks faith to let God lead, reveal, and provide. It relies on traditional and conventional ways for making decisions. It manipulates and controls to achieve its desired outcomes. Instead of seeking and hearing from God, it makes up its own strategies and asks God to bless them. (Mark 7:13) If you make decisions based on narrowly selected teachings and what you want to see happen, rather than by discerning what the Spirit is saying, you may have a religious spirit.

Religion operates on principle to the exclusion of presence.

Religion leads you to believe that Christianity is about living life based on biblical principles. It sets forth "how-to" methods and eight-step programs. Principle- based living lacks resurrection power. Whereas Christians seek guidance from biblical principles, they are first called to live in a relationship with the living God. This means maintaining a focus on His presence. The replacement of harmful habits is not achieved through self-help formulas, but through the indwelling presence of the Holy Spirit. If you rely on your own strength to live out the laws of the kingdom rather than the presence and power of the Holy Spirit, you may have a religious spirit.

Religion will wear you down and burn you out.

Human effort and performance are the basis for religion. It seeks to control outcomes through enforcement of rules and regulations that place heavy burdens on people (Matthew 23:2-4). When you do not perform to its standards, it will blame, intimidate, slander, judge, and reject. It will withhold honor, affection, and cooperation when expectations are not met. While appearing to be holy and righteous, it will backstab and betray. A religious spirit will be hypocritical, and divisive, creating an oppressive atmosphere that steals away joy. If your faith is based on your own efforts, you may have a religious spirit.

Religion feeds on the fear of man.

Religion promotes the fear of man more than the fear of God. It calls for strict adherence to laws and traditions. Any failure to conform results in punishment. Religious authorities seek to control their people by inducing fear, guilt, and shame. They use social norms to keep people in compliance with their rulings. If you fear religious authorities out of fear and guilt, you may have a religious spirit.

In John 12:42-43, Jesus delivers an indictment against those caving into such fear. He says, *"But for fear of the Pharisees they did not confess it, so that they would not be put out of the synagogue; for they loved the glory that comes from man more than the glory that comes from God."*

Religion will keep you ignorant.

Religion will keep you ignorant of God's righteousness and goodness. It will keep you from seeing how Jesus makes you righteous (Romans 10:3) and does not allow you to see yourself justified before God. Because you have received Jesus as your Savior, God considers you innocent (Romans 3:24). If you continually carry a sense of guilt, shame, and unworthiness you may have a religious spirit.

Jesus Opposed Religion

Jesus did not come to make you religious. He came to set you free from all spirits that keep you captive to sin. *"If the Son sets you free, you are free indeed"* (John 8:36). Jesus came to restore you to a right relationship with the Living God. Religious spirits are counterfeit, producing dead works. Jesus clashed with the Pharisees and Sadducees because of this. They resisted the work of the Holy Spirit by killing the prophets (Matthew 23:31; Acts 7:51). They focused on regulations rather than revelation and concentrated on law rather than relationship. Their religiosity kept people out of the kingdom. Jesus warned them, saying, *"Woe to you, teachers of law and Pharisees, you hypocrites! You shut the door of the kingdom of heaven in people's faces. You yourselves do not enter, nor will you let those enter who are trying to"* (Matthew 23:13).

Religious Spirits Feed on the Flesh

Jesus never cast a religious spirit out of anyone, not even a Pharisee. Instead, He called them out on their sins, calling them hypocrites, blind guides, white-washed tombs, and vipers. Jesus told Nicodemus, *"You must be born again"* (John 3:7). I do not think you can get rid of religious spirits simply by commanding them to leave. Like all demonic oppression, they feed on the sin of the flesh. Confession and repentance are required for someone with a religious spirit to be free.

The religious spirit describes a cluster of defiling spirits that fuel pride, legalism, traditionalism, antichrist, control, jealousy, intimidation, unbelief, and shame. Together they form a stronghold, keeping people captive to dead works. I do not believe there is a single religious spirit per se. The way to dismantle a religious stronghold is to follow the example of the Apostle Paul.

Dismantling the Religious Stronghold

Paul recognized that a religious stronghold held him captive. He publicly confessed that he was the chief of sinners and bemoaned the futility of dead religion. In Romans 7:15, he disclosed, *"I don't really understand myself, for I want to do what is right, but I don't do it. Instead I do what I hate"* (NLT). Paul recognized that the way to be set free from this dilemma was not by casting out demons, but by dying to self. He had to die to his sinful nature. He said, *"I have been crucified with Christ and I no longer live, but Christ lives in me. The life I now live in the body, I live by faith in the Son of God, who loved me and gave himself for me"* (Galatians 2:20).

Religious people need to die to self-righteousness, self-ambition, self-achievement, self-justification, self-promotion, self-driven agendas, and anything related to self-glorification. This was Paul's message in his letter to the Philippians. He acknowledged that he had previously put his confidence in his own ability to be righteous by adhering to the law but now understood that righteousness comes through faith in Jesus Christ (Philippians 3:4-6).

Declaring War on Performance, Rejection, and Religion

If the church is going to walk in victory and freedom, at a bare minimum, it needs to declare war on the strongholds of performance, rejection, and religion. No longer can this evil be allowed to prevent the saints from growing into full Christ-like maturity. The only way love and unity will be restored to the church is for believers to die to self and humbly put on the Spirit of Christ. Paul put it this way in Romans 6:6-8, *"We know that our old sinful selves were crucified with Christ so that sin might lose its power in our lives. We are no longer slaves to sin. For when we died with Christ, we were set free from the power of sin. And since we died with Christ, we know we will also live with him"* (NLT).

There are many strongholds from which believers need to be set free. They need liberation from fear, unbelief, grief, victimization, lust, greed, envy, occult, and others. However, for a local church to create an environment where freedom is a way of life, the church must begin with being liberated from rejection, performance, and religion.

The reason we need to begin with these three strongholds is that secular values, invasive technology, and unreliable media heavily influence believers. Western culture thrives on massive amounts of information that reinforces the rejection, religious, and performance mindsets. Everything must be bigger and better—otherwise you experience rejection. Performance determines success, as well as, personal identity and is the basis on which to build self-esteem. Our culture operates on the premise that we define ourselves based on how others judge our performance. This is the antithesis of what the Bible teaches. The Bible teaches our identity and self-esteem is based on God's Word.

Western culture routinely rejects others with harsh words and bullying behavior. Prejudice elicits rejection. Politics polarize people. Criticism, mocking, and insults are common in public discourse. Demeaning others becomes the primary way of elevating one's own status. This undignified behavior is the opposite of what the Bible calls for—humility, honor, grace, and love. Church leaders need to model these traits and concentrate on building them into community life. These traits should be values woven into the DNA of church culture.

When the local church defaults to Western culture, the result is dead religion. Doing takes the place of being. Performing good deeds in the flesh takes priority over life in the Spirit. Where the predisposition for freedom is absent, the church is reduced to social cliques competing for control. The goal becomes preserving self-interest, rather than advancing the kingdom of God. Sadly, the gospel deteriorates into heady doctrine. Preaching becomes entertaining self-help messages. Fellowship is turned into pleasant social outings. In contrast, the Bible speaks of the church as a house of prayer where God's power to heal, restore, redeem, reconcile, and deliver are released.

The Power of the Cross

We are people of the cross and must learn to live that way. Jesus said, *"Whoever does not take up their cross and follow me is not worthy of me"* (Matthew 10:38). Before conversion, we had a limited understanding of our sinfulness and the character of God. At conversion, we confessed our sin and received forgiveness for sin through Christ's work on the cross. By accepting Christ as Savior, we are saved.

However, we still have a limited awareness of the depravity of our sin and the glory of God's holiness. While we celebrate Jesus' redemptive work on the cross, it becomes a past tense experience. Its life-giving impact on the soul fades into the background. Slowly, we forget its relevance to our daily lives. We lose touch with its power. Subtly, without detection, we return to a cultural mindset.

We continue to believe intellectually that we are saved by faith and not by works, but practically strive for achievement and approval. God's grace is more talked about than lived out. Consequently, we deceive ourselves, pretending we are not all that bad. We say to ourselves, "I am a good person." Before we know it, pride slips in. Out of fear, embarrassment, and shame, we become reluctant to confess our sins to one another. Instead, we protect ourselves by doing things that make us look good on the outside while the inside remains corrupt. This is one way we get caught up in a religious spirit.

Only as we draw near to the cross on a daily basis, are we set free to embrace our true identity as sons and daughters of God. Our identity is not secured by doing good things but is secured in a Savior who makes us righteous. With the assurance of His acceptance, the pressure to look good and please others dissipates. We are free to own up to our sinfulness without shame. We are free to renew our minds and be transformed into Christ-likeness without incrimination. We are open to enjoy the fullness of God's blessings without the fear of rejection, the burden of performance, or the constriction of religion. For a diagram depicting this progression, see Appendix H. The more we move toward God's holiness, the more aware we become of our sin.

As a congregation becomes proficient in tearing down strongholds, people will be set free to enjoy the abundant life Jesus came to give. In my opinion, achieving victory over the performance, rejection, and religious strongholds will make it much easier to attain freedom in all other areas of life. As strongholds are regularly dismantled, believers are sanctified and clothed with expectant hope. In such an atmosphere, the kingdom of God is advanced. The people themselves become the signs and wonders that point to the very presence of God.

Strategies for Victory

- **Discern the presence of religious spirits.** Recognize how they are embedded in the culture. They are very subtle and can be overlooked as bad behavior (Luke 12:1).

- **Religious spirits are demonic entities separate from people.** People may exhibit bad behavior, but demons are motivating and re-enforcing the behavior (Ephesians 6:12).

- **Recognize you are in warfare with religious spirits not only at church,** but also in the culture (2 Timothy 3:1-6). The first place to do battle is with yourself. It is detrimental to point a critical finger at others. Seek first the kingdom of God to be manifested within you (Matthew 6:33; Romans 14:7). Seek cleansing and healing for yourself (2 Corinthians 7:1). Remember, you are purified by faith in the gospel through your relationship with Christ (1 Peter 1:22-25), not by compliance to the law through human effort. Then seek corporate cleansing.

- **Learn to die to the flesh. Religious spirits are most often linked to selfish ambition.** Demons can only influence you if you agree with their lies or grant them access through unforgiveness and unrepentant sin (Ephesians 4:26). Desire holiness.

- **Expose religious spirits with humility, compassion, and wisdom** (Galatians 6:1). Be committed to taking the log out of our own eye before trying to remove a splinter from the eye of someone else (Matthew 7:5; Luke 6:42). Learn to deal with offenses quickly (Luke 17:1; Matthew 18:7-9).

- **Be aware of how you resist, grieve, and quench the Holy Spirit.** Be alert to anything that detracts, denies, or derails your intimacy with the Father. Draw upon the four-step process to tear down strongholds. Seek help to overcome obstacles that keep you from hearing the voice of God clearly.

- **Maintain an attitude that says to your Christian brothers and sisters,** "If you see anything in me that is an obstacle or keeps me from intimacy with the Father, call it to my attention so I can repent. I don't want anything between me and the Father."

- **Do not think more highly of yourself than is healthy.** Look to the interests of others, treating them with respect and honor even when they don't deserve it. Do what you can to build a culture of honor. Practice the biblical "one another's."

- **Learn how to be strong in the Lord by putting on the full armor of God** (Ephesians 6:10-18). In this way, you will resist the devil and he will flee. Learn how to strengthen yourself in the Lord (1 Samuel 30:6). This involves prayer of thanksgiving, praise, and hearing the Word of the Lord. Decide to always rejoice, pray without ceasing, and give thanks in everything (1 Thessalonians 5:16-18). Celebrate testimonies of those who gain freedom.

- **Remember, you are not called to steward events, programs, institutions, or revivals.** You are called to steward the presence of God. Stop focusing on doing; instead focus on being and doing will follow. Do not let what you can achieve for Christ become a substitute for who you are in Christ.

- **Remember, you are called to excellence.** This does not mean executing flawless performances. It means stewarding the presence of Christ in all matters of work.

- **Refuse to absolutize the little truth you have by rejecting greater truth God wants to give you.** Be open, teachable, humble, and discerning. Be eager to discover more of God's mystery. The more you come to know God, the more love and grace you will have for people.

- **Maintain a hunger and desire to learn. Grow in your relationship with God.** Don't allow yourself to become complacent, comfortable, or self-limiting. The more you feed on the Word of God, the hungrier you will become to practice His ways.

- **Be aware of the death-producing attitude that says, "We never did it that way before."** Remember, there is more than one path to an answer. For example: 2+2+2 = 6, 3+1+1+1= 6, 4+2= 6, 4+1+1= 6. Recognize the validity of the way others arrive at the right answer. Don't insist on doing things your way. Allow for alternative approaches, sequence, combinations. and styles. Allow for diversity within the boundaries of truth. Remember, "Where the Spirit of the Lord is there is liberty" (2 Corinthians 3:17).

- **Be open to revelation.** Pray for the spirit of wisdom and revelation in the knowledge of Christ (Ephesians 1:17). Do not despise prophecy but test it, and where it proves to be good, hold on to it (1 Thessalonians 5:20-12).

- **Do not put loyalty to a denomination, church, or subgroup above your devotion to Christ.** Your identity is in Christ alone. Do not let anything else give you identity, for in doing so, you are committing idolatry.

- **Be sensitive to how you can be blind to and deceived by religious spirits.** Pray for yourself and intercede with and for others to be delivered from these spirits (Ephesians 6:18). Pray for protection from any religious spirit that would seek to control your thinking. Ask the Father to give you the mind of Christ.

Prayer to Overcome the Spirits of Religion

Gracious God, I come to you in the name of Jesus Christ. I give you praise and honor. You have saved me. You are a good, good Father. You are my provider, healer, deliverer, and sanctifier.

I ask your forgiveness for all my sins, both sins of commission and omission. I ask forgiveness for sins committed against You, others, and myself. I receive your forgiveness and declare I am covered by Jesus' blood and righteousness.

I confess, repent of, and renounce every known and unknown sin of my ancestors that has opened the door to any demons that take the form of a religious spirit. I break all agreements with forces of darkness that have a religious quality.

Father God, I reject the idea that you are distant, judgmental, and unkind. I repent for any way I have not believed in your goodness, compassion, mercy, and grace. Forgive me for any time I have been disappointed and blamed you and others. Even when my situation is filled with misery and heartache, I choose to believe you want nothing but the best for me. I accept your Word and promises as true.

I repent for those occasions when I relied on my own effort, talent, knowledge or ability rather than on the Holy Spirit. I repent for relying on my own understanding in worship, prayer, works of service, Bible study, giving, and spiritual warfare rather than connecting with your Spirit. Lord, grant me eyes to see and ears to hear what you are releasing from heaven. Give me godly wisdom from above that will glorify your name.

Lord, I repent and renounce legalism, the traditions of men, the fear of man, and self-imposed limitations. I repent for my hardness of heart, dullness of spirit, doublemindedness, and unbelief. I ask you to soften my heart, activate my faith, breathe life into my soul, and restore me to the joy of my salvation. Holy Spirit, open my eyes to all the Father wants for me. Grant me a renewed hunger to know the Son of God in the fellowship of His sufferings and the power of His resurrection. Increase my desire for intimacy with the Father.

I repent for allowing the opinion of others to define me in a way that is different from my heavenly Father's. I repent and renounce all deceptions, self-deceptions, hypocrisy, pride, arrogance, and self-righteousness. I repent and renounce all unforgiveness, jealousy, anger comparison, covetousness, critical attitude, gossip, judgment, manipulation, and control.

I repent for having compromised my convictions, making excuses for, rationalizing, and minimizing sin. I ask forgiveness for not receiving correction. I repent for becoming defensive when others point out my faults and even when they falsely accuse me. Please fill me with grace and power, so that I will not be shaken when others threaten or attack me.

I ask forgiveness and repent for all occasions where I have slandered, judged, mocked, intimidated, persecuted, or spoken ill of those who are filled with the Holy Spirit and those who have spiritual authority over me. I renounce the spirit of revenge, retaliation, and rebellion reinforcing the spirits of religion. Grant me humility and a gentle confidence to practice mutual submission in obedience to Jesus Christ.

I repent and renounce all fears and unbelief that has allowed spirits of religion to influence me. I especially renounce the lie that I must control things to feel in charge. I renounce the lie that I must earn the Father's love and acceptance and declare the truth that nothing can separate me from the love of God through Christ Jesus, who died for me.

I ask forgiveness and repent of my stubbornness, self-will, and selfish ambition. I declare my submission to God and His Word. I ask you, Holy Spirit, to keep me in alignment with the Lord's plans, purpose, and destiny for me. Teach me God's ways and convict me when I start to become introspective or demand that my agenda be met.

In the name of Jesus Christ and by the authority He grants me, I break every legal right that has allowed religious spirits to operate in my life and in my ancestors. I apply the blood of Christ to my life and I ask that you forgive me and cleanse me of all sins I have confessed both known and unknown. I receive your forgiveness and cleansing from all unrighteousness. In the name of Jesus, I command every unclean religious spirit to depart from me. I receive life-giving grace to live in victory over the powers of darkness.

Father, thank you for your mercy and grace. Please fill me with more of your truth and love, that I may walk in freedom. Restore to me all the enemy has stolen. Strengthen me for your service. Holy Spirit, come and have your way with me. Bestow upon me your gifts and help me to bear the fruit of your Spirit. Lord Jesus, I invite you to rule my life. May I decrease and your presence increase in my life. To you be all the glory, honor, and praise.

Amen.

Discussion Questions

1. What impressed you about Travis' story? How do you identify with his story?

2. Which of the "When I was perfect" statements could be true of you? What is God revealing to you about your identity? How have your family and culture contributed to this identity?

3. What does the Word of God have to do with your identity? What does God say about your identity compared to what your culture and your family say?

4. In what areas do you identify with an orphan heart? In what areas do you identify with the heart of a Son? How does the rejection stronghold apply to you? Do you struggle with judging yourself? In what ways?

5. In what ways do you see religious spirits operating in you? What about your church? What could your church do to overcome religious spirits?

6. How does the power of the cross keep you from falling prey to religious spirits? What are some strategies you can employ to overcome religious spirits?

7. What would happen if the church declared war on these three strongholds of performance, rejection, and religion?

Endnotes

1. https://www.goodreads.com/author/quotes/847789.Timothy_J_Keller
2. Leif Hetland, *Healing the Orphan Spirit*, (Global Mission Awareness, Peachtree City, GA, 2013)
3. Christ Hayward, *The End of Rejection*, Chris Hayward, (Regal Books, from Gospel Light, Ventura, CA, 2007)
4. Jack Frost, *Spiritual Slavery to Spiritual Sonship*, (Destiny Image Publishers, Shippensburg, PA, 2006), pp. 213-214, Used by permission.

18

Freedom Means
a New Identity

Being Born Again Secures a New Identity

When we are born again, we receive the Spirit of God (John 3:3-8). We take on the spiritual DNA of God and a new identity. God becomes our heavenly Father (Romans 8:15); we belong to Him. According to 1 Corinthians 6:19-20, we are not our own, we have been bought with a price. By virtue of the Holy Spirit living in us, we become children of God (1 John 3:2). God is a perfect parent and we are His perfect children (1 Peter 1:23). The word *perfect* in Greek means "complete." By accepting Christ as our Savior and Lord, we are completely His. We are made righteous through Christ, who has reconciled us to God (2 Corinthians 5:21). This does not mean we are holy. Holiness is something we grow into as we learn to submit and follow Christ's example in the Holy Spirit (Hebrews 10:14). Being born again, we take on the identity of a child of God. However, this identity needs to develop and mature into Christlikeness.

Personal Revival Strengthens Identity in Christ

For many years I had been meeting every Tuesday morning with a group of community pastors and lay people. For decades, we have been praying for revival for our churches and community. I cannot tell you how shocked I was the day revival came to me, personally.

Pastor Art Karick read a passage from Psalm 66. Verse 10 says, *"You have tested us, O God; you have purified us like silver."* At that moment, the Holy Spirit convicted me of a sin that I did not know I was carrying. It had been hidden, buried deep within my heart. As I listened to the Scripture, I suddenly became aware of bitterness and resentment I had ignored for years. I had repressed some woundedness that had become rooted in my soul. Overall, I did not think of myself as a bitter person, but the Holy Spirit revealed an ugly hidden truth.

Immediately, I began to confess the hidden hurt, frustration, grief, anger, resentment, and bitterness that resulted from past offenses. Immediately, I felt a surge of electricity pass through my body starting at the top of my head and traveling to the bottom of my feet. Something had been removed. I felt cleansed and refreshed. *Voila'!* And there was *revival*!

But that was not all. A few weeks later, at a conference I was attending, a lady came to pray for me, without me asking her. She simply took hold of my hands and began to pray that the love of the Father would come upon me. As she did, soft and gentle currents of electricity came flooding over me. It was like a warm waterfall. Wave after wave of liquid love began to flow over me. With each passing wave, I became weaker and weaker until I fell back into my chair. I could not stand up, nor could I move under the weight of God's glory.

Then, a young man I did not know came up from behind me and began to prophesy over me. His message was that all the pain, stress, and strife I had endured was over. The test was over and in the past. From now on, I would be walking in a new peace, power, and authority. I was wrecked. How could this be?

Strangely enough, I felt rewarded with a spirit of humility that unleashed a stream of compassion I had never known. I became a new person. Indeed, over the course of months, I began to notice that I would react to situations differently. Almost effortlessly, I began to think about things from a different perspective. I had a sense of greater peace and calm within. But this was not all. The way was paved for greater revelation in which the Holy Spirit revealed an even deeper layer of sin that had been hidden in my soul. It was a pattern of sin I had received through my family line. It involved, self-justification, self-defense, and self-righteousness. Once again, after repenting, I began to experience a new freedom that allowed me to see myself differently. I no longer viewed myself as a teacher and pastor of a church. I was now a more effective ambassador for Christ.

This process of transformation involves taking off the old man and putting on the new. Paul references this process in Ephesians 4:22-24, *"You were taught with regard to your former way of life, to put off your old self, which is being corrupted by deceitful desires; to be made new in the attitude of your minds; and to put on the new self, created to be like God in true righteousness and holiness."*

Taking off the old man and putting on the new man is essentially putting on the "mind of Christ." This means seeing and understanding things from God's perspective, instead of one's natural reasoning and emotional way of thinking.

A New Way of Thinking and Feeling

Through my personal experience of revival, I began to understand what the Apostle Paul wrote in his letter to the Romans. He said, *"We can rejoice, too, when we run into problems and trials, for we know that they help us develop endurance. And endurance develops strength of character, and character strengthens our confident hope of salvation. And this hope will not lead to disappointment. For we know how dearly God loves us, because He has given us the Holy Spirit to fill our hearts with His love"* (Romans 5: 3-5 NLT).

For the first time, I understood love to be greater than an emotion or a concept. It was something supernatural. It is imparted into us by the Holy Spirit. To be renewed in your mind involves more than learning spiritual ideas or biblical information. It has to do with increasing our capacity to love by taking off the old man and putting on the new through the transforming work of the Holy Spirit (Ephesians 4:21-24).

Incidentally, before this experience, I understood Paul's instruction in Romans 12:1-2, *"be transformed by the renewing the mind"* as a command to replace faulty intellectual thinking with correct doctrinal propositions. However, after this experience, I examined the passage more closely. I discovered the Greek word for "mind" is *nous*. It means to come to know something by using faculties of perception and understanding that involve feelings, thoughts, desires, purposes, intuition, and judging. In other words, transformation involves more than utilizing our rational faculties to grasp intellectual concepts. It involves all the elements of the soul including mind, will, emotions, and spirit.

When the soul is transformed by the Holy Spirit, the flesh loses its power, sin loses its appeal, and we take on a new identity that reflects the glory of Jesus Christ. And as a bonus, the hunger for righteousness increases dramatically and intimacy with the Lord becomes indispensable.

Union with Christ

The great missionary to China, Hudson Taylor, went through an excruciatingly painful time when he first established China Inland Mission. Just after three years of ministry, he wrote to his mother describing his situation. He reported that he was envied by some, despised by many, hated by others, and often blamed for things he did not do. He was an innovator in missions without much help. He was often sick, perplexed, and embarrassed by circumstances. He continually grieved over what he understood to be his failure in relating to the Lord. He often felt that he was so full of sin that he could not be a child of God. He grieved at how slow he was to imitate the Master. He was continually buffeted by temptation. He said, "I never knew how bad a heart I have."[1] It appears that Hudson was struggling with a spirit of rejection.

During that dark and difficult period, on September 4, 1869, Taylor received a letter from his friend and fellow missionary, John McCarthy. The letter's message revolutionized Taylor's life. He later wrote, "When my agony of soul was at its height, a sentence from dear McCarthy was used to remove the scales from my eyes, and the Spirit of God revealed to me the truth of our oneness with Jesus as I had never known it before."[2]

Taylor had experienced union with Christ before, but McCarthy's letter revealed a dimension of truth about his oneness with Christ that he had not previously considered. Feelings of rejection and striving ceased. Joy and rest filled his soul. He experienced the kind of rest Jesus spoke of in Matthew 11:28, *"Come to me, all you who are weary and burdened, and I will give you rest."* Abiding replaced his striving. The eyes of his heart opened to a fuller identification with Christ (Ephesians 1:18). This experience became known as the "exchanged life" in which there was a greater level of surrender to the Lord.

The apostle Paul speaks of this "exchanged life" in terms of his strong identification with Christ. In Galatians 2:20, he says, *"I have been crucified with Christ. It is no long I who live, but Christ who lives in me. And the life I now live in the flesh I live by faith in the Son of God, who loved me and gave himself for me."* Paul also references this same idea in Ephesians 4:13 where he speaks of *"attaining to the whole measure of the fullness of Christ."* He speaks of it again in Philippians 1:21: *"For me to live is Christ, and to die is gain."*

This understanding of oneness with Christ sustained Taylor throughout the remainder of his life and ministry. This was not a "flash in the pan" emotional experience. This union with Christ provided him a sense of security, sweetness and power that strengthened his faith. He was lifted to a life-sustaining plane of joy and peace. This deeper union with Christ inspired Taylor to devote his entire life to sharing the gospel with the Chinese people. Keeping the Word of Lord was no longer viewed as something that constrains. Instead, it set him free to be content and joyful despite harsh conditions. Psalm 40:8 mirrors Taylor's experience, *"I take joy in doing Your will, my God, for Your instructions are written on my heart."*

Any church seeking to develop a culture of freedom will have the lofty goal of bringing every believer to the place where they view the Word of God and union with Christ not as something that constrains, but as the source of unending contentment and joy. How can this be achieved?

Paul tells us this is accomplished by taking off the old self and putting on the new self, resulting in a new attitude of mind (Ephesians 4:21-24). The Bible refers to this as putting on the mind of Christ.

The Mind of Christ

Essentially every believer has the capacity to learn to think like Christ by virtue of the Holy Spirit that is within them. Having the mind of Christ enables the believer to see things from God's perspective. The believer rises above circumstances, problems, and trials without becoming overwhelmed. Jesus alluded to receiving God's perspective when he said, *"I tell you the truth, the Son can do nothing by himself. He does only what he sees the Father doing. Whatever the Father does, the Son also does"* (John 5:19 NLT).

Because believers have the same Spirit as Jesus within them, they too, can know what is on the Father's heart. Instead of deferring to the sinful nature, believers can enlist the help and guidance of the Holy Spirit. The Apostle Paul put it this way in 1 Corinthians 2:14-16, *"The natural man does not receive the things of the Spirit of God, for they are foolishness to him; nor can he know them, because they are spiritually discerned. For 'who has known the mind of the Lord that He [The Holy Spirit] may instruct Him?' But we have the mind of Christ."*

As Christians, we have the capacity through the Holy Spirit to hear from God, but it is not automatic. We must choose to put on the mind of Christ. Philippians 2:5 says, *"Let this mind be in you, which was also in Christ Jesus."* Putting on the mind of Christ is a matter of willful choice. This choice includes a lifestyle of humility (Philippians 2:8).

Many believers do not realize that the way they think is the way they live. Proverbs 23:7 says, *"For as a man thinketh in his heart, so is he"* (KJV). Your inner thoughts or attitude will determine how you engage others. The activity of your conscious, subconscious, and unconscious mind determines your response to the world around you.

Many people do not realize they can choose their thoughts, rather than be subject to whatever randomly falls into their heads. Others do not recognize the difference between their thoughts and God's thoughts (Isaiah 35:8). Our human way of thinking is not only different, but often it is the very opposite of God's. Without the mind of Christ, believers are vulnerable to thoughts that emanate from their own soulish desires, the world, and the demonic.

To put on the mind of Christ, we need to have saving faith in Christ, recognize His Spirit lives in us, surrender our wills to His, and allow Him to renew our mind with His Word. All of this involves the interplay between the Spirit, the Word and our own thinking. Paul wrote in 1 Corinthians 2:11-13, *"No one can know a person's thoughts except that person's own spirit, and no one can know God's thoughts except God's own Spirit. And we have received God's Spirit (not the world's spirit), so we can know the wonderful things God has freely given us. When we tell you these things, we do not use words that come from human wisdom. Instead, we speak words given to us by the Spirit, using the Spirit's words to explain spiritual truths"* (NLT).

What this means is this: If we allow the life of God within us (the Holy Spirit) to flow into our lives (the soul), then we will not be like the world – full of selfish-ambition; instead, we will reflect the mind of Christ. It is a mind that desires to bring glory to God, longs for the salvation of sinners, exhibits humility and obedience, has compassion for hurting people, and is prayerfully dependent on God. In addition, the Bible gives us four insights into how Christ's mind functions.

A Prophetic Perspective

The prophet Isaiah characterized the mind of Christ this way: *"The Spirit of the LORD shall rest upon him – the Spirit of wisdom and of understanding, the Spirit of counsel and of might, the Spirit of knowledge and fear of the LORD"* (Isaiah 11:2). Isaiah further clarifies how these traits would be appropriated: *"He will delight in the fear of the LORD. He will not judge by what he sees with his eyes, nor decide by what he hears with his ears"* (Isaiah 11:3).

Based on these words, we can deduce that Christ's thoughts originated from the Spirit of the LORD, the Holy Spirit. Instead of relying on His judgment, He would depend on revelation from God. And because He was not simply divine, but also human, His wisdom, understanding, counsel, power, and knowledge would be derived from the fear of the LORD.

Yes, that is right. Jesus feared God. He recognized God the Father as the One who holds supreme power of life and death, blessings and curses. Oddly enough, dread did not fill Jesus. Instead, He took delight in the fear of God. He valued His relationship with God so much that He submitted His will to the Father's will. The magnitude of God's tremendous power and authority inspired Him to love the Father in total obedience even to the point of suffering. He joyfully served the Lord even unto death on the cross. As Christians, we are called to follow Jesus' example and take delight in fearing God.

If the fear of the Lord was foundational for Jesus' mission and ministry, how much more important it is for us. Without the fear of the Lord, we cannot have the mind of Christ. Without the fear of the Lord, we are prone to follow our own will rather than God's. Without the fear of the Lord, we are apt to let the fear of man influence our decisions more than the Spirit of God.

Overcoming the Fear of Man

Whereas Jesus was fully God, He was also fully human. He was tempted in every way, just like we are. One of the greatest temptations believers struggle with is the fear of man. We want to trust God, but our desire for acceptance and approval of others often compromises our resolve. John tells us *"Many people did believe in him, however, including some of the Jewish leaders. But they wouldn't admit it for fear that the Pharisees would expel them from the synagogue. For they loved human praise more than the praise of God"* (John 12:42-43 NLT). The fear of man will keep us from demonstrating faith in God.

Proverbs 29:25 warns, *"The fear of man will prove to be a snare, but whoever trusts in the LORD is kept safe."*

Jesus overcame the fear of man by maintaining a healthy fear of God. His singular goal was to honor God the Father more than anything else. He took delight in pleasing the Father rather than pleasing people. Consequently, He suffered for it. He was despised and rejected by men, punished, and abused (Isaiah 53:3). Even though enduring their hostility, He disregarded their shame and joyfully anticipated His place on the throne of God (Hebrew 12:2-3). In this way, He was kept safe. Satan could not prevent Him from completing His purpose.

The way to overcome the fear of man is to fear God more than man. Jesus said, *"And do not fear those who kill the body but cannot kill the soul. Rather fear Him who can destroy both soul and body in hell"* (Matthew 10:28). Man can hurt us in many ways in the present. We can be bullied, threatened, and persecuted, but God controls the whole of eternity. If we keep this in mind, we can overcome any reluctance to be a witness for Christ.

The Fear of the LORD and the Mind of Christ

The Fear of the Lord has many benefits. It not only keeps one safe from the snare of Satan (Proverbs 16:6), it also unlocks the secrets of heaven. Psalm 25:14 declares, *"The secret of the LORD is with those who fear him."* Those who fear the LORD will live from a heavenly or Kingdom perspective. Similarly, Proverbs 1:7 says, *"The fear of the LORD is the beginning of knowledge."* Without the fear of

God, we cannot understand who God really is. But with the fear of the LORD, we come to know him in a profoundly personal way. We receive discernment, understanding, and wisdom that emanate from His thinking. Proverbs 2:5 states, *"Then you will understand the fear of the LORD, and find the knowledge of God."*

Having a revelation of God's character and His ways makes us able to receive godly instruction. Psalm 25:12 says, *"Who is the man that fears the LORD? Him shall He teach in the way He chooses."* This is the way Jesus lived, saying, *"Very truly I tell you, the Son can do nothing by Himself; He can do only what he sees his Father doing, because whatever the Father does, the Son also does"* (John 5:19). When one learns to live in the fear of the LORD as Jesus did, he will put on the mind of Christ and overcome the temptations of the world.

Being an Overcomer

John declares, *"For everyone born of God overcomes the world. This is the victory that has overcome the world, even our faith"* (1 John 5:4). Overcomers are those who draw upon their faith to prevail over their own feelings, desires, and thoughts. They listen to the counsel of the Spirit more than to their own limited perspectives and wishes. Revelation from above is the basis of their judgments, not appearances. They cling to the Word of God as the rock on which they stand. To fulfill the will of God they know they need to practice taking off the old identity and putting on the new (Ephesians 4:22-24). Employing this equipping process, as referred to in Ephesians 4:12, requires the overcomer to take off the old broken soul with all its dysfunction and restore it to wholeness so that it functions as it was designed.

To *equip* means "to mend broken nets." Think of it this way, a broken fishing net cannot catch fish because it has gaping tears through which the fish easily escape. It is only after mending the holes that the net can hold fish. Broken souls are the same. Only after they are mended and made whole can they function in a healthy, unified way so as to bring others into the kingdom and hold them there.

When the body of Christ comes together in love, having been healed and made new through the transforming power of the Spirit, the church is poised to bring others into the kingdom. As long as envy, jealousy, insecurity, and fearfulness exist, the wounded body remains dysfunctional. As long as people are judgmental, lustful, competitive, divisive, gossiping, and controlling, the body will not attract and hold lost people. When Jesus said, *"I will make you fishers of men"* (Matthew 4:19), He was doing more than simply instructing His disciples to convince people to confess their sin and to receive forgiveness. He was showing them a way of life by which they could engage people in loving relationships. Jesus said, *"A new commandment I give you: Love one another. As I have loved you, so you must love one another. By this everyone will know that you are my disciples, if you love one another"* (John 13:34-35).

What Does the Identity of an Overcomer Look Like?

In addition to the "fishers of men" analogy, the New Testament uses several metaphors to describe the nature of a Christian's identity. A Christian is:

- An ambassador for Christ (2 Corinthians 5:20).
- A co-laborer with Christ (1 Corinthians 3:9-17).
- An heir of God and a co-heir with Christ (Romans 8:17).
- A royal priest (1 Peter 2:9; Revelation 1:6).
- A saint (Philippians 4:21; Acts 9:13; Ephesians 4:12; 1 Corinthians 1:2).
- An adopted son/daughter of God (Romans 8:14, Ephesians 1:5).
- A member of a heavenly family (Ephesians 3:14-15).
- A citizen of Heaven (Ephesians 2:19).
- A soldier, athlete, and farmer (2 Timothy 2:3-13).
- Salt and light (Matthew 5:13-14).
- A branch (John 15:5).
- A temple in which the Spirit dwells (Ephesians 2:20-22).

This New Identity Has Authority

The Greek word for "authority" is *exousia*. It is a term used to denote legal right, privilege or ability over a jurisdiction or realm. Another term for *exousia* would be "dominion."

The Book of Genesis tells us that God gave Adam and Eve authority to rule over the earth. Satan tricked them into disobeying God. Having sinned against God, they lost their authority. Satan took the authority that was initially given to man, and he became the ruler over the earth. John 12:31 and John 14:31 indicate that Satan is called the ruler of this world. In 2 Corinthians 4:4, he is called the god of this world.

As the god of this world, Satan tried to tempt Jesus in the wilderness to disobey God by promising Him authority over the kingdoms of the earth (Luke 4:6). Unlike Adam and Eve, Jesus obeyed God and remained faithful to His mission. He taught the truth about God as one who had authority (Matthew 7:29). Jesus atoned for the sins of man and disarmed the spiritual rulers and authorities, making a public spectacle of them when He won the victory on the cross. (Colossians 2:15).

Because Jesus was obedient even to death on the cross, He ascended to the throne of God after His resurrection and was seated on God's right hand. Jesus received a special place of honor (Mark 16:19) and was given all authority, dominion, and power to rule over everything in this present age and the one to come (Ephesians 1:20-23; Colossians 2:10).

Jesus rules in this present age through His followers. He has conferred His authority onto them. God has raised them up along with Jesus and has seated them next to Jesus in a place of spiritual authority (Ephesians 2:6). Through Christ, the church has access to approach God in freedom and confidence (Ephesians 3:12). We have received the fullness of Christ (Colossians 2:9-10). His life is within us. He has given His followers authority to carry out His mission. We are Christ's ambassadors with authority to speak on His behalf (2 Corinthians 5:20; 1 Peter 4:11). Believers received the following authorities:

1. **Authority to forgive or not to forgive sins.** He said, *"As the Father has sent me, so I send you." And He breathed on them and said to them, "Receive the Holy Spirit. If you forgive anyone's sins, their sins are forgiven; if you do not forgive them, they are not forgiven"* (John 20:21-23).

2. **Authority to make disciples by way of baptizing and teaching obedience.** He said, *"I have been given all authority in heaven and on earth. Therefore, go and make disciples of all nations, baptizing them in the name of the Father and the Son and the Holy Spirit, and teach them to obey everything I have commanded you. And surely, I am with you always, to the very end of the age"* (Matthew 28:18-20).

3. **Authority to proclaim repentance and forgiveness in His name to all nations.** He said, *"and repentance for the forgiveness of sins will be preached in his name to all nations, beginning at Jerusalem"* (Luke 24:47).

4. **Authority to do miraculous things.** He commanded His followers to preach the gospel, cast out demons, speak in different tongues, recover from deadly poison, handle snakes and heal the sick by the laying on of hands in His name (Mark 16:15-20).

5. **Authority over poisonous creatures and demons.** He gave them His authority to overcome natural fears. He said, *"I have given you authority to trample on snakes and scorpions and to overcome all the power of the enemy; nothing will harm you"* (Luke 10:19).

6. **Authority to teach, encourage and rebuke.** Titus 2:14-15 says that Jesus *"gave Himself to redeem us from wickedness and to purify for Himself a people that are his very own, eager to do what is good. These, then, are the things you should teach. Encourage and rebuke with all authority. Do not let anyone despise you."*

7. **Authority to claim the promises of God.** Making Jesus Lord of your life entitles you to benefit from all of God's promises. Paul tells us, *"For all the promises of God in Him (Jesus) are Yes, and in Him Amen"* (2 Corinthians 1:20a). In other words, God has purposed that you will never face any negative circumstances without God's promises to help you overcome.

    • God's promises serve as your armor and protection. Psalm 91:4 declares: *"He will cover you with His feathers. He will shelter you with His wings. His faithful promises are your armor and protection"* (NLT).

    • God's promises enable you to share in His divine nature. Peter states: *"Through these He has given us his very great and precious promises so that through them you may participate in the divine nature, having escaped the corruption in the world caused by evil desires"* (2 Peter 1:4).

Charles Spurgeon, who suffered with depression much of his life, said, "All depressing circumstances lose their power for evil when our faith takes firm hold upon the promises of God." There are thousands of promises in the Bible that will help you overcome the perils and problems of this world. When you identify and claim God's promises, evil loses its power and you live in freedom.

This New Identity Has Power

Jesus has delegated His authority to His followers so that they can continue to carry out His mission. Along with the legal right to carry out His mission, He has given His followers power to accomplish the things He authorizes them to do. He gives them power to do the right thing when they don't feel like doing the right thing, keeps them going when they feel like giving up and overcomes evil with good. When they are weak, Jesus gives them power. Philippians 2:12-13 says, *"continue to work out your salvation with fear and trembling, for it is God who works in you to will and to act in order to fulfill his good purpose."*

The Greek New Testament word for "power" is *dunamis*. Various Bible dictionaries defines *dunamis* as miraculous power, ability (Strong's); act of power (Young's); natural capability, inherent power, capable of anything, ability to perform anything; and absolutely, not merely capable of action, but power in action (Bullinger's). *Dunamis* is found 121 times in the New Testament.

Scriptures depicts how *dunamis* power applies to the believer:

1. **Jesus has given His followers power to be His witnesses.** He said, *"But you will receive power when the Holy Spirit comes upon you; and you will be my witnesses"* (Acts 1:8).

2. **The Early Church believed that the manifestation of dunamis was an indication of God's approval.** Luke quoted Peter saying, *"People of Israel, listen! God publicly endorsed Jesus the Nazarene by doing powerful miracles (dunamis), wonders, and signs through Him, as you well know"* (Acts 2:22 NLT).

3. **Paul asserted that the gospel of the Lord Jesus Christ is one of power (dunamis) to bring salvation** (Romans 1:16). He wrote in I Corinthians 2:4, *"My message and my preaching were not with wise and persuasive words, but with a demonstration of the Spirit's power."* Paul believed that power was a standard by which to determine the authenticity of one's faith. He wrote, *"But I will come to you very soon, if the Lord is willing, and then I will find out not only how these arrogant people are talking, but what power they have. For the kingdom of God is not a matter of words, but of power"* (*dunamis*) (1 Corinthians 4:20 GNB).

4. **Paul proclaimed that the power of Christ was available to every believer.** He wrote to Timothy saying, *"For the Spirit God gave us does not make us timid, but gives us power (dunamis), love and self-discipline"* (2 Timothy 1:7). This power (*dunamis*) within the believer is the same power that raised Jesus from the dead (Ephesians 1:19-20).

   Speaking about God's light shining in the hearts of believers, Paul says, *"But we have this treasure in jars of clay to show that this all-surpassing power (dunamis) is from God and not from us"* (2 Corinthians 4:7). And in 2 Corinthians 12:9, he writes, *"So now I am glad to boast about my weaknesses, so that the power (dunamis) of Christ can work through me"* (NLT).

   To the Ephesians, he prays that they would have wisdom and revelation, they would know the hope of God's holy people, and the power (*dunamis*) that belongs to those who believe (Ephesians 1:17-20). Later in that same letter, he declares these words of praise, *"Now to Him who is able to do immeasurably more than all we ask or imagine, according to His power (dunamis) that is at work within us, to Him be glory in the church and in Christ Jesus throughout all generations, for ever and ever! Amen"* (Ephesians 3:20-21).

5. **Peter states the purpose divine power is given to us is to produce godly living,** declaring, *"His divine power (dunamis) has given us everything we need for a godly life through our knowledge of Him who called us by His own glory and goodness"* (2 Peter 1:3).

6. **Paul warns Timothy to avoid people who have a form of religion but deny its power.** After providing a laundry list of negative behaviors and attitudes indicative of people in the last days, he says these people will give the appearance of being religious but refuse to acknowledge its power. He then warns, *"Have nothing to do with such people"* (2 Timothy 3:1-5).

7. **Jesus taught the two things that cause believers to go into error, not knowing the Scripture and not knowing the power of God.** He said, *"You are in error because you do not know the Scriptures or the power (dunamis) of God"* (Matthew 22:29; Mark 12:24).

8. **Jesus intends for His disciples to have faith that takes hold of power.** It is written, *"When Jesus had called the Twelve together, He gave them power (dunamis) and authority to drive out all demons and to cure diseases and He sent them out to proclaim the kingdom of God and to heal the sick"* (Luke 9:1-2).

Today across America, most people in the church do not know or understand the authority or the power they have as a follower of Christ. And even if they know it intellectually, they are not walking in it regularly. Satan has blinded their eyes and stolen their true identity.

Satan Wants to Steal Your Identity

A thief who steals your personal information can rob you of your money and property. He can ruin your life, damaging your business, your marriage, and robbing you of your dreams for the future. It may take years to recover. In much the same way, Satan wants to steal your identity. Jesus warned us that Satan is a thief who comes to rob, kill, and destroy. He does not want you to know who you really are in Christ, because once you discover your identity, you become a threat. As you assert your authority and power as a son or daughter of God, Satan loses his authority and power. His kingdom diminishes, and God's kingdom expands.

Perhaps the best biblical example of this is the story of Job. In the first chapter of the Book of Job we are told Job was a righteous man. There was no one like him on earth. He was blameless and upright, a man who feared God and who turned away from evil (Job 1:1,8). In the court of heaven, God bragged on him before Satan. Satan challenges God's assessment of Job's identity and asks permission to test him. God grants Satan permission on one condition;

he could not take his life. Satan proceeds to ruin Job's life by destroying all his possessions, killing his children, and ravaging his health. Job is miserable as his wife tells him to curse God and die. Job refuses to denounce God, leaving him in a pile of ashes grieving his losses (Job 2:8-10).

Three of Job's friends come to console him. They sit with him in silence for seven days. Then Satan whispers into the ear of Job's best friend Eliphaz sometime in the night. Eliphaz tells what happened:

A word was secretly brought to me, my ears caught a whisper of it. Amid disquieting dreams in the night, when deep sleep falls on people, fear and trembling seized me and made all my bones shake. A spirit glided past my face, and my hair on my body stood on end. It stopped, but I could not tell what it was. A form stood before my eyes, and I heard a hushed voice: "Can a mortal be more righteous than God? Can even a strong man be more pure than his Maker" (Job 4:12-17)?

Previously, God had declared Job to be righteous and upright, but this spirit questioned that very identity. In a subtle and suggestive voice, Satan planted a devious thought into Eliphaz's mind when he was not fully awake. It was the same tactic he used on Eve, causing her to doubt God's words.

In this instance, Satan used the power of suggestion to steal Job's identity. Without any discernment, Eliphaz broke his silence and began to accuse Job of being a sinner. He argued that Job was once a strong and pious man who is now discouraged and depressed. He asserts God does not bring harm to the innocent and upright, but those who do evil reap trouble and perish (Job 4:2-9). With these incriminating words, Job's identity as a righteous man was no longer recognized. He is now considered a loser. He had lost favor with God.

How many Christians have had their identity stolen? Because of tragedies or hard times, they feel grief, guilt, and shame. They have heard that whispering voice say: "How can you, a mortal, be righteous?" Others have taken the advice of Job's wife. They become angry and blame God. In either case, they lose sight of their true identity.

Such people need to be reminded of the abundance of God's goodness (Psalm 31:19; Romans 8:28) and that their righteousness does not rest on their own piety. The truth is *"all have sinned and fallen short of the glory of God"* (Romans 3:23). Nonetheless, *"Therefore there is now no condemnation for those who are in Christ Jesus"* (Romans 8:1). Having faith in what Christ Jesus did on the cross, God declares them to be righteous. As 2 Corinthians 5:21 clearly states, *"God made him who had no sin to be sin for us, so that in him we might become the righteousness of God."*

Knowing our identity in Christ is crucial for breaking any false identity Satan and the world want to pin on us. Instead of letting the opinions of others define us, we must believe the truth of what God says about us. Believing the truth found in God's Word is what sets us free from lies and false identities.

Practical Steps

When confronted with difficult situations, we will choose to respond with the Spirit of God rather than the flesh. Instead of reacting out of human emotions and reason, we receive revelation that comes through the Holy Spirit. The key to knowing the mind of Christ is discernment, which includes these acts:

1. Empty yourself of all desired outcomes.

2. Crucify all instincts to want to judge.

3. Get rid of all sin in which you have quenched or grieved the Spirit.

4. Prayerfully listen and watch for the leading of the Spirit.

5. Ask the Spirit for clarification and additional information.

6. Test what you perceive.

7. Look for repeated messages that confirm your perceptions.

8. Engage the discernment of others.

9. Be willing to adjust or be corrected.

For additional insight in how to exercise discernment, I recommend Francis Frangipane's book, *The Three Battles*. In chapters 10 and 11, he provides an excellent explanation of key elements that constitute discernment.

Putting on the mind of Christ requires some preparation. Here are some general recommendations that will help you get prepared:

1. **Trust that God's way of thinking is better than our own.** We must believe that God will never lie to us and that He will always lead us in a way that is for our ultimate good. Next, we must be willing to do something adverse to our human nature, surrender our will over to Him. Proverbs. 3:5-6 says, *"Trust in the LORD with all your heart and lean not on your own understanding; in all your ways submit to Him, and He will make your paths straight."* Romans 8:28 puts it this way, *"And we know that in all things God works for the good of those who love Him, who have been called according to His purpose."* To put on the mind of Christ, the believer must decide not to rely on what seems reasonable, but instead have faith in the goodness

of God and submit to His purposes. This is what Jesus did. It was not His will but His Father's will to which He committed Himself.

2. **Commit to renewing your mind.** In Romans 12:2, Paul wrote, *"Do not conform to the pattern of the world, but be transformed by the renewing of your mind. Then you will be able to test and approve what God's will is – His good, pleasing and perfect will."* Corrupted cultural practices, philosophies, pleasures, values, partisan political agendas, humanistic views, idol worship, false religious teachings, and deceptions of the devil sculpt the patterns of the world. To renew the mind requires replacing all this corruption with the truth found in God's Word. The mind must be continually fed thoughts about God. God has revealed His thoughts most perfectly in the person of Jesus Christ and has deposited His wisdom in the Bible through the inspiration of the Holy Spirit. The way to renew the mind is to renounce the world's systems, take in God's Word daily by reading and studying the Bible, receive godly counsel and listen to God in prayer. Jesus said in Matthew 4:4, *"Man shall not live on bread alone, but on every word that comes from the mouth of God."* Feeding on the Word of God is not a casual or optional endeavor. It is as essential as breathing. Keeping your thoughts on God is to be a priority and a lifestyle.

Colossians 3:2-3 says, *"Set your minds on things above, not on earthly things. For you died, and your life is now hidden with Christ in God."* By setting your mind on godly things ahead of time, you cultivate an intimate relationship with the Lord and are more likely to resist temptation when it comes. Knowing what you will and will not do in advance of a compromising situation makes the decision easier. Having a love relationship with the Lord and having already laid the foundation for the right choices, you are less likely to be lured into making wrong decisions.

3. **Gird up the loins of your mind** (1 Peter 1:13 NKJV). This is a metaphor derived from the ancient practice in which a person would bind up long flowing clothing, wrapping it close around their body so that it would not impede their movement. The idea is to remove any obstacle that would keep you from functioning in Christlikeness. Rid yourself of all the junk in your mind that prevents you from running the race and winning the victory in Christ.

For the believer, this means ridding oneself of lies, ungodly beliefs, word curses, traumas, negative soul ties, generational iniquities, judgments, vows, offenses, disappointments, idols, fears, unbelief, strongholds, false identities, and any demonic influences. For all intents and purposes, this means regularly cleansing your soul of corruption through deliverance.

4. **Demolish strongholds and take every thought captive to Christ.** As 2 Corinthians 10:4-5 states, *"The weapons we fight with are not the weapons of the world. On the contrary, they have divine power to demolish strongholds. We demolish arguments and every pretension that sets itself up against the knowledge of God, and we take captive every thought to make it obedient to Christ."* I wrote extensively about strongholds in chapters 16 and 17. The way to deconstruct strongholds is through the power of the Holy Spirit. However, to take every thought captive to Christ, it is necessary to know the Word of God, to know who you are in Christ, make declarations in accordance with God's promises, and know the power and authority you have in Christ. Here are some more things a believer can do to put on the mind of Christ:

- Ask the Holy Spirit to help you put on the mind of Christ.
- Accept responsibility for your thoughts and know you can control them.
- Confess all ungodly thoughts to God, renounce all demonic associations, and receive forgiveness.
- Command unclean spirits to leave and cast your cares on the Lord.
- By faith, expect to receive grace and truth as revealed by the Holy Spirit.
- Daily take in the Word of God.
- Declare who you are in Christ.
- Make declarations in accordance with God's promises.

Making Declarations

Perhaps you have heard it said, "A man doesn't always practice what he preaches, but he will always practice what he believes." Any time we believe a lie in our heart, that lie will determine how we live. If your belief system says, "I am different. I am a reject. I am not good enough. I am not worthy," that is the message you will project to those around you. Based on those faulty beliefs, you will make assumptions and decisions that will shape your life. You will say and do things according to those beliefs.

To renew the mind, we must not only identify and renounce lies, we must also replace them with the truth. Making daily declarations is the most practical way to position truth in the mind. By verbally repeating the truth, we strengthen our beliefs, aligning them with God's Word. Hearing the Word over and over imparts grace. Ephesians 4:29 states, *"Let no corrupt word proceed out of your mouth, but what is good for necessary edification, that it may impart grace to the hearers."* Grace is empowerment to do the will of God.

What we say has the power of life and death (Proverbs 18:21). Jesus taught that words have consequences. He said, *"For by your words you shall be justified and by your words you shall be condemned"* (Matthew 12:37). Making positive confessions that agree with God's Word brings life. Revelations 12:11 tells us the way to overcome Satan is by the words we speak over ourselves. *"And they overcame him by the blood of the Lamb and by the word of their testimony"* (NKJV). When you continually tell yourself that what God says is true, you eventually begin to believe it. In this way, your faith enables you to overcome the world's influence (1 John 5:4). To defeat Satan, we must speak forth the Word of God that has been deposited in our hearts. King David put this way: *"I have hidden your word in my heart that I might not sin against you. Praise be to you, LORD; teach me your decrees. With my lips I recount all the laws that come from your mouth"* (Psalm 119:11-13).

When our hearts are right with God, we shall make a declaration and God will authorize it to happen. Job 22:27-28 says: *"You will make your prayer to Him. He will hear you and you will pay your vows. You will also declare a thing and it will be established for you; so light will shine on your ways"* (NKJV). King David made a similar assertion, *"Delight yourself in the LORD and He shall give you the desire of your heart; commit your way unto the LORD; trust also in Him; and He shall bring it to pass"* (Psalm 37:4-5 NKJV). James also writes, *"The prayer of righteous person is powerful and effective"* (James 5:16). Jesus put it this way, *"Whatsoever you ask in my name you shall have it"* (Matthew 18:19; Matthew 21:22; Mark 11:24; John 14:13; John 15:7, John 16:23). 1 John 5:14-15 says, *"This is the confidence we have in approaching God: that if we ask anything according to His will, He hears us. And if we know that He hears us – whatever we ask – we know that we have what we asked of Him."*

Within the New Testament, the Greek word *aiteo* appears eighty times to denote declarative prayer. It means, "I ask," or "I demand." Making demands of God is not a lack of reverence or humility. *Aiteo* describes one who has audacity, prays authoritatively and almost commands something from God. The person who prays this way knows what he needs and is not afraid to boldly ask, believing he will receive it. It is like when Moses declared, *"If Thy presence go not with me, do not lead us up from here"* (Exodus 33:15 NAS). Jesus taught His disciples to pray this way when He instructed them to say, "Father... give us... deliver us... forgive us." All three of these commands are stated in the imperative mood.

Jesus began His ministry by making a declaration. He repeated the words from Isaiah 61 and applied them to Himself, saying: *"The Spirit of the Lord is on me, because He has anointed me to proclaim good news to the poor. He has sent me to proclaim freedom for the prisoners and recovery of sight to the blind, to set the oppressed free, to proclaim the year of the Lord's favor"* (Luke 4:18-19).

Declaring what God has put into our hearts brings a sense of well-being. Paul wrote: *"If you declare with your mouth, 'Jesus is Lord,' and believe in your heart that God raised him from the dead, you will be saved"* (Romans 10:9). Once again, this scripture reinforces the principle that declaring biblical truths results in positive outcomes.

Declaring God's promises is a key component of Christian life. Steve Backlund, author of *Declarations: Unlocking Your Future*, boldly asserts, "Nothing happens in the Kingdom unless a declaration is made."[3] Backland has written several books that teach Christians how to appropriate the making of declarations into their daily life. Recognizing you are living under a lie and renouncing it is the first step. Here is a brief example of how making declarations can work.

State the lie:
My dysfunctional family will never change, and neither will I.

State the truth
I can change because with Christ I can do all things through Him who strengthens me.

Identify Supporting Scripture
"Though my father and mother forsake me, the LORD will receive me" (Psalm 27:10).

"I can do all things through Christ who strengthens me" (Philippians. 4:13).

"He is able to do immeasurably more than all we ask or imagine, according to His power that is at work with us" (Ephesians 3:20).

State Positive declarations:

My family is blessed and will be a blessing to others with the help of God.

My family will model healthy relationships with the help of God.

My family will rise above its limitations to do incredible things with God's help.

My descendants will be happy and productive with the help of God.

Let me make it clear that making declaration is not a formula for getting what you selfishly want. It is a means of aligning one's belief with God's promises, thereby increasing the likelihood of living a blessed and empowered life. Making declarations is not a way to ignore facts or circumstances. We are making a choice to focus on higher realities. Declarations draw upon God's Word to activate God's power. Hebrews 1:3 says, *"He sustains all things by His powerful word."*

Kyle Winkler speaks of God's Word this way, "It is a force that cannot be rivaled and is more dependable than gravity. It is a supernatural power that when tapped, radically transforms anything to which it is applied."[4] The spoken Word of God is what gave structure to the world (Genesis 1). Joshua recognized that it brought success (Joshua 1:8). The psalmist found it a source of prosperity (Psalm 1:3). It activates the work of angels (Psalm 103:20). David discovered God's Word as the key to strength and refreshment (Psalm 1:1-2). Jesus used it to resist Satan (Matthew 4:1-10). Peter used it to heal those who were crippled (Acts 3:1-10). Paul determined the spoken Word is the way to realize salvation (Romans 10:9).

When you welcomed Christ into your life, you became a new creation. However, to live in victory, more transformation needs to take place. Just as a caterpillar must first nestle himself in a cocoon before becoming a beautiful creature free to fly, so must Christian nestle himself in the Word of God. Learning to declare the spoken Word of God is the way to freedom and taking on a new identity in Christ.

Why is it important to know your identity in Christ?

Knowing who you are in Christ enables you to live life as God intended. It enables you to fulfill the destiny God has designed for you. In Christ, your need for acceptance, security, and significance is fully met. You are empowered to live a righteous and purposeful life, which is not possible with a false identity. In Christ, your life rests on a firm foundation, one that cannot be shaken by the uncertainty of worldly beliefs.

God's opinion of you is the only one that ultimately counts. The words and opinions of others are varied, biased, wrong, uninformed, contradictory, and always changing. Your boss may call you a genius after you close a big deal, while your calculus teacher may think you are stupid. Your current girlfriend may think you are prize catch, while your ex-girlfriend sees you as a loser. Your baseball coach may think your talent is worthy of the big leagues, while a talent scout refuses to give you a second look.

Even if you gather a group of your closest friends who know you best, they know only a fraction of your words, beliefs, actions, and inner thoughts. As 1 Samuel 16:7 declares, *"For the Lord does not see as a man sees; for man looks at the outward appearance, but the Lord looks at the heart"* (NKJ). No one knows everything about you except God. He is the only one who can make accurate judgment of who you really are.

Jesus based his identity on what God said about Him. Matthew 3:17 records, *"A voice from heaven said, 'This is my Son, whom I love; with him I am well pleased.'"* With these words firmly planted in His soul, Jesus refused to let His identity be altered by Satan when Satan challenged Him in the desert (Matthew 4:1-10). He came up against people who disagreed with Him, despised Him, and disparaged Him, yet was not deterred from His mission nor His identity.

People responded differently to Jesus. Some curiously listened to Him, some committed to follow Him, and others bitterly opposed Him. His own friends did not have a clear picture of His true identity as the Messiah. Judas betrayed Him, Peter denied knowing Him, and the disciples abandoned Him. Even when people did believe in Him because of the miracles He performed, He did not entrust Himself to them, because He knew what human nature is really like (John 2:23-25).

The opinions of men are inconsistent and unreliable. Your true identity is not based on what you are feeling, what you do, what you look like, what you own, what country you are from, what others say about you, or even what you say about yourself. What God says about you reveals your true identity. His Word is the one foundation on which to build a healthy identity. God says many things about us, but it is helpful to keep a few things in mind:

God says you are a new creation: *"If anyone is in Christ, the new creation has come. The old has gone, the new is here"* (2 Corinthians 5:17).

God says you are acceptable: *"Jesus treated us much better than we deserve. He made us acceptable to God and He gave us the hope of eternal life"* (Titus 3:7 CEV).

God says you are valuable. Jesus said: *"Look at the ravens. They don't plant or harvest or store food in barns, for God feeds them. And you are far more valuable to Him than any bird"* (Luke 12:24 NLT)!

God says you are lovable: *"We love because He first loved us"* (1 John 4:19); *"The mountains and hills may crumble, but my love for you will never end.... So says the LORD who loves you"* (Isaiah 54:10 GNT).

God says you are forgivable: *"I am the God who forgives your sins. I do this because of who I am. I will not hold your sins against you"* (Isaiah 43:25 GN).

God says you are capable: *"The capacity that we have comes from God. It is He who made us capable of serving the new covenant"* (2 Corinthians 3:5-6 TEV).

An Overarching Characteristic

One overarching characteristic of having the mind of Christ is found in Philippians 2:5-8. Paul exhorts the church to do nothing out of selfish ambition. Instead, they are to empty themselves, honor others, and be servants. This is what Jesus did in coming to earth. He did not look to His own interest but gave Himself to the divine purpose of procuring salvation for humanity. To have the mind of Christ means to work for the welfare of others even when it is costly. A Christian is a servant of God and others.

Attaining the mind of Christ is not only a task for individuals. It is also a collective endeavor. In 1 Corinthians 2:16 Apostle Paul said, *"**We** have the mind of Christ."* This is plural, not singular. No single person can have the entire mind of Christ. Each person has access to the fullness of Christ's thoughts, but each person can only assimilate a portion at a time. To have a more complete perspective, we need to connect with each other. We need to remind each other who we are in Christ, less we lose sight of our true identity. The degree to which we function as a unit will determine the level of access we have to the divine council of God. To advance the kingdom of God, unity is not optional. It is essential. We must have the same unity that Jesus had with the Father (John 17:23). This is only possible as each person dies to his own selfish ambition, puts on the mind of Christ, and is fully alive in the Spirit.

Discussion Questions

1. Share an occasion when you experienced a personal revival in which you took off the old man and put on the new man.

2. What do you think convinced Hudson Taylor of his union with Christ? How did this change his life? How would you describe your union with Christ?

3. What are some things you consider important when it comes to putting on the mind of Christ? How do you measure your progress?

4. How does Satan attempt to steal your true identity? What could be in your belief system that needs to be renounced and replaced?

5. What are some things a person can do to incorporate declarations into their Christian lifestyle? What would it take for you to become more confident in making declarations?

6. Why is it important to know your identity in Christ?

Endnotes

1. Dr. Taylor and Mrs. Howard, *Hudson Taylor's Spiritual Secret* (Moody Publishers, Chicago, IL, 2013), Kindle Edition, pp. 140-141.
2. Ibid, (p. 149) Kindle Edition
3. Steve Backlund, *Declarations: Unlocking Your Future,* (Igniting Hope Ministries, Redding, CA, 2013) back cover
4. Kyle Winkler, *Activating the Power of God's Word: 16 Strategic Declarations to Transform your Life,* (Charisma House Book Group, Lake Mary, FL, 2017), p. xv

19

Healing Trauma Brings Freedom

Trauma Shocks Us at the Core of Our Being

Have you ever experienced a traumatic event? Have you ever been involved in a car accident, a house fire, or natural catastrophe? Have you experienced the overwhelming grief from losing someone close to you? Have you ever been attacked and beaten, robbed, raped, or suffered abuse? Have you ever been hospitalized for a severe illness, caught up in war, or betrayed by someone close to you? Have you been impacted by divorce, poverty, or bankruptcy? Have you ever been a victim of bullying, rejection, abandonment, physical, mental, or emotional abuse, or ridiculed by a teacher or someone in authority? Have you ever experienced an abortion, been fired from a job, or felt overwhelmed by worry or stress?

Any of these events and experiences can shock a person at their very core, leaving them with long-term adverse effects including physical impairments, emotional wounding, psychological pathology, and spiritual dysfunction. These effects can drain the life out of a person, leaving them feeling helpless, hopeless, unloved, unworthy, trapped, and without purpose or confidence. A diminished sense of self and severely damaged sense of well-being shatter a person's beliefs, personal security, and trust.

When a person experiences trauma, almost nothing feels safe. Something happens deep within a person's brain and body that renders a person upset and in distress. Trauma deposits anxiety and pain deep into one's memory and can have long-term consequences. Most people are familiar with the term post-traumatic stress disorder (PTSD). This occurs when a person experiences a life-threatening event. The person processes the trauma in such a way that the inner pain from the initial trauma becomes amplified. Something inside becomes shattered and broken. The person's identity is distorted and life is disrupted.

In severe cases, a person can degenerate into what mental health experts call dissociative identity disorder (DID). In such instances, fragmentation occurs in which a person's identity or personality separates into pieces. These people develop alternate identities that come and go from a person's consciousness. Not all traumas are this severe and debilitating; however, anyone who has been traumatized can have pain stored in a memory that can be set off by a triggering event.

The severity and duration of the trauma and how resilient a person is will determine the nature of long-term effects. Various biological, psychological, social, and spiritual factors determine how resilient that person will be.

When a memory is triggered, persons experience symptoms like those of the initial trauma, causing them to believe things about themselves and others not warranted by the current circumstances. For example, I knew a person who was repeatedly raped as child by a construction worker whose truck had a specific sign. As an adult, every time the person saw a truck with similar signage, she would have a panic reaction. The truth is, there was no real threat, but the body went into a panic as though the danger was real. Panic attacks occur when the body comes under stress due to a threat. In this way, faulty beliefs systems are constructed. Lies become attached to painful emotions from the past. The person will make irrational responses and unhealthy choices based on the pain they feel rather than objective truth and actual circumstances. Because of their distorted perceptions, they remain trapped in a web of dysfunction. Deliverance from the pain and lies sets them free to enjoy life as God intended.

Secondary Trauma

Mental health experts recognize the negative impact secondary trauma can have on people, particularly first responders. Secondary trauma occurs when a person does not personally experience a trauma but witnesses someone else's trauma. When we see news reports featuring stories of terror, tragedy, or torture the graphic images can leave a lasting impression. Footage of survivors recounting their terrifying ordeals on social media can be paralyzing, creating an atmosphere of despair.

What's the Point?

A friend of mine, Ron Derr, teaches mathematics in our local high school. He shared with me an incident that occurred in his classroom. This is his account:

The situation began when I confronted a student about using a cell phone during class. With this student, it was not the first time we had discussions about this issue. Cell phone use in class is a constant battle with students, and I was trying to discuss with them the importance of knowing the appropriate time and place to use them. Local employers often say their biggest complaint is the struggle of young adults to put their cell phones down; this has become a distraction in the workplace.

As I was trying to make *my* point, one student made the comment, "What's the point?" I stopped to ask what he meant—I thought I was making my point clearly. Other students contributed and began to elaborate. They were not wondering about the cell phone issue in particular, but about following rules in general. This was not a discussion I anticipated. A pattern began to emerge. These young people were not trying to be rebellious. They were scared. One by one, they voiced concern about issues impacting their world: coronavirus, pending war, the current political climate, and climate change. As they continued, I began to detect something more than fear. It was a loss of hope. They saw no signs of things getting better. They were struggling with what to do because they have nothing to look forward to. In their words "what's the point?"

When people are exposed to constant trauma or even secondary trauma, they can become so anxiety-ridden that they have no hope. They see no point in doing anything that will make their lives better. The little faith they have begins to crumble under the weight of fear and despair. From there it is easy to sink into a victim mentality and be filled with self-pity. Setting people free from the effects of trauma can be a daunting task. It often requires long-term care and medical treatment.

Incidentally, my friend seized the moment and spoke truth into the situation. He reminded them of two things:

1. They are not the first generation to head into a scary or hopeless-looking future. All generations have had issues that made hope elusive. He described what it was like for him as a teen during the cold war. (This addressed the victimization and self-pity issue.)

2. He told them they needed to find a purpose to help them move forward and get through tough times. He then shared that all his hope and purpose come from his faith. (This addressed the fear and despair issue.)

Given the widespread exposure young people have to social media, the responsible thing for the Christian community to do is to learn about trauma and develop strategies to help free this generation from its effects.

Trauma Theory and Biblical Solutions

I have a friend who does extensive work in healing and deliverance. He shared with me an incident that occurred when he was working with a woman who had been severely abused. As she was remembering the brutal beating and getting in touch with the initial pain, suddenly her face began to swell and turn red. One eye was completely swollen shut. There appeared on the side of her cheek a handprint at the place where she had been struck in the initial attack. It took a couple of days for the swelling to subside and for her face to return to normal. Somehow as her memory was stimulated, her body reproduced the effects of the initial trauma.

There is currently an ongoing debate in the scientific and psychological communities as to where trauma is deposited. Some argue for body memory, asserting that trauma is absorbed into the body and remembered at the cellular level. Others contend that there is no scientific evidence for this and that only brain cells have the capacity to remember.

Body Memory

In ministry sessions, I have seen people experience pain in their legs, backs, head, chest, and stomach. They have reported having vibrations, feeling warm electrical currents, a sense of heaviness leaving their body, things in the room seeming brighter, changes in body temperature, and body contortions.

The medical field has long recognized the connection between the mind and body as psychosomatic conditions. Daniel Mintie, LCSW, an integrative trauma expert in Taos, New Mexico, states, "Psychological experience always has correlates throughout our physical structure. When we think a stressful thought or have a distressing memory our bodies participate in such activities every bit as much as our minds. Our emotions occur not only in brain structures as the amygdalae but throughout our bodies. It is impossible to experience feelings like fear, anger or joy 'from the neck up.' Our psychological lives are intimately bound up with activity in our endocrine, cardiac, respiratory and immune systems."[1]

Based on my limited experience and research, my bias is that each cell contains stored memory in the form of energy vibrations at the molecular level. This stored memory works in conjunction with messages sent from the brain.

When a smell, a visual, a touch, a sound, or circumstance triggers in a person, the brain sends messages to the body, setting off an alarm that is based on previously assimilated knowledge. This description is over simplified, but it recognizes the physiological component of trauma. Whether this theory is proven to be accurate or not remains to be seen.

In any case, the bottom line is that everyone has a past which contains some measure of pain due to trauma. Beliefs attached to that pain can have a detrimental effect on a person's self-image and relationships with others and God. At such points of vulnerability, demons can seduce a person to accept ungodly beliefs as truth. Unfortunately, this has the harmful effect of keeping a person captive to strongholds rather than walking in spiritual freedom. For a person to walk in freedom, the internalized pain needs to be removed. Lies need to be replaced with truth and a new identity established based on the Word of God. This is accomplished as the person experiences the presence of God and the life-transforming power of the Holy Spirit. The Bible calls this "abiding in Christ."

Key to the healing process is for the individual to stay connected to God over a sufficient period of time, allowing for complete healing and the emergence of a fruitful life (John 15:4-8). This requires a person to maintain faith in God's goodness and avoid the temptation to doubt (James 1:6-7). It requires the continual application of the Word and Spirit until all defilements are removed from the body and spirit (2 Corinthians 7:1). It requires tearing down old patterns of thought (strongholds) and replacing them with those of Christ (2 Corinthians 10:4-5).

"Hurting people hurt people" is a popular saying. And it is true. A traumatized person is a hurt person. Without healing these internal hurts and comforting the person, over time, the pain gets buried or repressed deep within a subconscious memory. Unable to process painful experiences from the past, the person will often resort to unhealthy ways of coping, including abuse of drugs, illicit sex, mishandling of money, dysfunctional relationships, joblessness, or many others.

If severe traumas occurred early in life, God often allows the person to mature to the point where they are able to face the hidden pain keeping them in bondage. Frequently, these hidden hurts will not surface until later. Much of the time, they are connected to psychosomatic illnesses. Most often, people find relief only in small increments because they cannot process it all at one time. King David understood the nature of hidden hurts and prayed that they be brought into the light. In Psalm 139:23-24, he says, *"Search me, O God, and know my heart; Try me and know my anxious thoughts; And see if there be any hurtful way in me, and lead me in the everlasting way"* (NASB).

A Helpful Tool

Currently, one of the most helpful tools in understanding the effects of trauma is the Adverse Childhood Experiences (ACE) study. Dr. Vincent Felitti from Kaiser Permanente's Obesity Program and Dr. Robert Anda, epidemiologist at the Center for Disease Control, undertook this study. It was conducted from 1995 to 1997 and involved 17,337 participants who answered a ten-question survey around abuse, neglect, and household dysfunction.[1] The traumas identified in the ACE study included:

- physical, emotional and/or sexual abuse
- neglect or abandonment
- divorce
- family violence
- alcoholism or drug addiction
- poverty, homelessness, lack of food and basic needs
- family member in prison
- family member with mental illness

The study correlated traumas in childhood with negative social, behavioral, and physical health outcomes in adulthood. These negative outcomes included alcohol and drug abuse, depression, suicidal thoughts, risky sexual behavior, sexual victimization, domestic violence, self-harm, physical inactivity, obesity, heart disease, cancer, liver disease, sexually transmitted diseases, teen pregnancy, homelessness, unemployment, and being either a victim or a perpetrator of violence.

The study revealed that the more traumas a person experienced in childhood, the higher the risk of exhibiting dysfunction in adulthood. This dysfunction included emotional suffering, lack of physical health, and mental illness. The impact of trauma depended on the age of the child when the adverse experience occurred and the protection, support, and social networks that were available.

Trauma not only has short-term but also long-term adverse effects on the quality of life.

Jesus and Trauma

Being human, Jesus experienced trauma. He experienced starvation in the desert for forty days. When the devil tempted Him to believe lies, Jesus overcame Him with the truth. Jesus also experienced rejection, abandonment, and physical abuse of the worst kind. He was publicly stripped, shamed, ridiculed, whipped, speared, and crucified. Yet, through all this trauma, He overcame. He remained faithful to God and fulfilled His mission. He restored humanity to a right relationship with God. He set humanity free from bondage to sin and oppression, healed bodies, and restored souls. Jesus taught His disciples that they, too, would have to endure trauma. He said, *"In this world you will have trouble. But take heart! I have overcome the world"* (John 16:33).

The Greek word for "trouble" is *thlipsis,* which means "pressure, affliction, anguish, burden, persecution or tribulation." This definition fits within the purview of trauma. In this verse, Jesus also promises that He has overcome the trauma found in the world. The Greek term for "overcome" is *nike.* It means "to carry off a victory as in winning a battle."

In Luke 4:18, Jesus quotes the prophet Isaiah as to the purpose for the Messiah coming to earth. This included setting the oppressed free. The Greek word for "oppressed" is *thrauo.* It means "to break into pieces or to shatter." Part of Jesus' fundamental mission was to heal those who were broken and shattered into pieces. Isaiah 61:1 puts it this way, *"He has sent me to bind up the broken hearted."* The Hebrew word for "broken hearted" is *shabar.* It means "to break, to break into pieces, or to wreck or crush." In other words, Jesus came to bring healing to the traumatized. He came to restore people whose identity is shattered into pieces. He came to heal and make them whole again.

Jesus came not only for broken people; He also came for those who are overwhelmed by stress and weighed down by dysfunction. The Greek word for *weary* in Matthew 11:28 means "exhausted by toil or burdens or grief." The Greek word for heavy-laden means "to be loaded up with spiritual anxiety."

All of this is in keeping with God's promise in Psalm 34:17,18, *"The LORD hears His people when they call to Him for help. He rescues them from all their troubles. The LORD is close to the brokenhearted; He rescues those whose spirits are crushed"* (NLT). In Psalm 23:2-3, we are told, *"The Lord makes me lie down in green pastures. He leads me beside quiet waters. He restores my soul"* (ESV). And in John 14:27, just before His crucifixion, Jesus told His disciples, *"Peace I leave with you; my peace I give to you. I do not give to you as the world gives. Do not let your hearts be troubled and do not be afraid."* Jesus came not only to forgive us of our sins but also to heal our broken hearts, to bear our burdens, rescue those with crushed spirits, and give us peace.

John 10:10 states that the devil, who is a thief, comes to kill, steal, and destroy our life. There is no better way to destroy a person's life than to subject them to trauma. When people are wounded by trauma, they lose hope, peace, faith, and joy. Their ability to give and receive love is greatly encumbered. They lose the abundant life Christ came to give them.

However, as believers remain connected to Christ in the face of opposition, hardships, trials, and tribulations they become overcomers. They endure all kinds of adversity with joy (James 1:5). They maintain hope when overwhelmed with problems because the Holy Spirit fills them with God's love (Romans 5:3-5). In the words of the Apostle Paul, they are more than conquerors (2 Corinthian 12:9).

The book of Revelation promises overcomers rewards. They receive authority over nations (Revelation 2:26). They sit with Jesus and the Father on the throne of heaven (Revelation 3:21) even as God dwells among them. They inherit blessings and freely drink from the waters of life (Revelation 21:1-7).

Believers have wonderful things to look forward to in the future, but for now, it is good to recognize that we do not live in a playground but a battlefield. We are fighting enemies that seek to destroy our souls. We can expect injuries and casualties, but are assured the victory is ours in Christ Jesus. He has already overcome our circumstances. He has overcome our pain and emotions. He has overcome our lack of finances, our addictions, and troubles. We must resolve to run the race of faith with Him and not give up. We must learn not only how to fight off temptation to sin, but also how to lay every weight or hindrance aside. Hebrews 12:1 says, *"Therefore, since we are surrounded by such a great cloud of witnesses, let us throw off everything that **hinders** (weight or encumbrance) and **the sin** that so easily entangles. And let us run with perseverance the race marked out for us."* To do this, we must keep our attention focused on Jesus, who is the author and finisher of our faith (Hebrews 12:1). He is the one who teaches us how to be an overcomer (John 5:4-5). Believing in His shed blood to wash away our sin and by giving testimony to what Jesus is doing in our lives, we overcome the evil one (Revelation 12:11).

Most people have a good idea of what sin is, but what does the writer of Hebrews mean when he says to lay aside everything that hinders? The Greek word for "hindrance" is *ogkos*. It refers to a burden or an encumbrance. Weights or hindrances are different from sins. When running a race, weights or burdens slow you down and keep you from performing at your best. Sins, on the other hand, are things you do that break the rules of the race. Although you finish the race (get to heaven), unrepentant sins disqualify you from receiving highly-prized rewards. In contrast, weights, burdens, or encumbrances do not disqualify you, but they make it difficult to win those rewards.

When it comes to running the race of faith, we must not only stop sinning but also need to lay aside the heavy burdens, stress, and emotional pain that accompany trauma. Casting our cares on God (1 Peter 5:7; Proverbs 12:25) includes dealing with encumbrances such as grief, disappointments, offences, injustices, curses, vows, and inherited iniquities. These things act as extra baggage that weigh down our spirits. However, the good news is Jesus has made a way for us to run our best race and to win rewards. He has provided a way for us to unburden ourselves through a divine exchange. For example, Jesus died that we could have life (2 Corinthians 5:15). He took on our condemnation and gave us eternal life (John 5:24). Jesus became sin so that we could become righteous (2 Corinthians 5:21). He became poor so that we could become rich (2 Corinthians 8:9).

This divine exchange occurs when we cast our cares upon Jesus. In exchange, He gives us grace in the form of cleansing, healing, restoration, revelation, hope, empowerment, authority, spiritual gifts, spiritual fruit, freedom, and many other blessings. Beauty, joy, and praise replace despair, grief, mourning, and sorrow through the grace of Jesus Christ, the Messiah (Isaiah 61:3).

The New Testament refers to this divine exchange in two places: Matthew 8:16-17 says, "*When evening came, many who were demon possessed were brought to Him, and He drove out the spirits with a word and healed all the sick. This was to fulfill what was spoken through the prophet Isaiah: 'He took up our infirmities and bore our diseases.'*" In 1 Peter 2:24 we read, "*He himself bore our sins' in His body on the cross, so that we might die to sins and live for righteousness; 'by His wounds you have been healed.'*"

When we come into Christ's presence in a spirit of consecration and surrender, He draws near to us. As we give Him the pain, sorrow, grief, guilt, despair, anger, fear, rejection, shame, abandonment, He gives back to us grace, healing, wholeness, truth, peace, joy, love, hope, and many more blessings. In this way, we unburden ourselves. We become free of negative emotional baggage that weighs us down. As a result, we are empowered to live the abundant life Jesus came to give us.

God is not limited by space or time. By asking the Holy Spirit to take the wounded person back in time to when the trauma first occurred and by inviting Jesus into the memory, the great exchange is made possible. When the exchange is fully complete, the people experience relief that is palpable and real.

Joni's Story

Joni, a fifty-six-year-old woman, was referred to me and Sue by a neighboring pastor. She had suffered severe trauma throughout her life. The initial wounding, sexual abuse, rejection, and neglect took place within her family. She eventually married, but tragically that ended in divorce. She sought to comfort her emotional pain in a variety of unhealthy ways. Her treatment history included admissions to hospitals for psychiatric care and professional counseling from numerous therapists She eventually married, but tragically that ended in divorce. Her treatment history included several rehabilitation programs, admission to hospitals for psychiatric care, and professional counseling from numerous therapists. She became estranged from her family and could not maintain a job. With a diagnosis of fibromyalgia, she had to rely on disability payments. Upon coming to us, she was drowning in debt, barely able to survive, and having suicidal thoughts. During ministry sessions, she would frequently be triggered and experience excruciating pain in her legs. This is her own testimony:

In my opinion, sexual abuse of a child is so damaging that it cannot be healed except by Jesus. This is a body/soul/spirit wound so deep that only our Maker can restore it. A child is completely shattered by what is happening, unable to process horror because their brain is not capable. The brain is not completely developed yet. The trauma is literally held in the cells of their bodies. They are unable to function as a "normal" human being for the remainder of their lives. Their life is basically destroyed! A counselor once showed me a marble that was shattered inside. She told me that this is what happens to a child's brain when they are sexually abused.

Recently, I have gone back into a memory in which I was traumatized by sexual abuse. This is what happened: Jesus came into the memory as a figure bathed in a golden yellow light. I saw myself shattering into a billion tiny pieces. These pieces were my body/soul/spirit. I watched these pieces float from me and into Jesus. He took them upon Himself. Then He replaced these shattered pieces with wholeness and restored me to the foundation of who I was meant to be. This is just one example of the many healings Jesus has done in the trauma I experienced as a child.

I've been through an extensive period of deliverance and healing. There was a lot of trauma and life-long wounding that needed to be healed. It takes time, patience, perseverance, faith, strength, the right prayer counselors, the absolute willingness to be healed, and of course, Jesus!

God is teaching me how to have healthy relationships. It's a slow process, but I guess it has to be in order for me to learn how to do this the right way. First, He is teaching me to rely on Him for all things, especially love. The love of the Father allows me to love myself, then I can love others. This is a normal process when a child is loved by their parents. God is teaching me this through His Father's heart of grace and loving kindness.

I am a work in progress. The transformation so far has been amazing and miraculous. The process works. Jesus works! Jesus is the healer. He heals all wounds. He brings light to the darkest of darkest places. He makes us whole, healthy, and restored to who we are meant to be in Christ.

Joni's testimony is an example of how Jesus can take a severe trauma from the past, in which a person's soul is fractured, and make it whole again.

Biblical Examples of Trauma

Both the Old and New Testaments give examples of men of faith who experienced trauma. Perhaps there is no better example than Job, who suffered one trauma after another. He lost all his possessions, servants, animals, children, and his health. His friends accused him of sinning and his wife encouraged him to turn against God. He said, *"I have no peace, no quietness. I have no rest; only troubles come"* (Job 3:26). In all this, he remained faithful to God.

However, Job did admit that the things he privately feared had come upon him. He cursed the day he was born. Complaining and blaming God for treating him as an enemy, he questioned the ways of God. In response, God corrected him. In the end, Job repented for having questioned God's ways and humbled himself before the Lord. He prayed for his friends and the Lord blessed him by giving him twice as much as he had lost (Job 42:10).

King David also experienced trauma. As the youngest son in the family, he was given the menial job of watching sheep. His bothers looked down on him and criticized him, believing he was prideful and deceitful (1 Samuel 17: 28-29). He fought with a lion, a bear, and the giant Goliath. King Saul, his father-in-law, tried to kill him with a spear. Saul's army hunted him down. The Philistines recruited him to fight for them but then distrusted his leadership. His own friends, his mighty men, turned against him and wanted to kill him. But David overcame these traumatic experiences. How? He strengthened himself in the Lord (1 Samuel 30:6).

When Paul was converted, he was struck blind. The disciples looked upon him with suspicion. In 2 Corinthians 4:8-9, Paul testified to his sufferings, *"We are hard pressed on every side, but not crushed, perplexed, but not in despair; persecuted, but not abandoned; struck down, but not destroyed."* In 2 Corinthians 11:23-28, he said, *"I have worked harder, been put in prison more often, been whipped more times without number, and faced death again and again. Five times the Jewish leaders gave me 39 lashes. Three times I was beaten with rods, one I was pelted with stones, three times I was shipwrecked, I spent a night and a day in the open sea. I have been constantly on the move. I have been in danger of rivers, in danger of bandits, in danger of my fellow Jews, in dangers from Gentiles; in danger in the city, in danger in the country, in danger at sea; and in danger of false believers. I have labored and toiled and I have often gone without sleep; I have known hunger and thirst and have often gone without food. I have been cold and naked. Besides everything else, I face daily the pressure of my concern for all the churches.*

Through all this trauma, Paul learned that God's grace is sufficient, and he boasted of his weakness, so that Christ's power might rest on him (2 Corinthians 12:9).

Clearly, the Bible teaches that trauma strikes people of faith. It can cause the most righteous of saints to question and to be disappointed with God. For this reason, Peter reminds us not to lose faith, but to see trials as a form of testing. He gives the assurance that having passed the test, believers will receive glory and honor when Jesus returns (1 Peter 1:6-7). We must view these trials and traumas not through the lens of "end -of-the-world thinking," but in expectation of joy that comes when the soul enters heaven.

To be healed of trauma, one must get past the temptation of blaming God for inflicting hurt. This means repenting from any way you have misjudged God. God is good and is always working for our salvation. The key to overcoming trauma is learning to strengthen yourself in the Lord. This involves making a divine exchange in which you cast your cares upon the Lord (1 Peter 5:7). In exchange, the Lord gives back grace to overcome the trials and tribulations. As you pour out your complaint to God (Psalm 142), including all negative emotions of frustrations, anger, and resentment, God releases healing and freedom.

Most often, when people go through adversity they react with sinful attitudes and behaviors of their own. These responses are a form of grief. Some people develop an attitude of anger, seek revenge, rebel, and make judgments while others suffer depression. Still others become bitter, cynical, and distrustful. Some withdraw, wallowing in self-pity, or become disconnected from others.

In any case, when people get hurt, they need to refrain from blaming, Otherwise, they will remain trapped in the negative emotions. Instead of blaming, they need to forgive and ask God's forgiveness for the sinful way they responded. Then they must receive God's forgiveness deep within their soul. This act of humility allows them to experience freedom from sin, ungodly beliefs, and from trauma. Equally important, the person needs to forgive themselves and renounce any agreements unconsciously made with the enemy. By doing these things, they are made clean from all unrighteousness (1 John 1:9). The Lord removes the pain in the memory and blesses the person with freedom, grace, and health.

The Apostle Paul writes about God's transforming work in Romans 5:3-5, He says because of our relationship with Jesus Christ we can rejoice, *"Not only that but we can rejoice in our sufferings, knowing that suffering produces endurance, and endurance produces character, and character produces hope, and hope does not put us to shame, because God's love has been poured into our hearts through the Holy Spirit who has been given to us"* (ESV). In other words, when we take off the old sinful self in this manner, God turns suffering into steadfastness and shame into hope. How does He do this? He pours out more of His supernatural love into us through the Holy Spirit. We continue to grow as new creations in Christ Jesus. For these reasons, we can look upon adversities as an opportunity for joy (James 1:2). The joy is not found in the trauma itself, but in the spiritual growth that comes from testing. Some understand this to be baptism with fire in which spiritual impurities are removed from the soul.

Trauma Prayer

It is important to recognize that trauma is not only recorded in the soul and spirit but deposited and remembered in the body (2 Corinthians 7:1). For this reason, prayer needs be rendered not only for soul and spirit but also for the body. Jim Banks from House of Healing Ministries suggests several things that should be incorporated in this type of prayer.[2]

Steps to Healing

1. Identify all traumatic events in a person's life.

2. Attain permission from the person to take authority to cut off all trauma from their life.

3. Command all short-term and long-term effects of trauma to come out of the body.

4. Ask the Lord to disconnect them from any second-heaven entities including principalities, powers, dominions, thrones, rulers, or any other demonic entity.

5. Take authority over all means of access or pathways in which the demonic may connect with the person and shut them down.

6. Ask the Lord to re-establish the connection between the right and left hemispheres of the brain and bring healing to other parts of the brain.

7. Ask the Lord to re-establish appropriate sleep patterns so that the person can be refreshed and rejuvenated (Proverbs 3:24).

8. Ask the Lord to dismantle any automatic responses gained from the initial trauma and to heal and restore all chemical and electrical functions that were broken due to the trauma.

9. Have the person instruct his own spirit to receive all the Lord has for him while he sleeps (Psalm 16:7).

A copy of Jim Bank's Trauma Prayer is provided in Appendix I.

Discussion Questions

1. What traumas have you experienced? How did you respond? How about secondary traumas?

2. What do you think about body memory?

3. What does the Bible teach us about trauma?

4. How does Satan leverage trauma to interfere in your relationship with God?

5. What is involved in making a "divine exchange?"

Endnotes
1. https://www.psychologytoday.com/us/blog/real-food-real-life/201810/trauma-and-the-body2.
   https://jimandpatbanks.com/

20

Ministry that Sets People Free

A Vision for Freedom Ministry

There are many ways God uses people to set others free. There is no single method or approach capable of meeting all the demand. A church may employ several different strategies to minister freedom. However, one thing remains constant: dependence on the Holy Spirit. It is the Spirit that brings healing and deliverance no matter what form the ministry takes.

God has made His light to shine in the hearts of believers. Even though they are fragile like clay jars, even though they are hard pressed, perplexed, persecuted, and struck down, God uses them to release His power. Despite their human weaknesses He uses them to advance His kingdom (2 Corinthians 4:6-9). It is the responsibility of each believer to keep the faith and live free.

Within each local church, believers are called to various kinds of ministries. Each one makes a unique contribution as the ministries collectively make for a powerful witness of freedom in Christ. Unfortunately, without a culture devoted to freedom, believers can come to see their ministry as mundane and unimportant. If an usher cannot see the relationship between his task and the ministry of rescuing someone from torment or pain, he will not see value in helping people find seats or a parking place. But, if he has experienced the joy of being set free from evil, ushering becomes significant as a way of helping others hear about the gospel of freedom. He has the privilege of placing people in an environment where they can personally receive freedom in Christ, and the ministry is now gratifying.

Following is an explanation of how to leverage different ministries in promoting a culture of freedom.

Pulpit

Preach messages and give people the opportunity to share testimonies on how Jesus Christ sets people free. The goal is to help people understand, appreciate, and desire the freedom that Christ promises.

Pastoral Staff

Provide prayer, a perspective, and a plan for people seeking greater measures of freedom. The goal is to set people on a pathway to freedom both in the short-term and the long-term.

Worship

Lead the congregation in celebrating God's goodness by singing about the freedom found in Christ. "Who I am in Christ" statements can be flashed on flat screens when giving announcements. The goal is to honor God and remind believers of their true identity in Christ.

Membership Orientation

When new people are introduced to congregational life, they are instructed in how the church seeks to provide for and live out the freedom Jesus promises. The goal is to establish an expectation for finding greater measures of freedom.

Media

Provide pamphlets and devotionals outlining scriptural teachings on freedom, both online and in literature racks. Provide links to other sites specializing in freedom ministry on the church website. The goal is to undergird the church's ministries with supplemental information regarding freedom.

Classes/Seminars/Retreats

Offer courses to introduce and train people in the ministry of freedom. The goal is to equip and empower every member of the congregation to engage in the ministry of setting people free.

Altar Ministry

Train prayer ministers to pray with people during or after the worship service. This is a short five-to-ten-minute period of prayer. The goal is to allow people an opportunity to immediately respond to God's Word and presence.

Weekly Prayer Meeting

Without making an appointment, people can walk to receive prophetic and deliverance prayers. This affords more ministry time for each person, ranging from twenty minutes to an hour. Also, it can serve as an outreach to the community. The goal is to relieve people of pain and distress while expressing comfort, love, and encouragement. If there are chronic issues, referrals are made to lay counselors for more in-depth ministry.

Small Group Ministry

Small group members pray for one another. The goal is to provide ongoing support for each other in the quest for more freedom. This creates a unity and a bond that sustains people through difficult times.

Every Believer's Ministry

Believers pray with their families, friends, neighbors, and co-workers. The goal is to present the gospel in power, manifest the presence of Christ and set people free by speaking the truth in love in the spirit of prayer.

In-Depth Ministry Sessions

People meet with trained lay counselors for at least a three-hour block of time. The goal is to explore the soul at deeper levels to receive greater measures of healing, deliverance, and freedom. In cases of severe pathology, referrals are made to Christian mental health professionals.

Leadership Training for "Issue Focused" and "Thorough Format" ministry is available at Restoring the Foundations.

Preparation for a Three Hour In-depth Ministry Session

The initial contact with a person who desires in-depth ministry includes asking about how they learned about the ministry and what has been happening in their life that causes them to seek freedom. After filling out an application, they are given a Receiver's Guide to read. These resources are available online for purchase through Restoring the Foundations International.

The application is a questionnaire that serves as a diagnostic tool. It asks for background information including personal history, family history, spiritual history, personal beliefs, and factors that characterize the condition of the person's life. The Receiver's Guide explains the four areas ministry and the biblical rationale for each. It also outlines the ministry steps in addressing each ministry area.

Depending where a person is in their faith walk, sometimes an initial meeting is scheduled to get acquainted and to go over the Receiver's Guide. What they can expect from each session is explained. They are encouraged to ask questions to make an informed decision as to whether they want to receive ministry. If they want to proceed, an appointment (for at least three hours) is scheduled. Receivers are encouraged to invite family and friends to pray for them during their healing and deliverance process.

The environment for the meeting is very important. It should provide private, free from intrusive noise and interruption. It should be well-lit, with a thermostat to set a comfortable temperature. Restrooms should be nearby. Inviting and relaxing seating, snacks, drinks, and blankets should be available. Having access to a copier is helpful in order to provide the person with handouts and resources.

The person needs to feel secure, protected, and safe with confidentiality strictly observed. A non-judgmental attitude is maintained. A spirit of acceptance and grace pervades the atmosphere. Sensitivity and concern for the person's physical and emotional welfare are continually communicated. Hospitality is evident in all proceedings. A spirit of peace and calm permeates the room. Prayer to cleanse the room from all defiling spirits is made before and after each session. The Holy Spirit is invited to rest in the room. A cross, wall hangings, and plaques with encouraging messages make for a faith-building atmosphere.

Before delving into ministry areas, a short interview is conducted to gain a fresh perspective on any new developments since the questionnaire was filled out. Each session begins with two prayers, a Consecration Prayer and a Submission Prayer. It concludes with thanksgiving and blessing.

Prayer Is Foundational

Prayer is foundational for freedom and underlies every aspect of this ministry. Prayer puts us in touch with the presence of the Lord. Paul in 2 Corinthians 3:17-18, declares, *"Now the Lord is the Spirit, and where the Spirit of the Lord is, there is freedom. And we all, who with unveiled faces contemplate the Lord's glory, are being transformed into His image with ever-increasing glory, which comes from the Lord, who is Spirit."* It is in the presence of God that people are changed into His glory.

We begin each session with a Consecration Prayer and Submission Prayer. For a sample of these prayers see Appendix J. Through prayer, we acknowledge our total dependence on the Holy Spirit inviting Him to be in charge and give direction in each session. The idea is to hold a three-way conversation between the one receiving ministry, the one's initiating ministry and the Holy Spirit who provides grace for transformation. Collectively, we listen for and follow the leading of the Holy Spirit who releases truth, love, and power. Connecting with the Spirit is what brings healing and deliverance, resulting in freedom and restoration.

Kinds of prayers utilized during a session

Intercessory Prayer

Family and friends of the person receiving ministry are asked to pray for the person before and during the session. These persons often serve as a support system after the session. During the session, one of the ministers is constantly interceding. They are seeking revelation and insight from heaven. Hearing back from God provides guidance, encouragement, perspective, and divine protection.

Prayer of Consecration

All sessions begin with consecration of the meeting and the person's spirit, soul and body to God. Evil is renounced through the exercise of spiritual authority. The Holy Spirit is welcomed and invited to take charge of the meeting.

Submission Prayer

The person receiving ministry submits himself to God. He recognizes his need for God to heal and deliver him. He admits his faults and takes responsibility for his condition. He admits he belongs to Christ and takes the authority Christ gives to break ungodly alliances. He acknowledges his need for God to take him through pain and hurt, to renew his mind, and to deliver him from evil. He positions his will in alignment with God's will to set him free.

Petition

This is making a request of God to do something on behalf of the person. A petition includes any number of graces including comfort, hope, insight, truth, cleansing, spiritual gifts, spiritual fruit, or many others

Declarative Prayer

This includes truth statements that replace ungodly beliefs. It also involves identity statements that reflect who a person is in Christ. Declaring God's promises for the person is also employed.

Commanding Prayer

Based on the authority Christ has given believers, demons are told to depart. In the name of Jesus, tormenting spirits are commanded to leave and go where Jesus tells them to go. No theatrics are permitted.

Prayer of Disappointment

The person releases any disappointment they have had toward God. They repent for having wrongly judged God.

Forgiveness Prayer

The person forgives those who have harmed him. He confesses his own sinful responses and receives forgiveness from God. The person forgives himself in the presence of God.

Praise and Thanksgiving

Adoration is expressed for who God is and gratitude is given for the healing and deliverance God has rendered.

Blessings

God's favor, peace, provision, power, and protection are pronounced over the person.

Forgiveness Is the Bedrock of Freedom

The poet Alexander Pope said, "To err is human; to forgive is divine." As humans we make mistakes. Because of that, we need to learn how to forgive. Jesus teaches us how to be divine by teaching us how to forgive.

Learning to forgive is essential to living the Christian life. Jesus taught His disciples the importance of forgiveness in the parable of the two debtors (Luke 7:36-50). He insists that forgiveness is necessary before worshiping God (Matthew 5:23-24). Jesus instructs us about praying for forgiveness in the Lord's Prayer (Luke 11:1-13), explaining that it is necessary to forgive others to receive forgiveness from God (Matthew 6:14-15). Jesus instills the need to forgive continually without ceasing (Matthew 18:21-22; Luke 17:3-4), and that forgiveness is connected to love (Luke 7:44-48). He connected the authority to forgive sin with the authority to heal (Mark 2:9-10, Matthew 9:2-8). Jesus explained that a lack of forgiveness results in torment (Matthew 18:23-35). He emphasized the paramount importance of forgiving instead of judging (Luke 6:37), just as He forgave those who crucified Him while on the cross (Luke 23:33-34).

Forgiveness is the bedrock of freedom. Without learning to forgive, asking for forgiveness, and receiving forgiveness we remain stuck. Forgiveness frees us to live in the present rather than in the hurtful past. Forgiveness is not a feeling. It is an act of the will that activates the grace of God, positioning us to receive healing. It does not excuse the wrong rather it leaves judgment of the offender up to God. We cannot progress in spiritual maturity without practicing forgiveness.

Forgiveness Comes in Three Tenses

Through faith in Jesus Christ we receive forgiveness for all our sins: past, present, and future (emphasis mine):

- *"By grace you **have been saved"*** (Ephesians 2:8).

- The message of the cross is the power of God *"to us who **are being saved"*** (I Corinthians 1:18).

- *"Since we have now been justified by His blood, how much more **shall we be saved** from God's wrath through Him!"* (Romans 5:9).

God applies forgiveness to our past, present and future. Having a full understanding of God's forgiveness is vital to realizing freedom. It plays a critical role in living out salvation.

Four Dimensions of Forgiveness

The New Testament uses four different words to convey different dimensions of forgiveness.

Aphiemi

Aphiemi sets us and others free from carrying a load of guilt and shame. Through His sacrifice on the cross, Jesus becomes our scapegoat, the one who bears our burdens. He is the Lamb of God who takes away the sins of the world. We no longer face condemnation with guilt and shame removed.

It is used 174 times in 133 verses in Greek Concordance KJV.

Example: Luke 17:4

Aphesis

Aphesis sets us and others free from the prison of hate and bitterness. We are released from captivity to malice due to our debt being paid. We owe nothing. Obligations for wrongs are erased; criminals are let go as though no crime has been committed. There is a remission of penalty. All reproach is forfeited as disapproval and disappointment are put to an end.

It occurs seventeen times in sixteen verses in the Greek Concordance KJV.

Example: Mark 3:29

Apolyo

Apolyo sets us legally free. It means "to dismiss, to loosen, let go, no longer detain, send away, depart, release, acquit of a crime, release from a debt, grant a prisoner leave, in cases of divorce to dismiss from the house and send oneself away."

It is used eighty-nine times in sixty-three verses in Greek Concordance KJV.

Example: Luke 6:37

Charizomai

Charizomai sets us and others free from the compulsion toward punishment. Instead of demanding vengeance for offenses, we are free to extend mercy and favor. Kindness replaces revenge. We are free to bless rather than curse, do something agreeable or pleasant, and offer grace instead of demanding justice.

It occurs twenty-four times in nineteen verses in the Greek Concordance KJV. Example: 2 Corinthians 2:7

In the Old Testament and in the New Testament, God's forgiveness is complete with mercy. It is as though He forgets it and never remembers it again.

- Psalms 103: 12 – He puts our sin behind Him as far as the East is from the West.
- Micah 7:19 – He hurls our sins to the bottom of the ocean.
- Isaiah 1:18 – He makes our scarlet sins as white as wool.
- Jeremiah 31:34 and Hebrews 8:12 – He forgives wickedness and remembers sin no more.

God's complete forgiveness is an act of mercy that brings us comfort. Knowing our forgiven sins can no longer be used against us, we are set free from any fear of judgment. On the other hand, if we do not forgive and do not show mercy, we shall receive judgment. Showing mercy is the way to avoid judgment. That is why James 2:12 says, *"Mercy triumphs over judgment."*

Similarly, according to Matthew 18:21-35 and Ephesians 4:26, if we do not forgive because we are angry, bitter and resentful, or demand justice, requiring others to repay what they owe us, then we ourselves will be tortured. This is the point of the parable found in Matthew 18. In verses 34-35 the king turns over the unforgiving servant to the jailer to be tortured and Jesus concludes, *"This is how my heavenly Father will treat each of you unless you forgive your brother or sister from your heart."*

In short, unforgiveness gives permission for demons to punish and inflict pain. This pain can be emotional, physical, or spiritual. If we refuse to forgive others from the heart, we will not be sanctified. We may be saved, but we will not receive blessings that accompany righteousness.

Indicators of Unforgiveness

- Desire for revenge or getting even
- Slander/gossip
- Rejection, avoidance, cold shoulder
- Resistance, lack of cooperation
- Sense of being owed something
- Transference of affection
- Bigotry
- Inability to bless the person
- Secretly wanting something bad to happen to the person
- Bitterness, anger, contempt

Sometimes we can become hurt and not recognize it as an offense. We then carry unforgiveness in our hearts without realizing it. We may even excuse, deny, and pretend we were not hurt to keep the relationship intact. However, unforgiveness will eventually surface, and failing to deal with the offense will cause the relationship to suffer.

Forgiveness is a Process

Forgiveness is a process that involves the four dimensions indicated in the four Greek words defined above. If you forgive someone who has hurt you, you no longer consider them guilty, but in your heart, you still feel they owe you something. You cannot bless them, and forgiveness is not complete. You have failed to forgive as the Lord has forgiven you, so you have more work to do. If you have forgiven and still demand justice, again, you have more work to do. If you have forgiven others but not yourself, yet again, you have more work to do. If you have forgiven but can't forget about it because of the pain, once more, you have more work to do. You need to keep forgiving until you have inner peace. It is not a one-time-done type of arrangement. Jesus makes this point in Matthew 18:21-22 when He tells Peter not to forgive just seven times, but seven times seventy. The idea is to be continually forgiving.

Sometimes our hurt and pain can be so severe that even though we have forgiven people who mistreated us, we still carry bitterness. We have not moved beyond memories of the injustice involved. We still feel the pain. Subconsciously, we may still be blaming God for letting such terrible things happen to us. We might hold on to grief that comes in the form of anger, self-pity, depression, distrust, resentment, blame, projection, demanding justice, withdrawal, or rejection of others. All this needs to be turned over to God before one realizes peace and freedom. Having the patience to peel back layers of inner pain, one layer at a time, is key. This requires learning to be gentle with yourself and believing God is working with you to bring healing a little at a time. Forgiveness is not healing, however, it is necessary for healing to occur.

Three Applications of Forgiveness in the Bible

1. **We are to forgive others who have sinned against us** (Matthew 6:15; Mark 11:25-26; Ephesians 4:32; Colossians 3:13).

2. **We are to ask God to forgive us for our sins** (Luke 18:13-14; 1 John 1:9).

3. **We are to forgive ourselves for having sinned against God, others, and ourselves** (Romans 10:9-11).

Critical to walking in freedom is the application of all three teachings. Before freedom can be realized in our lives, forgiveness must be accompanied by faith. We must know in our hearts, through faith, that we have received forgiveness. Acts 10:43 declares, *"All the prophets testify about Him that everyone who believes in Him receives forgiveness of sin through His name."* Similarly, Mark 11:24 declares, *"Therefore I tell you, whatever you ask for in prayer, believe that you have received it, and it will be yours."* If you asked for forgiveness, but don't believe you have received it, then you are still in captivity. You are not free until you have received God's grace by faith.

A Complete Understanding is Needed

Having a complete understanding of God's forgiveness is imperative if we are to become spiritually mature. Scripture commands us to forgive, but more than that, it instructs us how to forgive. Colossians 3:13 commands, *"Forgive as the Lord forgave you."* The Lord forgives by appropriating all dimensions of forgiveness, past, present, and future. Jesus forgives completely. Out of His mercy, He chooses to forgive and forget all our sins, forever. If we are to experience the healing and deliverance Jesus promises, we must learn to forgive the same way. Forgiveness is essential to the Christian faith. Putting it into practice is vitally important for living out our salvation. Forgiveness is foundational for deliverance. It is key to realizing freedom, health, and maturity.

Forgiving those who have caused us excessive pain can be very difficult, if not impossible. However, God's grace makes it feasible. The Holy Spirit will help us overcome the pain, anger, and contempt no matter how hurtful the circumstances. If you can't forgive, ask the Holy Spirit for help. He will give you the comfort you need to move beyond the pain. 1 John 3:20 explains, *"If our hearts condemn us, we know that God is greater than our hearts, and He knows everything."*

Forgiveness Prayer

Dear Lord,

You have shown me that you desire my freedom and healing. You require that I forgive so that I can receive forgiveness. Therefore, I choose to forgive _____ for _____. I forgive everyone who has provoked me to sin by hurting me. I release them from all debt. They owe me nothing. I let go of all judgments and punishments. I turn them over to you for judgment, mercy, and salvation. I bless them and ask you to reveal to them your righteousness, goodness, and love. Lord help me to continue to forgive as you have forgiven me.

This I pray in the name of Jesus Christ, my Savior and Lord.

Amen.

Four Basic Areas of Ministry

We need to consider four basic areas of ministry: generational sins, ungodly beliefs, trauma, and demonic oppression. These areas overlap and impact each other. Healing cannot be fully realized until all four areas are addressed. Each area holds a key to unlocking a door to a person's freedom. We cannot open one or two doors and expect complete freedom. An integrative approach is needed. For a complete biblical exposition of this approach to ministry, I recommend the book, *Restoring the Foundations: An Integrative Approach to Healing Ministry* by Chester and Betsy Kylstra. The following is a brief overview of each area:

1. Generational Iniquity

You shall not bow down to them (idols) or worship them; for I, the LORD your God, am a jealous God, punishing the children for the sin of the parents to the third and fourth generation of those who hate me (Exodus 20:5).

The LORD is slow to anger and abundant in lovingkindness, forgiving iniquity and transgression; but He will by no means clear the guilty, visiting the iniquity of the fathers on the children to the third and fourth generations (Numbers 14:18 NASB).

Generational sin and resulting curses are a significant source of oppression, but many Christians do not understand this. Generational iniquities are sins committed by previous generations that put pressure on future generations to repeat the same sins. The Bible identifies these pressures as iniquities. They are deeply entrenched unjust attitudes, prejudices, or values manifesting in wicked behaviors. The iniquities of our ancestors do not automatically force us to sin. However, they do create a natural bent or predisposition toward committing the same sins.

This problem is more easily noticed in families where alcoholism, drug addiction, sexual abuse, or poverty is passed down from one generation to the next. With less serious sins, the problem is not as recognizable. People understand the similarities of behaviors, traits, and characteristics within family lines as normal. They might say something like, "He is just like his father" or "The apple doesn't fall far from the tree." Fortunately, God provides a way to nullify the power of generational sins and curses. Ultimately, Jesus is the one who breaks curses (Galatians 3:13).

When a person confesses and repents of their iniquity, it breaks the chain, cancels curses, and restores blessings. If sin is not confessed and repented, the enemy has legal right to continue his torment. It is important to note that confessing the sins of your ancestors does not relieve them of their responsibility. Everyone is accountable to God for their sins and iniquities. But, by acknowledging and confessing iniquities, the propensity toward sin loses its power over us.

Steps to healing

- Confess the iniquity of your ancestors and your own to God.

- Forgive your ancestors for the iniquity that has been inherited. Be specific as to the nature of the iniquity.

- Ask God to forgive you for the ways you have repeated and responded to the iniquity. Receive the Lord's forgiveness.

- Forgive yourself for the ways you have sinned.

- Renounce all demonic spirits attached to the iniquity and sinful responses. Use your authority to cast out the unclean spirits.

- Receive grace to live in freedom.

2. Ungodly Beliefs

Let the wicked forsake his ways, and the unrighteous man their thoughts. Let them turn to the LORD, and He will have mercy on them, and to our God, for He will freely pardon (Isaiah 55:7).

Ungodly beliefs are anything we believe which is not in agreement with God's Word, character, or nature. A belief may be factual in feeling or perception, but if it is not in agreement with God's truth, it is ungodly.

Deeply embedded in every person's soul is a belief system. The convictions a person has about life comprise his belief system. These beliefs affect how a person views himself, how he sees the world, and how he relates to others and God. These convictions take the form of judgments, attitudes, expectations, vows, and agreements. From these convictions flow emotional responses and decisions. Some of these are rooted in lies the person has come to believe. Everyone is influenced by the corrupt messages of the world and the lies of Satan. Jeremiah 17:9 says, *"The heart is deceitful above all things and beyond cure. Who can understand it?"*

To bring healing and restoration to the soul requires the renewing of the mind. Uncovering the lies and replacing them with the truth found in God's Word renews the mind. Renouncing lies and breaking all agreements with demons attached to the lies nullifies legal grounds for torment. To firmly plant truth into the person's belief system, meditation is needed. Through meditation the truth is rehearsed until it becomes rooted in memory. Making repeated verbal confessions and catching oneself when drifting back into old patterns of thought prevents lies from resurfacing. None of this happens automatically. It requires personal discipline and often needs the encouragement and prayers of others.

Steps to healing:

- Identify and confess the lie you have believed.

- Forgive those who have contributed to you forming this wrong belief.

- Ask the Lord to forgive you for receiving the lie and living your life based on it. Receive the Lord's forgiveness.

- Forgive yourself for believing the lie.

- Renounce and break all agreements with the lie. Break and cancel all agreements made with demons around this lie.

- Command all defiling spirits to leave.

- Choose to accept and believe the truth. Write out the biblical truth to replace the lie. Meditate on this truth until it becomes the auto default in your belief system.

3. Traumas

He heals the brokenhearted and binds up their wounds (Psalm 147:3).

The LORD is close to the brokenhearted and saves those who are crushed in spirit (Psalm 34:18).

He has sent me …to set at liberty them that are bruised (Luke 4:18 KJV).

Traumas are emotional hurts embedded inside the heart. They are wounds to the soul. They cannot be seen from the outside. These hurts are lodged in memories from the past. When a situation, event, or circumstance occurs that is similar to the original trauma, it triggers the hurt and pain over again. The way to heal these wounds is through a divine exchange in which the person casts his cares upon the Lord (1 Peter 5:7; Psalm 55:22). He pours out his complaint as David did in Psalm 142 and lays all his pain and sorrow upon the Lord, according to Isaiah 53:3-6. In exchange, Jesus bestows His grace. He crowns the person with beauty instead of ashes, the oil of joy instead of mourning, and the garment of praise instead of the spirit of heaviness (Isaiah 61:2-3). This is all accomplished through the presence and power of the Holy Spirit.

Steps to healing:

- Ask the Holy Spirit to reveal the hurt deeply embedded in the memory.

- Listen and watch for what the Spirit reveals.

- Identify all the pain and hurt associated with the past trauma.

- Invite Jesus to come and be with you.

- Give all the pain and hurt over to Jesus. You may need to do this many times before all the pain is taken away.

- Receive back from Jesus the comfort, healing, and grace He wants to give you.

- Give thanks to God for His goodness and grace.

Demonic Oppression

For this purpose, the Son of God was manifested, that He might destroy the works of the devil (1 John 3:8 KJV).

And these signs will follow those who believe; in My name they will cast out demons (Mark 16:17).

…How God anointed Jesus of Nazareth with the Holy Spirit and with power, who went about doing good and healing all who were oppressed by the devil, for God was with Him (Acts 10:38).

Then He called his twelve disciples together, and gave them power and authority over all devils, and to cure diseases (Luke 9:1).

Demons cannot possess Christians, but they can oppress. Demons are invisible spirit entities with minds, emotions, and wills of their own. They have their own personality and are organized in ranks under Satan's control. They do his work for him by tormenting, distracting, deceiving, tempting, distressing, and accusing, in an effort to inflict harm. They negatively impact every part of our life: body, mind, and spirit. Demonic oppression is pressure exerted by demons to try to get us to sin, thereby limiting our ability to witness for Christ. They try to prevent people from receiving salvation and keep people from maturing in Christlikeness. Demons gain access to Christians through generational curses, ungodly beliefs, traumas, unrepentant sin, and occult involvement. They are active in the occult and new age movements. They are constantly influencing Christians, but for the most part their influence goes unrecognized by Americans indoctrinated in humanism.

Some behavioral indicators of demonic oppression include inability to feel joy, agitation in worship services, unable to stop sinning, shame based identity, extreme emotions, family breakdown, accident proneness, insomnia, financial lack, abnormal sex life, self-inflicted injury, super human strength, foul odors, change in personality, night terrors, poltergeist activity, voices prompting sin, and more.

Steps to Deliverance:

- Work through generational sins, ungodly beliefs, trauma, and all unrepentant sin to take away all legal rights and close all doors of access.

- If this is not successful, do the following:

  1. Confess all sin and forgive those who influenced you to sin.
  2. Confess and repent for allowing demons to have place in your life.
  3. Forgive yourself for allowing the pain and limitations that come from demons forgiving yourself for not submitting to God and not resisting the devil.

- In the name of Jesus, break off and renounce all agreements made with demons, both consciously and unconsciously.

- In the name of Jesus, use your authority to command all demons by their name or function to leave you. Command all demons connected to a stronghold to leave you based on the finished work of Christ on the cross. Command them not to return.

- Ask the Holy Spirit to fill you with more grace. Then receive what the Holy Spirit pours out.

- Give thanks for the goodness of God.

Related Areas of Ministry

Inner Vows

Do not judge, or you too will be judged. For in the same way you judge others, you will be judged, and with the same measure you use, it will be measured to you (Matthew 7:1-2).

But I say to you, make no oath at all, either by heaven, for it is the throne of God, or by the earth, for it is the footstool of His feet, or by Jerusalem, for is the city of the great King. Nor shall you make an oath by your head, for you cannot make one hair white or black. But let your statement be 'yes, yes' or 'no, no'; and anything beyond these is of evil (Matthew 5:34-36).

Inner vows are pronouncements or judgments a person speaks over himself in response to hurt, unmet expectations, and unmet needs designed to protect himself from more pain. It serves as a promise to self. An inner vow often uses words like "always" or "never." For example, "I will never be like my father who cares for nobody except himself." These vows can lay dormant for years until something is triggered, and the person begins to experience the effects of the vow. The Bible instructs us to avoid making vows.

Word curses

The LORD's curse is on the house of the wicked, but He blesses the home of the righteous (Proverbs 3:33).

...Let fire come out from Abimelek and consume you, citizens of Shechem and Beth Millo, and let fire come out from you, the citizens of Shechem and Beth Millo, and consume Abimelek (Judges 9:20).

The tongue has the power of life and death, and those who love it will eat its fruit (Proverbs 18:21).

A curse can come from God as a penalty for sin. Deuteronomy 11:26-28 says God either blesses or curses according to our obedience to His law. Men can also speak a curse. A word curse is a wish or negative statement pronounced over a person by someone who desires evil to come upon another. Witchdoctors make these proclamations, but so do ordinary people. Parents tell their children in a moment of frustration, "You will never amount to anything." A teacher tells a student, "You are stupid." When the person agrees with these curses in his heart, they become self-limiting beliefs that wreak havoc in life. The Scriptures teach that we are not to curse but to bless.

Steps to nullifying vows and curses

1. **Forgive yourself for speaking a vow or the other person for speaking a curse over you**. Try to identify the exact words that were said. Example: I forgive_____ for saying _____.

2. **Ask the Lord to forgive you for saying the vow or receiving the curse,** and for living your life based on it. Receive the Lord's forgiveness.

3. **Renounce and break off all legal rights of the vow or curse** based on the shed blood of Jesus Christ and His finished work on the cross.

4. **Based on the finished work of the cross and your authority as a believer in Christ, cancel all judgments** and stop the work of all demons connected to the vow or curse.

5. **Speak a blessing over yourself or the other person**. In this way, overturn evil with good.

Soul Ties

After David had finished talking with Saul, Jonathan became one in spirit with David, and he loved him as he loved himself (1 Samuel 18:1).

Do you not know that he who unites himself with a prostitute is one with her in body? For it is said, "The two will become one flesh" (1 Corinthians 6:16).

God is a covenant-making and covenant-keeping God. In his kingdom, covenants are considered serious agreements that must be kept. Covenantal bonds are emotional or spiritual attachments that could have godly or ungodly ramifications. God recognizes and honors these agreements even when they are made without any formal recognition. The term "soul tie" is not found in the Bible. However, the Bible refers to it when it speaks of souls being knit together (1 Samuel 18:1 NKJ) and becoming one flesh (Genesis 2:24; Mark 10:7-8; Ephesians 5:31; 1 Corinthians 6:15-16).

To cut off negative influences, a person needs to break ungodly soul ties. These could be influences marked by co-dependence, inversion, manipulation, intimidation, control, or abuse. Soul ties can be established through sexual relationships, platonic relationships, or familial relationships. You can have both godly and ungodly soul ties with the same person.

Steps to Freedom from Ungodly Soul Ties

1. **Confess** all emotional and spiritual ungodly soul ties with others. Identify them by name.

2. **Forgive** the other person for their part in the ungodly soul tie.

3. **Ask the Lord to forgive** you for your part in the ungodly soul tie.

4. **Renounce and break** each ungodly soul tie. Release yourself from each person you have named.

5. **Renounce and cancel** the assignments of demons associated with these ungodly soul ties.

6. **Ask the Lord to bless the other persons** and to remove all ungodliness from them.

7. **Give thanks** unto the Lord for his goodness.

Expect Resistance

Any effort to advance the kingdom of God will be met with resistance from the kingdom of darkness. Jesus gave Peter the keys to God's kingdom so that the gates of Hades would not prevail against his efforts to build the church. He instructed him to bind and to loosen what is on earth as it already had been done in heaven (Matthew 16:18-9). The New Testament records that wherever the apostles went, they were met with some opposition or resistance. The same is true today.

People who come for ministry inherently bring a measure of resistance with them. Even when they sincerely want to be healed, forces operating against them resist healing. Ignorance, fear, and unbelief make it difficult for them to receive truth. Also, faulty belief systems riddled with lies often block the truth. Deep hurt-filled memories surface, triggering emotional reactions that shut down the person's capacity to receive. When persons feel unsafe, condemned, or judged they cannot focus on what God is doing and are reluctant to surrender control. Additionally, demons interfere by bringing confusion or physical manifestations. Occult demons are especially resistant. These are some of the general inhibitors you can expect to encounter in the ministry of healing and deliverance.

Some specific inhibitors include lack of trust, the inability to forgive, bitterness, shame, guilt, pride, self-deception, denial, rationalization, intellectualism, not accepting responsibility, and blaming others. Other inhibitors include unworthiness to receive, misconceptions about God, false identities, partial healings from the past, lack of expectation, and lack of faith in God's grace. If there is a lack of scriptural knowledge, misunderstanding of spiritual authority, or lack of understanding of healing and deliverance process, this can also inhibit ministry. Lastly, inability to hear God's voice, occult connections, and mental disorders like DID, OCD and PTSD all contribute to the resistance.

To overcome resistance, the minister needs to exercise patience and discern the voice of the Holy Spirit, who gives direction and wisdom. Drawing upon prophetic gifts at this juncture is very helpful. Asking the Lord for revelation to identify where blockages lie helps prevent the restoration process from stalling. The minister must recognize and accept the fact that overcoming resistance is part of the healing process. Often, this will mean waiting for the person to surrender control over to God. If the person is not ready to deal with a specific area of hurt, the minister needs to look for an alternative area in which the person is ready to receive.

A lifeguard will tell you that you cannot rescue anyone as long as they're trying to save themselves. If you try, they will pull you down with them. You just need to wait and tread water until they finally give up. When that happens, things become easy. You just wrap your arm around their shoulder and swim to shore.

The same is true for ministers of freedom. The way ministers "tread water" is to gently instruct the person to stop fighting through their troubles alone (2 Timothy 2:25). Instead of resisting, they need to surrender and work with God, who promises to heal, deliver, and restore.

Maintaining Healing

Freedom cannot be taken for granted. It is like your health. After having cleaned and bandaged a wound, it must be maintained. Otherwise, infection will creep back in. Galatians 5:1 says, *"Stand fast therefore in the liberty by which Christ has made us free and do not be entangled again with a yoke of bondage"* (NKJV). Each person must maintain a right relationship with the Lord. Engaging in sin and self-deception will cause a relapse. The person's eternal salvation is not at stake—that is secure in Christ's finished work on the cross. However, living in victory will be tenuous at best. Vigilance and discipline are needed to keep the faith and to live free. Healing and deliverance should be understood as a lifestyle, not an event. Freedom is a daily choice, and each day we have the option to repent or to let our hearts grow hard. Every time a person says, "No" to doing what is right, they put themselves in prison. Seeking the kingdom of God and His righteousness is what keeps us free (Matthew 6:33).

Composition of an In-depth Ministry Team

God can use individuals to bring deliverance, but it is best to do ministry in teams. Jesus sent His disciples out in teams of two and Paul conducted ministry as part of a team. Teams have the advantage of mutual support, diversity of gifts, accountability, and discernment.

Team ministry also provides a measure of legal and spiritual protection. When conducting ministry in private settings, it is best to have another person present. Having two team members in the same room reduces the risk of false accusations around sexual misconduct or the temptation toward inappropriate sexual intimacy.

It works well for husbands and wives to minister as a team or to have two men or two women to serve on a team. Again, this reduces the temptation toward sexual misconduct. If a man and woman are to serve on a team, they must have the trust and support of their spouses and families. The character of these persons needs to very solid and be verified by spiritual leaders.

In-depth ministry requires the skills and experience of a staff person or highly-trained lay counselor. At this level, ministry can be very challenging and time consuming. It might lead to long-term relationships.

Ministry can be conducted anywhere that has a measure of privacy, safety, and hospitality. It is possible to do ministry in a home, but I recommend a church building for several reasons. First, it removes the specter of impropriety, especially for a team of mixed-gender ministers. Second, it maintains privacy of the ministers and their families. Third, it avoids the appearance of the ministry being viewed as something independent of the church. Fourth, it provides access to office equipment, supplies, and resources. Fifth, it gives the ministry greater visibility and public validation by the congregation.

Authorization and Supervision

Ideally, authorization for this ministry will come from the elders or governing body of the church. This body not only gives permission but could also establish training requirements and venues for freedom-oriented ministry. This could include small groups, altar ministry, prayer nights, or in-depth scheduled sessions. Believers need to be encouraged to minister freedom to their families, neighbors, and co-workers once they have been trained.

Supervision for the ministry may vary depending on the size of the church. It can take different forms. In smaller churches, the pastor or a laity team could provide supervision. In larger churches, a staff member or a designated ministry team could provide supervision. Each ministry should have a level of accountability that corresponds with the depth of ministry provided. For example, accountability for small group leaders should be at one level, altar team members another level, prayer night participants still another level and those doing in-depth ministry yet another level. Each type of ministry should have someone to hold them accountable. Church members who minister outside the formal structures of the church should find accountability in their small groups.

Discussion Questions

1. How would you rate the various ministries within your church when it comes to advancing the gospel of freedom? What ministries need to be made stronger if your church were to establish a culture of freedom? What needs to happen for that to occur?

2. The author says prayer and forgiveness are foundational for the ministry of freedom. What makes prayer so important? What makes forgiveness so important? Is there anything in the author's treatment of forgiveness that caught your attention? What difference could this make in your life?

3. The author claims that before freedom can be fully realized, four basic areas of ministry need to be addressed. Do you agree or disagree? Why? What do you think could happen if some area of ministry is overlooked?

4. Why do you think it is necessary to expect resistance when seeking to help others receive freedom? How do you experience it working in your life?

5. What would it take for your church to consider a comprehensive vision that includes an altar ministry, small group ministry, weeknight prayer and in-depth counseling? What would be the best place for your congregation to start?

21

Building a Culture of Freedom

Why a Culture of Freedom?

According to Scripture, the purpose of life is to glorify God by developing godly character. We are called to be holy as God is holy (1 Peter 1:16). We are called to be conformed to the image of his Son (Romans 8:29). We are told it is the will of God that we be sanctified (1 Thessalonians 4:3). Being instructed to purify ourselves from everything that contaminates the body and spirit (1 Corinthians 7:1), we prepare ourselves in anticipation for Christ's return (1 John 3:3). We are instructed to love from a pure heart and a good conscience and a sincere faith (1 Timothy 1:5). None of this happens apart from being set free from sin, the world, and evil. This freedom is realized within the context of a faith community devoted to the glory of God (Acts 2:42-47). As Peter clearly states, *"Live as people who are free"* (1 Peter2:6).

The Need for a Culture of Freedom

Dr. Marcus Warner, President of Deeper Walk International, tells a story about a student who attended Trinity Evangelical Divinity School in Deerfield, Illinois. By way of background, the student had graduated from Moody Bible Institute and was furthering his theological education in preparation for ministry. Asked by his professor to write a report on the book *Victory Over the Darkness* by Neil Anderson, the student wrote:

> I have never been discipled, and I have been a Christian for 20 years. Be   cause of not knowing who I am in Christ, I did not know how to walk according to the Spirit. Therefore, I have been living my life according to the flesh, while getting a lot of head knowledge about the Bible and God. I have struggled so long because of my weakness to say no to myself and I have really been ineffective for Christ. I was always told what to do by those I opened up to, but I never had any power in my life. I know a lot of theology. I know everything I should

do, but I do not bear much fruit. And I do not love others the way God wants me to. I have prayed a long time that God would show me how to get my head knowledge into my heart. And now, He has shown me the way. I feel like a baby Christian because I have to start at the basics again. But I will swallow my pride and learn how to reprogram my faulty ways of thinking. I have grown up with poor self-esteem, self-condemnation, self-hatred, bitterness, rebellion, perfectionism, anxiety, and a weak functional faith. I had needs that I tried to have fulfilled by lust, pornography, eating, acceptance by others, withdrawal, and façade. My life is filled with hurts and I responded to them incorrectly. I used to really struggle because of my view of how God views me. By reading a couple of helpful books on God's grace I have been freed from the mentality of perfectionism for God's acceptance and love. Yet my life is still powerless because of my faulty patterns of thoughts, many of which are strongholds."[1]

This story points to the profound need for people of faith to discover the power to overcome strongholds, wounds, lies, and faulty thought patterns that keep them in bondage. It is these things that keep them stuck or plateaued in their Christian growth. Churches are filled with believers who are perplexed as to why their faith is not working for them. Could it be that current church cultures neglect the inner life and should be reconfiguring their culture to bring freedom and new life to the soul?

Traditional Discipleship Culture

Typically, churches in America utilize a traditional discipleship approach. Traditional discipleship incorporates five characteristics:

1. **"All Welcome"** or **"Y'all Come"** approach – The emphasis is on identification with the way we live. There is no intentional strategy other than to invite people to church and make them feel welcome. Simply by their attendance and participation in our way of life, they will absorb what it means to be a disciple of Christ. The limitation of this approach is its reliance on ethnic background, style, and personal preferences for maintaining the local community instead of greater identification with Christ.

2. **"Learn with Us"** approach – The emphasis is on academics. By learning Bible content and Christian doctrine, you can be a disciple of Christ. The more knowledge you accumulate, the more you are seen as an expert in the faith and recognized as spiritually mature. The limitation of this approach is

that it appeals to the intellect, which can foster elitist thinking. The formation of a culture of puffed up and condescending people is the result.

3. **"Do What We Do"** approach. The emphasis is on behavior. By practicing spiritual disciplines such as worship, giving, serving in a ministry, participating in rituals, programs, and events, you can be a disciple of Christ. Your performance profile deems you a fruitful person. The limitation of this approach is that it relies on human achievement and lends itself to selfish ambition.

4. **"Be Good"** approach – The emphasis is on morality. You can be a disciple of Christ if you learn to comply with the shoulds and should nots, stay within the sphere of what is right, avoid what is wrong, and engage in suitable activities. The more strictly you observe the boundaries of the ethical and legal code, the purer you are. The limitation of this approach is that it relies on self-policing, which inevitably fails and leads to hypocrisy, guilt, and shame. It reduces the gospel to works righteousness rather than reliance on grace.

5. **"Make It Happen"** approach – The emphasis is on training people to invest in the church. People are trained to invite others, volunteer for service, and join a small group. The idea is to keep people involved in order to keep the institution operational. In using your gifts to serve and encouraging others to do the same, you are a disciple of Christ. The more you invest in doing ministry, the more you are valued and appreciated. The limitation of this approach is that a church turns inward, focusing on developing its own attributes and comfort rather than taking the risk of sharing the gospel with resistant and hostile people.

What Is Missing?

The descriptions used above are not meant to be pejorative. Each approach is needed and has a unique role in making disciples when appropriated correctly. However, these approaches together do not address the need for inner transformation of the heart. Reliance on these approaches alone result in a religious culture that produces carnal Christians. People look good on the outside—but it doesn't do much for the inside. They learn how to dress, what words to say, and how to fit in the church culture, but remain stagnant in Christian growth. They appear polished on the outside, but the inside remains corrupt. Consequently, an atmosphere of pretense emerges. This lack of authenticity has a detrimental impact on many among the younger generations. For them, the church over-promises and under-delivers.

What is missing in the traditional model is what I call the **"Be Set Free"** approach. This approach emphasizes the need for the Holy Spirit to heal the heart. This transformation of the soul is not accomplished by referring people to mental health experts who teach them how to manage their pathology. No, this is accomplished by equipping every believer to minister restoration to the heart. As valuable as psychologist and counselors are, they are no substitute for the body of Christ implementing the healing ministry of Christ to the soul. By creating a culture that utilizes the apostolic, prophetic, evangelistic, pastoral, and teaching gifts in every aspect of church life the body builds itself up in love. Thus, the person becomes a disciple of Christ, who walks in the Word and the power of the Spirit. The limitation of this approach is determined by the limits people place on the Holy Spirit. The Bible identifies this as quenching and grieving the Spirit. When sin is embraced, the Spirit is grieved. When the presence of the Spirit is neglected, the Spirit is quenched.

A Culture of Freedom Is Planted in the LORD

To build a culture of freedom requires plowing up hard soil and planting good seed. Building a culture of freedom is not simply about revival. Revivals are needed because spiritual freedom is not maintained. Revivals tend to be local and short-lived. To build a culture of freedom requires a reformation. Old religious practices, belief systems, organizational priorities, and educational methods need to be plowed under. New church structures need to be raised up, not only to accommodate freedom, but to sustain it.

This plowing under and raising up cannot be accomplished simply by the noble intentions of men, but by submission to the power of the Holy Spirit. It is written, *"Unless the LORD builds the house, those who labor build it in vain"* (Psalm 127:1). Continual refreshment in the Spirit is essential to build the house of the Lord. The labor required to build the LORD'S house involves more than planning, setting goals, and strategizing. It requires the hard work of prayer. Jesus said, *"It is written, 'My house shall be called a house of prayer'"* (Matthew 21:13; Isaiah 56:7; Jeremiah 7:11). This means more than shouting out an occasional prayer request or a perfunctory praying before a meeting. It means cultivating intimacy with the LORD that results in a constant awareness of His presence. The Bible calls this prayer without ceasing (1 Thessalonians 5:17). Making the church a house of prayer calls for collective gatherings for prayer. These are occasions in which people not only make petitions, express gratitude, and worship, but also listen, discern, and make prophetic declarations for the restoration of the soul. Unfortunately, the busy pace of today's society and lack of spiritual hunger results in prayer meetings being the least attended event on the church calendar. This neglect renders the body spiritually malnourished and susceptible to spiritual disease. In contrast, freedom feeds on prayer, making the body strong.

A Culture of Freedom Seeks Righteousness

Freedom does not seek permissiveness. Freedom is not a license to sin or to be apathetic. On the contrary, it seeks righteousness in surrender to the Holy Spirit. Isaiah prophesied there would be a people who would be set free to pursue a life of righteousness. He said, *"captives will be released and prisoners will be freed... The time of the LORD's favor has come. In their righteousness, they will be like great oaks that the LORD has planted for His own glory"* (Isaiah 61:1-3 NLT). In other words, anything done in a church to promote freedom resulting in righteousness will enjoy the favor of God. Similarly, the prophet Hosea also invokes the pursuit of righteousness. He wrote: *"Sow righteousness for yourselves, reap the fruit of unfailing love and break up your unplowed ground; for it is time to seek the Lord, until He comes and showers His righteousness on you"* (Hosea 10:12). Building a culture of freedom will require plowing up the soil of the soul to reap God's unfailing love and righteousness. This is not an easy task, but if the church will make it a priority to seek the Lord until He comes, God will shower blessing upon His people. Jesus said, *"Seek the Kingdom of God above all else, and live righteously, and He will give you everything you need"* (Matthew 6:33 NLT).

A Culture of Freedom Results in Good Fruit

Freedom results in prosperity. Psalm 1:1-3 declares, *"Blessed is the one who does not walk in step with the wicked or stand in the way that sinners take or sit in the company of mockers, but whose delight is in the law of the LORD, and who meditates on His law day and night. That person is like a tree planted by streams of water, which yields its fruit in season and whose leaf does not wither - whatever they do prospers."* Freedom results in bearing good fruit, specifically the fruit of the Spirit. A church culture that emphasizes freedom for the soul will transform lives that bear the good fruit of love, joy, peace, patience, kindness, goodness, faithfulness, gentleness, and self-control (Galatians 5:22-23).

Mike Gribble's Story

During a Sunday morning worship service Deryl Hurst, pastor of DOVE Westgate Church in Ephrata, Pennsylvania, spoke on the need to be planted in a local congregation. He read from Psalm 92:13-14, *"Those who are planted in the house of the Lord shall flourish in the courts of our God. They shall still bear fruit in old age; they shall be fresh and flourishing"* (NKJV).

To illustrate the importance a local church plays in the acquisition of freedom he told the following story:

> Several years ago, Mike was in a very dark place in his life. He had a long history of alcohol and substance abuse. He had gone through a secular rehab program and achieved temporary reprieve, but as with most secular programs where there is no genuine heart change, it didn't stick. Soon he fell back into some of his old ways. Along the way, during a time of sobriety, he began to attend DOVE Westgate Church. When the wheels came off the wagon again, he did the right thing. He fully engaged, I mean fully engaged! He began to attend Celebrate Recovery at another local church. He began meeting with a mentor from our church twice a month who led him through the Biblical Foundation Series. He and his wife Deanne began attending a small group that met weekly in addition to meeting the small group leaders for counsel and guidance. He attended our men's retreat. He went for Isaiah 61 ministry (a ministry of healing and deliverance). He and his wife attended Sunday morning worship services faithfully. Along the way, he grew in faith and stability. He became a member of our worship team. Today, Mike and his wife are small group leaders, mentoring and discipling others. They are excited to be used by God in even greater ways. Mike and his wife are fully planted in the house of God and are now in a place where they can minister to others.

Mike's story demonstrates that for individuals to fully experience personal freedom, they need to be immersed in a culture of freedom. They need leaders to connect them to a God who wants to heal the deeply wounded places in their hearts. They need a church culture that is safe, loving, and speaks truth. They need a church culture where the Holy Spirit's power is released, not just talked about. They need a church where the power of God's love is demonstrated through many different ministries. They need a church where healing and deliverance are practiced by engaging all five of Christ's gifts.

Generally, churches that recognize the gifts of teaching, pastoring, and evangelism tend to rely on intellectual and verbal communication skills to share the truth of the gospel. Emphasis is placed on preaching, doctrine, caring relationships, and social programs as a means of witnessing to the lost. Whereas these ministries are valued and needed, exclusive dependence on them can leave a void, often having the form of religion but denying its power (2 Timothy 3:5).

There is a need to recover and engage the apostolic and prophetic gifts. These gifts have the added advantage of seeing the gospel communicated and confirmed through revelation and power (Mark 16:17-20). These gifts point to the presence and power of God in a way that exceeds human effort. Paul made this clear in writing to the Corinthians. He said, *"the message of the cross... to us who are being saved it is the power of God"* (1 Corinthians 1:18). And in 1 Corinthians 4:20 he declared, *"The kingdom of God does not consist in words, but in power."* Similarly, he told the Thessalonians, *"Our gospel did not come to you in word only, but also in power and in the Holy Spirit"* (1 Thessalonians 1:5).

A Different Story

Mike's story is encouraging, but not all who experience a measure of freedom have such a positive outcome. For example, an elderly lady came to us on the recommendation of a relative who had benefited from our ministry. She was in a miserable state, suffering from agoraphobia. She had been shut up in her house for years. She barely went outside and when she did it was mostly to see her doctors. The woman had a strained relationship with her husband and long-standing issues of regret with one of her daughters. She had carried resentment in her heart against some other Christians for over twenty years. We made a strong connection with her and ministered to her soul for nearly eight months.

During the sessions, she connected with the Holy Spirit and there were visible breakthroughs. After every session, she experienced a measure of relief and freedom. Eventually, she became well enough to attend worship services at a nearby church. Her husband was delighted with her progress. When she felt she was well enough to stop receiving ministry we celebrated her progress and sent her on her way with blessings.

However, I learned sometime later through her husband that she had regressed into old patterns. Once again, she confined herself to her bedroom and her attitude drifted into negativity. Her relationship with her husband deteriorated. She suffered a fall requiring her to be admitted into a personal care facility. Although she had experienced some degree of freedom, without ongoing support, stimulation, and the encouragement of a local church her condition deteriorated over time.

Restoration requires involvement in a congregation where you can receive ongoing counsel, comfort, and encouragement. According to 2 Corinthians 1:4, *"God comforts us in all our troubles so that we can comfort others. Then when others are troubled, we are able to give them the same comfort God has given us"* (NLT).

Charles Spurgeon said, "Friendship is one of the sweetest joys of life. Many might have failed beneath the bitterness of their trial had they not found a friend."

Freedom Focuses on Discipling the Heart

Freedom-focused discipleship deals with the inner life—with what is going on inside of a believer's heart. Inside the heart is a person's belief system. It is composed of memories, will, ideas, expectations, opinions, traditions, values, judgments, attitudes, perceptions, desires, thought life, and self-talk. A person's beliefs influence their emotional reactions and behavioral responses. Beliefs are not simply creeds that one intellectually subscribes to. Beliefs are heart-felt convictions that determine what you feel and what you do. Proverbs 4:23 states, *"So above all, guard the affections of your heart, for they affect all that you are. Pay attention to the welfare of your innermost being. For from there flows the wellspring of life"* (TPT).

God has given each person the responsibility to steward their own heart. The condition of our heart determines the direction and quality of life. Circumstances do not determine the condition of the heart, rather they reveal what is already there. What we believe determines how we respond to life's circumstances and challenges. The decisions we make flow from what is inside the heart, whether filled with truth or lie, anxiety or peace, faith or unbelief, wickedness or righteousness. In speaking to the Pharisees Jesus said, *"You brood of vipers, how can you who are evil say anything good? For the mouth speaks what the heart is full of"* (Matthew 12:34 NIV).

Freedom-focused discipleship seeks to create an environment where people feel safe to take the lid off their hearts and expose what is happening beneath the surface. By revealing deeply embedded wounds, lies, vows, and strongholds, a person can be set on a path toward healing and freedom. However, before this can happen, a culture must exist that invites this kind of vulnerability. Such a culture is built on the fear of the Lord and is enlivened by His grace. When people genuinely fear the severity of God's judgment and at the same time are enamored with His kindness (Romans 11:22-23), they are apt to continually ask God to examine their hearts for unbelief and corruption. They are like King David, who prayed, *"Search me, God, and know my heart; test me and know my anxious thoughts. See if there is any offensive way in me, and lead me in the way everlasting"* (Psalm 139:23-24).

The main reasons people don't open their hearts to freedom-focused discipleship is either because they think they don't need it or they are afraid of it. The fear of man and unbelief harden their hearts. They are not in touch with the condition of their souls. They are self-deceived and are like Peter who declared his faith in Christ was so strong that he would never deny the Lord, yet denied knowing the Lord three times.

The truth is, every believer needs freedom from their sin, the world's lies, and the devil's schemes. The reality is everyone hurts. Everyone has wounds and trauma. The cares of life weigh everyone down with emotional baggage. Everyone has hidden sins and has made vows that have shaped their life's direction. Obstacles that block their spiritual growth keep them from living a victorious life. Everyone falls short of the glory of God. Not one among us does not need sanctification, restoration, and healing. We all need the impartation of more grace.

If people are going to live the good news found in Christ, it is important that they feel secure, accepted, and valued. They need to feel they can trust their community with their heart. They need to be convinced that when they take their mask off and become vulnerable, they will be cared for and protected. Before they will take the risk of being real and honest, they need to be assured gossip is strictly prohibited and confidentiality is maintained. Before they share what is going on under the surface, they need to believe they are loved unconditionally, regardless how messy their lives have been.

A major feature of a freedom-focused culture is recognizing that the people around them are themselves wounded healers. Most believers, and especially leaders, have an ongoing testimony of being healed and delivered from the effects of sin and the powers of darkness. There is an unspoken recognition that those gathered for worship go through much heartache will be comforted. And with the comfort they have received they are willing to reach out and comfort others in need (2 Corinthians 1:4). Going a step further, these wounded healers not only exhibit the ability to mend broken souls they also display a high level of integrity. They are not only familiar with the powers of the spiritual realm, they also model the character of Christ.

A culture that facilitates freedom is characterized by honesty, forgiveness, humility, compassion, accountability, hope, patience, joy, and gentleness. It engages the full power of the Holy Spirit. There can be no tolerance for pretense or denial of sin (Acts 5:1-11). The depravity of man is not underestimated nor minimized. At the same time, the goodness of God and the sovereignty of God cannot be elevated nor celebrated enough.

Worship

Central to the culture of any church is its worship. It follows that if free-dom is to be infused into the DNA of church culture, it must be reflected in its worship. Giving praise and thanksgiving to God for who He is and what He has done is expressed most powerfully through the singing of psalms, hymns and spiritual songs (Ephesians 5:19). Singing songs about how God has set us free pays homage to the goodness of God. The lyrics used in worship reveal what a community values and believes about God. When a church values freedom found in Christ, it will take great delight in singing about it. The more that wor-ship includes these type songs, the more people will identify with freedom. The music style may be different, but the message is the same. The following is a list of some contemporary and traditional songs that lift up themes of freedom.

Contemporary Songs

"Raise a Hallelujah" by Jake Stevens, Jonathan and Melissa Helser, Molly Scaggs
"Hallelujah for the Cross" by Chris McClarney
"No Longer Slaves" by Jonathan David Helser and Brian Johnson
"Trading My Sorrows" by Darrell Evans
"Yes and Amen" by Christ Tomlin
"Where the Spirit of the Lord Is" by Hillsong Worship
"Living Hope" by Phil Wickham
"Let the Redeemed" by Josh Baldwin
"Holy Spirit" by Jesus Culture
"This is Amazing Grace" by Phil Wickham

Traditional Songs and Hymns

"What a Friend We Have in Jesus" by Charles Crozat Converse and William Bolcom
"Come Thou Fount of Every Blessing" by Robert Robinson
"Because He Lives" by Bill and Gloria Gather
"It is Well with my Soul" by Horatio Spafford
"Standing on the Promises" by Russell Kelso Carter
"There is Power in the Blood" by Lewis E. Jones
"Blessed Quietness" by M.P. Ferguson
"Victory in Jesus" by E.M. Bartlett
"Come Thou Long Expected Jesus" by Charles Wesley
"Lord Prepare Me to be a Sanctuary" by Randy Lynn Scruggs

Teaching and Preaching

What is taught and proclaimed as truth will give shape to a culture. Christians universally draw upon the authority of Scripture as the primary source of truth. Doctrines of faith and principles that define the kingdom are all derived from Scripture. Whereas there are differences in interpretation, the Scriptures are fundamentally viewed as truths that reveal God's nature and activity in the world, past, present, and future. When the local church neglects to teach how God works for each person's freedom and how He equips each person to bring freedom to others, the culture becomes a depository of truth without power.

Along with basic doctrines of the Christian faith, a few other topics are critical to build and maintain a culture of freedom. The church curriculum needs to include the following the topics:

- How to fear the Lord
- How to hear the voice of God
- How to engage in spiritual warfare
- How to exercise discernment
- How to deal with offenses
- How to apply the three levels and four dimensions of forgiveness
- How to make divine exchanges
- How to take down strongholds and renew the mind
- How to strengthen yourself in the Lord
- How to assert your authority as believer to cast out demons
- How to die to the flesh
- How to be accountable to others
- How to give honor to those who don't deserve it
- How to live out the fifty-plus "one another's"
- How to pray the six types of biblical prayers
- How to use the gifts of the Spirit for the benefit of others
- How the five-fold ministry operates
- How to overcome tests of faith
- How to pray for someone's healing and deliverance

This list does not represent an all-inclusive curriculum but is a start toward building a culture of freedom. Please note the use of the "How's" in these topics. This implies not only explanation but also demonstration.

The building of any culture requires leadership, the topic of the next chapter.

Discussion Questions

1. Of the six models of discipleship presented in this chapter, with which one do you have the most experience? What are the strengths and weaknesses of that model? What does it take to disciple someone's heart?

2. Why is it important to belong to a freedom-oriented congregation with support groups? What would keep someone from getting involved? How should a congregation help others overcome their hesitancy?

3. If you were looking to join a freedom-oriented congregation, what would you be looking for? What would hold you back?

4. It has been said that Christ comes to disturb the comfortable and to bring comfort to the disturbed. Do you agree? What does the character of Christ look like? How do you recognize it in a person and a congregation?

5. What criteria would you use to identify a wounded healer? Have you ever thought of yourself as a wounded healer? How do you see yourself helping someone else achieve freedom?

6. What are the top ten songs your church sings? What are their themes? What does that say about what your church values and believes about God?

7. What biblical teachings from this chapter could benefit your church? What topics would you personally benefit from? How would you go about generating interest in these topics?

22

The Role of Leadership in Freedom

Leaders Gives Shape to Culture

John Maxwell, author, teacher, and leadership consultant is fond of saying, "Everything rises and falls on leadership." A leader's influence plays a key role in shaping culture. Leaders not only cast vision for the future, they also equip people with knowledge and ability to make the vision a reality. Leaders instill confidence. Leaders do more than manager systems. They are change agents and model what they want others to do. Leaders cannot take their followers any further than they have gone themselves. Unless they have personally experienced freedom in their own lives, they have no credibility in recommending it to others. Leaders must first be an example. They need to submit themselves to the healing and deliverance process and embrace it as an ongoing lifestyle. It is not to be a one-time event. They need to share their testimony of how the presence, power, and love of Jesus Christ transforms life.

Having a personal testimony, however, is only the beginning. Leaders must also be competent and confident in their ability to set others free. And beyond that, they must provide training to equip others. Freedom ministry is not lectured or talked about; freedom ministry is demonstrated. It is not something to be acknowledged and then farmed out to mental health professionals. The ministry of freedom belongs to the body of Christ. It is something that is to be lived out and practiced as part of one's faith. Granted, it can be messy and a bit scary. Nevertheless, it is at the heart of what it means to be a Christian.

Dan Reiland, author and pastor, says, "The essence of leadership involves the unknown. If you're truly out in front leading and taking new territory, you will absolutely experience uncertainty. Making measurable progress in leading others to places where you, and they have, not traveled before creates questions, doubts, and wavering confidence."[1] In this uncertain period, between what has been and what is yet to come, flow the turbulent waters of unbelief, causing some to flounder. Within the heart of every leader, there is an underground stream of unrest and spiritual struggle. Will he capitulate to threats and fear, or will he hold onto faith? Freedom for himself and for those he leads hangs in the balance. The outcome of this inner battle will determine whether he has what it takes to lead his people into spiritual warfare or remain content maintaining the institutional church.

Having a vision for the future is not enough. There needs to be boldness and courage to take risk. People must see the leader's faith in action to be convinced the vision is from God rather than a pipe dream of the leader. The leader must inspire faith. Even though the people may not see the big picture or fully understand its implications, they must be willing to set aside their timidity, trust the leader, and commit themselves to God's vision.

To gain an understanding and a vision for the healing and deliverance ministry necessary for freedom, I recommend the book, *The Biblical Guidebook to Deliverance* by Randy Clark. He writes, "Our congregations are assaulted daily by an increasingly godless culture, with both the believer and the unbeliever alike swimming in a sea of New Age and occult activity like the West has not seen for centuries. It is my greatest desire to see the entire Church awakened afresh to the knowledge that deliverance is a New Testament reality that springs from the compassionate heart of God as revealed in Jesus."[2]

Admittedly change is uncomfortable, especially when dealing with spiritual matters that upset our assumptions about reality. Introducing such a vision brings a measure of pressure and stress that is painful. When organizations go through significant transition, roles change, beliefs are challenged, practices are altered, and a sense of place and worth is re-stablished. People are afraid of both of what lies ahead and of being left behind. In such an uncertain environment, leaders must instill confidence and inspire hope. They must repeatedly remind people the vision belongs to God and that He alone has put within them the grace to make it possible. Before a new culture becomes visible, the people must first have faith to see the invisible.

Seeing with Spiritual Eyes

Perhaps the greatest challenge leaders face in building a culture of freedom is helping people see with spiritual eyes. Helen Keller, author and political activist, was the first deaf-blind person to earn a Bachelor of Arts degree. She was a remarkable person who is remembered for this famous quote: "There are none so blind as those who will not see." Inherent in this statement is not so much a reference to limitation of sight but reluctance of the will.

Throughout the Bible, God's prophets, apostles, and even Jesus encountered stubborn resistance to the reforms God was calling for. God's people had hard hearts, stiff necks, ears that could not hear, and eyes that could not see (Deuteronomy 29:1-4; Isaiah 6:9-10; Jeremiah 5:21; Matthew 13: 10-17; Mark 8:17-18; Acts 7:51; Acts 28:23-27; Romans 11:1-10). Ezekiel 12:2 states clearly, "*You are living among a rebellious people. They have eyes to see but do not see and ears to hear but do not hear, for they are a rebellious people.*"

The Apostle Paul recognized the inherent difficulty the human heart has toward perceiving spiritual realities. He had spent three years teaching and discipling the church at Ephesus. One of the very first things he said in a letter written to them is that he is praying for them. He prays that God would give them wisdom and revelation so that they would know Christ better (Ephesians 1:16-17). Continuing, Paul prays that the eyes of their hearts would be opened so that they could know three things:

1. The confident hope that God has called them to, including the expectation of heaven and a life of holiness.

2. The rich inheritance they have in being united with Christ, including the fruit of the Spirit and gifts of the Spirit

3. The power available to those who believe—the kind of power that raised Jesus from the dead and gave Him authority to rule over every other spiritual power (Ephesians 1:16-23).

For Christians to walk in freedom, they need to become more intimately acquainted with Christ. This requires the ability to receive revelation and wisdom from God. It means acquiring an unshakeable confidence in the promises of God. It means being familiar with Christ's gifts and assimilating the fruit of the Spirit into one's character. It also means demonstrating Christ's power and authority to forgive sins, heal the sick, and cast out demons. The eyes of the heart need to be open to the supernatural work of the Holy Spirit who uses ordinary people to do extraordinary things.

Perhaps the primary reason people have difficulty seeing with the heart is what psychologist call "cognitive dissonance." This is a state of mind in which a person's thoughts, beliefs, behaviors, and attitudes toward change are inconsistent. They waffle back and forth in their convictions and have divided loyalties. The Bible calls this double-mindedness (James 4:8).

Some things that cause double-mindedness are the sinful nature, worldly influences, demonic schemes, and fears.

Some specific sins that contribute to double-mindedness include self-righteousness, selfish ambition, self-deception, insecurity, pride, and unbelief.

Some worldly influences connected to double-mindedness include a humanistic worldview and worldly distractions and pleasures.

Some demonic schemes that promote double-mindedness include distrust for leaders, divisive arguments, competing factions, and clinging to personal agendas or preferences.

Some fears that advance double-mindedness include fear of the unknown, fear of being deceived by false teachers, fear of change, and fear of losing control.

Other contributing factors include ignorance of the demonic, ignorance of spiritual authority, and a desire to grow while maintaining the status quo. Maintaining the status quo is often reflected in stubborn mindsets that say things like: "If it ain't broke, don't fix it," "We never did it that way before," and "This is my church, you can't have it." How can these challenges be overcome?

Profile of Church Leadership

All of Christ's gifts need to be activated to overcome these obstacles. The gifts of pastors, teachers, and evangelists are needed but these gifts alone are not sufficient. The apostolic and prophetic gifts are also required. To realize the ministry of freedom, these gifts need to be activated and imparted into the congregation.

The apostolic is needed to confront the powers of evil, to exercise spiritual authority, bring correction, establish order, delegate responsibility, institute accountability, introduce new initiatives, and establish organizational priorities and structures.

The prophetic gift is needed to hear from heaven, provide revelation and insight, uncover that which is hidden, call forth gifts, provide encouragement, speak truth in love, speak into existence what God has ordained, and equip others to hear from heaven.

For churches unfamiliar with these gifts, it will mean a step of faith in an uphill direction. Educating people in these gifts is crucial for them to be accepted and trusted. Because these gifts embrace facets of the supernatural, they will need to be tested and given some time to mature. These gifts already exist within most congregations. They need to be recognized, cultivated, activated, nurtured, and appreciated. If these gifts are not evident within a congregation, the thing to do is to ask God for them prayerfully. Leaders must not deny their existence, ignore them, or allow them to remain dormant. For churches that lack this kind of experience, they can seek outside help from more seasoned leaders who are able to provide supervision.

No one leader can change a culture. It requires a team of leaders who hold the same vision, hunger, passion, and love for the freedom Christ provides. This team of leaders refuse to compete with each other. Instead, they recognize the need to complement and support one another. They realize they cannot usher in a culture of freedom without the gifts of others. They learn to depend on each other for insight, encouragement, and counsel. They demonstrate humility and honor toward each other, especially when they disagree. They understand and desire biblical accountability. They see it as essential in maintaining their own freedom and spiritual growth. These leaders are not content with maintaining the operations of the institution or its numerical growth. They have an insatiable desire to join with the Holy Spirit to raise sons and daughters to spiritual maturity.

This team of leaders perseveres and remains steadfast amid all kinds of testing and temptations. They remain:

- hopeful and confident in the face of opposition, resistance, and offense;
- unoffended, patient, and calm when blamed for things going wrong;
- respectful and honoring to their opposition;
- content in the battle for the acquisition of trust and cooperation;
- approachable, loving and kind toward their detractors;
- accountable to each other and governing authorities;
- prayerful and vigilant against the schemes of the devil;
- connected, nurturing, and comforting to the fearful;
- intolerant toward gossip or breach of confidentiality;
- united in the face of divisive power plays and factions;
- committed to the freedom of others even when falsely accused;
- encouraged by other leaders who have known their struggle;
- resilient amid failures, setbacks, and disappointments;
- faithful not to the abdicate the vision, call, and authority of leadership;
- dependent on the Holy Spirit for wisdom, discernment, and direction.

Equipping Is Needed

Presently, many churches are not able to provide this kind of community because their pastors and leaders have not been equipped to build this kind of culture. Seminaries and Bible Colleges have not adequately prepared them for this kind of freedom-based ministry. For churches that have not known this kind of discipleship, it will take a bold commitment to implement such a vision over a long period of time. This is not a program that can easily be installed into current church structures. To establish such a community, it will take years. And to become consistently effective, it may take decades.

Where can this kind of training be found? Spread across the United States are Antioch-type churches who have established schools of ministry to equip people for this kind of discipleship. Whereas the primary goal of these churches is to plant churches, they recognize the necessity of the five-fold ministry gifts and the power of the Holy Spirit. The Association of Related Churches (ARC) has an impressive record of establishing life-giving churches. I am not in a place to endorse any of these churches. However, there are two churches I am most familiar with, Ephrata Community Church and DOVE Westgate Church. These two churches leave a big footprint in Lancaster County, Pennsylvania. I can speak favorably of these ministries. I know both senior pastors and have benefited greatly from their church's ministry. Freedom in Christ is a major focus for both of these churches. I would encourage you to visit their websites.

Some international networks have schools of ministry. A few that I am aware of include, HarvestNet International, DOVE International, Global Awakening, Iris Global, and Bethel School of Supernatural Ministry. For more information you can conduct a google search for schools of supernatural ministry.

There are parachurch organizations that also do training, much of it online. Some of these equipping ministries include Freedom in Christ Ministries, Deeper Walk International, Restoring the Foundations, Elijah House, Cleansing Streams, Strait Paths Foundation, Biblical Counseling Coalition, Be in Health, and Heart of the Father Ministries. Most of these ministries are non-denominational.

Finally, there are some life coaching ministries for those who desire one-on-one mentoring. One such ministry located online is Christianlifecoaching.co.uk

Spiritual Fathers and Spiritual Mothers

Spiritual fathers and mothers are needed to help others walk in freedom. They are leaders who are spiritually mature in Christ. They are not perfect, yet they have allowed their failures to instill a greater dependence on God. These leaders can teach the Bible, but their calling involves a lot more than the just communicating information. These folks have consistently surrendered their life over to the Holy Spirit to the point where their identity is deeply rooted in Christ. They are secure in the Father's love. Having undergone healing and deliverance for themselves, they walk in much personal freedom. They see with spiritual eyes. Not limited by reason alone, revelation guides them. God has bestowed on them a level of spiritual authority and power that enables them to help others find freedom.

No matter their age, young or old, they are recognized by church leaders as having been called to a position of influence. They have Christlike character and maintain an intimate relationship with the Lord. These folks have made great sacrifices of time and energy, pouring their life into those who want mentors. Without regard for recognition, they find great purpose and gratification in setting others free from bondage. They take great delight in nurturing and counseling others to maturity. Their ministry carries much responsibility, but it also has great reward. Watching the Holy Spirit transform people into new creations, right before their eyes, gives them much happiness. They are like a midwife who assists in the birth of a baby. They have great joy partnering with the Holy Spirit to bring new life to a besieged soul.

The challenge facing many churches today is the same problem Paul faced at the church in Corinthian. He told them, *"For though you might have ten thousand instructors in Christ, yet you do not have many fathers"* (1 Corinthians 4:15 NKJV). There is a substantial difference between the way instructors operate as opposed to how fathers function. Instructors teach, lecture, and sermonize. They impart content. Spiritual fathers and mothers nurture, correct, sacrifice, and counsel others into freedom. Instructors educate students. Spiritual fathers and mothers love and believe in their children. There is a desperate cry among the younger generations for spiritual fathers and mothers. They are looking for someone to confide in and provide mentoring.

If the church is going to inch its way toward becoming a bride without spot or wrinkle with each new generation, it needs to make the raising up of spiritual fathers and mothers a priority. Larry Kreider has written an outstanding book entitled *The Cry for Spiritual Fathers and Mothers*[3] that goes a long way to equip the body of Christ in this area. It offers a vision, strategies and practical considerations that aid in the development of spiritual fathers and mothers.

Spiritual parenting involves the whole package of loving, training, modeling, motivating, correcting, restoring, and imparting. At the heart of spiritual parenting is teaching your spiritual children how to steward the inner life. Only as one learns to walk in freedom from strongholds can spiritual maturity be attained.

Small Groups

Spiritual fathers and mothers can best impact believers is in a small group. The small group functions like an *oikos*. This New Testament word means "household" or "home." Acts 5:42 reports, *"And daily in the temple, and in every house (oikos), they ceased not to teach and preach Jesus Christ"* (KJV). A welcoming home establishes close relationships. In this setting, small group members practice the fifty-plus one another's, discuss biblical teachings, share testimonies, refine spiritual gifts, and cultivate the fruit of the Spirit. People learn to live out the kingdom of God.

Getting believers to commit to small groups can be a challenge in modern society. People have many options and opportunities that compete for their loyalty. The combination of vocational demands, family responsibilities, and recreational events lead to a hectic lifestyle. These interests often conflict, forcing people to make difficult decisions about how to use their time. Adding another evening out for a small group can seem taxing. Another factor that could discourage people from joining a small group is the thought of having to talk with people you don't know. For some, this can be very intimating. In addition, people live guarded lives and are hesitant to share their hearts. It can take a long time to establish mutual trust. Despite these hindrances, small groups are well worth the effort. They are vital to the spiritual health and wellbeing of the church. The contribution they make to the discipling process is indispensable. Developing small groups where spiritual fathers and mothers exert their influence should be a high priority for church leaders. Today this can be accomplished with the aid of small group resources in which study guides and DVD courses are available. For a brief list of some recommended recourses, see Appendix K.

To develop spiritual fathers and mothers within a congregation requires accountability. This accountability cannot be the kind found in the world. It needs to be the kind found in the Bible. The next chapter focuses on biblical accountability.

Discussion Questions

1. What kind of leadership does it take to establish a culture of freedom within a church? How important is it for a leader to conquer his own fears before attempting to lead others in the battle for their souls?

2. Paul prayed that the Ephesians would have the eyes of their hearts opened. What did he mean by that? How do leaders help others to see into the spiritual realm? Based on his prayer, what were Paul's expectations for the disciples at Ephesus? What implications does this have for the way you live out your faith?

3. When a church sets its sights on freeing people from captivity it will encounter resistance and obstacles. What are some of the things you would anticipate encountering and how would you overcome them?

4. What kinds of leaders are needed to implement a vision for freedom in a congregation? What kind of attributes should they have? How can they function as a team? What do a spiritual mother and father look like? What role do they have in building and maintaining a culture of freedom?

5. Small groups function like New Testament house churches (*oikos*). What do you think should happen in a small group? How do small groups contribute to building and maintaining a culture of freedom?

Endnotes

1. Dan Reiland, *Confident Leader*, (Thomas Nelson Books, Nashville, TN, 2020), p. xix.
2. Randy Clark, *The Biblical Guidebook to Deliverance*, (Charisma House, Lake Mary, FL, 2015), p. xvi.
3. Larry Kreider, *The Cry for Spiritual Fathers and Mothers*, (House to House Publications, Lititz, PA, 2000)

23

Leaders Function in Freedom Through Accountability

Biblical Accountability

Earlier in the book, I cited a late friend, Frank Ferrari. He said, "There are two questions people ask when they enter your church for the first time: Is there anyone here who will love me? Is there anyone here who will tell me the truth?" The answer to those questions is found in the way a church goes about implementing accountability.

Most of what I have learned about biblical accountability comes from having failed to implement it. I hope others can benefit from my mistakes. I am grateful to my Amish friends who have modeled biblical accountability for me. I offer the following in the spirit of much humility and gratitude.

There is a story of two fishermen drifting down the river in a boat. As they approached a nearby bridge that spanned the width of the river, they noticed it was falling apart. Every time a car would go across, another piece of the bridge would shake. Finally, a huge truck passed over the bridge and the entire middle section of the bridge crumbled into the river. The fishermen knew that the next car to come around the bend would not see the bridge was gone and would come crashing down into the river, damaging the car and injuring the driver.

One of the men turned to his friend and said, "We've got to do something. What would be the 'Christian' thing to do?" The friend thought for a moment and said, "Build a hospital?"

This is a crazy thought, yet many in the church would rather build a hospital than put up a warning sign. We are prone to deal with things after the fact rather than take preventive measures. We often wait until a person gets into a bad condition before we do anything. At that point, we want to hold them accountable, and in effect, we say, "Get your act together" or "You need to get some help."

Sad as it is, we do not understand biblical accountability. Biblical account-ability is as proactive as it is reactive. It seeks to provide a protective covering that shields people from themselves. We are our own worst enemy. We are driven by ego. We are self-centered and will resort to anything to advance our own credibility and agenda.

The prophet Jeremiah wrote, *"The heart is deceitful above all things and beyond cure"* (Jeremiah 17:9). The truth is we have an uncanny ability to de-ceive ourselves through rationalization, denial, excuses, and exaggeration. It is amazing how we forget, suppress, and minimize the truth. We embellish and elevate what we know to be false. We beautify ugly realities to paint ourselves in a favorable light. We lie to protect our pride. We will do all these things to pro-tect ourselves and get what we desire. A person's pride is his greatest stumbling block. The Bible warns, *"Pride goes before destruction, a haughty spirit before a fall"* (Proverbs 16:18).

To illustrate the insidious nature of pride, Daniel Coyle, in his book *The Culture Code,* records an experiment conducted by Peter Skillman in several universities. He organized business school students in groups of four to build the tallest structure possible using twenty pieces of uncooked spaghetti, one yard of transparent tape, one yard of string and one standard-size marshmallow. There was only one rule. The marshmallow needed to be at the top. He challenged the students to complete with a group of kindergartners to see who could build the tallest structure. He did the same exercise with a group of lawyers and CEOs.

In every case, the kindergartners out-performed the professionals. The kindergarten groups averaged twenty-six inches, the business students averaged ten inches, lawyers averaged fifteen inches and CEOs averaged twenty-two inches.

It would seem that those with more education, sophistication, strategizing skills, and experience would perform better. But apparently, the level of individual skill was not the determining factor. What mattered was the interaction between participants. The professional groups were engaged in what psychologists call "status management." They were more concerned with who was in charge, who could be criticized, and what the rules were. This resulted in competition, inef-ficiency, and hesitation. The professionals focused more on the uncertainty of their relationships than on solving the problem. In contrast, the kindergartners appeared disorganized, unafraid of offending and willing to try whatever they could. Instead of being competitive or comparing themselves with each other, they focused on problem-solving and helping each other. They took risks and noticed outcomes which helped them to come up with effective solutions. The kindergartners proved to be more effective not because they were smarter, but because they worked smarter together.[1]

When you remove issues of status, achievement, competition, and comparison groups work better together. In other words, when you can eliminate pride and selfish ambition embedded in the carnal nature, people are free to achieve much together. For this reason, it is necessary that the Spirit convict us of our self-conceit, self-ambition, and self-deception. Accountability helps us get over ourselves, especially our pride. In this way, we are set free to live in righteousness and heavenly wisdom (James 3:14-17).

The sinful nature of man requires accountability, and accordingly, the Bible instructs us to pay close attention to the inner man. In 1 Samuel 16:7, *"The LORD said to Samuel, 'Do not consider his appearance or his height, for I have rejected him. The Lord does not look at the things people look at. People look at the outward appearance, but the LORD looks at the heart.'"* Psalm 51:6 declares, *"God desires truth in the inward parts and in the hidden part the Lord will reveal wisdom."* Zechariah 8:16 says, *"These are the things you must do: Speak the truth to each other, and render true and sound judgment in your courts."* Jesus himself emphasized the importance of truth in the heart of man. He said, *"Out of the abundance of the heart the mouth speaks"* (Matthew 12:34).

Even further, the Lord calls upon leaders of the church to be honest (Acts 6:3) and to equip people to speak the truth in love in order to grow to maturity (Ephesians 4:11-15). These Scriptures clearly indicate that it is God's intention for the local church to be focused on the transformation of the inner man and that accountability is essential for this to work.

If the church is going to facilitate the healing of the inner man, it must practice accountability as a balance between love and truth. Timothy Keller beautifully states the need for both. He says, "Love without truth is sentimentality; it supports and affirms us but keeps us in denial about our flaws. Truth without love is harshness; it gives us information but in such a way that we cannot really hear it. God's saving love in Christ, however, is marked by both radical truthfulness about who we are and yet also radical, unconditional commitment to us. The merciful commitment strengthens us to see the truth about ourselves and repent."[2]

Merriam-Webster dictionary defines *accountability* as "being subject to giving an account: answerable; capable of being explained." Explanation for one's behaviors, motives, and attitudes is a matter of reporting what you did, why you did it, what you were thinking and feeling. It is a means of analyzing both the external and internal conditions of a person's behavior. It does not have to be an emotionally-charged event filled with fear of condemnation. For some people, however, accountability has a negative feel to it. It is seen as a beating down that holds you liable for every little action or inaction. In other words, you are judged by your weaknesses and faults.

From a business point of view, this is understood as a necessary practice to maximize production. You are expected to clean up any deficiency to be acceptable to those passing judgment on your performance. In the work world, if you don't meet the standards, your job is in jeopardy. Accountability in search of a fault can easily put you on the defensive, or at the very least, make you nervous and guarded. All you want to do is survive the dreaded evaluation. Where there is a lack of trust, honor, and safety no real honesty can be expected. No real life-giving change will occur. Some minor behavioral adjustments may happen, but no internal shift will transpire.

The church needs to practice accountability, but not as it is typically practiced in the world. Jesus warned His disciples they were not to use their power and position to rule over others as the Gentiles did. Instead, they were to serve others by putting forth a good example (Matthew 20:26). The church must conduct accountability in the Spirit of Jesus Christ, who serves others by seeking their well-being. Rick Warren puts it this way, "Great leaders genuinely care for and love the people they lead more than they love leading itself."

Doing ministry with excellence is important. However, the primary focus must remain on the person's well-being rather than conformity to a set of expectations around a task. Ministry should employ accountability in a way that motivates and empowers. Hebrews 10:24 says, *"And let us consider how we may spur one another on to love and good deeds."* Similarly, 1 Thessalonians 5:11,14 says, *"Therefore, encourage one another and build each other up, just as in fact you are doing.... warn those who are idle and disruptive, encourage the disheartened, help the weak, be patient with everyone."* In an atmosphere of safety and honor, it is possible to strike a balance between guilt and grace.

Biblical accountability involves a willingness to be open and vulnerable. If a high level of trust exists, there will be a willingness to share personal and sensitive information. Examination of complaints can occur without critical accusation. There is no concern about betrayal or breach of confidentiality. There is not the slightest whisper of gossip. Instead, there is a climate of respect and mutual submission. There is no hint of "I am right and you are wrong." Instead, biblical accountability preserves each person's dignity while focusing on their healing and freedom. This kind of openness is achieved not by holding a once-a-year evaluation, but by frequent meetings in which personal heart issues are shared together in prayer. Ephesians 6:18 says, *"Praying always with all prayer and supplication in the Spirit, and watching thereunto with all perseverance and supplication for all the saints"* (KJV). James 5:16 says, *"Therefore, confess your sins to each other and pray for each other so that you may be healed. The prayer of a righteous person is powerful and effective."* Crying out to God together from the depths of your heart creates a strong bond and unity. It is in this kind of environment that the wisdom of Proverbs comes to fruition. Proverbs 27:17 says, *"As iron sharpens iron, so one person sharpens another."* Working and praying together makes accountability effective and serves as a centerpiece for the gospel of freedom.

Working Together in Anticipation of Ultimate Accountability

The Bible teaches that every person will have to give account to God on how they lived their life on earth. Romans 14:12 says, *"So then each of us shall give account of himself to God."* Holding each other accountable within the church should be conducted with this one goal in mind; helping each other do well when standing before God at the final judgment. Galatians 6:1 provides guidance in this principle, *"Brothers and sisters, if someone is caught in a sin, you who live by the Spirit should restore that person gently. But watch yourselves, or you also may be tempted. Carry each other's burdens, and in this way, you will fulfill the law of Christ."* There are several notable things worth pointing out in this verse.

First, those who are holding others accountable must *"live by the Spirit."* These are leaders who have died to their carnal nature. Their emotions or personal agendas do not drive them. They remain anchored in the Word and are discerning. They are able to filter out sin. The Spirit of Christ not only resides in them, they are able to hear His voice and receive wisdom. Because of their dependence and obedience to the Lord, they have developed a sense of righteous judgment, making them spiritually mature.

Secondly, their task is to *"restore gently."* *Restore* here means "to mend or restore to proper functioning." It is the same term used for the equipping of the saints for ministry in Ephesians 4: 12. In the classical Greek, this same word is used as medical term referring to the mending of broken bones. The idea is to heal and restore to proper functioning through realignment. This is accomplished with the precision of a doctor, who gently resets broken bones with minimal pain.

Thirdly, Galatians 6:1 warns, *"But watch yourselves, or you also may be tempted."* Those who are administering healing must be careful not to commit sin in their efforts to restore. When someone is in pain, they will often lash out at those who are helping them. In the heat of the moment, it is easy to take offense and respond out of the flesh rather than the Spirit. Caution and discipline are advised.

Fourthly, according to Galatians 6:2, *"Carry each other's burdens, and in this way, you will fulfill the law of Christ."* Every attempt at restoration must done in Christlikeness. Jesus identified Himself with sinful man. He took upon Himself the burden of man's sin. In providing for man's salvation, He bore the weight of God's judgment on the cross. Filled with compassion, He suffered on their behalf. To bear the burdens of others is to feel the weight of their sin and to ask God for forgiveness on their behalf. Jesus did this on the cross with great compassion.

This kind of burden bearing does not eliminate the need for each person to ask forgiveness. Instead, it is an act of love that moves the heart of God to restore the sinner. The law of Christ is put into effect when this kind of love for our neighbor is operative. As the righteous stand in the gap for those in bondage, the Lord hears their prayers and is obliged to respond. Out of His mercy and grace, He releases the gift of repentance (Acts 11:18; 2 Timothy 2:25). This is the spirit and goal of biblical accountability.

An Example of Biblical Accountability

Sue Shank became the administrative secretary at my church in 1994. For over ten years, we had a professional relationship. Gradually, through many strained and difficult periods, this evolved into an accountability relationship, and we learned to work together. The relationship went to a new level in 2006 when we began to apply to our relationship what we learned in Restoring the Foundations training. Things shifted. She was no longer my secretary taking orders from me. I no longer evaluated her on how well she could type and file information. We became partners in a shared ministry. We learned that God uses our weaknesses to help us realize we need each other. Jokingly, she became my "humbler," telling me things I did not want to hear about myself.

Humblers Verses Cripplers

Everyone needs to have a "humbler," someone who tells you the truth when it is uncomfortable to do so. A "humbler" is someone who humbly speaks into your life, bringing a word of correction. The word is spoken directly and pointedly, but also with love and tenderness. Constructive criticism is offered in a way that you feel honored, valued, and lifted up. Proverbs 27:6 NLT says, "*Wounds from a sincere friend are better than many kisses from an enemy.*" A friend helps you become your best self. You can receive their criticism because you know they are not out to hurt you. You are confident that you are being loved like a brother. 1 John 4:21 says, "*And He has given us this command: Whoever loves God must also love his brother.*" Love for God requires humility. This humility makes the honor of others possible. It would then follow that where there is a lack of honor there is also a lack of humility.

Humility and honor go hand in hand. In Philippians 2:3, Paul instructs his listeners to be humble and then to honor others above themselves. He writes, "*Don't be selfish; don't try to impress others. Be humble, thinking of others as better than yourselves.*" Humility precedes honor. It is impossible to honor others above yourself if you have not first died to the flesh. The sinful nature is so self-centered it only looks to its own interest. Comparison, competition, condemnation, criticism, and control fuel the sinful nature. Unless we renounce these things, honoring someone above yourself becomes impossible.

When your attitude is, "I am going to straighten out that guy" or "I will reject them before they reject me," you are not ready to hold another person accountable. You lack humility and you become a crippler, not a humbler. Cripplers damage relationships. Despite good intentions, they create distance, build walls, and foster distrust. The crippler sees himself as the one chosen to fix another person. In this role, he subconsciously elevates his own importance. Cripplers do not take into consideration the need to honor and preserve the dignity of others. Their primary interest is in exercising their own superior wisdom and knowledge, convincing themselves of how much good they are doing.

Cripplers are those who critique others while still having the splinter in their own eye. The irony is that they don't know it. Often, they are trying to correct someone else out of their own pain. The very issues they see as detrimental in the life of others are the very ones that are unresolved in their life. Jesus warned against this in Matthew 7:1-5, "*Do not judge, or you too will be judged. For the same way you judge others, you will be judged, and with the measure you use, it will be measured to you. Why do you look at the speck of sawdust in your brother's eye and pay no attention to the plank in your own eyes? How can you say to your brother, 'Let me take the speck out of your eye,' when all the time there is a plank in your own eye? You hypocrite, first take the plank out of your own eye, and then you will see clearly to remove the speck from your brother's eye.*"

Vulnerability

Accountability requires a willingness to be open and vulnerable. Vulnerability is achieved in an atmosphere of trust where respect and mutual submission are fostered. Accountability is not a one-way street. Whereas positional authority is honored, relational authority must also be practiced. In other words, there is a freedom for both parties to speak into each other's lives. It is not a matter of a superior exercising power over a subordinate. In the kingdom, power is used not to manipulate or control people but to develop spiritual maturity and set them free.

When you know your brother is helping you to be your best self in preparation for the final judgment, it is only natural to confide and pray for one another. Healing relationships do not happen simply by meeting together socially or strategically. They are developed by sharing heart issues and praying together. Crying out to God from the depths of your heart creates a powerful bond of affection and trust. This kind of accountability builds strong unity.

Listening (really, really listening)

Another element of biblical accountability is listening. Listening allows the person being held accountable to feel understood. This also keeps one from rushing to judgment. James 1:19 says, *"My dear brothers, take note of this: Everyone should be quick to listen, and slow to speak and slow to anger."* Actively listening to a person's inner struggles, without an attitude of judgment, conveys the love of God and the grace of the Jesus. It helps set the stage for healing and freedom.

Safety from Judgment

Biblical accountability holds to a non-judgmental attitude. It employs correction without making the person feel condemned. The goal is to bring out the best in others, not to make them feel weak, inferior, or inadequate. Biblical accountability has a prophetic quality. 1 Corinthians 14:3 states, *"But one who prophesies speaks to men to edification, and exhortation, and comfort."* (NAS). Prophetic ministry removes the dirt, and thereby uncovers the gold within a person. When the prophet Nathan confronted David, he did not accuse and condemn. He gently led David to the revelation that he had compromised his own principles and beliefs. David repented, proving himself to be a man after God's own heart.

Nathan confronted his superior respectfully and gently. The New Testament speaks of approaching those in positions of leadership the same way. 1 Timothy 5:1 declares, *"Do not rebuke an older man harshly, but exhort him as if he were your father. Treat younger men as brothers."* And 1 Timothy 5:19-20 says, *"Do not entertain an accusation against an elder unless it is brought by two or three witnesses. But those elders who are sinning you are to reprove before everyone, so that the others may take warning."*

One helpful approach to calling people to give an account is to draw upon the THINK approach. This is an anacronym for a series of questions to ask oneself before speaking into another person's life.

T: Truth – Is what I am about to say the truth?

H: Helpful - Is what I am about to say helpful?

I: Inspiring – Is what I am about to say inspiring?

N: Needed – Is what I am about to say needed?

K: Kind: – Is what I am about to say kind?

Examining one's own attitude will ensure you are serving the other person in the Spirit of Christ.

Those who engage in healing and deliverance ministry need to be people who have significantly worked through pain and strongholds in their own life. Having done so, they are less likely to be judgmental of the people they seek to help. They can say without hesitation, "I've been where you are, and I desire freedom for you just as I have been set free myself." This is the kind of spiritual leadership needed in the church.

Measuring Up?

In most church settings, markers of institutional growth measure success. A church is deemed successful based on the number of baptisms, budget, and buildings. These indicators point to institutional success but have little bearing on the spiritual growth of individuals.

Common business mantras like, "measure what matters" or "what gets measured gets managed" are helpful when evaluating performance. But this begs the question: What should we be measuring in order gauge how well the church is doing when it comes to building God's kingdom? If you consider building God's kingdom on earth as the work of freeing people from sin and evil, then how do you measure freedom?

The best way to assess progress toward spiritual maturity is to ask questions focused on the inner life. This cannot be measured statistically but anecdotally. Holding interviews, one-to-one accountability meetings, and small group discussions can provide the setting to share personal stories.

Accountability Questions

To evaluate how you or your church are doing at setting captives free, here are some accountability questions to consider.

- What strongholds do you struggle with?
- To what degree have you overcome them?
- What grace have you incorporated into your life?
- What truths are you attempting to apply to your life?
- What are some lies you have discovered about yourself?
- What new beliefs have you incorporated into your life?
- What are you doing to renew your mind?
- In what areas have you received a measure of spiritual authority?
- How has your identity changed?
- How have you become more loving, kind, peaceable, joyful, gentle, patient, and self-controlled?
- How much healing have you experienced from past wounds and trauma?
- How have you become more of a blessing to others?
- How has your hearing the voice of God improved?
- How have you grown more content?
- How have you grown in managing stress?
- How have you exercised compassion and mercy for others?
- What has been the most difficult thing to forgive?
- What has happened to embarrass or humiliate you and what did you do about it?
- What do you perceive to be the greatest threat in your life?
- What thought keeps nagging you and keeps coming back?

Leo Tolstoy once said, "Everyone thinks of changing the world but no one thinks of changing themselves." Perhaps if we practiced more biblical accountability, people would be willing to change themselves.

Discussion Questions

1. What has been your experience with accountability at work, at home, and in the church?

2. What is the difference between accountability practiced in the world and biblical accountability? How does proactive accountability function? How does reactive accountability function?

3. Is there anything that needs to change in your church to make biblical accountability more effective? What is the difference between a "humbler" and a "crippler?"

4. How important is biblical accountability in forging a culture of freedom? What kind of attitudes are needed to implement biblical accountability? How can those attitudes be developed within the church?

5. What role does biblical accountability play in measuring spiritual growth? How do you think spiritual growth should be measured? How important is it to have a different set of eyes and ears to help analyze your spiritual growth?

6. What are the connections between loving people, telling them the truth, and biblical accountability? How does this set people free?

7. What example or evidence can you point to that would indicate Leo Tolstoy is right in saying "Everyone thinks of changing the world but no one thinks of changing themselves"? What would it take for people to change themselves before attempting to change the world?

Endnotes

1. Daniel Coyle, *The Culture Code*, (Bantam Books, USA, a division of Penguin Random House LLC, New York, 2018).
2. Timothy Keller, *The Meaning of Marriage: Facing the Complexities of Commitment with the Wisdom of God* (Penguin Group, New York, NY, 2011).

CHAPTER 24

Leaders Work Together in Freedom

Dealing with Offenses

By virtue of living in a broken, sin-infested world, offences are going to occur whether we want them to or not. Jesus said, *"It is impossible that no offenses should come, but woe to him through whom they come"* (Luke 17:9 NKJV).

Jesus tells a parable that explains what happens when a person does not handle offenses with the grace that God requires. The bottom line is this: if you do not forgive those who offend you, your life will be filled with misery. If out of bitterness, you want to see those who have hurt you being punished, then you will be tormented by demons (Matthew 18:23-35). What a sobering thought. It behooves us to learn how to process offenses.

Similarly, in Ephesians chapter four, Paul makes a dire admonition. He gives instruction in how to avoid sinning when you are provoked to anger. He warns that if you do not resolve your anger quickly, you will be giving your heart's territory over to the devil. He says, *"In your anger do not sin: Do not let the sun go down while you are still angry and do not give the devil a foothold"* (Ephesians 4:26-27).

The Greek word for "foothold" is *topos*. It is the word from which we get the English word "topography." It refers to a place or space and carries the idea of an inhabited place like a city or town. In other words, Paul is saying that if you don't let go of your anger, you will give place for demons to operate in your life. Once again, this is very sobering message. It is something every Christian needs to understand if he is going to live in freedom.

Definitions for Offense

What constitutes an offense? A dictionary defines it as "a breach of the law or an illegal act; an annoyance or resentment brought about by a perceived insult to or disregard for oneself or one's standards or principles."

The Bible uses two words for "offense:" *scandalon* and *proskomma*. Both have the connotation of sinfulness or stumbling block.

Offenses can be intentionally or unintentionally imposed. A person can be offended by something said or done to them by someone else, even though there was no malicious motivation involved. It is a matter of perception derived from one's belief system. For example, I was talking with someone concerning a controversial theological topic: Covenant Theology versus Dispensationalism. A third person who was listening to the conversation suddenly became upset at something I said. He interjected into the conversation and accused me of judging his theology as inferior. There was no intention on my part to say such a thing. Nevertheless, he was insulted. Later I learned that he was in a ministry situation where a group of self-righteous superiors were continually putting him down. He had been emotionally wounded and was very sensitive to the slightest hint of self-righteousness in another person. Out of his emotional wounding, he took offense to something that was neither directed at him nor intended to be malicious.

People can become offended without realizing it. Instead of acknowledging their standards were disregarded, their expectations were not met, their honor was insulted, or their feelings were hurt, they try to minimize their experience by saying, "I am not angry. I am not upset. I am just a little frustrated. It's no big deal." Essentially, they are not being honest. To avoid rocking the boat or causing a disturbance, they deny being offended. To maintain the appearance of peace, they repress their anger and explain away their irritation. The truth is, anytime you have been disappointed, distressed, or disturbed you have been offended, even in the slightest way.

Another consideration is what I call "pet offenses." Just as people have pet peeves that cause frustration, we can have pet offenses. We find certain things that annoy, irritate, and offend us, but others that don't bother us so much. Having people talk with their mouth full may not offend you, but being cut off in heavy traffic by a reckless driver may send you through the roof. A pet offense I have discovered in myself is that I can have a lot of patience with people who disagree and don't cooperate with me, but I easily become offended when those people become hypocritical. Hypocrisy invokes anger within me that other things do not. I used to justify this as righteous indignation. The sad truth is, such anger is rooted in self-righteousness and pride deeply seated in the soul. James 1:20 says, *"Human anger does not produce the righteousness that God desires."* Learning to repent of this has given me a measure of freedom and a peace I had not known. Admittedly, I am still trying to apply Proverbs 4:23, *"Above all else, guard your heart for everything you do flows from it."*

How do you know if you have been offended? As a rule of thumb, I have found that if I become frustrated in the slightest way, I have already been offended, whether I want to acknowledge it or not. The best way to determine if you have been offended is to take stock of your inner peace. If your inner peace has been disrupted or if you feel unsettled, there is a high probability you have been offended. Instead of letting the offense simmer into bitterness, it is best to process it immediately. Processing the offense will go a long way in helping you increase your ability love others. I believe it was this ability to process offenses that led outsiders to say of the early Christians, "Behold, see how they love one another."

In dealing with offenses, it is necessary to consider secondary offenses. These offenses occur when people who are close to an offended person feel offended even though the initial offense was not directed at them. For example, someone verbally attacks my wife and she is deeply hurt. Because I love her and identify with her, I also feel attacked. It is as though the offense was levied at me. My protective instincts kick in. I declare war and enter into battle with the one who committed the offense. I use every tactic I can to neutralize the threat and defend my wife.

One person may get offended in a congregation, but that is not the end of the story. Their family and their friends are likely to become offended as well. Resolving the initial offense is not enough to keep bitterness at bay. Every person connected to the offended person also needs to work through the offense. Like contact tracing that is done in the COVID–19 pandemic to limit the virus' spread, the same is needed in a congregation. Unfortunately, there are not enough leaders in a congregation to trace all offenses and treat every person therapeutically. It is much more useful to equip every person in the congregation to process their offenses and to enlist other believers' help. Hebrews 12:15 instructs, *"See to it that no one falls short of the grace of God and that no bitter root grows up to cause trouble and defile many."*

To *defile* means to "make unclean or impure." It involves being corrupted by sin. Religious leaders of Jesus' day were concerned with external behaviors that make a person impure. But Jesus was concerned with the heart. In Matthew 15:11;18, He said, *"It is not what goes into the mouth that defiles a person, but what comes out of the mouth; this defiles a person… What comes out of the mouth proceeds from the heart, and this defiles a person"* (ESV). The sinful words and deeds that emanate from within is what defiles a person. How a person responds to an offense will reveal the godly or ungodly content of a person's heart.

Basically, there are four ways people respond to an offense committed against them.

1. **Retaliate.** They can retaliate, seek revenge, or try to get even.

2. **Repress.** They can bury or suppress their feelings rather than release them. Anger turned inward often leads to anxiety, panic attacks, or depression.

3. **Redirect.** They can transfer their emotions to innocent parties.

4. **Render.** They can turn over their emotions to God. They can release their emotions over to the Lord in prayer.

To overcome offenses in a godly way requires goodwill. When someone offends us, it is easy to make them our enemy. We want to strike back and get even. We want justice. Instead of retaliating, Jesus says we are to love those who persecute us (Matthew 5:43-44). This seems unreasonable to the carnal mind. The truth is that both the offender and the offended will be miserable and filled with hate unless love intervenes. Paul defines love this way: *"Love is patient, love is kind. It does not envy, it does not boast, it is not proud. It does not dishonor others, it is not self-seeking, it is not easily angered, it keeps no record of wrongs. Love does not delight in evil but rejoices with truth"* (I Corinthians 13:4-6).

For both Jesus and Paul, love is *agape*. It is not a feeling; rather, it is characterized as goodwill. Goodwill is more than warm fuzzy feelings for another. It is an act of the will that selflessly seeks the good of another despite hurt feelings. Goodwill is expressed five ways in Scripture: forgiveness, blessing (saying positive words), doing good deeds, restoring gently, and prayer. By doing these things, we show ourselves to be children of God. These acts of goodwill are indicators of having overcome Satan's schemes.

Satan uses offenses to bait us into committing sin. In response to an offense, people react out of hurt. You have heard the expression, "Hurt people hurt people." In response to pain, people commit sin against each other. Sin can take the form of withdrawing affection, refusing to cooperate, holding grudges, believing a lie, or becoming afraid. Other forms sin can take include making judgments, speaking a curse, declaring a vow, acting in revenge, spreading gossip, or becoming passive aggressive. Even blaming, betrayal, control, and rejection are forms of sin resulting in broken relationships. John Bevere in his book *The Bait of Satan* explains in detail how Satan uses offenses to take people captive and keep people from doing the will of God. Bevere asserts that when offenses are handled correctly, you will be made stronger rather than bitter.[1]

Some deliverance practitioners estimate that at least 80% of all demonic activity in a person's life is due to offenses. You can imagine how unprocessed offenses negatively impact the life of a congregation. Where there is a lack of growth and unity in a congregation, it can usually be traced back to offenses that have gone unaddressed. It is the responsibility of church leaders to both model and teach how to handle offenses in a godly way.

Jesus prophesied that in the last days the love of many will grow cold. He indicates there will be many reasons for this, and among them will be a turning away from the faith. Christians will betray and hate each other (Matthew 24:9-12). I believe this hate and betrayal will be fueled by social media that will infect the minds of many with lies, distortions, and misinformation. To prevent or at least offset the love of church members from growing cold, it will be incumbent upon church leaders to teach their congregants how to overcome offenses.

Indicators Offenses Remain in the Heart

Most Christians know the way to deal with offenses is to forgive. They intellectually agree that they should forgive and will verbally say "I forgive so-and-so for having done thus and such." But this is not the same as forgiving from the heart (Matthew 18:35). The heart involves emotions, and emotions need to be healed. We may agree to forgive but still hold on to the hurt. Brian Brennt explained in *Culture of Revival* that he realized he could forgive someone but remain with something under the radar that was undermining his walk with Jesus. He identified four things indicating an offense remained in his heart: dwelling on the offense, avoiding the person, criticizing the person, and holding strong opinions about what others should do.[2]

The Bible has in-depth instruction in forgiveness that a humanistic clinical approach does not afford. Secular clinical psychologists acknowledge the need for forgiveness in therapeutic settings, but they do not acknowledge the divine element in forgiveness. They approach offenses on a person-to-person level as a way to restore justice. This does not take into consideration that all offenses rooted in sin are offenses against God. God's grace replaces injustice with righteousness and hurt with healing; otherwise a vicious cycle of offense persists. This cycle becomes self-defeating unless God is invited in.

My friend Ed Hersh wrote a book entitled *Escaping the Pain of Offense* in which he explains the "Cycle of Defeat" and how to break free of it. He writes, "Without God's help we try to rectify situations in many ways including revenge, obsessing for justice, forgetting, excusing, 'moving on,' self-inflicting condemnation, or finding some other way of replacing the negative feelings with positive ones."[3] Without God, freedom cannot be achieved. It is accomplished through the Holy Spirit (Romans 8:2). See Appendix L for a diagram of the offense-defeat cycle.

Paul tells us that God has called all Christians to the ministry of reconciliation (2 Corinthians 5:18-19). Anyone who has been involved in the healing of a broken relationship knows this can be very difficult. Sometimes the hurt can be so deep, the injured parties want nothing to do with each other. In such cases, the hurt needs to be healed before reconciliation can take place. To get rid of the pain and torment, they often need the help of someone who can tap into the healing power of Jesus and the Holy Spirit. Healing hurt emotions, forgiveness, and deliverance from evil go hand in hand. They are prerequisites for reconciliation.

Disappointment with God

Sometimes life can be overwhelmingly harsh. Under the weight of tragedy, betrayal, abuse, and injustice of all kinds a soul can grow so weary from hurting that God does not seem real. He does not seem to be the one He says He is. The God of blessing, promise, and prosperity becomes so distant that He can't be trusted. Any expectation that God would, could, or should rescue us from our distress is crushed under a ton of disappointment. When hope is lost, we become offended with God.

We tend to think that because God is all powerful and good, our life should be that way also. We tend to confuse the character of God with the condition of the world. God does promise salvation, including provision, protection, prosperity, healing, and deliverance, but He does not promise there will be no pain, sorrow, and disappointment. Living in this world, we must contend with the destructive forces of sin and evil. When life doesn't go as we expect, we are prone to lose hope in our relationship with God. We resort to blaming Him or abandoning our belief in His existence. In order to live a victorious life as Christ did, we must learn to overcome the temptation to become bitter, blame God, or abandon our faith in Him. Instead of rejecting God, we must do what is counterintuitive and run to Him.

Phillip Yancey makes this point in his book, *Disappointment with God*. He writes, "One bold message in the book of Job is that you can say anything to God. Throw at him your grief, your anger, your doubt, your bitterness, your betrayal, your disappointment—he can absorb them all. As often as not, spiritual giants of the Bible are shown contending with God. They prefer to go away limping, like Jacob, rather than to shut God out. In this respect, the Bible prefigures a tenet of modern psychology: you can't really deny your feelings or make them disappear, so you might as well express them. God can deal with every human response save one. He cannot abide the response I fall back on instinctively: an attempt to ignore him or treat him as though he does not exist. That response never once occurred to Job."[4]

When people are severely wounded, they can become bitter and angry with God. This disappointment needs to be dealt with before they are ready to receive freedom and healing from the hurt and pain incurred at the hand of others. To do this, I recommend the person be led in a prayer in which they acknowledge bitterness and repent. For a sample of a Disappointment with God Prayer, see Appendix M.

Overcoming Offenses

This outlines a process that will guide you to freedom over offenses:

Steps to Dealing with Offenses

1. **Acknowledge you were offended.** Do not deny or repress "anger." If you are frustrated, you have been offended. If you have lost your peace, you have been offended. This can be very subtle and you may not be aware of it.

2. **Forgive the person who offended you.** You do not necessarily have to tell them you have forgiven them. However, if you care about them you may gently rebuke them (Matthew 18:15). Your forgiveness does not excuse them for their sin. They are still accountable to God. Nor does forgiveness mean you are reconciled to them. Forgiveness simply means you are letting go of the debt they owed you. If the hurt is so damaging that you don't have the strength to forgive, you may need to first make a divine exchange. Ask Got to give you the grace to forgive completely. Then give Jesus the pain and let Him give back to you grace enabling you to forgive. You may need someone else to help you walk through this process.

3. **Ask God to forgive you for the sinful way you responded** (in thought, word, or deed).

4. **Receive Jesus' forgiveness for your sinful responses.**

5. **Forgive yourself and receive forgiveness for yourself.**

6. **Declare that the debt has been paid** and the offender owes you nothing.

7. **Release all injustices to the Lord** (undeserved hurts and wounds).

8. **Renounce all agreements and cancel all assignment of demons** connected to the offense.

9. **Take authority over all defiling demons and cast them out.**

10. **Receive God's grace.**

11. **Break negative soul ties with the person.**

    - I confess all emotional and spiritual ungodly connections/soul ties with _____.

    - I forgive_____ for their part in my ungodly soul ties.

    - I ask your forgiveness, Lord, for my sin resulting in ungodly soul ties. I receive your forgiveness.

    - I renounce and break all ungodly soul ties. I release myself and _____.

    - I renounce and cancel the assignments of all demons associated with these soul ties.

12. **Bless the person and begin to pray for them** (Matthew 5:44; Romans 12:14).

13. **When appropriate, begin the work of reconciliation.** Pray for opportunities to be reconciled.

    When it is safe, under the leading of the Spirit you can try to reconcile.

    Each party takes their responsibility for the estrangement. Speak truth in love, forgive, affirm, and bless.

Things to do that could help lead to reconciliation.

- Love and do good to the offender (Romans 12:9).
- Ask God to change your heart (Ezekiel 36:26-27; Psalms 51:10-13).
- Don't speak poorly of the offender (Romans 12:14).
- Release them from your punishment (Romans 12:17-19).
- Don't celebrate their failures (Proverbs 24:17).
- Treat them the way you want to be treated (Luke 6:31).
- Stop dwelling on the past (Isaiah 43:18).
- Pray blessings on them (Matthew 5:43-47; Luke 6:27-28).

Something to Remember

In Colossians 3, Paul told the church how to take on Christlikeness. After telling them what to take off and what to put on, he said, *"Let the peace of Christ rule in your hearts, since as members of one body you were called to peace. And be thankful"* (Colossians 3:15). You know that you have adequately dealt with an offense when the peace of Christ is restored.

"Jesus does not cherish an offense, loving us as well after the offense as before it." Charles Haddon Spurgeon

Dealing with Injustice

At a meeting of HarvestNet International, I was greeted by J.C. Alzamora, the Director of the HarvestNet School of Supernatural Ministry. He asked me how I was doing. I responded by saying that I was doing well, except for my arm. "I can hardly move it," I explained. "I am in a lot of pain."

"I have a bunch of students that are on fire," he said. "Let me have them pray for you."

We went to an adjacent room where a group of four or five students began to pray for my arm. They began to pray as per their training, speaking healing to my arm muscles, bones, nerves, and blood vessels. They prayed for a while and asked me to move my arm to see if there was any difference. I slowly raised my arm, but the pain was still there. They prayed some more and asked me to try it again. I tried moving it, but unfortunately there was no difference. So, they prayed once more, and again, nothing changed.

About that time two young men walked by and stuck their head in the door. I asked them, "Do you have any spiritual muscle?"

They responded, "Yea, we got spiritual muscle."

"Come in here and pray for my arm," I told them. So, they came in and began to pray.

One of the young men said, "I see a bag of bricks chained to your shoulder." He began to break off the chains in Jesus' name. I tried moving my arm, but nothing happed.

A young woman to my right said, "It is a spirit."

"Name that spirit," I said to her.

A young woman from behind me answered, "It is the spirit of injustice." At that point something in my spirit resonated with what she said. She began to pray against the spirit of injustice, but nothing happened.

Now I knew what I was dealing with. Somewhere in my past, I agreed with and accepted the injustices. Before I could be set free, I had to be the one to break my agreement and give those injustices to the Lord. So, I prayed. As I did, I raised my hands and arms above my head, giving those injustices over to God. At that moment, I felt a heavy weight lift off my shoulders. Something left my body. I felt lighter. I tried moving my arm, it was still filled with pain. I heard an inner voice saying it would be healed in the months to come. At that point, the students went back to the main meeting.

In the weeks and months ahead, I began to do physical therapy for my arm. Gradually, over a period of two months, my range of motion increased and the pain left.

I shared this story with some pastor friends that I pray with. They encouraged me to do some research into the idea of a spirit of injustice. I spent several weeks researching this and learned some things I believe are important for church leaders to understand.

First, God rules justly. Psalm 103:6 says, *"The Lord works righteousness and justice for the oppressed."* Secondly, the Bible speaks of the scales of justice. Proverbs 11:1 says, *"A false balance is an abomination to the LORD, but a just weight is His delight."* Thirdly, the Bible uses two Hebrew words in the Old Testament for "injustice." *Mishpat* refers to treating people equally and without partiality in legal matters. This also includes providing and protecting the poor and less fortunate in the community so that they can be effective community members. *Tsadeqah* refers to a life of righteous relationships. This means treating people fairly, generously, and equitably. Deuteronomy 16:20 says, *"Follow justice and justice alone so that you may live and possess the land the LORD, your God is giving to you."* In other words, your very life and receiving the promises of God depends on how you treat people around you.

Treating people unfairly or unjustly is an offense to God. Injustice happens when people agree with Satan in perverting God's Word. In Isaiah 59:5, the term *tsepha* depicts those who commit injustice. It means "viper, a poisonous snake." It infers that injustice is the work of demons. Demons influence people to be unjust. Isaiah 5:21 indicates those who commit injustice are those who call evil good and good evil. They do what is wise in their own eyes instead of God's. In other words, they operate from the carnal nature and open the door for demons to influence their decisions. In Romans 1, the Apostle Paul identifies several sins that relate to injustice. They include covetousness, malice, envy, strife, deceit, gossip, slander, haters of God, insolent, haughty, boastful, inventors of evil, disobedient to parents, foolish, faithless, ruthless, and heartless. In 1 Corinthians 6:9-10, he includes thieves, greedy, and swindlers as being those who will not inherit the kingdom of God.

Anyone who serves in a leadership position in a Christian organization is subject to injustice. Jesus himself experienced injustice from His enemies, but also from His friends. His disciples abandoned Him and Judas betrayed Him. As a church leader, if you are going to follow Jesus, you can expect injustice from those close to you. Demons can use religious people to engage in gossip, slander, maliciousness, strife, covetousness, envy, and many other sins that undermine or hurt those in leadership. The Pharisees were experts in God's law, but they perverted the truth through their carnal nature. They falsely accused Jesus and maliciously got rid of Him--thinking all the while that they were acting righteously.

Injustices will inevitably occur in the church. They come in the form of offenses. The question is: How do leaders deal with injustices and avoid being weighed down by them? Certainly, forgiveness needs to be applied, involving all four biblical dimensions. But that is not enough to walk in freedom that is characterized as love and righteousness. As Angela Strong says, "We must be freed from all damaging roots left by the malignant spirit of injustice."[5] Freedom is realized by healing inner wounds, renouncing lies, and eliminating spirits associated with the injustice.

Unintended Consequence

Spirits of injustice will linger and weigh you down long after you have forgotten the incident and forgiven the offender. If you agree with and hold on to those injustices, your Christian walk will be encumbered. It will be as if you were carrying a bag loaded with bricks, weighing down your spirit, without you knowing it.

A church had just replaced their pastor with a new preacher. Everyone was pleased and said he was so much better than the previous preacher. Someone in the community asked one of the church members why this new preacher was preferred. The church member said, "He preaches the truth. He preaches powerfully against sin."

The person asked, "Didn't the previous minister preach against sin?"

"Yes, he did preach against sin, but this one preaches with tears in his eyes" replied the church member.

If you unknowingly carry spirits of injustice, you may speak the truth. You may preach the right message, but your tone will not have the right feel. As a minister of the gospel, your message must come from the Lord, who sits on His throne of justice and righteousness. Psalm 89:14 declares, *"Righteousness and justice are foundations of your throne. Unfailing love and truth walk before you as attendants"* (NLT). Love always accompanies godly justice.

Freedom Preserves Unity

Jesus Christ never changes. He is the same yesterday, today and forever (Hebrews 13:8). However, He is constantly working to change His creation to reflect His glory (2 Corinthians 3:18). Meaning, we are always being made into new creations. Change is not easy. Many folks resist change, preferring to hold unto what is familiar and comfortable.

Saints who have passed through many seasons of life are a great asset to a pastor. However, they can also be a great liability. These persons tend to look back to when God first stirred their hearts and see no need for change. They think the way they came to faith is adequate for the current generation. Valuing tradition, they critique the innovations the younger generation want to incorporate into church life. True maturity, however, sets aside personal preferences in order to accommodate spiritual growth in others.

On the other hand, being full of zeal, the younger generation tends to act impulsively. They are eager to incorporate new methods and new styles without regard to tradition. These young leaders see themselves as change agents without giving much thought as to how their actions impact the congregation. Full of ambition, they lack patience. They need to honor their elders without being limited to the past. This inherent tension between generations can manifest in destructive conflict unless careful attention is given to preserving the unity of the Spirit in the bond of peace (Ephesians 4:3).

Typically, there are eight things that destroy unity within a congregation. Among them are poor communication, gossip, lack of closure to disagreements, lack of shared purpose, lack of trust, incompetence, unmet expectations, and unresolved offenses. The sinful nature inherent in these need to be crucified. If these go unaddressed, disrespect, jealousy, suspicion, competition, power grabs, and malice can boil up to the surface until conflict spills over into the congregation. Unity is threatened. Setting people free from these hindrances preserves unity. When conflict arises, each person needs to search their soul to see if there is any wickedness within (Psalm 139:23-24). When sin is exposed, they can repent of it, paving the way for restored fellowship. 1 John 1:7 says, *"If we walk in the light, as He is in the light, we have fellowship with one another."*

Where fellowship is broken and relationships are strained, someone must be walking in darkness. Someone must have sinful attitudes. Someone must subscribe to ungodly motives. Unity cannot be maintained where humility and honor are lacking. It cannot be achieved where truth and love are absent. It cannot be realized where critical spirits and hardened hearts go unchecked. A leader's highest priority is the care of souls in his charge. Unity is preserved as defilements are cleansed and peace permeates the soul.

Leaders must get everyone facing the same direction and rowing at the same time. This can be a challenge when everyone has an independent mindset and a personal agenda. Like herding cats, the task becomes Herculean when you add together the carnal nature and the eight things that destroy unity. A leader will need the anointing of Moses to accomplish a vision. And consider this; even Moses did not make it across the finish line into the Promised Land.

That said, unity within the body does not rest on uniformity. Neither does it rest on conformity to the leader's will. There will always be different points of view and various opinions. This variety is a good thing. What makes for unity is not conformity to the leader's will, it is conformity to the Spirit. When people yield to the Spirit rather than their own selfish ambition, they submit to one another. They honor and respect each other, especially, the senior leader. When people become ornery—and they will—it is the Spirit that brings them to the place of repentance, reconciliation, and renewal. Where the Spirit of the Lord is, there is freedom. Where there is freedom, there is unity.

Braveheart

In 1995, Mel Gibson directed and coproduced the film, *Braveheart*. The film is based on the life of William Wallace, a warrior and patriot of Scotland during the late 13th century. Whereas the film is a fictional story, Mel Gibson, who plays the lead role, forcefully captures the spirit and character of William Wallace. His depiction of him as a legend, living by the courage of his convictions, is riveting.

History records that Wallace fought many battles with the English. They had invaded and occupied his native Scotland. Knighted as Guardian of the Scots, he led the fight for their independence. Eventually, he was betrayed by Robert

Bruce and was captured in August 1305. Charged with treason, he underwent a trial at Westminster Hall. Being found guilty, he was sentenced to death. His execution was to be carried out in the most gruesome manner. He was to be hung, drawn, and quartered. After being disemboweled, his entrails were to be burned. His body parts would be sent to Newcastle, Berwick, Stirling, and Perth as a warning to all who would commit treason against England.

In the final scene of *Braveheart*, Wallace is about to be executed. A great crowd of people have come to witness his death. Wallace is lying on his back, gasping for air and struggling to speak. His executioner addressed the crowd, "The prisoner wishes to say a word." With his last ounce of strength, Wallace summons one final cry. In defiance of oppression, he shouts out a single word, *"freedom!"* It is a word that shatters the atmosphere, pierces the heart, and is heard echoing throughout the land.

Wallace gave his life in pursuit of freedom for the Scots. Jesus gave His life to procure freedom for the human race. The question remains: What are you giving your life to? As a Christian, how will you live out your faith to bring freedom to yourself and others? Remember what the Scriptures say, *"You my brothers and sister were called to be free"* (Galatians 5:13). Therefore, *"Live as people who are free"* (1 Peter 2:16).

May the Lord strengthen you to keep the faith and live free.

Discussion Questions

1. What are some of the ways people react to offenses? How do you typically respond to offenses? Do you have a pet offense?

2. What is the connection between offenses, injustices, and demons? What are some indicators that offenses are held in the heart? How important is it to deal with offenses properly? What do you think of the process the author suggests?

3. Have you ever been offended by God? How did you resolve the offense?

4. In what ways have you suffered injustice? How did you handle it?

5. The Bible uses two Hebrew terms for justice. James 1:27 captures both concepts in one Scripture. Which concept do you identify with most? How can you incorporate both concepts into your life?

6. What do you think about the possibility of hosting spirits of injustice and not knowing it? How does that make you feel?

7. What is your concept of justice? How does that impact the way you speak?

8. What is the connection between peace among a body of believers and personal freedom? How do peace and freedom impact evangelical outreach?

9. William Wallace gave his life in the cause of political freedom for the Scots. Jesus gave his life for your freedom. Going forward, how do you see yourself incorporating freedom into your life? How can you bring freedom to others?

Endnotes:

1. John Bevere, *The Bait of Satan*, (Charisma House, Lake Mary, FL, 2004)
2. Andy Byrd and Sean Feucht, *Culture of Revival: A Revivalist Field Manual* (Fire and Fragrance Publishers, Kona, HI, 2012)
3. Edward Hersh, *Escaping the Pain of Offense: Empowered to Forgive from the Heart*, (Intermedia Publishing Group, Millersville, PA, 2011), p. 4.
4. Philip Yancey, *Disappointment with God*, (Zondervan, Grand Rapids, MI, 1992)
5. Angela Strong, *Unmasking the Spirit of Injustice: The Truth Never Before Revealed Behind our Daily Struggles*, (WestBow Press, Bloomington, IN, 2019), p. 95

Greek Verses Hebrew

GREEK	HEBREW
Cognitive	**Cognitive**
Appeals to intellect	Appeals to the heart
Is analytical	Is intuitive
Emphasizes Knowledge	Emphasizes Experience
Religion	**Religion**
Creed	Application of living Word
Emphasizes good works	Emphasizes God's empowerment
Divides Secular & Religious	Unifies Secular & Religious
Salvation	**Salvation**
Goal is going to heaven	Goal is to make earth fit for God to dwell
God's kingdom is in heaven, not earth	God's kingdom is reigning with His people
Jesus will return to take us to heaven	Jesus is coming to rule over this world
Say yes to Jesus or miss your ride to heaven	Prepare self to reign with God on earth
Discipleship	**Discipleship**
Emphasis on Program	Emphasis on spiritual growth process
Priority on Education	Priority on personal transformation
Relies on oratory and speaking skills	Relies on age and wisdom
Conveys information	Connects by modeling
Utilizes resource materials	Mentoring is method of learning
Personal relationships are optional	Personal relationship is essential
Leadership by organizational need	Leadership is by personal example
Leader's personal life not crucial	Character of the leader is crucial
Biblical Application	**Biblical Application**
Belief without any personal investment	Belief is being and doing the Word
Bible is a source of truth to be taught	Bible is truth that must be actualized
Focus is on do's and don'ts (rules)	Focus is on developing Christlikeness
Emphasizes theological doctrines and denominational uniqueness	Emphasis is on unity and freedom
Lifestyle	**Lifestyle**
Casual friendships at place of worship	Close relationships at church
Trained professionals employed	Each believer is trained to serve
Produces spectators	Produces mature disciples
Led by logic	Led by revelation of Holy Spirit
Identified by "what you know"	Identified by who you are in Christ

Ten Reasons Why the Bible is a Reliable Source of Truth

1. **Manuscript Evidence.** There are many more copies of the biblical manuscripts, with remarkable consistency between them, than there are for any of the classics written by persons such as Plato, Aristotle, or Socrates. "There is no body of ancient literature in the world which enjoys such a wealth of good textual attestation as the New Testament." F.F. Bruce, The New Testament Documents: Are They Reliable?

2. **Archaeological Evidence.** Again and again, archaeological discoveries have verified the accuracy of the historical and cultural references in the Bible. The more they find, the more the Bible is confirmed. "It is important to note that Near Eastern archaeology has demonstrated the historical and geographical reliability of the Bible in many important areas." E.M. Blaiklock, The New International Dictionary of Biblical Archaeology

3. **Eyewitness Accounts.** The Bible was written by people who witnessed the events it describes; many were persecuted or martyred but never changed their story. Would you die for something you knew was untrue? "It is no moderate approbation of Scripture that it has been sealed by the blood of so many witnesses, especially when we reflect that they died to render testimony to the faith …with a firm and constant, yet sober, zeal toward God." John Calvin, Institutes of the Christian Religion

4. **Corroborating Accounts.** There are plenty of references in non-biblical sources to the events described in the Bible. The Jewish historian Josephus, born in 37 AD, "provide(s) indispensable background material for the student of…New Testament history. In them, we meet many figures well known to us from the New Testament. Some of his writings provide direct commentary on New Testament references." J.D. Douglas, ed., The New Bible Dictionary

5. **Literary Consistency.** The Bible contains sixty-six books written over 1,500 years by forty different writers, but it tells one "big story" of God's plan of salvation that culminated in Jesus Christ. You can't even pass a secret around a circle of twelve people and get the same message at the end. "There is indeed a wide variety of human authors and themes (in the Bible). Yet behind these…there lies a single divine author with a single unifying theme." John R.W. Stott, Understanding the Bible

6. **Prophetic Consistency.** There are over three hundred specific prophecies in the Old Testament that are fulfilled in the life, death, and resurrection of Jesus Christ in the New Testament. "The very dimension of the sheer fulfillment of prophecy of the Old Testament Scriptures should be enough to convince anyone that we are dealing with a supernatural piece of literature....God has Himself planted within the scriptures an internal consistency that bears witness that this is his Word." R.C. Sproul, Now That's a Good Question

7. **Expert Scrutiny.** The early church had extremely high standards for what books were judged to be authentic and therefore included in the Bible. A book had to have been written by an apostle or someone in their immediate circle, had to conform to basic Christian faith, and had to be in widespread use among many churches. This was a careful process of "the people of God in many different places, coming to recognize what other believers elsewhere found to be true"; these writings were truly God's word. G.J. Wenham, J.A. Motyer, D.A. Carson and R.T. France, *The New Bible Commentary*

8. **Leader Acceptance.** A majority of the greatest leaders and thinkers in history have affirmed the truth and impact of the Bible. "I believe the Bible is the best gift God has ever given man. All the good from the Savior of the world is communicated to us through this book. But for it we could not know right from wrong." Abraham Lincoln.

9. **Global Influence.** The Bible has had a greater influence on the laws, art, ethics, music and literature of world civilization than any other book in history. Can you think of one that even comes close? "Christianity", as set forth in the Bible "is responsible for a disproportionately large number of the humanitarian advances in the history of civilization—in education, medicine, law, the fine arts, working for human rights and even in the natural sciences...." Craig L. Blomberg, in Christian Apologetics: A Comprehensive Case for Biblical Faith.

10. **Changed Lives.** From St. Augustine to Martin Luther to Joni Eareckson Tada to countless men, women, and children, the words of the Bible have transformed lives unmistakably and forever. "As unnamed masses of Christians down through the ages have shown us, the Bible is the most reliable place to turn for finding the key to a life of love and good works." T.M. Moore, The Case for the Bible

Used by permission from Whitney T. Kuniholm.
https://essentialbible.org/2018/09/top-10-reasons-the-bible-is-true/

Ten R's to Maintaining Freedom and Wholeness

1. **Recognize** – Ask God to help you recognize what has you in bondage. Psalm 139:23, Isaiah 5:13, Hosea 4:9, Hebrews 5:14

2. **Respond** - Take responsibility for what you recognize. Psalm 32:5, Psalm 51:3-4, Proverbs 28:13

3. **Repent** - Confess it to God, be forgiven and cleansed, change your thinking. Nehemiah 9:2, Ezekiel 18:30, Acts 3:19, 1 John 1:9, Revelations 2:5, Revelations 2:16, Revelations 3:19,

4. **Renounce** – Make it your enemy and verbally renounce it. Psalm 97:10; 119:4,28; Proverbs 8:13, Proverbs 13:5, Amos 5:15, Romans 12:9, Ephesians 4:26-27, 1 Peter 1:15, Jude 1:23

5. **Remove it** – Get rid of it by commanding it to leave and not return. Psalm 101:3, Ezekiel 18:31, 2 Corinthians 7:1, I Peter 5:7

6. **Receive** – By faith, receive the grace God imparts. Matthew 10:8, Romans 8:32, 1 Corinthians 2:12, Ephesians 2:8, Hebrews 11:6, James 1:17

7. **Rejoice** – Give God praise and thanks for setting you free and blessing you. Psalm 34:1-4; 54:6, Philippians 4:4

8. **Resist** – When it tries to come back, assert your authority and reject it. Matthew 12:44, Luke 11:25-26, John 5:14, Ephesians 6:11-19, James 4:7, 1 Peter 5:8-9

9. **Restore** – Testify to what God has done for you and help others get free. Matthew 28:20, 2 Timothy 2:2, Acts 1:8

10. **Repeat** – Continue practicing this process until it becomes a lifestyle. John 8:31-32, 2 Corinthians 7:1, Philippians 1:6; 2:12; 4:9, 1 Peter 1:15-16

Christians are called to keep the faith and to fight the good fight. They are always fighting for freedom (2 Timothy 4:7).

Seven D's of Discipleship

- **Doctrine** – Learn biblical teachings, especially what Jesus taught about the kingdom of God and all reality. Rely on sound doctrine and teach it to others. (Matthew 7:9; Mark 1:15; 2 Timothy 2:2)

- **Discipline** - Put into practice spiritual habits like prayer, giving, worship, fellowship (one another's), confession, repentance, service, the Word, and others. Experience spiritual growth. (Hebrews 13:7; 2 Thessalonians 3:7; 1 Corinthians 11:1; Philippians 3:17)

- **Dependence on the Spirit** – Rely on the Spirit for revelation of truth through both *logos* and *rhema*. Rely on the fruit and gifts of the Spirit for power in order to live a holy life and to witness to the world. Turn to the Spirit for guidance in decision making. (John 14:16; Acts 1:8)

- **Devotion** – Develop an intimate relationship with the Father, Son and Holy Spirit through prayer, hearing God's voice and being obedient, worship, thanksgiving, and service. Practice the presence of God which results in radiating peace and joy. (John 10:27; John 14:15 John 14:15; Hebrews 4:16; James 4:8)

- **Die to self** - Crucify corrupt desires rising from the carnal nature in order to have more of Christ's nature manifested. Desire the Spirit-filled life greater than satisfaction derived from fleshly desires. Identify as a son or daughter of God. Become less self-centered, having an increased capacity to love. (Luke 9:23-24; Romans 6:6, 2 Corinthians 4:11; 1 Corinthians 15:31; Galatians 2:20)

- **Discernment** – Draw upon natural abilities, scriptural truths, spiritual gifts, other mature believers, and wisdom from heaven to learn to distinguish between good and evil. Perceive things from a heavenly perspective (Matthew 7:1-5; Hebrews 5:13-14; James 3:13-18;)

- **Deliverance** – Be set free to live a Christlike life (Colossians 1:13; 1 John 2:14). This includes deliverance from penalty of sin (Romans 6:6-7, 1 Thessalonians 1:10); deliverance from the sinful nature (Romans. 7:23, 1 John 1:9); deliverance from inner strongholds (2 Corinthians 10:5-6); deliverance from the worldly systems of thought (Romans 12:2); deliverance from fear of death (Hebrews 2:14-15); deliverance from the evil one.

The Johari Window

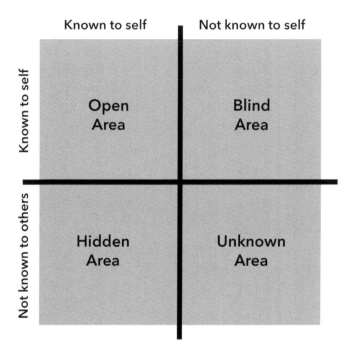

Known to self   Not known to self

Known to self

Not known to others

Open Area

Blind Area

Hidden Area

Unknown Area

The Open area is information about yourself known to you and to others. (This is where "the one another's" have significance)

The Hidden area is information about yourself known to you but not to others. (This is where "confession and repentance" have significance)

The Blind area is information about yourself known to others but not to you. (This is where "speaking the truth in love" has significance)

The Unknown area is information about yourself that is known only by God. (This is where "prophetic revelation" has significance)

Daniel 2:22 declares: *"He reveals deep and secret things; He knows what is in the darkness, and light dwells with Him."* Therefore, ask God for revelation.

Ten Basic Love Needs

1. **The Need for Security** — Freedom from harm, danger, and fear; Placing beyond hazard, loss; want, or deprivation; Confidence and harmony in relationships.

   "Perfect love drives out fear" (1 John 4:18).

   "He will shelter you with his wings. His faithfulness is like a shield or a protective wall" (Psalm 91:4 NET).

2. **The Need for Comfort** — Gives strength and hope; Easing grief or pain; Hurt with console.

   "The God of all comfort, who comforts us in all our troubles, so that we can comfort those in trouble" (2 Corinthians 1:3-4).

   "Mourn with those who mourn" (Romans 12: 15).

3. **The Need for Attention** — Taking thought of another and conveying appropriate interest and concern; entering another's world.

   "Let each of you look not only to his own interests, but also to the interest of others" (Philippians 2:4 ESV).

4. **The Need for Acceptance** — Deliberate and ready to receive; Reception with a favorable response; Receiving willingly; Regarding someone as good and proper.

   "Accept one another, then, just as Christ accepted you, in order to bring praise to God" (Romans 15:7).

5. **The Need for Appreciation** — Recognizing with gratitude; Communicating with words and gestures of personal gratefulness for another person; Praising.

   "I praise you" (1 Corinthians 11:2).

   "Honor one another above yourselves" (Romans 12:10).

6. **The Need for Encouragement** – Urging forward; Positively persuading toward a goal; Inspiring with courage, spirit, or hope; Stimulating.

   "Therefore encourage one another and build each other up"
   (1 Thessalonians 5:11).

7. **The Need for Affection** — Communicating care and closeness through physical touch and affirming words.

   "Having thus a fond affection for you, we were well-pleased to impart to you not only the gospel of God but also our own lives"
   (I Thessalonians 2:8 NASB 1977).

   "Greet one another with a holy kiss" (Romans 16:16).

8. **The Need for Respect** – Valuing and regarding highly; Conveying great worth; Esteeming

   "Show proper respect to everyone" (l Peter 2:17).

9. **The Need for Approval** — Affirming as satisfactory; Giving formal sanction to; Expressing a favorable opinion; Approving of.

   "Anyone who serves Christ in this way is pleasing to God and approved by men" (Romans 14:18).

10. **The Need for Support** — Coming alongside and gently helping to carry a problem or struggle; Assisting; Providing for.

    "Carry each other's burdens, and in this way, you will fulfill the law of Christ" (Galatians 6:2).

APPENDIX G

When I Was Perfect

When I was perfect, nothing was too difficult for me. I could do it all myself.

When I was perfect, I lived by the law. There was no grace and little love. Now I live by faith resting in God's love.

When I was perfect, I wasn't kind. I didn't care if I hurt others with words because I was right.

When I was perfect, I judged others by my doctrines. Now I don't judge others or even myself until I have checked and removed my ungodly beliefs.

When I was perfect, I was a fixer. I told others what was wrong and what they needed to do to fix it. Now I ask, "How we can we work together to find a solution to a problem?"

When I was perfect, I had no need to pursue God's presence, now I desire Him all the time.

When I was perfect, it was all about me because I was the center of the universe. Now I look at things from the perspective of others.

When I was perfect, I did everything myself because others could not measure up to my standards. Now I value the contribution of others even when it may not meet my expectations.

When I was perfect, I could not function on a team because no one else did things right. Now I see the value of enlisting the gifts of everyone.

When I was perfect, I told everyone else what to do and how to do it. Now I let people make their own decisions.

When I was perfect, I was in control of everything and everybody. Now I allow God to be in control.

When I was perfect, I didn't need to change, everybody else did.

When I was perfect, I needed to change others. Now I let them be themselves.

When I was perfect, I was easily offended by others who criticized me. Now I no longer need to defend myself.

When I was perfect, if someone pointed out I was wrong, I turned it around on them and made them regret they tried to correct me. Now I look for the sliver of truth in their criticism.

When I was perfect, I had little patience with others. Now I am more kind and understanding.

When I was perfect, I judged others perfectly. Now I have compassion to show them grace.

When I was perfect, I didn't need to apologize. Now I am quick to admit my faults.

When I was perfect, I didn't need to pray. Now I pray without ceasing.

When I was perfect, I was blind. I didn't see anything except that which I wanted to see. I didn't see how badly I was treating others. Now I am quick to examine my own heart before I speak truth to others.

When I was perfect, I had no joy. I manufactured false contentment by playing the clown. Now I am free to enjoy each day without putting on a false face. I am free to be honest and transparent.

When I was perfect, I took on false responsibility. I needed to control everybody to make sure they met my standards of perfection. Now I no longer carry the burden of being the judge of others.

When I was perfect, I had the right answers. I was a depository of knowledge and experience. I told people how to do things.

When I was perfect, I was quick to correct. Now I am patient and pray for them. I am more apt to encourage than to critique.

When I was perfect, I withheld my blessing until others met my standards. Now I bless others not because they deserve it but because they need it.

When I was perfect, I was inflexible. Everyone needed to adjust their plans around my schedule. Now I am more flexible.

When I was perfect, I could not say, "No.: No one could do it like me. Now I realize "No" is not a bad word. It is healthy to have boundaries.

When I was perfect, my idea of accountability was to find fault with someone, not to make them better but to prove myself superior.

When I was perfect my prophetic gift showed itself in a biting judgmental tongue. Now that my heart is healed, my words are encouraging.

When I was perfect, people did not trust me with their confidences. Now they want my input on the most sensitive and significant decisions.

When I was perfect, I did not realize how wounded I was. I did not think I needed ministry. Now that I have received a measure of healing, I desire even more ministry and freedom.

When I was perfect, I only half understood the gospel. Because I was forgiven of my sin, I did not think I needed to look for any imperfections hidden deep within my soul.

When I was perfect, I was more anxious to get details of a task right than I was concerned about others' interests. Now I have more passion for getting relationships right.

When I was perfect, making myself look strong and capable was a necessity to protect myself. Now I can show weakness without feeling threatened or inferior.

When I was perfect, I was highly competitive. Now I am free to honor, appreciate and call out the talents of others.

APPENDIX H

Cross Chart

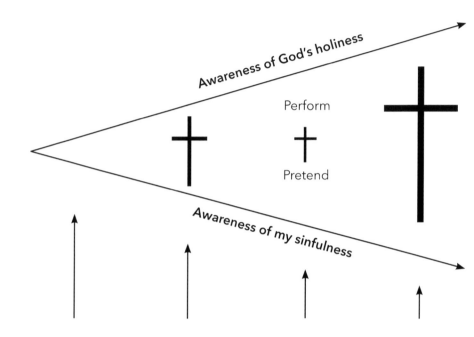

Before Conversion	At Conversion	Shrinking the Power of the Cross	Boasting in the Cross
Before entering a relationship with Jesus the person has a limited awareness of his sinfulness and the holiness of God.	Upon salvation, the person realizes his need for Jesus to die for his sin and has a growing awareness of his sinfulness and God's holiness.	The person's awareness of Christ's work on the cross diminishes. He looks to his own righteousness to justify his salvation.	Christ's work on the cross becomes a daily awareness. He takes his identity from Christ's righteousness.

Adopted from the Cross Chart, Sonship, 2012 World Harvest Mission /Serge

Trauma Prayer

by Jim and Pat Banks

(Before praying, ask the person or persons' permission to take authority on their behalf.)

RELEASING TRAUMA FROM THE SPIRIT, SOUL, AND BODY

Lord Jesus, I ask that you would come as the Prince of Peace and bring Peace to _____. Come and establish your dominion of peace in him/her and manifest yourself in such a way that _____ will know that you are here, and allow him/her to feel the depths of your love.

I ask that you rebuke any forces of darkness that seek to harm _____ in any way, or have tried to keep him/her locked in this prison of trauma. You have not given _____ a spirit of fear, but of love, power and soundness of mind, and that is what I claim for him/her today.

As we pray, I ask that you would be as a poultice, and draw from _____ all the pain, trauma, shock, fear, terror and shame, bringing it all to death on your cross. You suffered and died for _____and we appropriate all that you accomplished for him/her.

Pour in your love and grace and by the power of the Holy Spirit remove any traumatic memory that has been stored in the cells of _____ 's body and restore the cells to perfect order and vibration.

Lord, I bless the very moment the egg and the sperm came together and _____ came to be. I bless the conception and every moment that _____ was in his/her mother's womb. Holy Spirit I ask that you brood over the original DNA and restore all vibrations, frequencies, tones and colors within _____ and remove anything that is not of you.

Heavenly Father, I ask that you remove any trauma experienced in the womb; absorbed from the womb; or passed down through the generations, I ask that You would heal the very DNA and remove all shock, trauma, fear, terror and shame that has come through his/her generational flow.

Together we plant the cross of Jesus Christ firmly between_____ and his/her generations and ask that all iniquity be stopped at the cross of Christ. Forgive those in his/her generations who traumatized others, or manipulated, dominated or controlled through fear and torment. Release your precious blood and heal all unresolved grief and pain.

_____, I bless your birth and call you forth into newness of life. I say that you are welcome on this earth. There is a place for you here. Your heavenly Father has a purpose for you and a plan to give you a future and a hope; to prosper you in every way.

Heavenly Father, bring your healing and please remove any shock, trauma, fear or terror that _____ experienced in the birthing process or in the moments following and help him/her to fully embrace the life that you have given.

I ask You to come into _____'s conscious memory, unconscious memory and subconscious memory and remove all shock, trauma, fear, shame, and the pain that has caused so much torment.

Heal the Amygdala, and remove all shock, trauma, fear, terror and shame from the emotions.

I ask that you bring healing to the "fear center" of _____'s brain. Turn off the alarms that have been ringing for so long, and replace the fear, dread and hyper- vigilance with godly discernment. Let him/her know when there is true danger and give him/her wisdom to know how to deal with it. Bring peace and rest to that part of _____'s heart that has always had to stand guard and be alert; remove any pervasive low-level anxiety. Heal the immune system and remove all toxins that remain from any chemicals or hormones that have poured through his/her body for so many years.

Heavenly Father, please remove the trauma from _____'s eyes and ears. Wash over any images "seared" upon the soul, with the blood of Jesus Christ. Remove the trauma from any words spoken and remove any dis-harmony, dis-ease, or dis-order that these words or images have caused. Sing your song of love over _____ and bring everything within him/her into agreement with your song and original design. In the name and by the Blood of Jesus Christ, I prophesy order and healing; into your spirit, soul, and body.

Remove any trauma or shame that is associated with scent.

Remove any trauma from the skin.

Lord, trauma has shaken _____ to the very core of his/her foundations, and I ask that you heal every crack with your love. Restore trust and the grace to believe in you and receive your promises, and to trust others.

I ask, Lord Jesus, that you would remove all shock, trauma, fear, terror and shame from the will and spirit of _____. Restore his/her will and strengthen it in every way.

I ask, Lord Jesus, that you would remove all shock, trauma, fear, terror and shame from the muscles, ligaments, tendons, bones and bone marrow. Bring your healing power to every area where _____'s spirit has been crushed or broken, and restore health, vitality and vigor. Make his/her bones and connective tissues strong.

I ask that you would remove all shock, trauma, fear and terror off the organs of _____'s body. (Ask the Lord to reveal any organs that you should pray specifically for.)

Lord, I ask that you would sever all fear bonds, trauma bonds, and all unhealthy and unholy soul ties that have been created through trauma.

I break every assignment of trauma against this person and bind and send away every "guard" assigned to _____. We receive and appropriate the love; power and soundness of mind that you have promised to give him/her.

Lord Jesus, bring to death any "old ways" of responding and reacting to shock, trauma, fear and terror. Dismantle the ungodly structures of defense and establish new neurological connections to the joy center. Rebuild within _____ new godly structures of defense based on scripture; trust in you; and true understanding of his/her spiritual authority as a daughter/son of the Most High God.

Fill every cell with your peace and healing grace. Displace any darkness with your light. Keep _____ in your perfect peace, especially in the night seasons and bring rest. Send heavenly hosts to guard _____ as he/she sleeps and quite him/her with your love. Amen.

https://jimandpatbanks.com/trauma-prayer/ Used with permission

APPENDIX J

Consecration Prayer

Thanksgiving

Lord, we thank You for the gift of salvation, including full healing and freedom from all that negatively affects us. We consecrate this day and our very selves to You. We consecrate our bodies, spirits, and souls. We thank You for the gift of eternal life. We thank You for manifesting Your love, power, presence, promises, and anointing in order to bring forth what You desire in _____ 's life. We thank You that there is no condemnation for those in Christ Jesus. We thank You, that by His shed blood, we are cleansed of all guilt and shame and made righteous through His sacrifice on the cross. We declare Your goodness and mercy over_____ today.

We bring _____ boldly into your throne of grace so that he/she will experience Your presence, peace and love, healing, and deliverance. We dedicate all our gifts and abilities to You. We give You all glory and praise for what You are going to do through us to restore _____ and to advance your kingdom in this session.

Submission to God

Lord, we choose to submit to You as our Father God. We willingly step into that place of authority that You promise in Your Word to give us as we submit to You. We ask You to open our ears and eyes to receive what you are releasing from heaven by way of revelation, knowledge, understanding, consolation, confidence, wisdom, perception, identity, healing, and deliverance. Open the eyes of our hearts. Expose any areas of our heart that are hard and soften them by Your Spirit of truth.

Authority over Satan and his demons

Lord Jesus Christ, we yield to your control. We commit ourselves to Your will. If we have been deceived in any way by the voice of Satan, we pray that You will open our eyes to the deception.

We choose to use the authority You give us against Satan and his army. We command in the name of Jesus Christ that all deceiving spirits depart from us, and we renounce and reject all counterfeit gifts (or any other spiritual phenomena). We resist you, Satan, and all your demons. We stop all communication between demons and their authorities right now in the name of Jesus Christ. We bind all demonic voices and forbid any distraction, confusion, interference, accusation, distortion, shaming, harassment, or critical spirit. We bind any spirit of stupor and mocking and disconnect and forbid you to manifest. We prohibit any outside demons from invading this space and spying on what happens here. We put blinders over the eyes and earplugs in the ears of all outside demons prohibiting you from seeing or hearing what happens in this ministry room. We forbid any astral projection into this room. We especially bind demons of occult, fear and unbelief. We especially command demons of fear and unbelief attached to rejection, pride, unworthiness, religious spirit, or intellectualism not to interfere in any way.

Lord Jesus, we ask You to release greater revelation of Your love, the grace of faith, humility and courage that will enable _____ to receive the gifts You want him/her to have.

Lord, we thank You for Your divine protection. We apply the blood of Jesus over each one of us, our health, our spouses, our homes, our children, our possessions, our finances, our dreams, our future, our vocations, our ministry, and over this ministry room. We place the cross between us and any outside negative influence. We declare this to be holy ground. We declare this to be a safe place. Lord, we ask You to post Your holy angels around us so that any weapon formed against will not prosper. We restrict any demon when commanded to leave from entering any other human or any pet. You are not to go to any shared host. You are to go to where Jesus tells you to go and nowhere else.

Invite the Holy Spirit to be in charge

Holy Spirit, we invite You to come and be in charge of this meeting. We depend on You to lead, guide, and direct us. We depend on You for wisdom, comfort, and truth. We ask You to bring forth Your will, purposes, change, transformation, healing, revelation, restoration, strength, knowledge, cleansing, imputed grace and righteousness, renewed spirit, renewed mind, and renewed body. We ask you to bestow upon us honor. We ask that you would implant within us seeds of reconciliation and fountains of joy. We ask that You impart to us discernment, power, and peace.

Lord, we thank You for ministering to us. We give You all honor, praise, and glory for what happens here during this ministry session. Amen.

Surrender Prayer by Ministry Recipient

Father God, I am here because I need Your help. I want You to be here with me as I go through this time of healing and deliverance. I want You to put fresh hope into my spirit. I give You thanks for loving me just as I am and loving me too much to let me stay the way I am. Help me to take responsibility for all that belongs to me. Open my eyes to where I have been blind.

Father God, I confess my sin. I confess the sins of my ancestors, and I choose not to hold them responsible for the effects of their sins on my life. I release them from any blame I have placed on them for my sins. I renounce my ancestors' sins and release myself from all negative effects of their sins, according to Christ's finished work on the cross. I also break the power of every curse against my descendants and me because of my ancestors' sins. I cancel all legal rights of demons to torment my descendants and me. I cancel all dedications made by my ancestors of their descendants, including myself and my descendants. I declare that I am completely owned by Jesus Christ, who paid the price for my sins on the cross. I declare He is always with me. He is for me and never will forsake me.

Father God, I thank You for Your help in revealing the lies I have believed. I want my mind to be renewed. I am grateful for the grace You give me to help me find freedom.

Father God, please comfort me as I go through the pain and hurt. Please uncover the lies I have believed and grant me clarity in my perceptions. Bring healing to all my "held-in" pain. Lord, when I have been frustrated, angry, upset, and separated from You, show me whether the true blame belongs—on my flesh or on Satan.

Lord Jesus, You are my Deliverer. I ask that You set me free from all demonic influence in my current issues. I choose to use the spiritual authority You have given to me to exercise power of the enemy. I declare I will walk in freedom according to Your Word and Your grace.

Holy Spirit, you are the Revealer of Truth and my Comforter. Come and pour more of the Father's love into me. I yield full control over to you in the name of Jesus Christ. Amen.

Resource Books

An Ancient Blueprint for the Supernatural by Doctors Dennis and Jennifer Clark, (Destiny Image Publishers, Inc., Shipensbeurg , PA 2020).

Biblical Healing and Deliverance by Chester and Betsy Kylstra, (Chosen Books, Bloomington, MN, 2005).

Biblical Foundations for Life by Larry Kreider, (House To House Publications, Lititz, PA, 2020).

Dressed to Kill: A Biblical Approach to Spiritual Warfare and Armor by Rick Renner (Teach All Nations, Tulsa, OK, 2007).

Fivefold Ministry by Ron Myer, (House to House Publications, Lititz, PA, 2006).

Growing in the Prophetic: A biblical guide to Dreams, Visions, and Spiritual Gifts by Mike Bickle, (Charisma House, Lake Mary, FL, 2008)

Hearing God 30 Different Ways by Larry Kreider, (House to House Publications, Lititz, PA, 2005).

Restoring the Foundations: An Integrated Approach to Healing Ministry by Chester and Betsy Kylstra, (Proclaiming His Word, Inc., Henderson, NC, 2008).

Sonship by Serge, (New Growth Press, Greensboro, NC, 2013).

The Biblical Guidebook to Deliverance, by Randy Clark (Charisma House, Lake Mary, FL, 2015).

The Bondage Breaker by Neil T. Anderson, (Harvest House Publishers, Eugene, OR, 2000).

Truly Free: Breaking the Snares that so Easily Entangle by Robert Morris, (W Publishing Group, an imprint of Thomas Nelson, Nashville, TN, 2015).

Understanding Prophetic People by R. Loren Sandford, (Chosen Books, Bloomington, MN, 2007)

Victory Over the Darkness by Neil T. Anderson, (Regal Books, Ventura, CA, 1990 1st Edition, 2000 2nd Edition).

Video Courses

"Basic Training for Prophetic Ministry" by Kris Vallotton

"Cleansing Streams" by Cleansing Streams Ministries

"Courts of Heaven" by Robert Henderson

"Culture of Honor" by Danny Silk

"Demolishing Strongholds" by Mike and Sue Dowgiewicz

"Freed to Lead" by Rod Woods and Steve Goss

"Strengthening Yourself in the Lord" by Bill Johnson

"The Bait of Satan" by John Bevere

"The End of Me" by Kyle Idleman

"Transformed: How God Changes Us" by Rick Warren

"Translating God: Hearing God's Voice for Yourself and the World Around You" by Shawn Bolz

"True Spirituality" by Chip Ingram

"Truly Free" by Robert Morris

The Cycle of Defeat

We live in a broken (disappointing, wounding, hurtful, offensive) world.

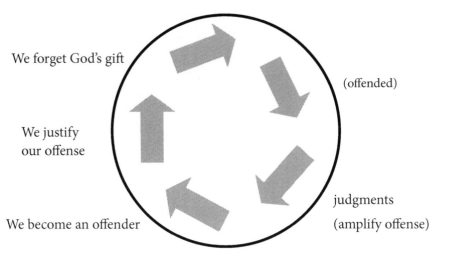

We forget God's gift

(offended)

We justify
our offense

judgments
We become an offender   (amplify offense)

We grumble and complain and wander in the wilderness (Hebrews 3:7-18).

We behave in ways that offend God and people—including self (1Corinthians 10:1-13). Misbeliefs and expectations become disappointment, judgments, discouragement, confusion, depression, loss of vision, disorientation, withdrawal, despair, and defeat.

This cycle is common to every human being alive. Because we live in a fallen, broken, and imperfect world, experiencing hurtful emotion is inevitable.

- *We become disappointed (offended)* by peoples' mistakes, misunderstandings, mistreatments, betrayals, injustices, abuses, or even crimes.

- *We make critical judgments (amplify the offense)* by rehearsing in our minds what coulda', woulda', shoulda' been done to avoid the pain. Many times our anger is directed at God for allowing bad things to happen. Some blame self and become imprisoned by self-rejection.

- We believe lies instead of God's truth and behave in ways that offend God, ourselves, and other people. Thus, *we become an offender*. Bitterness, resentment, and blame become an accepted way of life.

- Without God's help we try to rectify situations in many ways including revenge, obsessing for justice, forgetting, excusing, 'moving on', self-inflicting condemnation, or finding some other way of replacing the negative feelings with positive ones.

- In our quest of human effort, we may even find some relief and so *we justify our offense.*

- Unable to trust, surrender to God the sole right to judge the one(s) who disappointed us, we reject God's provision through Jesus to break the cycle.

- Having agreed with the lie that holding offense solves our problem, we become offensive to someone else who becomes offended, and the cycle spirals hopelessly on.

There is hope! Our hope is in Jesus and what God has done through Him (John 3:16). Through God's gift of forgiveness, we not only have hope to redeem this cycle in our own lives, but we can reverse this spiral in the lives of others as well.

You do not have to be enslaved by this victim/ predator cycle/ spiral. Stress, anxiety, and depression no longer have to remain when you allow Christ Jesus into the deepest parts of your heart to break this cycle down.

Used by Permission: Dr. Ed Hersh, author of Escaping the Pain of Offense: Empowered to Forgive from the Heart.
See http://authorededhersh.blogspot.com

Disappointment with God Prayer

Father God,

I admit that I have misjudged You and blamed You for things You did not do. I now choose to stop doing this. I repent and declare that your judgments are righteous.

I ask You to forgive me for blaming You. I declare You are a good God and that You always want what is best for me even when I don't fully understand my circumstances.

I agree and declare that You are in charge of my life. I believe You make all things work together for my good. You use all things for my spiritual development and maturity. You are equipping me to be a son/daughter who is able to rule with You as holy priestly king in eternity.

I will put the responsibility where it belongs, either on my fleshly self or on Satan's kingdom. I will no longer avoid responsibility but will now take responsibility for my life under the guidance and control of the Holy Spirit. I receive your guidance and grace….. (wait and receive by faith from the Lord).

Father God, thank You for this new freedom. I am grateful that my relationship with You is now restored. I receive both this freedom and renewed relationship in the name of Jesus Christ, my Savior and Lord.

Amen.

APPENDIX N

Discipleship Chart

	Stage 1 Come and See John 1:38-39	Stage 2 Come and Follow Me (Mark 1:16-20)
1	Approach is invitational	Approach is educational
2	Impartation is by relationship and events	Impartation is by teaching and modelling
3	Receives faith by hearing the gospel preached and taught	Receives instruction through teaching, reading, study and discussion
4	The heart's soil is hard and needs to be softened to receive the seed of the Word	The heart's soil is soft on the surface but needs to be softened at deeper levels by the Spirit
5	Understands salvation as conversion to Christianity (faith in Christ)	Understands salvation as a theological doctrine of justification/ sanctification
6	At conversion, is indwelt by the Holy Spirit	Is learning to respond to the Holy Spirit's convicting of sin and direction
7	Watches what is modelled	Implements what is being modelled
8	Engages the faith community	Imitates spiritual disciplines being modelled
9	Functions as a spiritual orphan in search of a family	Functions as servant and friend of God in the church family
10	The goal is to resolve hindering questions about faith	The goal is having assurance of salvation without doubt
11	Relies primarily on reason to understand spiritual truth and make application	Relies on reason and general revelation to understand spiritual truth and make application
12	Looks to pastors, teachers, and evangelists for spiritual nurture	Looks to pastors, teachers, and evangelists for spiritual nurture, but desires more
13	Has a worldly view of life, but is seeking a greater perspective of truth by which to live	Is learning a biblical worldview as the way to understand truth and live a godly life
14	Is being schooled in the Word and biblical authority	Is being schooled in the Word and kingdom principles

Stage 3
Come and Be with Me
(Mark 3:13-14)

Stage 4
Come and Remain in Me
(John 5:7-8)

Stage 3	Stage 4
Approach is transformational	Approach is collaborative
Impartation is by mentoring and accountability	Impartation is by mutual accountability
Receives inner strength to live out the faith by the presence of God	Receives encouragement to persevere in the faith by the presence of God
The heart's soil is soft at deep levels but must work to keep weeds and thistles out	The heart's soil is fertile producing much fruit in character and the adding of disciples to the kingdom
Understands salvation as personal freedom from sin, death, and evil	Understands salvation as faith of Christ; enjoys favor, blessing and abundant life
Is baptized in the power of the Holy Spirit and is strengthened for ministry	Continues to be baptized in Holy Spirit and is equipping others in ministry
Does what is modelled with help of a leader	Does what is modelled without leader's direction
Identifies as the Father's son or daughter	Is Jesus' ongoing witness and ambassador to the world
Functions as a co-laborer in ministry with God to strengthen the family	Functions as an ambassador and is on a mission to bring others into God's family
The goal is to be cleansed of defilements and become holy	The goal is to live a holy life and to be faithful to God's call and destiny
Learning to trust direct revelation, and discerning good from evil; operates in the supernatural	Is confident in direct revelation, able to test the spirits and regularly flows in supernatural
Looks to prophets and apostles for spiritual nurture and equipping	Looks to Holy Spirit and the Word and 5-fold ministers for nurture and equipping
Has a firm biblical worldview and is able to consistently apply its truth to life situations	Consistently lives out biblical truth and is able to teach others a biblical worldview
Has learned things in the Word and Spirit and is a vessel of God's power	Is able to school others in both the Word and Spirit to be a vessel of God's power

Stage 1 Come and See *(Continued)*	Stage 2 Come and Follow Me *(Continued)*
15 Exhibits sinful behavior in the struggle to win over sin, overcoming the carnal nature	Is learning obedience, how to die to self, and is acquiring a hope that instills a desire for purity and heaven
16 Is vulnerable to Satan's schemes	Is learning some of Satan's schemes
17 Is subject to spirit of religion, legalism, fear, and unbelief	Is subject to works and self-righteousness, fear, and unbelief
18 Considers kingdom rule	Consents to kingdom rule
19 Growth stage is that of a baby (1 Corinthians 3:1)	Growth stage is a little child (1 John 2:12)
20 Drinks the milk of God's Word (Hebrews 6:1-2)	Starts to eat a solid diet of God's Word (2 Timothy 3:16)
21 Gives reluctantly	Gives dutifully
22 Prayers are occasional, private, formal, and focused on personal needs	Prayers are heart-felt, worshipful, thankful; intercedes with and for others
23 Has little or no knowledge of their spiritual inheritance but is looking for fulfillment	Is learning about their spiritual inheritance in Christ (the sum total of God's promises given to us in salvation)
24 Views adversity and suffering as something to be avoided	Views adversity and suffering as something to be tolerated until heaven
25 Recognizes need for God's help	Is learning how to receive from the Lord
26 Demands personal rights and strongly resists submitting to others; remains independent	Considers the rights of others but struggles to submit to others; tries to be cooperative
27 Resists repentance out of a desire to protect the self; blinded by dead works	Reluctant to repent out of ignorance and fear; is prone to dead works
28 Sees relationship as a means to get his or her agenda accomplished and has little regard for how others may be offended	Values relationships in order to achieve mutual goals, however, challenged in overcoming offenses

Stage 3
Come and Be with Me
(Continued)

Stage 4
Come and Remain in Me
(Continued)

Stage 3	Stage 4
Takes off old man, puts on Spiritual man; practices confession, renewing the mind, healing, and deliverance	Continually walks in righteousness, peace, and joy in the Holy Spirit; enjoys a victorious life
Is overcoming Satan's schemes	Walks in authority, power, and love, thus overcoming Satan
Is set free of strongholds. Is operating in grace, spiritual gifts, spiritual fruit, and boldness	Sets affections on things above; sees self as citizen of heaven living on earth
Capitulates to kingdom rule	Conforms to kingdom rule
Growth stage is that of a young man (John 2:13-14)	Growth stage is that of a father (1 John 2:13-14)
Is digesting the meat of God's Word (James 1:22)	Nurtures others with God's Word (2 Timothy 2:2)
Gives joyfully	Gives generously
Prayers are strategic, precise, declarative and warfare in nature	Prayers are powerful, without ceasing and effective
Claims spiritual inheritance as a co-heir with Christ through obedience in the fear of the Lord	Possesses their spiritual inheritance by exhibiting intimacy with the Father like Jesus did, which is the mark of maturity
Views adversity and suffering as a necessity for Christlikeness	Views adversity and suffering as something to be counted as joy
Is able to receive from the Lord to strengthen self	Teaches others to strengthen self in the Lord
Yields rights to God and practices mutual submission with others; is compliant	Practices mutual submission and seeks mutual accountability; is interdependent
Readily repents. Is refreshed. Is set free to produce fruitfulness	Rushes to repent. Sees it as a lifestyle, allowing them to walk in holiness
Relationships are empowered by the Holy Spirit's love; able to process offenses in a positive manner	Relationships are characterized by an offense-free lifestyle; at peace with those who remain offended

Stage 1 Come and See *(Continued)*	Stage 2 Come and Follow Me *(Continued)*
29 Is exposed to people who are living out the biblical "one another's" and is drawn into the church community	Is learning the biblical "one another's" and is beginning to implement them while participating in the church community
30 Experiences worship through the eyes of others; observes at an event and is drawn to the worship of God	Experiences the worship of God in truth, by praising, praying, and receiving the Word of God in public and private settings
31 Is committed to finding out if Christianity is what it says it is; cautiously tests it.	Has chosen to follow Christ and is learning to make sacrifices but at his or her own convenience
32 Selfishly seeks to bring honor to self but is discovering the futility of such effort	Is learning to be humble before God and to honor others in the way of Christ
33 Depends on worldly wisdom to make decisions but is attracted to godly wisdom	Is discovering godly wisdom but does not fully walk in it; is still friendly with the world's wisdom
34 Is trying to make sense of how a good God can exist in a world filled with evil	Recognizes everything good is a gift from God and makes all things work for good
35 Desires to be loved and to love others but feels inadequate and is looking to receive more love	Has received God's love and is learning to love self and others but is encumbered by an impure heart

Stage 3
Come and Be with Me
(Continued)

Lives out the biblical "one another's" and plays a key role in maintaining a redemptive community

Experiences worship of God in spirit and in truth by engaging the manifest presence of the Holy Spirit in any setting

Has experienced Christ's faithfulness and is committed to becoming Christ-like by dying daily to self

Is bringing honor to Christ by protecting, nurturing, and calling out honor in others

Is able to receive heavenly wisdom for daily living; has declared war on the world and Satan

Expects to receive good things from God and is looking for how God is showing favor

Is receiving greater outpourings of love from the Holy Spirit; loves self and others with a pure heart

Stage 4
Come and Remain in Me
(Continued)

Lives out the biblical "one another's" and is able to teach and encourage others to live out the same

Experiences the worship of God in every aspect of life by way of spirit and truth in all settings; inspiring others to do likewise

Habitually dies to self and is empowering others to change the culture to reflect the kingdom of God

Is intentionally creating a culture of honor with the help of others in the power of the Holy Spirit

Uses heavenly wisdom to help others to overcome sin, the world, and the forces of evil

Walks in God's favor and helps others to recognize and appropriate God's grace

Helps others to discover and receive God's love for themselves and others with a pure heart in the Holy Spirit

Contact Information

Craig Snow
email revsnow@ptd.net

Made in the USA
Columbia, SC
19 February 2021